22nd EG-ICE International Workshop on Intelligent Computing in Engineering (EG-ICE 2015)

Eindhoven, Netherlands
13 – 15 July 2015

ISBN: 978-1-5108-0956-7

Printed from e-media with permission by:

Curran Associates, Inc.
57 Morehouse Lane
Red Hook, NY 12571

Some format issues inherent in the e-media version may also appear in this print version.

Printed by Curran Associates, Inc. (2015)

For permission requests, please contact the European Group For Intelligent Computing in Engineering (eg-ice) at the address below.

European Group For Intelligent Computing in Engineering (eg-ice)
c/o Andre Borrmann
Arcisstrasee 21
80333 Munich
Germany

Phone: 498928-925117
Fax: 498928-948789

anything@eg-ice.org

Additional copies of this publication are available from:

Curran Associates, Inc.
57 Morehouse Lane
Red Hook, NY 12571 USA
Phone: 845-758-0400
Fax: 845-758-2634
Email: curran@proceedings.com
Web: www.proceedings.com

Overview

Contact

TU Eindhoven
Design Systems Group

++31 40 247 2280
eg-ice-2015@tue.nl

BIM Technology in the Maintenance of Building Components

Alcinia Z. Sampaio, zita.sampaio@tecnico.ulisboa.pt
Dep. Civil Engineering and Architecture, University of Lisbon, Lisbon, Portugal

Diogo Simoes, simoes_diogo@hotmail.com
Dep. Civil Engineering and Architecture, University of Lisbon, Lisbon, Portugal

Abstract
The aim of the proposed work was to analyse the benefits provided by Building Information Models (BIM) as a methodology to support buildings maintenance. During an inspection activity for maintenance purposes, the implemented application, containing a rigorous database, allows the user to identify each anomaly present in building components, directly onto the BIM model, automatically associating them with probable causes, repair methods and a photograph of the anomaly uploaded at the site. Therefore, gains in productivity and a decrease in the error probability can be achieved. The inspection data is stored in the BIM model, making it suitable for consultation when planning maintenance. Additionally, it was case study the interoperability between BIM modelling and visualizing software, regarding the preservation of information, especially in the standard format Industry Foundation Classes (IFC)

Keywords: Building Information Model (BIM), BIM software, interoperability, maintenance

1 Introduction

Building Information Modeling (BIM) is the digital representation of all the physical and functional characteristics of a facility, being used as an information repertoire, which can be shared and updated throughout the facility's life-cycle (NBS, 2013). The parametric creation process of the BIM model provides a chance of performing an automatic detection of conflicts, of promoting a link between the model and the schedule planning stage (the creation of the 4D model), of interconnecting the model with budgeting data (5D model definition) (Hartmann et al. 2011) and of relating the modeling with different processes regarding the facility management and maintenance throughout its life span (referred as the 6D model) (Eastman et al. 2011). The aggregation of several types of information on a single platform provides tremendous value to the model, functioning as a resource that can be accessed directly by countless people, avoiding the expense of time and money in work duplications and allowing the constant update of information.

There is currently a growing concern about the maintenance and upkeep of buildings, not only due to regulatory standards set out in the project, but also the requirement of the users in terms of safety, health and building comfort (IST, 2013). BIM models have revealed themselves to be an excellent tool not only during the stage of planning and construction, but also in the maintenance phase, mainly because of its large capacity for storing information associated with the three dimensional (3D) representation (Goedert and Meadati, 2008). The fact that it is possible to access all the information of the building, through a single platform, combined with the automatic update of the model whenever changes are made, makes the BIM model very advantageous and promising during the exploration stage of a building, for this way, more reliable and accurate maintenance operations can be achieved (Martins and Cachadinha, 2012).

If on one hand, getting an accurate and omission free update of the models using the Industry Foundation Classes (IFC) standard, is one of the main difficulties encountered when using BIM models during the exploration stage of a building (Goedert and Meadati, 2008), then on the other, maintenance of buildings has proved to be a rather complex task to accomplish, because the identification and analysis of all kinds of failure in construction requires a considerable effort of the agents responsible for maintaining the facility (IST, 2013). As such, in this work we have developed an innovative software tool, aimed to support the inspection operations of buildings, making them more efficient and error-free, due to its rigorous database, allowing the user to identify anomalies in the construction components directly on the BIM model, and associate them with the probable cause, recommended solution, repair method and a photograph. Additionally, it was case study the interoperability between BIM modeling and visualizing software, regarding the preservation of information, especially in the IFC standard.

This work contributed to demonstrate, not only that there are still problems concerning the interoperability between BIM software, but also the advantages of employing BIM for building maintenance purposes.

2 BIM Model

The architectural BIM model was created, using the Revit Architecture software. In order to illustrate how to carry out the modeling of a building using a BIM based software, a small fraction of real estate development in Cascais, near Lisbon, Portugal, was chosen as case study. The building consists of three floors; the ground floor consists of two dwellings and the remaining floors, four duplex dwellings. Each dwelling consists of bedrooms, toilets, kitchen, living room, hall and balcony.

In the model, all elements represented as walls, floors, ceilings, roof, doors, windows, and handrails, were created by adapting existing 3D parametric objects in the Revit library. The components of decorative character and equipment, such as sofas, chairs, toilets, tables were used directly, merely taking into account the scale factor during their inclusion in the model. Table 1 presents the orderly steps in the creation of architectural BIM model.

Table 1 Steps in the creation of architectural BIM model.

Steps	Procedure
1st step	Defining sill elevations of the flooring
2nd step	Importing dwg files
3rd step	Defining the construction platform
4th step	Modifying the contour lines
5th step	Creating, editing and inserting the walls
6th step	Creating, editing and inserting the doors and windows
7th step	Creating, editing and inserting the pavements and the false ceilings
8th step	Creating, editing and inserting the roof
9th step	Creating, editing and inserting the staircases
10th step	Creating, editing and inserting the guardrails
11th step	Inserting the components

Some drawings and projections can be obtained from the established model. Figure 1 shows a plan and a cut and Figure 2 illustrates the main facade, a general perspective of the model, and one view shot of the interior.

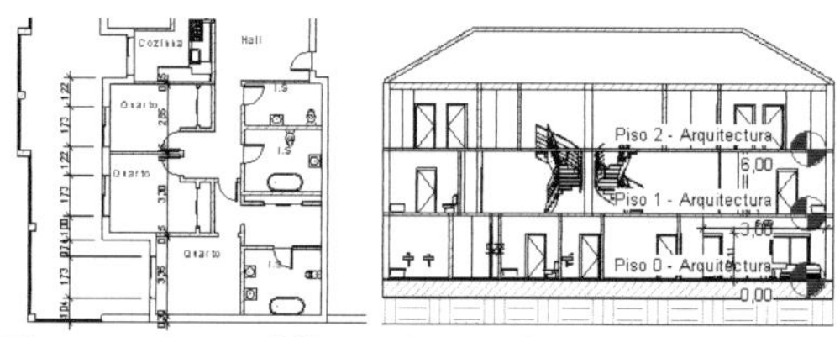

Figure 1 Ground floor plan and vertical cut

Figure 2 Main façade, general perspective and interior projection of the 3D model

3 Program of maintenance

The interactive inspection operations sheet, created using the Visual Basic software, has as main objective to support the implementation of an inspection. In its development the database that was used consisted in the compilation of information from other dissertations also developed for maintenance purposes. The information provided in this work relates to anomalies, causes, solutions and repair methodology concerning constructive components: exterior walls (Gomes, 2010); interior walls (Rosario, 2011); pitched roofs (Afonso, 2013). Therefore, during an inspection, the maintenance technician, when observing an anomaly, can consult the database support to fill out the inspection sheets and select the identified anomaly on the site.

Subsequently, the completed inspection sheet is then converted to the *pdf* format and inserted into the BIM model. This model should be constantly updated, in order to accurately support the facility with repair and maintenance plans. The developed computer application has its interface illustrated in Figure 3. An inspection sheet must include some initial information such as identification of the technician, the date of the inspection and the identity and characteristics of the building (address, city, number of floors, year of construction, etc...).

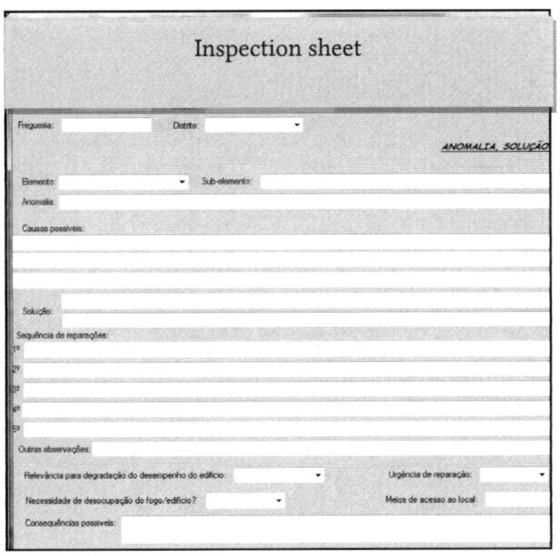

Figure 3. Interface of the inspection sheet.

A sheet of the inspection must include some initial information such as identification of the technician, the date of the inspection and the identity and characteristics of the building (address, city, number of floors, year of construction, etc...). Most of this information is selected from *ComboBox* elements, so your registration is carried in a fast way. A *ComboBox* element is defined with a combination of a text box and a list box, allowing the filling of the text box with one of the options provided in the list that appears as a descending menu.

In addition, a *ComboBox* element allows the user to group relations of dependence between them, providing different lists depending on types of elements, that is, the box lists differ according to the option selected in advance. In the developed software tool, this feature is observed between the elements and sub-elements, among the verified sub-elements and anomalies and between anomalies and possible causes, solutions and repair sequences (Figure 4).

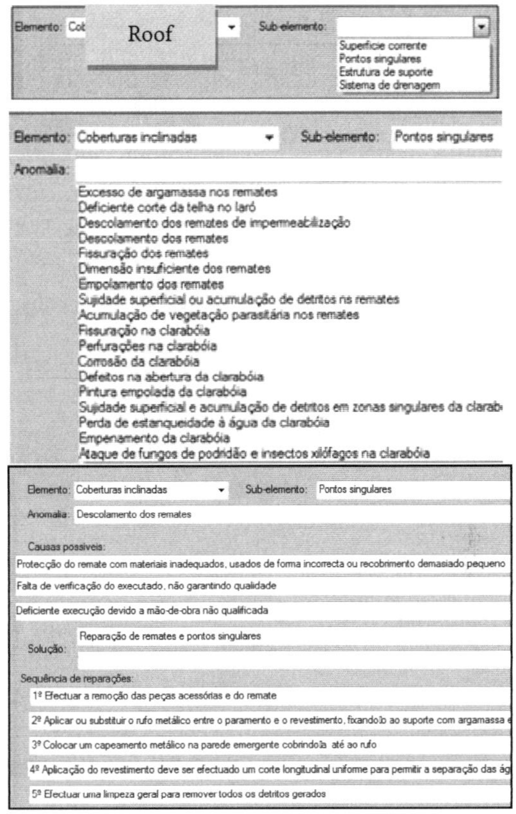

Figure 4. Lists of available anomalies according to the chosen element and sub-element and Causes, solution and repair sequence automatically filled after choosing the element, sub-element and anomaly.

The application also allows you to include a photograph of the anomaly taken at the site and convert the information presented in the sheet of inspection to a document in pdf format. Such possibilities are essential for an inspection sheet, because the addition of a photograph allows the user to recognize the anomaly, its severity and location, and conversion to pdf format enables the user to save the inspection form in an universal format.The result of filling the form and its presentation in pdf, are illustrated respectively in Figure 5.

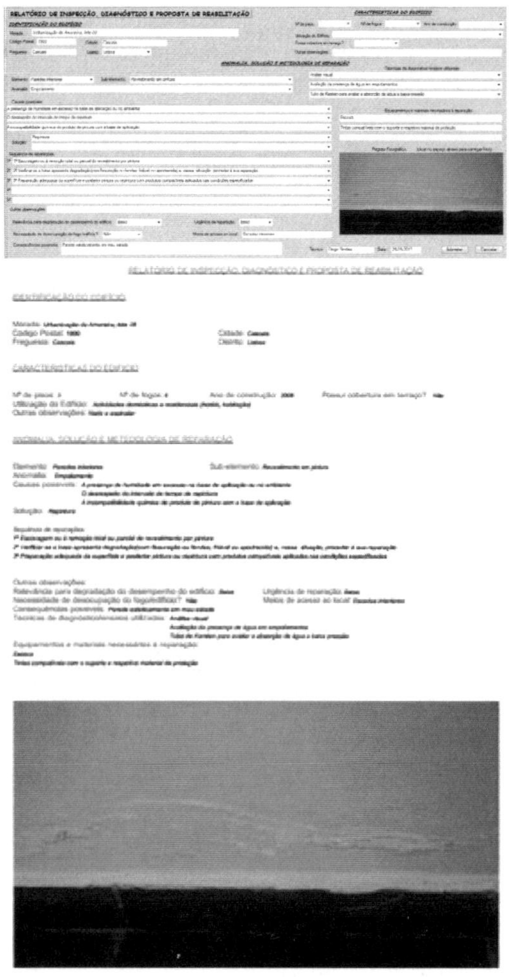

Figure 5. Interface of the filled out inspection form and Inspection sheet in pdf format.

4 BIM Model and Program

A BIM visualizer is an application that enables access to all information created in the BIM model. Unlike the modeling software, navigation and interaction with the model is performed quickly and lighter, and can also be accessed from mobile devices such as smartphones or tablets. This type of application also allows integrating the diverse information from architectural designs, structures, building installations and budgeting, and also allows the analysis of conflict detection. This chapter covers how to combine the BIM model of the building, the information from the inspection form, using a BIM visualizer. This study requires the analysis of interoperability between the BIM modeler and the BIM visualizer (*Navisworks*), regarding in particular data and information transfer in the IFC format.

Furthermore, an inspection form is filled in and, afterwards, saved and included in the model, so that it can be used as a basis for consultation when planning maintenance operations.

The data transfer between the BIM modeler and visualizer, in IFC standard, resulted in complete preservation of information and error free. The only limitations observed were the clutter of information and a lack of storage capacity of the previously predefined colors, which led to the total deprivation of color of the model, as illustrated in Figure 6.

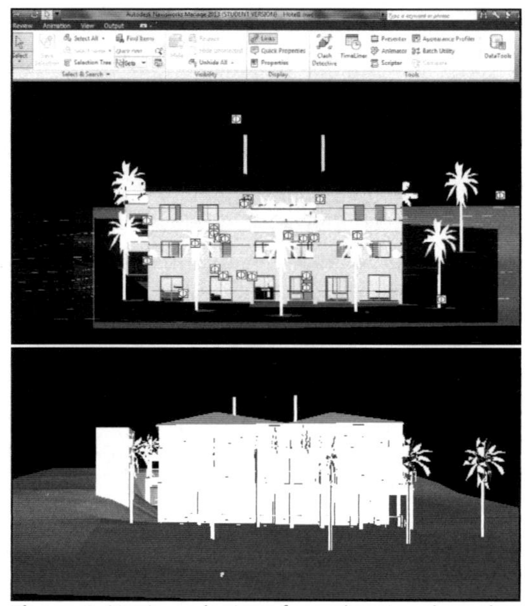

Figure 6. Navisworks interface showing the color deprivation in the IFC format.

In an inspection activity the maintenance technician, using the developed application, selects the element where an anomaly was observed, in this case an interior wall (shown in blue in Figure 7). Through the BIM model, the service technician can identify the constituent materials of the interior wall (Figure 7) and has the possibility to run the inspection program, by selecting the link "Program", fill out the inspection form and store it in the BIM model, through the creation of a new link. Let us assume for example, that the inspection sheet was recorded under the name "Inspection 29 Oct. 2014- Anomaly- paint blistering".

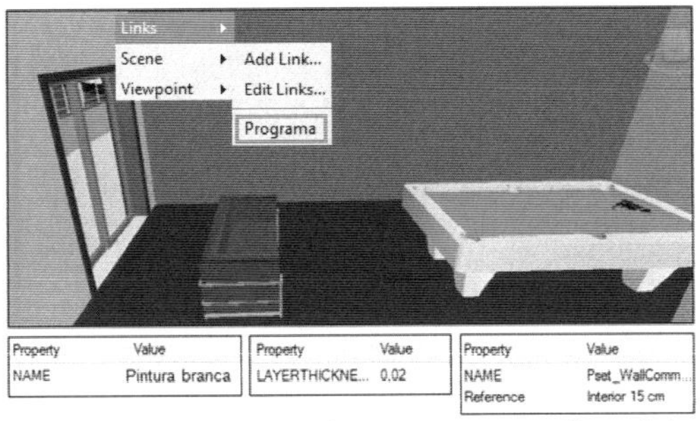

Figure 7. Selection of an exterior wall and its associated features, and of the link "Program".

Whilst planning for maintenance operations, or any other inspection activity, the choice of the element in which lies the anomaly (the wall inside the room depicted in blue in Figure 7) identifies two associated attachments: the inspection program and a sheet of the inspection carried out on the 29 Oct. 2013, concerning an anomaly called paint blistering (Figure 8).

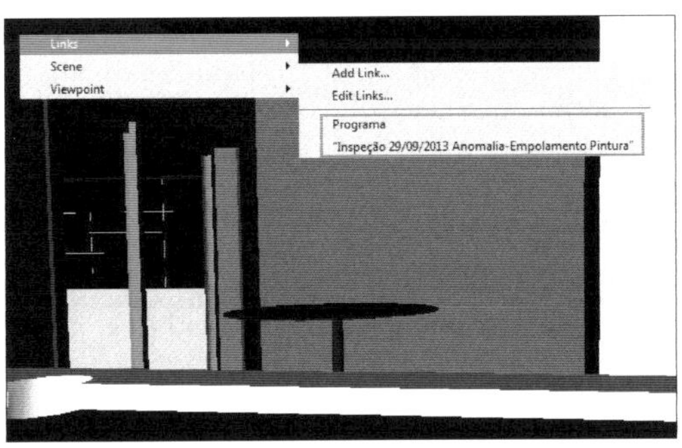

Figure 8. Selection of the inspection sheet of the anomaly associated with the inner wall.

By choosing the link "Inspection 29 Oct. 2013 - Anomaly- paint blistering", the user is automatically opening the *pdf* document related to the associated inspection form, i.e. the sheet shown in Figure 8.

This consultation allows us to better understand what the probable causes that originated the new anomaly are. If the problem shows a degree of severity or has been subjected to some kind of repair, the materials used and the exact location of the anomalies that have already been registered (through photography). An interaction with the application can be seen in reference (http_youtube, 2014).

5 Implementation Problems

The creation of the inspection sheet had some problems, particularly concerning the creation of a routine that allows the insertion of any picture on the form, and in obtaining the *pdf-sharp* library that would allow its conversion to *pdf* format.

However, the creation of an inspection sheet to support the maintenance of buildings, based on a BIM model would be unsuccessful if the digital modeling of a building wasn't performed. Therefore, parallel to the creation of the inspection form, an architectural BIM model was developed from scratch, being described every step of its development, illustrating the procedures of its establishment and insertion of distinct data type, with the objective of providing the building relevant information, which could be reused. Then, the modeling was exported using the IFC format to a BIM visualizer so that it could be displayed in a fast and efficient manner. The implementation of the model was done not only as a necessity, but also in order to study one of the major obstacles to the implementation of BIM, its interoperability under the IFC format. In fact, this work confirms that the IFC format is not yet fully developed in order to properly implement the information models, as, despite not losing any information, it features it in a disorganized manner, not retaining the color added to the model.

A BIM visualizer allows the representation of BIM models in a simple and fast way, allowing the user to add different models and different documents, programs or notes. As such, a program that supports the inspection of buildings was added to the BIM visualizer software. This combination's main objective is to aid in the maintenance activity of a building, because it allows the maintenance technician to perform inspections with the developed software by automatically running it after selecting the building element in the model. You can also save the inspection form in *pdf* format by entering it again in the model. So any maintenance technician can consult all the information concerning a given building element, not only its materials, dimensions and physical characteristics, but also its historical anomalies, any intervention that it has been subjected to and their exact location on the element, providing an important aid in keeping the building and therefore the comfort of their users.

Adding the program to the BIM visualizer of is done in a fairly simple way, however, it was observed that some visualizers do not support certain applications, which indicates difficult defect to overcome, when the main purpose of these is the aggregation of information in any form. It was also noted that it still wasn't possible to automatically save the inspection sheet onto the building element selected in the BIM visualizer. Overcoming this obstacle would result in even greater productivity, when filling out the forms and then associating them to the model, this being just one more aspect that would support the association between the inspection program and the BIM visualizer.

6 Conclusions

Effective facility maintenance is based on a thorough inspection for anomalies. Therefore, an inspection sheet was developed, with the purpose of enhancing the technical inspection, of a tool that lists anomalies, for the constructive element selected, automatically providing, the repair procedure, its main causes and respective solution. Thus inspections are carried out in greater detail, and hence greater chronological and productivity gains can be achieved. The ability to write in *pdf* format reveals itself most important for subsequent addition to a BIM model. It can be concluded that with this work, a useful program was established to support building inspections and future maintenance operations, which associated with an architectural BIM model, and taking into consideration that the benefits would be greater if the BIM model integrated various specialties, it was demonstrated that the great potential inherent in BIM, as a methodology, can be revealed in the actions of maintenance of a building..

References

Afonso, L. (2013) Maintenance of buildings supported on virtual reality technology (in Portuguese). *Master thesis in Civil Engineering*, Technical University of Lisbon, Portugal.

Eastman, C., Teicholz, P., Sacks, R,. Liston, K. (2011) *BIM Handbook - A Guide to Building Information Modelling*. Second Edition. New Jersey: John Wiley & Sons, Inc.

Goedert, J., Meadati, P. (2008) Integrating Construction Process Documentation into Building *Information Modelling. J. Constr. Eng. Manage.*, 134(7), pp. 509–516.

Gomes, A. (2010) Virtual reality technology applied in the maintenance of facades (in Portuguese). *Master thesis in Civil Engineering*, Technical University of Lisbon, Portugal.

Hartmann, T., Gao, J., Fischer, M. (2008) Areas of Application for 3D and 4D Models on Construction Projects. *Journal of construction Engineering and Management*, pp. 776–785. http_youtube (2013) http://www.youtube.com/watch?v=tkiqsoHk_UI (Accessed in September 2013)

Martins, F., Cachadinha, N. (2012) New uses of BIM capabilities: support for the work carried out measurement and production of as-built models reliable and rich in information to the maintenance phase (in Portuguese). *4th National Construction Conference*, FCT, University Nova, Lisbon, Portugal.

NBS (2013) National Institute of Building Sciences - www.wbdg.org/ pdfs/NBIMSv1_p1.pdf (Accessed in September 2013)

Rosario, D. (2011) Virtual reality technology applied in the maintenance of buildings: interior walls with paint coating (in Portuguese) *Master thesis in Civil Engineering*, Technical University of Lisbon, Portugal.

*** Formatting Issue - Best Available Paper/Graphic ***

Graph-based generating systems in urban space design

Barbara Strug, barbara.strug@uj.edu.pl
Jagiellonian University, Poland

Grażyna Ślusarczyk, gslusarc@uj.edu.pl
Jagiellonian University, Poland

Abstract
In this paper a mechanism supporting the design process of urban spaces is presented. The proposed system of graph grammars allows to separate generated structures describing arrangements of city components from their shape geometry and overall appearance. A great number of unique city designs with similar layout structures can be easily obtained and then filled with previously modelled 3D components. The system of cooperating distributed grammars operates on one common attributed graph, while the communication between grammars is realized through a set of communication labels. The proposed approach is illustrated by the case study of generating a city quarter using the specified graph grammar system.

Keywords: Urban design, graph representation, grammar systems

1 Introduction

The problem of automatic modelling of large urban environments is widely studied in literature. In (Parish & Muller, 2001; Greuter et al., 2003, Wonka et al., 2006) procedural methods of city modelling are presented. As there are many recurrently repeating patterns in urban geometry, various types of grammars are often used to generate city components. 2D shape grammars, which allow to derive building layout zones are described in (Susinno, 2003), while generating realistic building fronts with the use of split grammars is presented in (Wonka et al., 2003). Using L-systems in building city layouts is described in (Parish & Muller, 2001).

In this paper graph grammars are proposed as a generative tool for designing urban spaces. They give a large amount of freedom in composing city designs as they allow to separate the generated structure describing the arrangement and relations between components from their shape geometry and overall appearance. A relatively small set of rules can be applied to generate a great number of unique city designs with similar layout structures. The obtained designs can be then filled with previously modelled 3D components of a given repository or exported to a chosen rendering engine or visualisation system.

It can be observed that one of the main problems of graph generation using graph grammars lies in the complexity and size (understood as the number of rules) of grammars that are needed in real world problems. Such grammars tend to be both difficult to define and not very intuitive, resulting in being difficult to understand. Thus the use of a number of simpler grammars cooperating together (called a grammar system) seems to be a good solution to a great part of the above mentioned problem.

The work presented here is motivated by a need for a mechanism supporting the design process of complex, real-world artifacts. It also deals with the problem of coordinating different and independent graph grammars, responsible for different aspects of design, but at the same time operating on the shared areas of design.

A grammar system consists of a finite number of grammars (called components of the system) which together modify an environment by applying some operations to it. At a given moment the state of the system is described by the current environment (sub-environments).

In the theory of formal languages two main types of grammar systems are researched: parallel communicating grammar systems (PC grammar systems, Csuhaj-Varjú & Vaszil, 2001) and cooperating distributed grammar systems (CD grammar systems, Kelemen, 1991). The main difference between these types of grammar systems consists in the model of environment they work on. In PC grammar systems components operate on their own copies of the structure being derivated and they only exchange information on request. In case of CD grammar systems the grammars operate on one common structure, one grammar at a time.

As in computer aided design domain complex objects composed of many elements are usually developed, the CD grammar systems seem more appropriate here. They allow for a number of grammars to work together on one object. At any given time step there is only one structure being generated. Each component grammar operates on this structure according to a communication protocol called the derivation mode. The protocol may allow a single component to perform a predefined number of steps or to work until no production of this component can be applied. The method of selecting which grammar should be used as the next active component is also important. Such cooperating grammars can be seen as independent cooperating agents solving a large problem by modifying a common environment (often compared with the blackboard model in artificial intelligence). The use of graph grammar systems for floor layouts has been already researched (Grabska & Strug, 2005, Grabska et al. 2009).

In this paper the urban designs are represented in the form of attributed graphs, where nodes represent streets, buildings and other infrastructure elements, while edges describe relations between them. These graphs are generated by the proposed system composed of several grammars. The grammars of the system operate on the common attributed graph. First, the whole city layout is divided into zones of different types, i.e., commercial, residential, industrial, recreational, communication, administrative. Building density in zones is specified by attributes assigned to graph nodes representing zones. Then each graph grammar of the system independently creates the arrangement of components belonging to one type of zone. Then, solids selected of the set related with a given zone are located in places determined by grammar rules.

This paper proposes a grammar-based model for a computer-aided distributed design system which facilitates the automatic modelling of urban environments. The communication of the system of graph grammars is realized through a set of variables assigned to grammars and allowing for their activation. The resulting graph structure can be passed to the interpretation module and then visualized. The proposed distributed model of computing allows us to quickly generate different city layouts compatible with criteria encoded in grammar rules.

The proposed approach is illustrated by the case study showing several possible solutions of the criteria based design of the city quarter generated by the graph grammar system.

2 Graph-based design representation

In this paper the urban designs are represented in the form of attributed graphs. A graph is formally defined as a pair (V, E), where V and E are sets of graph nodes and edges, respectively.

In case of using graphs as representations of designs generated by a design system, a node in a graph usually represents either an object or a group of objects or, more generally, it may be seen as a "container" for a part of a design that may be designed at later time. For example, in a house design system a node can represent a floor of a house that in turn will be divided into rooms. Each node of a graph is labelled by a symbol from a predefined set (alphabet) that is later used to add some semantics to the representation.

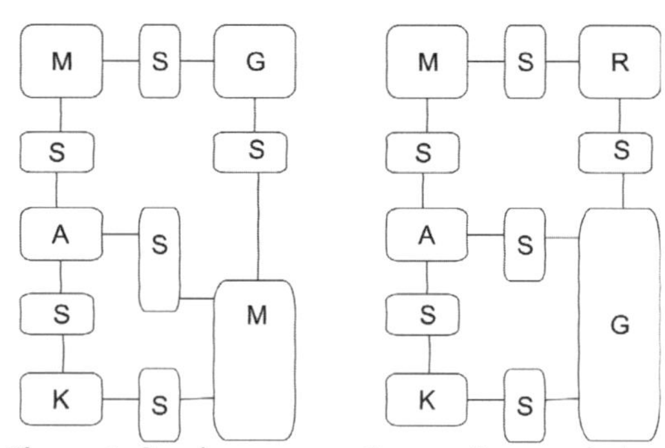

Figure 1 Graphs representing a city area being designed and obtained by applying different productions

Edges represent relations between objects. They are labelled by symbols being names of the relations. Labels are assigned to nodes and edges by means of node and edge labelling functions.

Moreover, as there is a need to represent some particular features/parameters of the objects and relations between them attributing of both nodes and edges is used. Attributes represent properties of an element represented by a given node (for example size, position, colour or material) or edge (for example distance).

Attributes are assigned by node and edge attributing functions. Formally, an attribute is a function $a: W \rightarrow D_a$, where W is a domain of the attribute and D_a is a set of possible values of the attribute.

Let Σ_V and Σ_E be the sets of node and edge labels, respectively, $\Sigma = \Sigma_V \cup \Sigma_E$. Let A and B be sets of node and edge attributes, and D_a and D_b be sets of possible values of attributes of nodes and edges, respectively.

Definition 1. A **labelled attributed graph** over Σ is a 6-tuple $G = (V, E, lab_V, lab_E, att_V, att_E)$, where:

- V and E are sets of graph nodes and edges,
- $lab_V : V \rightarrow \Sigma_V$ is a node labelling function,
- $lab_E: E \rightarrow \Sigma_E$ is an edge labelling function,
- $att_V: V \rightarrow 2^A$ is a node attributing function assigning a set of attributes to each node,
- $att_E: E \rightarrow 2^B$ is an edge attributing function assigning a set of attributes to each edge.

In Figure 1 two graphs representing an area composed of five zones (living (M), recreational (R), commercial (G), administrative (A) and communication (K)) and streets (S) connecting zones are depicted. Graph nodes represent zones of the area to be designed and edges represent communication possibility between them and distances or relative placements. These graphs may be further developed to add more details, for example the node representing a living zone (M) can be replaced by nodes representing actual buildings of different types. For the clarity of the figure attributes are not shown, but they include sizes, position and other features specific for the elements.

To represent an actual design we must define a graph instance, which is a labelled attributed graph in which for all attributes assigned to nodes and edges values of these attributes are determined. For example attributes assigned to graph nodes of the urban design representation and specifying sizes and locations of the corresponding areas should have determined values.

The instance graph makes it possible to obtain a whole class of designs with the similar structure but different geometry. To obtain such visualisations of different design solutions an interpretation of this graph is necessary.

An interpretation of a graph G is defined as a pair of functions (I_V, I_E), where I_V assigns to nodes geometrical objects determined by values of attributes associated with these nodes, while I_E establishes a correspondence between edges and relations between these objects. The objects assigned by I_V may be either simple geometrical objects or more complex objects. The geometry of these objects may be internally represented by means of any known representation. Objects used depend on the domain of application. In an urban design system a set of objects can contain such elements as buildings of different types, roads, lamps, benches or trees.

3 Design generation

The graphs representing designs may be dynamically generated by means of so called graph grammars. These grammars allow for generating many graphs with structures compatible with the syntax of grammar rules.

Let G and H be two labelled attributed graphs, such that $G \subseteq H$. Let $EMB(G,H)$ denote a set of edges connecting nodes of G with nodes of $H \backslash G$, called the embedding of G in H. Let $\Sigma_V = N \cup T$ be an alphabet of node labels composed of non-terminal and terminal ones, respectively.

A graph grammar is composed of a set of productions (rules) and an axiom being an initial graph. Each grammar production has the form $p = (L, R, \pi, C, F)$, where L and R are graphs with at least one node in L with a non-terminal label, π is a predicate of applicability, C is an embedding transformation, and F is a set of attribute transfer functions. A direct derivation step in a graph grammar (application of a production p) consists of replacing a subgraph L' isomorphic with L of a host graph H by R, and embedding R in the rest of the host graph $(H \backslash L')$ according to the embedding transformation C defined for this production. Values of attributes assigned to nodes and edges of R and edges of $EMB(R, H \backslash L')$ are specified by the functions of F.

Let G_A be a family of attributed graphs defined over Σ and $H \in G_A$. Formally a production is defined in the following way:

Definition 2. A **production** is a system $p = (L, R, \pi, C, F)$, where:

- L and R are graphs over Σ, and such that there exist a node v of L, such that $lab_V(v) \in N$,
- π: $G_A \rightarrow$ {TRUE, FALSE} is an applicability predicate, which on the basis of the values of attributes of host graph H determines whether a production can be applied,
- $C \subseteq \Sigma_V \times \Sigma_E \times \Sigma_V$ is an embedding transformation, where each triple of the form $(\sigma_1, \sigma_2, \sigma_3)$ denotes that an edge labelled σ_2 should be created between each node of R with the label σ_1 and nodes labelled σ_3 of $H \backslash L'$, where L' is a subgraph of H isomorphic with L.
- $F = \{f_a \,|\, f_a : V_R \longrightarrow D_a\} \cup \{f_b | f_b : E_R \cup EMB(R, H \backslash L') \longrightarrow D_b\}$, where $a \in A$, D_a is a set of values defined for a, $b \in B$, D_b is a set of values defined for b, and $EMB(R, H \backslash L')$ is composed of edges obtained by replacing edges of $EMB(L', H)$ according to C, is a set of partial attribute transfer functions.

Figure 2 depicts an example production responsible for adding more details to the living zone. It adds two buildings (represented by nodes labelled b) and also introduces a node with a non-terminal label B, which can be further developed by adding other nodes representing buildings. This production can always be applied so the predicate of applicability is set to TRUE. The embedding transformation C establishes the connection of the new nodes with the rest of the host graph in the derivation process.

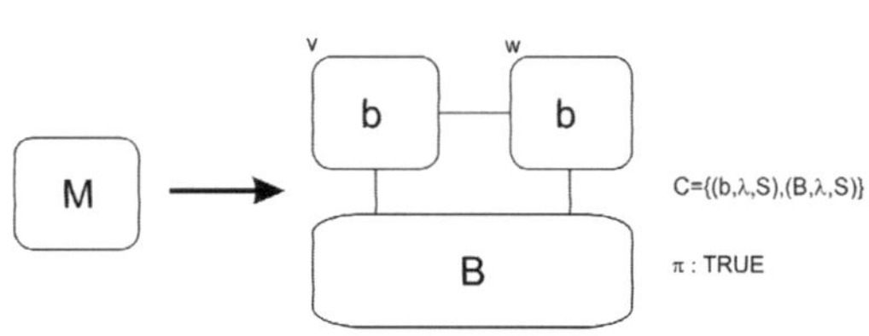

Figure 2 An example of a production from grammar G_2

Definition 3. A **graph grammar** over Σ is defined as $G = (P, x)$ where:

- P is a finite set of productions $p = (L, R, \pi, C, F)$, and
- x is a node with $lab_V(x) \in N$, called the axiom of the grammar.

In many design situations there is a need to preserve or even to propagate some information throughout the generation process, that is some sort of communicating between productions is needed. In this paper we propose an approach similar to the blackboard method in artificial intelligence i.e., all the productions of a given grammar can access and/or modify a common set of variables. This set will be called *memory*.

Formally a graph grammar with memory is defined in the following way.

Definition 4. A **graph grammar with memory** is a pair $GM = (M, G)$, where:

- M is a set of variables, $M = \{m_1, \ldots, m_n\}$, such that for $i = 1, \ldots, n$, a set of all possible values for m_i is denoted by D_i, and
- $G = (P, x)$ is a graph grammar, where P is a set of productions of the form $p = (L, R, \pi, C, F, k)$ defined as follows:
  - L, R, C, and F are defined as in Definition 2,
  - π: $G_A \times 2^M \rightarrow \{TRUE, FALSE\}$ is an applicability predicate, which determines the possibility of the production application on the basis of the values of both attributes of host graph H and variables of M,
  - $k = \{k_1, \ldots, k_n\}$ is a set of functions responsible for changing values of memory variables, where $k_i : 2^M \times L \rightarrow D_i$.

For the productions of the graph grammar with memory their applicability predicates take into account not only the values of attributes of the host graph but also values of memory variables. The functions of the family k modify values of the chosen subsets of memory variables in respect to attribute values of the left-hand side graph L. It also important that the above definition does not put any additional constraints on the type of grammar G, i.e. it can be a context-free or context grammar.

In the graph grammar responsible for the development of the living zone the memory consist of one variable m_f which contains the maximum number of flats within the area. Thus, the production depicted in Figure 2 changes the value of m_f according to the function k: m_f -(v.size+w.size), where *size* is the attribute assigned to nodes v and w of the production right-hand side and represents the number of flats within buildings.

In this paper a modification of CD grammar systems is proposed. It can be observed that while absolutely justifiable in string grammars the requirement that only one grammar can operate on a given temporary form (called sentential form) seems too strong in case of graph grammars. Moreover in design systems it would be useful to allow more than one grammar to operate on the same, common, sentential form. The proposed system of graph grammars can be seen as an equivalent of many design teams or agents working on different parts of the same design. To maintain the consistency of the design it must be ensured that no two agents work at the same time on the same part of the design, i.e., no two grammars (components) operate on the same nodes of the sentential form.

Moreover, some way of activating particular component grammars must be defined. This problem is solved by using a set of communication labels for graph nodes. In this paper a so called terminal derivation mode is used, i.e., each grammar works as long as it contains a production that can be applied to a current graph.

Let $Y \subseteq N$ be a set of communication node labels.

Definition 5. A **graph grammar system** over Σ is defined as $GGS = (GM_1, GM_2, \ldots, GM_s, g_0)$, where:

- $GM_i = (M_i, (P_i, x_i))$, for i = 1, ... s, are graph grammars with memory over Σ_i such that
    - $\Sigma_i = T_i \cup N_i$, where $N_i \supseteq Y_i$, is a set of terminal and non-terminal labels which include communication labels for the i-th grammar component, respectively,
    - $N = \sum_{i=1}^{s} N_i$, $T = \sum_{i=1}^{s} T_i$, $Y = \sum_{i=1}^{s} Y_i$
    - L_i of each P_i (i.e., its left-hand side) is the attributed graph labelled over $\Sigma_i \backslash Y_i$, while R_i (i.e., its right-hand side) is the attributed graph labelled over Σ_i,
    - $\forall v$ with $lab_V(v) \in Y_i$ $\exists$ j $\neq$ i such that $lab_V(v) \in N_j$,
    - $\forall v$ with $lab_V(v) \in N_i \backslash Y_i \; \exists \; p \in P_i$ such that L_i contains v,
    - $\prod_{i=1}^{s} M_i = \varnothing$,
- g_0 is an initial graph labelled over $T \cup Y$ and such that there exists at least one node in g_0 with the label of Y.

The nodes of the graphs of the right-hand side and left-hand side of the productions are labelled by terminals and non-terminals, but on the left-hand sides there do not exist nodes with communication labels. The nodes with non-terminal labels can be intuitively understood as representing parts of the design that are not finished but a given grammar knows how to deal with them further. Taking this intuition further a communication label means that a particular grammar knows that some part of the design is not finished but it is not specialist in this part and thus it communicates with other grammar that knows how to deal with this part. Terminal labels represent parts of the design that are considered to be finished (at least by the set of available rules).

The definition of a grammar system guarantees that if any grammar introduces a communication label into the host graph, then there exists the other grammar which contains the same label in its set of non-terminals.

Similarly as in the single grammar case, when applying a grammar system to real life problems a need to communicate between grammars may occur. To provide for such a situation we introduce a grammar system with memory.

Definition 6. A **graph grammar system with memory** is a triple $GSM = (GGS, M, K)$, where:

- GGS= (GM_1, GM_2,..., GM_s, g_0) is a graph grammar system,
- M is a memory which contains variables shared by all grammars of GGS, and such that $M \cap \bigcup_{i=1}^{s} M_i = \varnothing$,
- K = $\bigcup_{i=1}^{s} k_i$ is a family of functions allowing each production of each grammar in GGS to change the value of elements of system memory M.

In the proposed urban design system the component graph grammars of GSM are context-free, i.e., the left-hand side of each production of GM_i is composed of only one node labelled by the element of $N_i \setminus Y_i$. In each derivation step of a graph generation using such a system of grammars, when the node with the label σ is replaced, either a rewriting step in a grammar GM_i is performed, if σ belongs $N_i \setminus Y_i$ (i.e., σ is not a communication label), or a rewriting step in a grammar GM_j is performed, if σ belongs to Y_i and to $N_j \setminus Y_j$ (i.e., σ is a communication label of GM_i).

Definition 7. Let H_1 and H_2 be two labelled attributed graphs of G_A. Let v with $lab_V(v) \in N$ be a node of H_1. Let $GSM = (GM_1, GM_2, \ldots, GM_s, g_0, M, K)$ be a context-free graph grammar system with memory.
H_2 is **directly derivable** from H_1 using GSM ($H_1 \Rightarrow H_2$) if there exist a production $p = (L, R, \pi, C, F, k)$ of GM_i such that the node of L has the label $lab_V(v)$ and π is satisfied by H_1, and H_2 is isomorphic with the result of replacing v in H_1 by R and embedding R in the graph $H_1 \setminus v$ according to the embedding transformation C. Values of attributes assigned to nodes and edges of R and edges of $EMB(R, H_1 \setminus v)$ are specified by the functions of F. Moreover variables of M are modified by using functions k of K.

To demonstrate advantages of the proposed graph derivation method the sample grammar graph system with memory is proposed. The purpose of this system is to design an urban area, first dividing it into different zones, and then arranging these zone in various possible ways. The system is composed of seven grammars. The memory of the system consists of two elements and is defined as $M = \{Mp, Mb\}$. Mp represents the number of parking spaces within the designed area. As opposed to the maximum number of flats, which can only be changed by the grammar responsible for the living zone, the variable Mp can be changed by other grammars, as parking places can be added within different zones of the area. Mb determines the number of benches to be placed within the area (in different zones). Its initial value is specified by the designer.

The grammar G_1 is responsible for generating the initial subdivision of the area into zones of different type (like residential, commercial and so on). In Figure 1 two examples of graphs obtained by its application and representing area subdivisions are presented. The node labels which denote different zones (labeled as M, G, A, R, K) are communication labels, while the other labels (S) are terminal ones and denote streets which are to be located between zones. The grammars G_2 – G_6 of the system determine the arrangements of the mentioned zones (G_2 is responsible for designing the living zone, G_3 - for the administrative zone, G_4 - for the commercial one, G_5 - for the recreational zone, G_6 - for the communication one), while G_7 is responsible for designing parking areas which can be located in each zone. Memory of each grammar contains variables important for the development the considered zone. Additionally, the predicates of applicability are used for some productions to cover the requirements for the placement of selected elements. The embedding transformations of system grammars allow for connecting the nodes representing components of zones generated by grammars with the nodes representing nearest streets taking into account values of attributes specifying locations of urban components.

In Figures 2 and 3 some productions of the graph grammar, which develops the living zone, are depicted. In Figure 3 five productions of the grammar G_2 are shown. All four of them are applicable if the current number of required flats in this zone is greater than the building size. The fifth production is applicable if the current number of required flats in this zone is greater than the building size and the number of required parking spaces is greater than 0. This production allows to add a node representing a low building and a node representing a parking area with the

***** Formatting Issue - Best Available Paper/Graphic *****

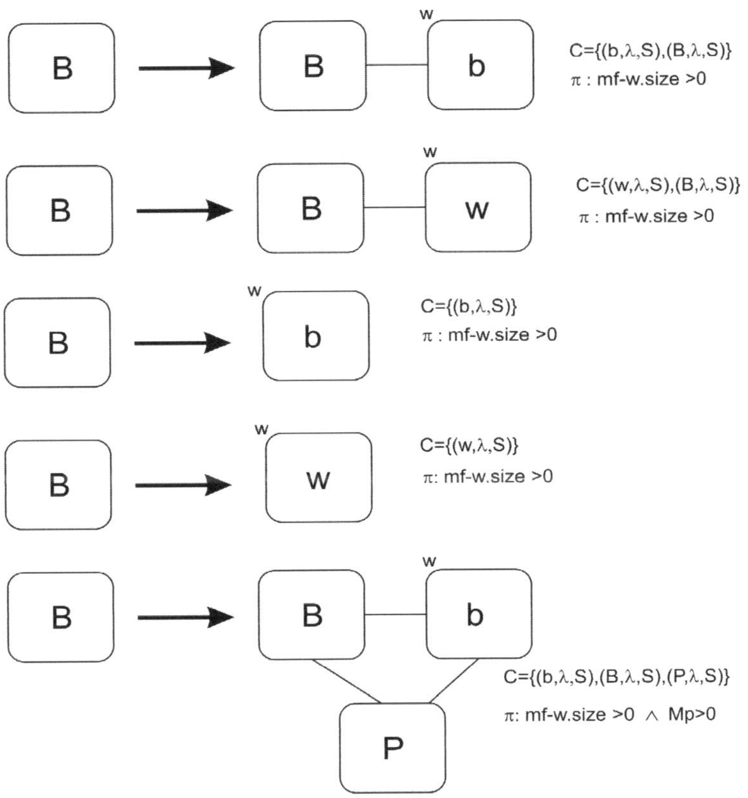

Figure 3 Examples of productions of the grammar G_2

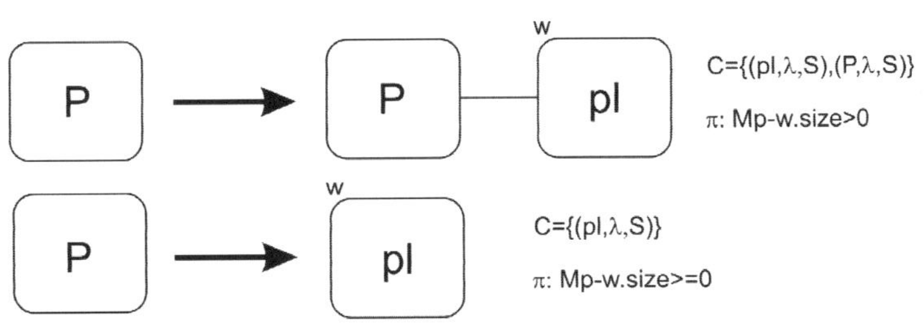

Figure 4 Examples of productions of the grammar G_7

Figure 5 Screenshot of the partial design (a) and the finished project (b)

label P, which is a communication label. This means that the parking area will be designed by another grammar (G_7).

In Figure 4 two productions which allow to add parking lots assuming that each lot does not exceed the required parking space.

Definition 8. Let $GSM = (GM_1, GM_2, ..., GM_s, g_0, M, K)$ be a context-free graph grammar system with memory. The language generated by GSM is a set
$L(GSM) = \{H \in G_A \mid g_0 \Rightarrow^* H \wedge \forall v \in H\ lab_V(v) \in T\}$.

The approach was implemented in the form of the test system which allows for developing an area and shows the graph structure during the development process. In Figure 5a a screenshot of the application is presented. It depicts the partial design, where the administrative and recreational zones are not yet developed. At the top of the screen the productions, which can be used in the next derivation step, are presented. Figure 5b shows the graph representing the finished design of the considered urban area.

4 Conclusions

In this paper an idea of intelligent, computer supported design by the use of cooperating grammar systems is proposed. This method is illustrated by a problem of design the city quarter. This example shows the usefulness of equipping individual grammars and all system of grammars with memory. The elements of memory solve the problem of dealing with resources shared by different grammars.

In future the theoretical results related to the expressive power of the proposed grammar system will be studied. Nearly all such results, as for example ability of a small number of context-free grammars to generate a language of identical or similar expressive power with the one produced by non context-free grammar, are now available only for systems composed of string grammars.

In this paper simple graphs and graph grammars were used. However it seems that adding a hierarchical structure to the graph would largely extend its understanding. Hierarchical graph representation of design structures will reflect the top-down way of design and simplify arrangements of graph elements. We will research the possibility of extending the proposed approach to hierarchical graphs and hierarchical graph grammars.

*** Formatting Issue - Best Available Paper/Graphic ***

References

Parish, Y. I. H. & Muller, P. (2001). Procedural modeling of cities. *Proc. of ACM SIGGRAPH 2001*, ACM Press, E. Fiume, Ed., pp. 301-308.

Grabska, E. & Strug B. (2005). Applying Cooperating Distributed Graph Grammars in Computer Aided Design. *Proc. of* PPAM 2005, LNCS 3911. pp 567-574.

Grabska, E., Strug B. & Ślusarczyk, G. (2009). A Multiagent Distributed Design System. *Proc. of* PAAMS 2009: Advances in Intelligent and Soft Computing 5. pp. 364-373.

Greuter, S., Parker, J., Stewart, N. & Leach, G. (2003). Real-time Procedural Generation of 'Pseudo Infinite' Cities. *Proc. of GRAPHITE 2003*, ACM SIGGRAPH, pp. 87-94.

Muller, P., Wonka, P., Haegler, S., Ulmer, A. & Van Gool, L. (2006). Procedural Modeling of Buildings. *Proc. of ACM SIGGRAPH 2006, ACM Transactions on Graphics.*

Wonka, P., Wimmer, M., Sillion, F. & Ribarsky, W. (2003). Instant architecture. *ACM Transactions on Graphics 22.* pp. 669-677.

Susinno, J. (2003). Citygen - a system for creating large city datasets using grammars. M.Sc. Thesis, Johns Hopkins University.

Kelemen, J. (1991). Syntactical models of cooperating/distributed problem solving. Journal of Experimental and Theoretical AI. 3 (1). pp. 1-10.

Csuhaj-Varjú, E. & Vaszil, Gy. (2001). On context-free parallel communicating grammar systems: Synchronization, communication, and normal forms. Theoretical Computer Science. 255 (1-2). pp. 511-538.

Mid-span connection of a deployable tensegrity footbridge

Nicolas Veuve, nicolas.veuve@epfl.ch
Swiss Federal Institute of Technology (EPFL), Lausanne, Switzerland

Seif Dalil Safei, seif.dalilsafei@epfl.ch
Swiss Federal Institute of Technology (EPFL), Lausanne, Switzerland

Ian F.C. Smith, ian.smith@epfl.ch
Swiss Federal Institute of Technology (EPFL), Lausanne, Switzerland

Abstract

This paper describes a near full-scale deployable tensegrity footbridge. Tensegrity structures are pre-stressed structures composed of tension elements (cables) surrounded by compression elements (struts) in equilibrium. Deployment of two bridge halves is assisted by the energy stored in spring elements. Five active cables control the deployment of each half. This paper presents a two-stage control methodology for determining control commands for mid-span connection of the two bridge halves. The control methodology determines active cable length changes based on computational control on a simplified analytical model and including measurement of the structural response to cable-length changes. Both halves are successfully connected at the end of deployment. Active control strategies provide effective solutions for completing deployment of multi-degree-of-freedom structures.

Keywords: Tensegrity, footbridge, computational control, active structures

1 Introduction

Motro defined tensegrity structures as self-stressed and pin-jointed assemblies of compression elements inside a network of tension elements (Motro, 2003). Skelton classified as "class k" according to, the maximum number of k struts connected to the nodes (Skelton et. al., 2001). Tensegrity structures are good candidates for deployment because structural elements can be used as active elements. In addition, Caluwaerts and Carbajal (2015) showed that the stress distribution can be modified in redundant tensegrity structures without altering the equilibrium shape and conserving a constant energy level.

Ziegler (2005) presented analytical and simulation results of a method for shape control of discrete structures such as a truss that does not result in additional stress. Domer et. al. (2003) controlled the deflections of a tensegrity grid under several load cases. The control commands were obtained from stochastic search methods combined with structural analysis. Adam and Smith (2008) showed the ability of a tensegrity grid to improve the performance of adaptation to new load cases through reinforcement learning. Dalil Safaei et. al. (2012), showed that the bending stiffness of a tensegrity boom can be improved with appropriate actuator placement and computed the actuation with genetic algorithms combined with non-linear finite elements methods. Shon et. al. 2014 studied numerically the shape adjustment of a Geiger dome using a control method based on the force method. Kmet et al. 2014 studied and tested a tensegrity module which is able to adapt its geometrical form and pre-stress properties to external conditions. Experimental results verified theoretical predictions done with closed-formed solutions. These studies demonstrate efficient control strategies in terms of shape and stress adaptation. However, tensegrity structures that undergo only small shape changes have been studied.

Vibration attenuation and shifting the natural frequencies away from the excitation range have been successfully tested (Amouri et. al., 2015, and Bel Hadj Ali and Smith, 2010). These studies showed that dynamic behavior can be improved by activating the elements in tensegrity structures.

Caluwaerts et al. (2014) studied control methods for the locomotion of a compliant spherical tensegrity robot on complex terrains. They showed that simulations of the locomotion of the spherical tensegrity were in good agreement with prototype measurements. Bliss et. al. (2013) demonstrated the robustness of a central pattern generator control for the motion of a tensegrity swimmer where cables were used to be simultaneously actuators and sensors. Although successes are achieved in the field of robotic tensegrity structures, civil tensegrity structures differ in requirements since there are more restrictive needs related to stiffness and other serviceability criteria.

Pinaud et al. (2004) studied the deployment of a small-scale class 2 tensegrity tower. Schenk et. al. (2007) used springs in order to design and test a statically balanced deployable tensegrity structure. The deployment of a near-full scale class 1 tensegrity reflector was analysed and tested by Zolesi et al. (2012). Tests of this structure showed deployment repeatability. Zhang et. al. (2014) described the cable-controlled reconfigurations of tensegrity structures based on a symmetrical state of self-stress maintaining a constant strain energy level. Possible non repeatable deployment was not addressed.

Most studies on locomotion and deployment are related to tensegrities where no joint modelling is required either because they are built at a small scale, or joint-related modelling challenges are small because they belong to class-1 tensegrity structures. A recent study by the authors (Veuve et. al. 2015) on tensegrity deployment demonstrated that joint eccentricities and friction in a near full-scale tensegrity structure of class 2 and higher cannot be neglected.

Rhodes-Barbarigos et. al. (2012a) studied the mechanism-based approach for the deployment and the design aspects (2012b) of a deployable tensegrity footbridge composed of four tensegrity ring modules. Challenges related to the mid-span connection of the footbridge have not yet been examined.

This paper proposes a control methodology for the connection of both halves of a near full-scale deployable tensegrity footbridge. Control commands that are computed from a combination of stochastic search and quasi-static analyses of the structure assuming frictionless and dimensionless joints are then tested. Finally, an additional control command search based on measurement of the real structural response to active cable length changes during deployment is verified experimentally.

2 Structure and simulation descriptions

2.1 The near full-scale structure

The structure is a ¼ scale model of a deployable tensegrity footbridge (Figure 1). The structure is composed of steel struts, steel cables and spring elements. The structure is actuated with active continuous cables. These cables are supported by intermediate nodes through which they slide over (Moored and Bart-Smith 2009). The combination of continuous cables and springs is an actuation scheme that reduces the number of actuators required for deployment and has the advantage of actuators located only at the ends (Rhode-Barbarigos et. al. 2012a). The total span of this ¼-scale structure is 4 [m]. The empty space inside the structure is intended for a pedestrian deck. The authors have shown that the deployment is not reproducible using the same control commands (Veuve et. al. 2015).

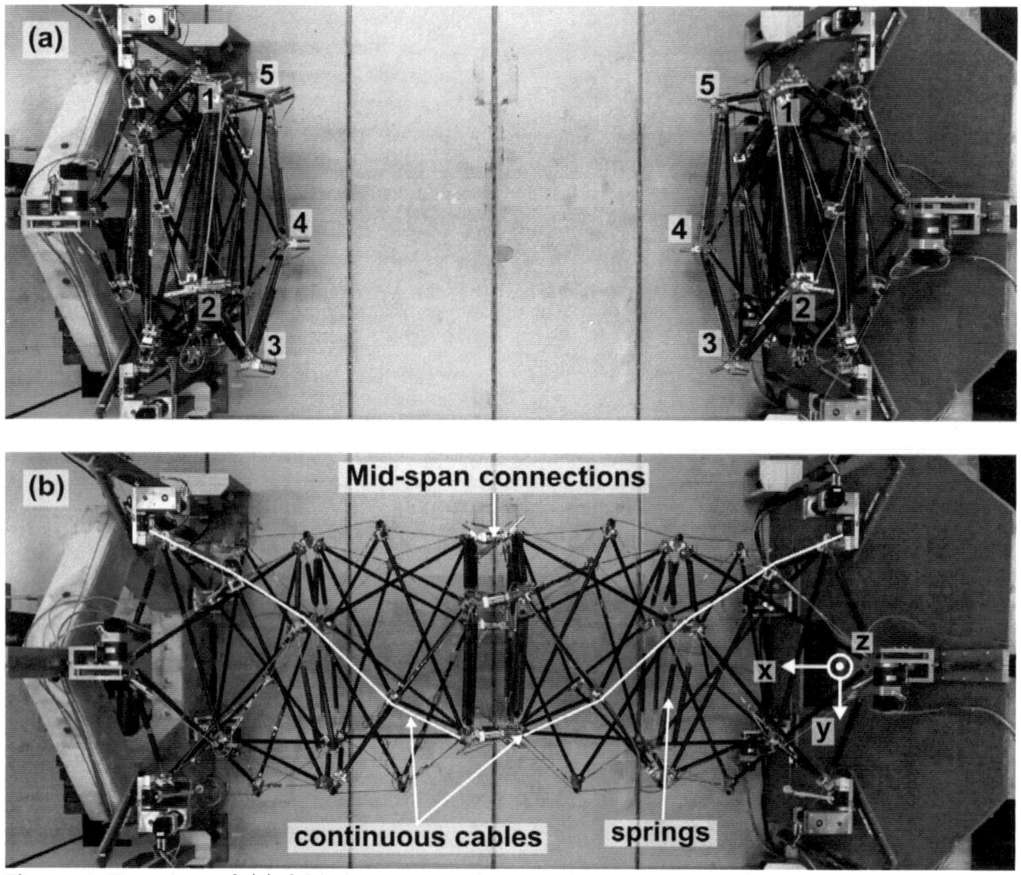

Figure 1 Top view of (a) folded structure showing the numbering of mid-span nodes and (b) deployed structure connected at mid-span

The mid-span connection system consists of a cylinder with a cone shaped hole of 30 [mm] internal radius and a rod with a round head. Both pieces are connected to the joints of the structure. In addition, they are supported by small springs in order to maintain their horizontal orientation. After successful control commands are applied, the connection pieces are locked together with a pin. This design of the connection is a first prototype made in order to develop and then test an active control methodology. In addition, after all five mid-span connections are completed, degrees of freedom in the joint shall be locked in order to prevent relative movements between the tip of both bridge halves. These degrees of freedom cannot be eliminated for connection since they are required development of the control algorithm. A connection joint with shorter length is the subject of future work.

2.2 Numerical simulations

Simulation is based on the dynamic relaxation (DR) with kinetic damping (Barnes, 1999). DR is a static analysis method. Static equilibrium is the same as the equilibrium state that a structure reaches under damped oscillations. DR is based on the equation of movement and it identifies the static equilibrium state with the equation of motion. DR has been used successfully for hundreds of tent structures and cable-stayed bridges. Most modern analysis software packages include DR modules.

The influence of continuous cables on the mechanics of tensegrity structures was first described by Moored and Bart-Smith (2009) under the term "clustered cables". Bel Hadj Ali et. al. (2011) proposed a modified dynamic relaxation algorithm that is able to include clustered cables. This study employs this algorithm.

Quasi-static actuation is assumed since deployment of the structure is slow and therefore, the inertia of the moving mass is not needed in simulations. The effect of a sequence of cable length change on the equilibrium state of the structure is simulated by a sequence of static analyses. In simulations, joints are assumed to be dimensionless and frictionless.

A stochastic search method is employed for obtaining initial control commands. This stochastic search algorithm is called PGSL (probabilistic global search Lausanne) (Raphael and Smith, 2003). This algorithm searches for sets of better solutions assuming that they are in the neighborhood of previously evaluated good solutions. The search process is guided by updating probabilities associated with regions of the solution space. For the search of good control commands, each solution generated by the stochastic search algorithm is evaluated with a DR simulation.

2.3 Computational control for mid-span connection

This section describes the strategy for mid-span connection. No solution could be found for a simultaneous connection of all five mid-span joints since the distance between mid-span node pairs is non uniform. Thus, a sequential strategy for mid-span connection is studied, where each node is connected in series.

Figure 2 shows the flowchart of the control methodology for each mid-span connection. The initial control command (Figure 3) is applied incrementally on the structure so that no cable length change exceeds 10 [mm] during each increment. The position of the two mid-span nodes is measured after the application of each increment of the control command. The connection is performed when the distance between nodes is less than or equal to the length of the mid-span joint. If all increments have been applied and the connection cannot be done, the additional control command search starts (Figure 4).

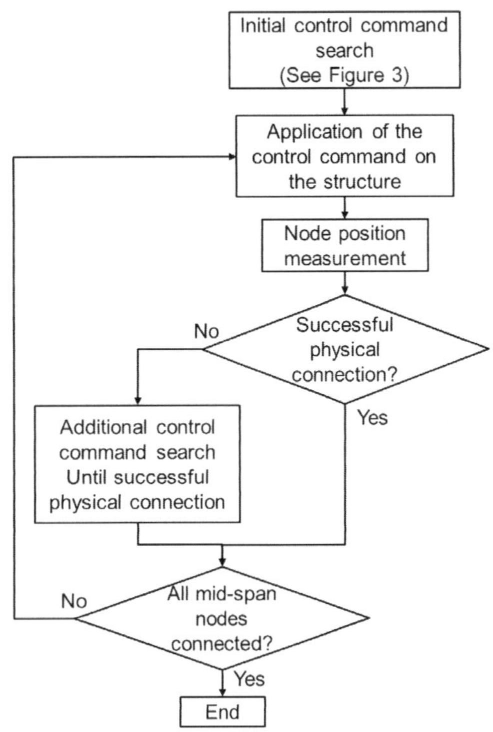

Figure 2 Flowchart of the control methodology for executing mid-span connection using real-time node-position measurements

Figure 3 shows the flowchart for computing initial control commands for each mid-span connection. Assuming that the length change of active cables is between -30 [mm] and 80 [mm] for the first mid-span connection with a resolution of 10 [mm], the size of the solution space becomes $12^{10} = 6.2\ 10^{10}$ which corresponds to the number of combinations. Hence, a search technique should be employed. The random solutions are length changes of the ten active cables in both halves. Quasi-static simulations are performed to compute the positions of mid-span nodes for each solution (control command). These simulations are calculated with the dynamic relaxation algorithm under the assumption that joints are dimensionless and frictionless. The evaluation of each solution is based on the distance between a pair of mid-span nodes. When the distance along the x axis is equal to the length of the mid-span node prototype and the distance in the y and z plane is less than 30 [mm], the solution is retained.

After the stochastic search, the corresponding mid-span nodes are linked in the model according to the best solution found. The configuration of the structure with the new mid-span connection is computed by dynamic relaxation. This configuration of the structure is used as an input for the computation of the next mid-span connection. Mid-span connections are successfully begun through employing initial control commands.

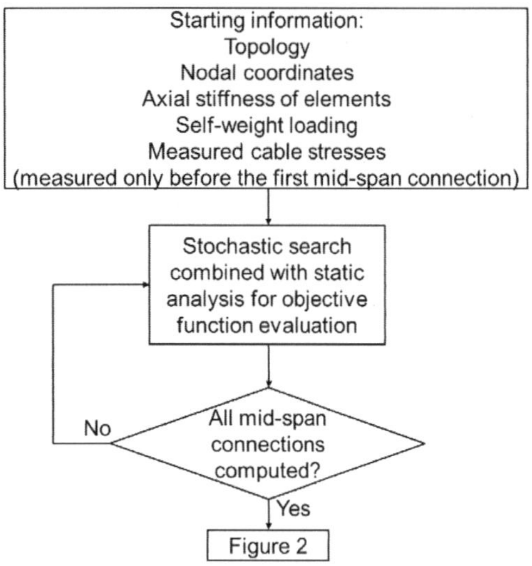

Figure 3 Flowchart for computing initial control commands using dynamic relaxation

In the case where initial control commands do not result in a successful connection, additional control commands are required. The additional control command search is based on node position measurement after application of active cable length changes. The search for additional control command starts by checking the distance between nodes.

If the remaining distance along the x-axis between both connection pieces is less than 10 [mm], the centering of the rod connection piece is checked in order to ensure that the rod will enter inside the cone hole of the cylinder connection piece. Depending on the remaining distance between connection pieces and centering (geometric criterion), the additional control command is the length change of either one or two active cables. In the case of two active cables, there is one cable on both halves and they end at the same mid-span connection. Therefore they are called a pair of symmetric cables in Figure 4.

Aside from the fact that the additional control commands consist of one or two active cables, the search process is the same. First a length change of one or two active cables is applied and the effect on the distance between connection pieces is measured. Then a reverse cable length change is applied and another active cable or pair of symmetric cables is tested. This three step process is repeated for all single cables or pair of symmetric cables. The active cable or the pair of symmetric cables resulting in the smallest connection distance is selected as the additional control command.

Figure 5 shows the length change of active cables of each bridge half for mid-span connection events 1 and 3. The initial control commands are shown in black and the additional control commands in grey. Figure 5 shows that control commands follow similar patterns for both halves of the footbridge. The first mid-span connection is successfully executed without requiring additional control commands. The third mid-span connection is the one that require most additional control commands. Among the five mid-span connection events, only two are successfully executed without requiring additional control command.

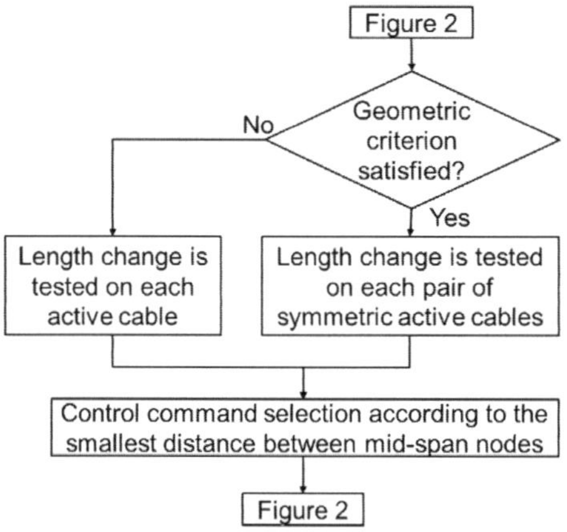

Figure 4 Additional control command search flowchart

Additional control commands are required when simulations deviate from the real behavior of the near full-scale model. This is due to the joint eccentricities and friction effects that are neglected in the simulations. Despite the simplifying assumptions of the simulation, initial control commands provide good initial solutions that are successfully completed with additional control commands. The additional control commands are efficient since they are based on real-time nodal position measurements.

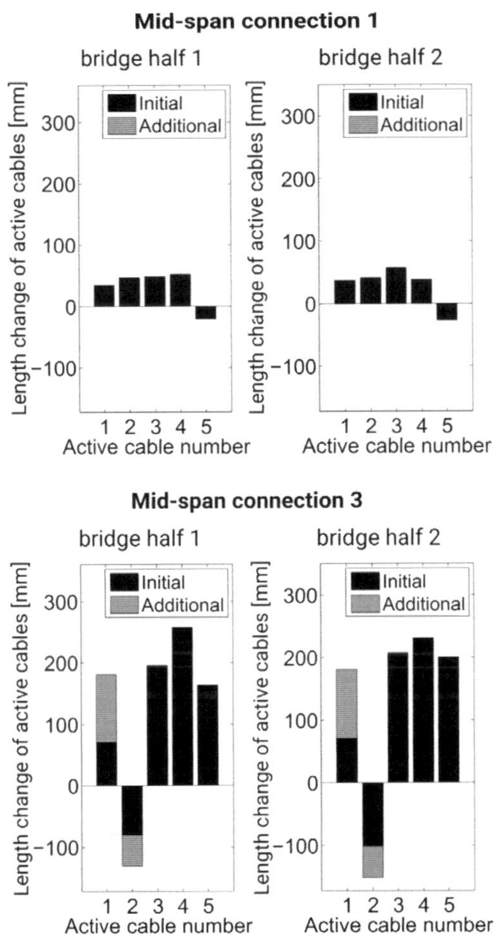

Figure 5 Initial (Figure 3) and additional (Figure 4) control commands of each bridge half for mid-span connection events 1 and 3

Figure 6 shows a top view of the first and the last mid-span connection events. Figure 6 shows the distances between mid-span nodes when the first mid-span connection is performed. The distances between lower mid-span nodes are more than those at the top because of the deformation due to self-weight. After each mid-span connection, the shape and the behavior of the footbridge change.

3 Discussion and conclusions

3.1 Discussion

Although a previous paper (Veuve et. al., 2015) has shown that the deployment behavior cannot be modelled with the assumption of dimensionless frictionless joints, modelling of joints is time consuming. Work that attempted to model joint more accurately lead to excessive computation time and only small accuracy improvement. Control command search is associated with long execution times since

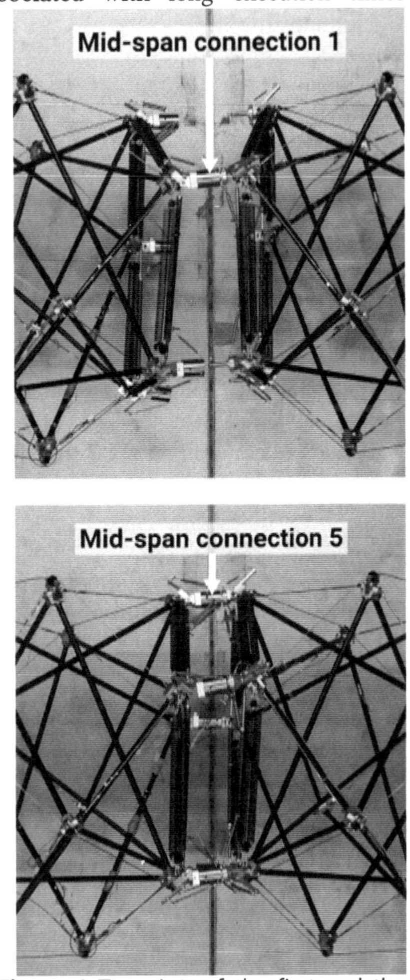

Figure 6 Top view of the first and the last mid-span connection event

quasi-static simulations are performed in order to evaluate each stochastic solution.

This research has shown that combining simplified computational control with real-time measurement of the structural response leads to successful outcomes. This result is expected to be applicable to any full-scale structure having many degrees of freedom.

3.2 Conclusions

Active control strategies provide effective solutions for completing deployment of multi-degree-of-freedom structures.

Initial control-command solutions generated using simulations that include assumption of dimensionless and frictionless joints are not accurate enough to complete all five physical mid-span connections.

Additional control search leads to successful mid-span connection. Additional control commands are determined successfully through nodal position measurement on the structure in real time.

Future work will involve designing a robust control methodology to accommodate changing environments, damage and in-service response.

Acknowledgements

Authors are thankful to the Swiss National Science Foundation for supporting this work through contract number 200020_144305. This work builds on a study that was begun in collaboration with Professor René Motro, University of Montpellier, France.

Finally we thank the technicians (P. Gallay, C. Gilliard and G. Guignet) for their contributions. This paper is part of a more detailed article that has been submitted to the journal, Engineering Structures.

References

Adam, B., and Smith, I. F. C. (2008). Reinforcement learning for structural control. Journal of Computing in Civil Engineering, 22(2), pp. 133–139.

Amouri, S., Averseng, J., Quirant, J., Dube, J.-F. (2014). Structural design and control of modular tensegrity structures. European Journal of Environmental and Civil Engineering. (In press)

Barnes, M.R. (1999). Form finding and analysis of tension Structures by dynamic relaxation. International Journal of Space Structures. 14, pp .89-104.

Bel Hadj Ali, N., Rhode-Barbarigos, L., and Smith I.F.C. (2011). Analysis of clustered tensegrity structures using a modified dynamic relaxation algorithm. International Journal of Solids and Structures. 48(5), pp. 637-647.

Bel Hadj Ali, N., and Smith, I.F.C. (2010). Dynamic behavior and vibration control of a tensegrity structure International Journal of Solids and Structures, 47(9), pp. 1285-1296.

Bliss, T., Iwasaki, T., Bart-Smith, H. (2013). Central pattern generator control of a tensegrity swimmer. IEEE/ASME Transactions on Mechatronics, 18 (2), 6291790, pp. 586-597

Caluwaerts, K., Despraz, J., Işçen, A., Sabelhaus, A.P., Bruce, J., Schrauwen, B., SunSpiral, V. (2014). Design and control of compliant tensegrity robots through simulation and hardware validation, Journal of the Royal Society Interface, 11 (98).

Caluwaerts, K., and Carbajal, J.P. Energy conserving constant shape optimization of tensegrity structures, Internationa Journal of Solids and Structures, (In press)

Dalil Safaei, S., Eriksson, A., and Tibert, G. (2012). Improving the bending stiffness of tensegrity booms. International Journal of Space Structures, 27(2-3), pp. 117-130.

Domer, B., Raphael, B., Shea, K., and Smith, I. F. C. (2003). A study of two stochastic search methods for structural control. J. Comput. Civ. Eng., 17(3). pp. 132–141.

Kmet, S., Platko, P. (2014). Adaptive tensegrity module. II: tests and comparison of results, Journal of Structural Engineering, 140 (9).

Moored, K.W. and Bart-Smith H. (2009). Investigation of clustered actuation in tensegrity structures, International Journal of Solids and Structures, 46(17), pp. 3272-3281.

Motro, R. (2003). Tensegrity: structural systems for the future. London: Kogan Page Science

Pinaud, J.-P., Solari, S., Skelton, R.E. (2004). Deployment of a class 2 tensegrity boom, Proceedings of SPIE - The International Society for Optical Engineering, San Diego, California.

Raphael, B., and Smith, I. F. C. (2003). A direct stochastic algorithm for global search, Applied Mathematics and Computation, 146(2-3), pp. 729–758.

Rhode-Barbarigos, L., Bel Hadj Ali, N., Motro, R., and Smith I.F.C. (2012a). Design aspects of a deployable tensegrity-hollow-rope footbridge, International Journal of Space Structures, 27(2), pp. 81-96.

Rhode-Barbarigos. L., Schulin. C., Bel Hadj Ali, N., Motro, R., and Smith I.F.C. (2012b). Mechanism-based approach for the deployment of a tensegrity-ring module. Journal of Structural Engineering, 138(4), pp. 539-548.

Schenk, M., Guest, S.D., Herder, J.L. (2007). Zero stiffness tensegrity structures, International Journal of Solids and Structures, 44, pp. 6569-6583.

Shon, S., Kwan, A.S., Lee, S. (2014) Shape control of cable structures considering concurrent/sequence control. Structural Engineering and Mechanics, 52(5), pp. 919-935.

Sultan, C. (2014). Tensegrity deployment using infinitesimal mechanisms, International Journal of Solids and Structures, 51(21-22), pp. 3653-3668.

Veuve, N., Dalil Safaei, S., and Smith I.F.C. (2015). Deployment of a tensegrity footbridge, Journal of Structural Engineering, in press.

Zhang, P., Kawaguchi, K., Feng, J. (2014). Prismatic tensegrity structures with additional cables: Integral symmetric states of self-stress and cable-controlled reconfiguration procedure. International Journal of Solids and Structures, 51(25–26), pp. 4294-4306.

Ziegler, F. (2005). Computational aspects of structural shape control. Computers and Structures, 83(15-16), pp. 1191-1204.

Zolesi, V. S., Ganga, P. L., Scolamiero, L., Micheletti, A., Podio-Guidugli, P., Tibert, G., and Ghiozzi, M. (2012). On an innovative deployment concept for large space structures, Proceedings of 42nd International Conference on Environmental Systems, San Diego, California, USA.

Simplifying the Analysis of Building Information Models Using ^{t}QL4BIM and ^{v}QL4BIM

Simon Daum, simon.daum@tum.de
Chair of Computational Modeling and Simulation, Technische Universität München, Germany

André Borrmann, andre.borrmann@tum.de
Chair of Computational Modeling and Simulation, Technische Universität München, Germany

Abstract
This paper presents a new approach to analyse Building Information Models. Firstly, a domain-specific language in its textual notation is introduced. It is tailored to domain experts with little programming experience. Based on an uncomplicated pattern, the language offers a formal and general method of BIM-analysis. Additionally, its imperative nature and its sequential layout makes a stepwise execution and inspection of intermediate results possible. Thus, complex queries may consist of comprehensible and verifiable statements. As an alternative to textual definitions, we introduce a visual notation for BIM queries. Both the textual and the visual notation are based on the identical abstract syntax and offer the same range of functionalities.

Keywords: BIM, IFC, CityGML, Query Language, VPL

1 Introduction

The paradigms of Building Information Modeling (BIM) promote the use of comprehensive digital building representations. Instead of previously adopted approaches, which focus on geometric data, a BIM comprises not only the 3D shapes of elements and enclosed spaces, but also type information and the relationships between elements (Eastman et al., 2011). Therefore, a BIM has the potential to serve as an interface and data pool for exchanging information across the disciplines involved in the design, construction and operation of a building. The research presented in this paper is based on the data model *Industry Foundation Classes* (IFC), an open, evolved and universal schema for representing building models (Liebich, 2013).

However, various issues can arise when BIM processes are introduced in construction projects. In the context of data handling and the transfer of interdisciplinary information, the following issues are of central importance for domain experts such as architects and engineers:

- Building models have to be analysable and their quality must be verifiable.
- The extraction of submodels from an overall model must be supported.
- The effort involved in performing these analyses and transactions must be reduced.

The currently used BIM tools do not support a formal analysis of building models. Instead, manual work has to be dedicated to extracting the necessary information. Due to the diverging characteristics of analyses, these tasks have to be continuously repeated using changed parameters. This manual work is time-consuming and error-prone, especially in data intensive models. The same holds true for the extraction of submodels and post-processing.

Due to these weak points in a BIM-based workflow, new methods have to be invented. They should be developed with domain experts rather than programmers in mind and their application should be intuitive without requiring an extensive learning effort. At the same time, a general approach capable of supporting different types of projects with different boundary conditions should be adopted. Finally, the structure of data and its scope must be taken into account if new strategies for analysis, quality checking and data processing are to be introduced to BIM.

This paper is based on the hypothesis that a formal, domain-specific query language can solve the aforementioned deficits. Accordingly, the novel BIM query language *QL4BIM* and its runtime, the *QL4BIM System*, are presented. The language offers advanced operators and data structures for a comprehensive analysis of building information models. It comprises semantic operators for type/attribute extractions and relational operators for analysing the links between entities. Additionally, temporal operators for examining the installation times of building elements are introduced (Daum and Borrmann, 2013). Spatial operators for evaluating topological, directional and metric predicates are also included in the language (Daum and Borrmann, 2014).

The focus of previous research in the *QL4BIM* project was on spatial operators and a query interface which is based on Microsoft LINQ and .NET languages such as *C#* and *Visual Basic*. The comprehensiveness of this approach increases complexity in query definition, making the interface primarily suitable for users with a background in programming.

To realize a simplified approach to BIM analysis and processing, two new interfaces for the query system are introduced. The first one is the textual query notation ^{t}*QL4BIM*. In addition, with ^{v}*QL4BIM*, a visual query notation is integrated in the system, primarily dedicated to users who want to steer analysis using a graphical user interface rather than code. Both notations are based on a single abstract language syntax provided by the *QL4BIM* language. Despite the simplicity of the language, it allows comprehensive BIM queries.

This paper is structured as follows: Firstly, general and domain-specific query languages are discussed in brief. Then, the novel, textual query notation ^{t}*QL4BIM* is presented and the incorporated type system used by the runtime is addressed. Section 5 then describes the possibility of operator overloading in the system. Subsequently, an overview of the runtime components is provided. Section 7 shows the deduction of the visual notation ^{v}*QL4BIM*. The paper finishes with a conclusion on the research presented.

2 Related Work

The analysis of extensive data sets is covered by databases and their query languages. The *Structured Query Language (SQL)* is the de-facto standard in this domain (ISO, 2011). The sound theoretical foundation for this language is provided by Relational Algebra (Codd, 1990). However, the IFC data models are defined by the EXPRESS modelling language and there is no standardized mapping of this kind of schema to a relational structure (Schenck and Wilson, 1994). The propagation of XML-based modelling has led to the development of the XQuery language (Robie et al., 2013). ifcXML represents an XML-based variant of IFC which can be analysed without pre-processing by an XQuery implementation (Liebich, 2001).

In order to examine the application of general query language such as SQL and XQuery to the analysis of building models, a test bed has been implemented. In short, the experiments have shown that an analysis of a building model based on general query languages can result in tedious coding. For example, a query stated in XQuery that extracts walls and their material from an ifcXML file comprises 18 lines. A direct mapping of EXPRESS to SQL also produces a complicated structure of tables, which hampers this approach to data analysis (Borrmann and Rank, 2009).

A domain-specific language for BIM can provide more direct access to the required data, as it is tailored to the domain model and hides the details of the internal data representation. The Building Information Model Query Language (BIMQL) achieves such a domain-specific approach (Mazairac and Beetz, 2013). The language is inspired, inter alia, by SPARQL which is a query language for semantic web content (Prud'Hommeaux et al., 2008). In **Listing 1** a BIMQL query is presented that extracts the floor area of two spaces. This type of query is easily understood by individuals with knowledge of SQL and SPARQL but may confuse

Listing 1 BIMQL query returning the floor area of spaces

```
Select ?mySpace
Where ?mySpace.Attribute.GlobalID = 3Dn6BYWjfErxE1JocogMGQ Or
   ?mySpaceAttribute.GlobalID = 0tLttARJ1F1esyGJSeaTmd
Select ?netFloorArea
Where ?netFloorArea := ?mySpace.property.NetFloorArea
```

domain experts. Additionally, the connection between each space and its floor area is lost as no relational results are produced. For a review of additional query languages please refer to (Daum and Borrmann, 2014).

A complex query can be composed of one or more statements. Each statement is built up by an assignment which binds a variable to the result of an operation. In addition, an operation can be subdivided into its operand and its parameters. Constants such as strings, numbers and floats as well as assigned variables can be used as concrete parameters. Furthermore, predicates evaluating attributes of entities are used to steer operators.

Listing 2 A query example in ^{t}QL4BIM

```
1 model = GetModel("C:\Institute.ifc")
2 allWalls = TypeFilter(model , "IfcWall")
3 someWalls = AttributeFilter(allWalls.Name = "Wall-002")
4 allWindows = TypeFilter(model, "IfcWindow")
5 rel[wall, window] = Touch(someWalls, allWindows)
```

3 ^{t}QL4BIM: The Textual Query Notation of the QL4BIM System

In previous research, a query interface based on LINQ was provided (Daum and Borrmann, 2013). It enables the end user do define queries in Microsoft .NET languages. While this is appropriate for programmers, domain experts such as architects and civil engineers are unable to use the query system intuitively. To resolve this restriction, a new streamlined language has been developed in accordance with the following paradigms:

- The language introduces a general and formal approach to BIM analysis.
- At the same time, only a few formal patterns are used in the language.
- An imperative query definition is intended, defining the ordering of statements and driving a sequential, comprehensible evaluation of subqueries.
- Type handling and low-level control flows are hidden from the end user.

Taking these requirements into account, an appropriate grammar for the textual notation *^{t}QL4BIM* is developed. Parts of it are shown in **Figure 1**.

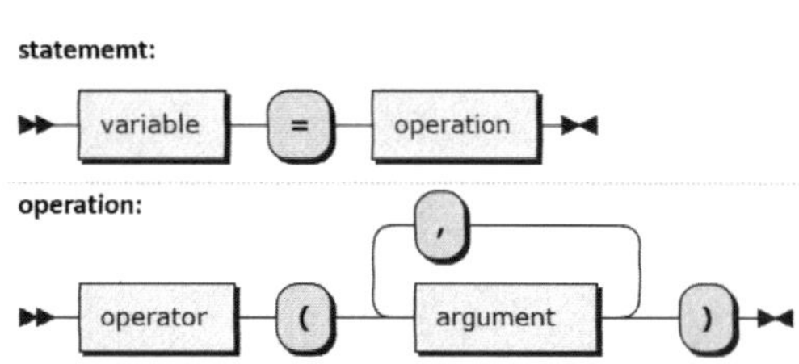

Figure 1 A section of the ^{t}QL4BIM grammar

Listing 2 illustrates an example stated in *^{t}QL4BIM*. In the query, an IFC instance file is loaded and all walls are selected (Line 2). The result is then restricted by applying a predicate to each entity. Only walls with an attribute entitled *Name* with the value "Wall-002" are retained in the process. To access an attribute of an entity, the point operator is facilitated in the predicate definition (Line 3). After receiving all windows with a second *TypeFilter* (Line 4), the sets of walls and windows are topologically analysed by the *Touch* operator. The result is saved in a relational variable which comprises pairs of a wall and its touching window.

This demonstrates the main pattern of *^{t}QL4BIM*: Repeated variable assignment combined with the calling of an operation. In this way, subsequent operations process variables assigned by previous calls. Despite its simplicity, this pattern enables a flexible and detailed analysis of building models by chaining manageable operations. The complexity of information retrieval is hidden in the interior processing of each operator. As a result, the domain expert can concentrate on the semantics of each operator instead of on low-level data handling.

4 Typing in the QL4BIM System

The type system of this novel QL4BIM version comprises four native types. These are *Constant*, *Entity*, *Set* and *Relation*. Denotation as native types highlights the presence of other types in the system. These additional types are introduced by the data model under examination. Currently, the *QL4BIM System*

Listing 3 A ^{t}QL4BIM query which selects partial rooms with gross floor areas greater than 40 m²

```
1 model = GetModel("C:\Institute.ifc")
2 spaces = TypeFilter(model, "IfcSpace")
3 pSpaces = AttributeFilter(spaces.CompositionType = "partial")
4 rel1[space, prop] = PropertyResolver(pSpaces, model, "SpaceCommon")
5 rel2[space, prop] = AttributeFilter(rel1[prop].GrossPlannedArea > 40)
6 largeSpaces = Projection(rel2[space])
```

supports IFC files as data pool but the developed methods are not closely coupled to this data model. To enable an analysis of buildings using additional data on their surroundings, an extension to the CityGML model is in progress.

As mentioned above, a variable introduced in a ^{t}QL4BIM query can be typed as *Entity*, *Set* or *Relation*. All of them act as wrappers for externally defined types stored in the current data pool. The following three examples demonstrate the interaction of the native and external types. (1) A variable can represent one entity, e.g. a wall. This is realized by a *QL4BIM Entity* which itself references an IfcWall. (2) A variable can refer to a set of entities. In this case a *QL4BIM Set* is used. This kind of variable acts as a container for (semantically-related) entities, e.g. windows which are located in the second storey. Internally, the set variable references *Entity*-instances each incorporating an IfcWindow. (3) A *QL4BIM Relation* is used to combine Entity instances and to express relationships between them. In contrast to a set variable, the relationship occurs between *Entity*-instances combined in a single tuple whereas many tuples are stored in one relation. A tuple refers to an ordered list of entities. A single *Entity* in the tuple can be accessed by a user-defined literal. To concretize the relational concept in use, **Listing 2** is considered once again. In Line 5, the variable rel[wall,window] is introduced, storing pairs of an IfcWall and its touching IfcWindow. The notation of literals for index access corresponds to the lower branch of the syntax diagram shown in **Figure 2**.

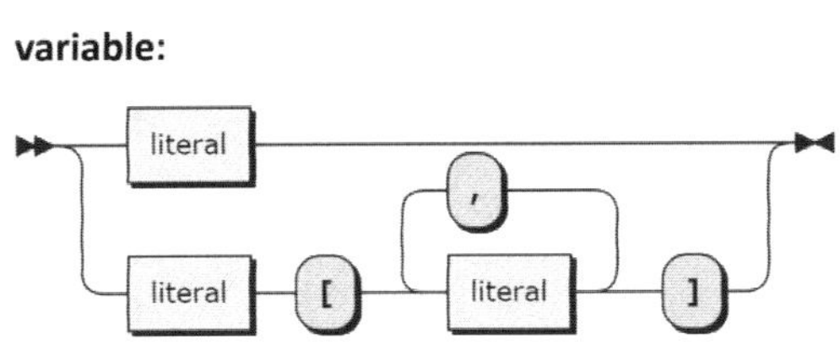

Figure 2 Syntax diagram of variables in QL4BIM

In the further processing, e.g. during predicate definition and parameter transfer, the window in each tuple can be accessed by rel[window].

A *QL4BIM Constant* is the base type for immutable and simple data structures. Like variables, constants are used as input for query operators. They are not fetched from the data pool but directly stated by the end user during query definition. Therefore, the values of these structures are independent from the data pool. *Constant* acts as a base type for *cstring*, *cnumber*, *cfloat* and *cid*. The first stands for strings and enumeration values. A *cnumber* represents an integer and *cfloat* a floating-point number. The last constant type *cid* is used to express a symbolic identifier. For the IFC model, a *cid* is an integer prefixed with a # token.

The query shown in **Listing 3** demonstrates the use of constants in *^{t}QL4BIM*. The query identifies all rooms attributed as partial which have a gross floor area greater than 40 m². In Line 3, the use of a *cstring* as an enumeration value is depicted. The attribute filter in Line 5 evaluates a *cnumber* in its predicate parameter.

One paradigm of *QL4BIM* is hiding its type handling. Therefore, the language is designed to cope without the need to explicitly type keywords and variables are simply introduced by initial use of a literal. The appropriate type of variable is inferred by the operator called in the assignment. So the distinction between *Entity* and *Set* variables is completely implicit. This is evidenced in **Listing 4** on the next page which presents a fragment from **Listing 2** together with a modification. In the original version (a), two sets are passed to the *Touch* operator. In modification (b), one *Set* and one *Entity* are handed over. In both examples, the textual syntax stays identical. Instead, the user can concentrate on the different semantics of the overloaded *Touch* operator. Section 5 depicts the concept of overloading operators in detail. Whereas there is no syntactical difference between entities and sets, the necessary definition of index literals for relational results and parameter handovers makes the use of relations more explicit. The presented approach relieves the user in that the user is not required to handle native types in the language. semantics can be realized by the types used in operator calls.

Listing 4 The implicity between entities and sets in the QL4BIM System

```
1a allWindows = TypeFilter(model, "IfcWindow")
2a rel[wall, window] = Touch(someWalls, allWindows)

1b theWindow = GetInstance(model, #2456)
2b rel[wall, window] = Touch(someWalls, theWindow)
```

This should also hold true if external types, e.g. from the IFC data model, are processed. Externally typed attributes are examined if predicates are passed to operators. Here the runtime has to convert external types to native types. To facilitate the definition of predicates, these conversions are performed automatically. This is done by recursively traversing the IFC schema until simple types of the *EXPRESS* language are reached. **Listing 5** containing fragments from the IFC4 schema, clarifies the used recursive processing. As shown here, the definition of IfcNonNegativeLengthMeasure is based on IfcLengthMeasure and finally ends up at the simple REAL type. As the query runtime incorporates a mapping for simple *EXPRESS* types to native *QL4BIM* types, the user is not restricted to explicitly instantiating an IfcNonNegativeLengthMeasure. If an entity attribute of this type is used in a predicate, a *cfloat* that maps to an *EXPRESS REAL* can be used during comparisons.

This is demonstrated by four applications of the *Touch* operator in **Listing 6**. In this case two sets (walls, windows) are extracted from the overall model. Additionally, the entity *wall2456* is fetched by the *GetInstance* operator. In the Lines 5-8, different overloads of the *Touch* operator are called. In the first variant the set of walls is used as a parameter. This results in a processing which finds all pairs of touching walls by evaluating the Cartesian product of set elements. In the second call of *Touch*, the instance *wall2456* is tested against each element of the window set. If *n* is the number of elements in the passed set, *n Touch* tests are performed. In Line 7, the operator is called with two sets. In this case only touching constellations between entities contained in different sets are examined. If *n* walls and *m* windows are passed, $n*m$ test are evaluated. Finally, a one-to-one test should also be supported by the system. In this case a relation containing pairs of entities is passed to *Touch* (Line 8). In the following topological processing, each tuple will be examined individually. In this way *element1* is tested for touching *element2*. If *n* is the number of tuples in the relation, *n* tests are executed.

This example shows that different processing can be realized by simply changing the types of parameters passed to an operator. Thus,

Listing 5 Fragments of the IFC4 EXPRESS schema used for type conversions

```
TYPE IfcNonNegativeLengthMeasure = IfcLengthMeasure
TYPE IfcLengthMeasure = REAL
```

5 Operator Overloading in ^{t}QL4BIM

As mentioned in the language paradigms, the user should be able to state queries at a high level of abstraction. No patterns for repeated execution of subqueries such as *for*-statements therefore exists in the language. Different query semantics can be realized by the types used in operator calls.

Listing 6 Overloads of the Touch operator

```
1 model = GetModel("C:\Institute.ifc")
2 walls = TypeFilter(model, "IfcWall")
3 wall2456 = GetInstance(model, #2456)
4 windows = TypeFilter (model, "IfcWindow")
5 rel1[wall1, wall2] = Touch(walls)
6 rel2[wall, window] = Touch(wall2456, windows)      //creation of
7 rel3[wall, window] = Touch(walls, windows)         //rel0 is ommited
8 rel4[element1, element2] = Touch(rel0[element1, element2])
```

overloaded variants are available to the majority of *QL4BIM* operators. For example, the *AttributeFilter* is present in three versions and can execute on a single entity, a set or a relational variable. The amount of semantical difference between the overloads varies for each operator. A detailed description of all available operators including information on each overloaded version will be provided in the *QL4BIM Manual* which is currently being drafted.

6 The QL4BIM System and its Components

This section describes the runtime for interpreting *^{t}QL4BIM* queries known as *QL4BIM System*. **Figure 3** shows the internal components of the runtime and their interrelationships.

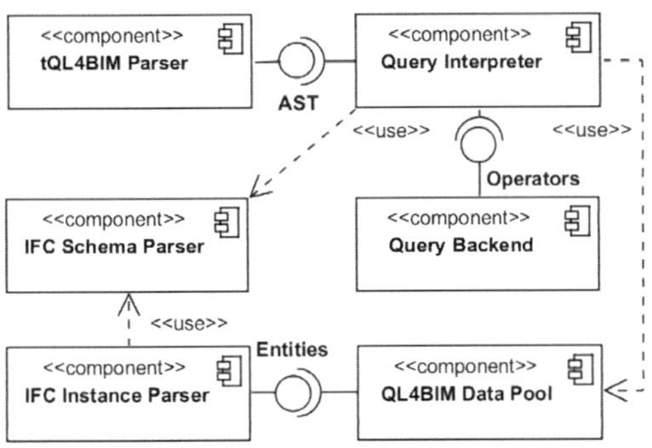

Figure 3 UML component diagram of the QL4BIM System

The system includes three parsers. They are used for the syntactic analysis of query input, for importing the underlying pool data and for examining the schema of the pool data. In general, a query is initiated by importing an IFC instance file to the current data pool via the *GetModel* operator.

The IFC instance parser is responsible for interpreting the referenced file and for creating an in-memory representation of IFC entities. The runtime uses a late binding approach to representing these external entities. Instead of specific classes for IFC types, entities are set up dynamically using generic parts. Fine-grained elements such as object identifiers, lists of symbolic references and values of simple types are stored in these parts. The late binding used has the advantage that all IFC versions can be supported ad-hoc. Additionally, the integration of further data models such as CityGML is facilitated.

The IFC schema parser supports query execution when external IFC types have to be compared with *QL4BIM* types (see **Listing 3**). Additionally, meta information such as attribute names of entities can be directly read out from the schema without the computationally expensive use of reflection mechanisms.

Once a query has passed syntactic analysis, the *^{t}QL4BIM* parser translates it to an *abstract syntax tree* (AST) (Parr, 2010). This intermediate representation of a query is consumed by the query interpreter. It is a streamlined structure deduced from the textual query input without lexical helpers. Instead, a tree structure is set up that can be processed for query validation and query execution.

Figure 4 shows a *^{t}QL4BIM* query and its representation as AST. The *S*-nodes correspond to the four subquery statements. As query execution is triggered by the user, the interpreter traverses the AST, collecting results and calling the appropriate function in the query backend with referenced variables. The imperative style of the language combined with the forced saving of interim results allows a step-wise query execution. Instead of processing all statements in the AST, the runtime interprets one statement after another, continuing by user request. In this

```
model = GetModel ("C:\Institute.ifc")
walls = TypeFilter (model, "IfcWall")
windows = TypeFilter (model, "IfcWindow")
r1[wall, window] = Touch(walls, windows)
```

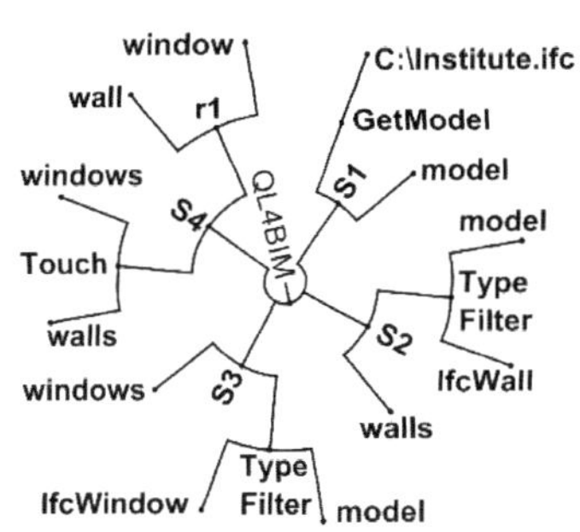

Figure 4 A query in ^{t}QL4BIM and its abstract syntax tree used by the runtime

step-wise execution, the content of the current intermediate variable can be shown in the *QL4BIM* user interface. This is done in a textual manner and extended by a 3D visualisation if the variable refers to geometrical information. The approach is similar to a debugging session in an IDE and a general programming language. It supports domain experts in defining complex queries as the influence of each single statement is testable.

7 The Visual Notion ^{v}QL4BIM

A *Visual Programming Language* (VPL) uses a graphical notation to represent the intent of the user rather than typed code. The concept first emerged in the 1970s but is currently adopted increasingly in modern applications (Sutherland, 1966). In the domain of model-based planning, *Dynamo* and *Grashopper* are examples of VPL-equipped tools (Yazar, 2014). The general approach of a VPL is to place visuals on a canvas and to establish a connection between these items. A network structure is thereby set up. The semantic of this structure is specific to each VPL.

Nowadays, rich graphic user interfaces are the primary access points to applications for non-programmer. In contrast, users may face obstacles when it comes to textual programming languages. This holds true for domain experts such as architects and civil engineers and a language such as *^{t}QL4BIM* despite its minimal amount of patterns. Thus, a VPL which reuses the methodology of the presented textual query notation is introduced. It is called *^{v}QL4BIM* and the following characteristics and services are borrowed from its textual sibling:

- the general paradigms used in the design of *^{t}QL4BIM*,
- the native type system, the handling of external types and operator overloading,
- the intermediate representation of a query in the form of an AST.

For the graphical syntax, visuals are defined, representing constants, variables and operators (**Figure 5**). Constants are defined as rectangles, variables as rounded rectangles and operators as hexagons. The assignment of operational results and parameter handovers are both denoted by arrows. The connection between a relational variable and its index literals are defined by lines with diamonds at their endpoints.

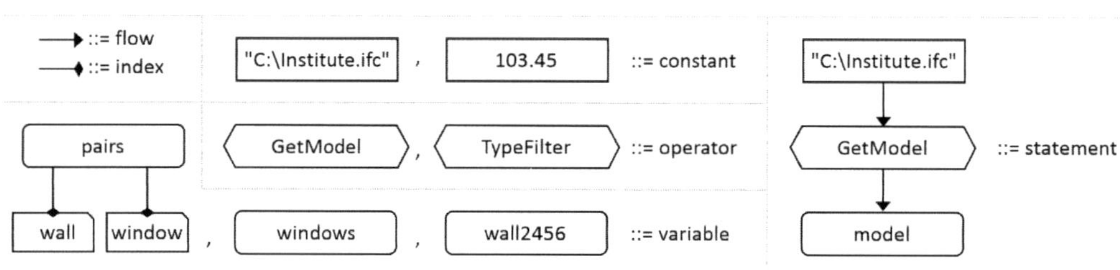

Figure 5 Visuals to express queries in ^{v}QL4BIM

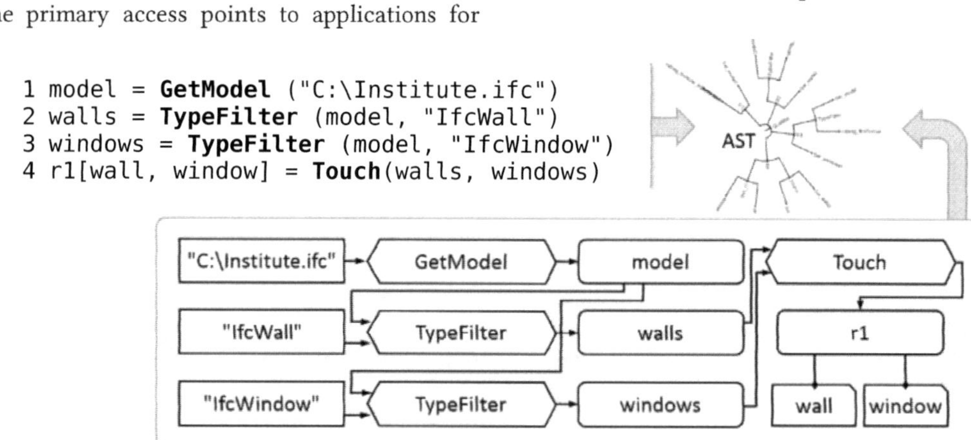

Figure 6 A textual and its equivalent visual query resulting in a common AST

The visual ^{v}*QL4BIM* and the textual ^{t}*QL4BIM* share the same intermediate representation in the form of an AST. The important fact is that a bijective relationship exists between a ^{t}*QL4BIM* query and its AST. As a ^{v}*QL4BIM* query and its resulting AST are also bijective connected, this tree structure can be used to synchronize both notations. Thereby an altering of the current query in both notation is possible at any time. If the query is changed in one notation, the obsolete representation is automatically renewed by traversing the AST and calling a visual, or respectively a code creation backend. **Figure 6** shows two equivalent queries: The first one is stated in ^{t}*QL4BIM* with the second arranged by ^{v}*QL4BIM* visuals. Both queries result in an identical AST.

8 Conclusion

BIM and its underlying data models, especially the IFC, have evolved over the past two decades. Today, they provide a well-grounded foundation for representing a wide range of buildings and the processes of their planning, construction and maintenance. On the other hand, there are gaps in analysis and data handling, particularly in relation to the formal exploration of models and the extraction of submodels.

This paper presents a novel query language in two notations that is designed to overcome these issues. The query language is focused on usage by domain experts and supports a straightforward, albeit formal and comprehensive examination of complex models. Together with the previously developed spatial and temporal operators of the system, a novel level of methodical support for analysing, verifying and processing of BIM data is achieved. This increases the efficiency of model-based processes and promotes a BIM-based methodology.

References

Borrmann, A. and Rank, E. (2009) 'Query support for BIMs using semantic and spatial conditions', Handbook of Research on Building Information Modeling and Construction Informatics: Concepts and Technologies: Concepts and Technologies, p. 405.

Codd, E. F. (1990) The relational model for database management: version 2, Addison-Wesley Longman Publishing Co., Inc.

Daum, S. and Borrmann, A. (2013) 'Definition and Implementation of Temporal Operators for a 4D Query Language', Proc. of the ASCE International Workshop on Computing in Civil Engineering.

Daum, S. and Borrmann, A. (2014) 'Processing of Topological BIM Queries using Boundary Representation Based Methods', Advanced Engineering Informatics, vol. 28, no. 4, pp. 272–286.

Eastman, C., Teicholz, P., Sacks, R. and Liston, K. (2011) BIM Handbook: A Guide to Building Information Modeling for Owners, Managers, Designers, Engineers and Contractors.

Liebich, T. (2001) 'XML schema language binding of EXPRESS for ifcXML', International Alliance for Interoperability.

Liebich, T. (2013) IFC4 specification [Online], no. 4. Available at http://www.buildingsmart-tech.org/ifc/IFC2x4/rc4/html/index.htm.

Mazairac, W. and Beetz, J. (2013) 'BIMQL – An open query language for building information models', Advanced Engineering Informatics, vol. 27, no. 4, pp. 444–456 [Online]. Available at http://www.sciencedirect.com/science/article/pii/S1474034613000657.

Parr, T. (2010) Language implementation patterns: Create your own domain-specific and general programming languages, Raleigh, N.C., Pragmatic Bookshelf.

Prud'Hommeaux, E., Seaborne, A. and others (2008) 'SPARQL query language for RDF', W3C recommendation, vol. 15.

Robie, J., Chamberlin, D., Dyck, M. and Snelson, J. (2013) 'XQuery 3.0: An XML Query Language', W3C Last Call Working, July.

Schenck, D. and Wilson, P. R. (1994) Information modeling: the EXPRESS way, Oxford University Press New York.

Sutherland, W. R. (1966) On-line Graphical Specification of Computer Procedures, DTIC Document.

Yazar, T. (2014) 'Design of Dataflow', Nexus Network Journal, pp. 1–15 [Online]. DOI: 10.1007/s00004-014-0222-8.

Conceptualization in Designing with the Use of Many-Sorted First-Order Logic

Wojciech Palacz, wojciech.palacz@uj.edu.pl
Jagiellonian University, Kraków, Poland

Ewa Grabska, ewa.grabska@uj.edu.pl
Jagiellonian University, Kraków, Poland

Szymon Gajek, szymon.gajek@gmail.com
Jagiellonian University, Kraków, Poland

Abstract

This paper is a continuation and extension in developing the knowledge-based decision support design system HSSDR (Hierarchical Graph System Supporting Design and Reasoning) which communicates with the designer via drawings displayed on the monitor screen. Graph-based modeling of conceptualization in CAD process is considered. Design drawings generated on the monitor screen are automatically transformed into appropriate graph-based data structures. In this paper the enrichment of the graph data structure is proposed. This is done by hierarchical graphs with bonds which correspond to arguments of existing (engaged bonds) and potential relations (free bonds). This distinction of bonds is essential in definitions of operations on graphs that reflect modifications of design drawings. This type of graphs provides an ontological commitment between drawings and its internal representations. Moreover, the first-order logic of HSSDR is replaced by many-sorted first order logic that makes it possible to define different sorts in specification of functions and predicates in semantics and design constraint verification.

Keywords: CAD, design constraints, graph data structures, many-sorted first-order logic

Introduction

This paper is focused on assisting the conceptualization in CAD process. Conceptualization concerns objects, concepts, and other entities that are assumed to exist in the considered domain of discourse, and the relationships that hold among them. A CAD system communicates with the designer via drawings displayed on the monitor screen. The drawings are usually converted to some internal data structures. In many CAD programs those structures are graph-based, because graphs are well-suited to model subcomponents of the designed object and relations between those subcomponents. An example of such a system is HSSDR (Hierarchical Graph System Supporting Design and Reasoning), whose first version is described in (Grabska et al. 2009). It was developed as a tool for designing floor layouts and validating their correctness in respect to an adjustable set of rules.

Every action undertaken by the designer modifies HSSDR's internal data structures, and this modification is in turn reflected in the displayed drawing. HSSDR uses a hierarchical graph as its main data structure, which allows for straightforward representation of recursive space splits. Every modification done by the designer triggers a constraint verification round. Design constraints are specified as logic formulas. The (Grabska et al. 2009) paper showcases two constraint sets which verify compliance with fire code regulations and check if all paths leading to certain important rooms are monitored by cameras.

Experiences gained during implementation and testing of the original version of HSSDR have suggested two potential improvements. The first one is concerned with the way of modeling parts of the layout. Areas and rooms were treated as elements of the domain of discourse, while other objects, like doors and cameras, as properties (attributes) of these elements. Such lack of ontological commitment between conceptualization and its hypergraph representation was problematic. This paper proposes a new representation which uses hierarchical graphs with bonds. This type of graphs makes it possible to include all of the objects as elements of the domain of discourse.

Another proposed improvement concerns the language in which the design constraints are specified. The first-order logic is replaced by many-sorted first-order logic. It makes writing the logic formulas a bit easier. It also allows for enhanced syntactic checking of the constraints.

This paper is organized as follows: Section 2 gives some insights in human-computer interaction in the context of computer-aided design. Section 3 presents the current modeling system and then proposes its modifications. In Section 4 a new type of hierarchical graphs, so called the graphs with bonds are defined. Section 5 considers the reasoning mechanism of HSSDR based on many-sorted first-order logical language. Section 7 concludes the paper and outlines future work.

Human-Computer Interaction in CAD

During the conceptual design the designer has to describe the domain of discourse being a subset of his/her cognitive domain. There exists the need to keep in mind objects, concepts, and other entities that are assumed to exist in the considered domain of discourse, and the relationships that hold among them. Conceptualization is one of the most challenging aspects of designing because it forces designers to considers many disparate factors. It is perhaps for this reason the sketching is such a popular tool of initial stages of designer's conceptualization. Sketches, being externalization of designer's conceptualization, are seen as thinking aids (Suwa & Tversky 1997). It seems helpful if there exists a commitment between the sketch and the level of certainty in the designer's mind at the time (Lawson 1997).

During the computer aided design process sketches are replaced by design drawings. A CAD system communicates with the designer via the drawings displayed on the monitor screen. They are generated by the designer with the use of a visual editor and constitute the first type of representation storing information about design solutions. The designer communicates with the design system using a visual design language, i.e., a set of design drawings being configurations of basic shapes. A majority of visual languages is characterized by a vocabulary being a finite set of basic shapes and a finite set of rules specifying possible configurations of these shapes. The basic shapes of visual languages and their spatial relationships correspond to concepts and relations defined by the conceptualization of the domain of discourse. Each specialized design domain has its own visual languages related to concepts used in this domain (Grabska et al. 2012).

The designer has a kind of conversation with design drawings (Goldschmidt 1994). During the designer's dialogue with the drawings on the monitor screen perceptual actions, such as discovering of visual features of drawings and spatial relations, and searching for differences or similarities between visual elements can be reinforced by editor functions like zooming, specifying a camera view point, etc., meanwhile physical actions such as drawing, copying and erasing elements of design drawings are imposed by possibilities and constraints of the visual editor and are also extended to include new actions as resizing, moving and inserting visual elements. Designer's dialogue with her/his drawings can be characterized by the cycle of actions. After performing physical actions leading to a design drawing, this drawing is inspected by means of perceptual actions which can also take into account the feedback from the computer system. In the next step of this dialogue conceptual actions, which determine the need of drawing modification take place. In the alternative course of actions, functional actions after perceptual actions are used. At the time meaning is associated with features discovered in perceptual actions or drawings are evaluated. Then, conceptual actions which consist of forming new or revising previous ideas, are performed. In both cases the cycle repeats by redrawing again using physical actions.

In the framework of the computational ontology the designer on the base of the conceptualization can generate an observable world state. The designer's world is defined as an ordered set of world states (Guarino et al. 2009). The approach presented in this paper describes the world in the form of a sequence of drawings on the monitor screen. The notion of

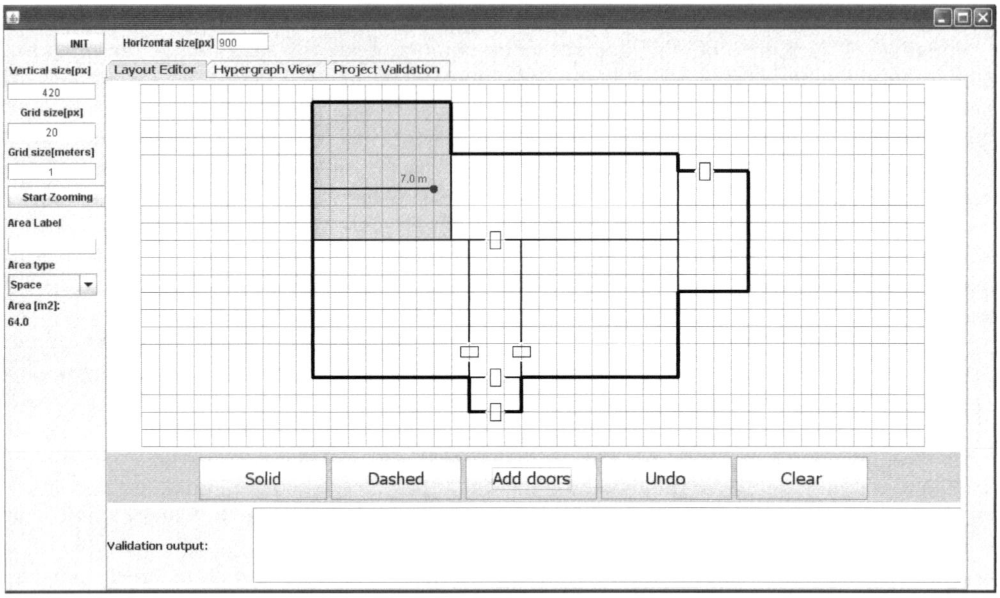

Figure 1 HSSDR with a floor layout diagram being sketched.

conceptualization is extended for all observable world states. In each step of design process for the same domain of discourse the designer changing number of elements of the domain of discourse and/or relations on it can devise a new conceptualization.

Let us consider the specialized CAD editor for designing floor layout composed of polygons which are placed on an orthogonal grid. These polygons represent functional areas or rooms. According to designer's convention each line shared by polygons in the drawing is associated with one of two relations. Lines with door symbol on them represent the accessibility relation among components, while continuous lines shared by polygons denote the adjacency relation between them. An example of a floor layout generated by the designer with the use of the editor is shown in Figure 1.

One of the main difficult problems in computer-aided design is creating visualizations of 3D objects. The general approach to construct 3D objects in human-computer interaction of CAD systems is using existing well-known CAD tools such as for instance Revit or SketchUp which communicate with the considered CAD system through plugins. Plugins gather the project data, pass it to the system, obtain the system response concerning the project validity and present them to the designer.

The Current Modeling System

The Hypergraph System Supporting Design and Reasoning described in (Grabska et al. 2009) is a system for designing floor layouts using the top-down methodology. HSSDR communicates with its users by means of a simple visual language of diagrams. It also checks if the current state of the layout satisfies design constraints specified as a set of first-order logic formulas.

A user starts by drawing an outline of an apartment. This outline is then divided by drawing a polyline. The resulting areas are further divided into sub-areas. The user continues dividing them, stopping when she reaches the level of rooms. Doors and cameras can be added either during, or after this process.

HSSDR internally uses a hierarchical hypergraph as its main data structure (see Figure 2). Every user action modifies this hypergraph, and these modifications are then reflected in the displayed diagram.

The hypergraph consists of two types of hyperedges: those representing rooms and areas, and those representing adjacency and accessibility relations. Functional areas and groups of rooms are at higher hierarchy levels, while single rooms are at the bottom. Graph nodes correspond to walls. Attributes are used to store rooms positions, as well as wall lengths, number and positions of doors and cameras, room labels, etc.

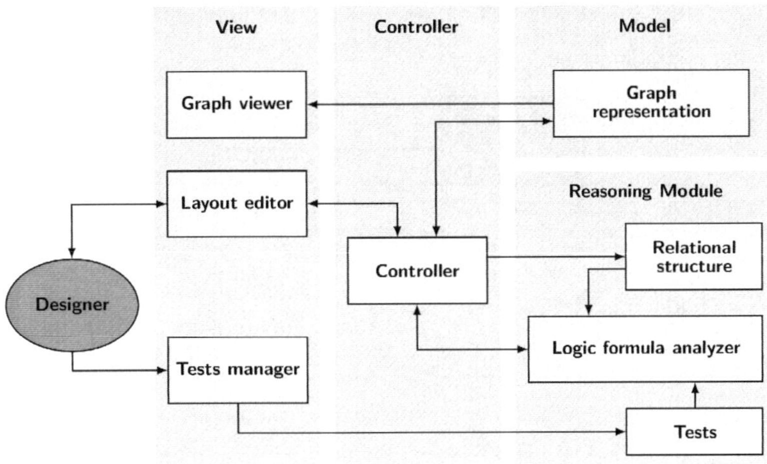

Figure 2 The internal architecture of HSSDR.

The design constraints are stored in external text files, thus they can be easily modified or replaced at any time, even in the middle of a design session. Constraints can refer to elements of the layout (rooms, walls, doors and cameras) and to a fixed set of relations and functions (adjacency between two rooms, room type, distance between two doors, etc.). Thanks to the use of widely known first-order logic formalisms they are readable by developers, experts and users.

The constraints are logic sentences, and as such can be evaluated as true or false in context of a specific relational structure (Fagin et al. 2003). HSSDR defines a structure which reflects the current state of the hypergraph. Results of evaluation are presented to the user; all false results are flagged as constraint violations.

An example of such results can be seen in Figure 3. The text field near the bottom shows the name of the file and the message associated with the failed test. The layout element which failed this test is marked red on the diagram.

The New System

Experiences gained during implementation and testing of the original version of HSSDR have pointed to several areas of potential improvement. One of them was the type of graph used as the main data structure and the way elements of discourse were modeled in this graph. The original way of representing an area or a room by a special kind of hyperedge together with its attached nodes was convenient for representing accessibility and adjacency relations between areas/rooms, but became problematic when the representation was extended to doors and cameras. From an ontological point of view areas and rooms are treated as elements of the domain of discourse, while other objects as doors and cameras as properties (attributes) of these elements. In other words, there does not exist ontological commitment between conceptualization and its representation in the form attributed hypergraph. Therefore, this paper proposes a new model which uses hierarchical graphs with bonds. This type of graphs makes possible to include all of the object as elements of the domain of discourse. Bonds are specific graph nodes which can specify arguments of relations on different levels of detail.

Another proposed improvement concerns the language, in which the design constraints are specified. The original HSSDR used first-order logic; it can be replaced by many-sorted first-order logic, which is used in semantics and program verifications, definition of programming languages, databases, computer aided problem solving, and logic programming and automated deduction. Although it does not change the class of constraints which can be formulated, but it makes the knowledge expert's job easier. Introduction of sorts divides the domain of discourse into subsets: the subset of rooms, the subset of doors, the subset of numbers, the subset of room types, etc. Predicates and functions used in formulas are annotated with information about sorts of their arguments and results. This allows for enhanced syntactic checking of formulas.

The new system keeps the name "HSSDR", but the first letter now stands for "hierarchical graph", not for "hypergraph". So, it can refer to

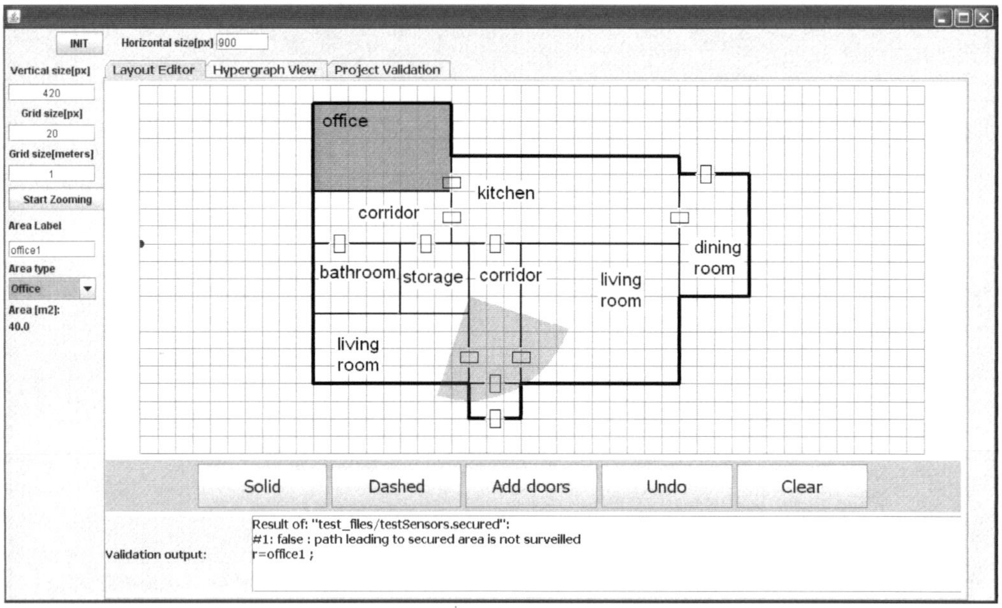

Figure 3 A finished layout which does not fulfill one of design constraints.

any kind of hierarchical graph, from graphs described in (Palacz 2004), through hypergraphs used by the previous version of HSSDR and B-graphs proposed for the new version, to as yet unknown kinds which may be used in the future. For example, multi-hierarchical graphs described in (Ślusarczyk et al. 2015) seem promising as models for multi-storey buildings and other cases where single hierarchy based on spatial containment is insufficient.

Hierarchical B-Graphs

B-graphs are meant to represent objects and their fragments or elements (known as bonds) that can be used as arguments of relations. Relations are defined between bonds (Grabska 1993). We distinguish two kinds of bonds: engaged and free bonds which correspond to arguments of existing and potential relations, respectively. This distinct of bonds is essential in definitions of operations on graphs that reflect modifications of design drawing.

B-graphs used in this paper are hierarchical, because of the need to represent nested areas. Hierarchy also allows for sub-bonds (for example, a room has walls as its fragments and one of them has a door – this door is a fragment of the room, but also is subordinate to the wall).

Instead of one set of nodes, B-graphs have two: a set of object nodes and a set of bond nodes. They also have a set of edges. Every edge connects bonds belonging to two different objects.

HSSDR needs to store additional information about layout elements, therefore B-graphs used in this paper allow for labels and attributes on nodes and edges.

Let Σ be a finite alphabet used to label object nodes, bond nodes and edges.

Let A be a nonempty, finite set of attributes. For every attribute $a \in A$, let D_a be a fixed, nonempty set of its admissible values, known as the domain of a.

A B-graph G is a tuple G = (O, B, E, bd, s, t, ch, lab, atr), where:

- O, B, E are pairwise disjoint finite sets, whose elements are respectively called object nodes, bond nodes, and edges;
- $bd : O \longrightarrow 2^B$ is a function assigning sets of bond nodes to object nodes such that $\forall x \in B\ \exists!\, y \in O : x \in bd(y)$, i.e., each bond belongs to exactly one object;
- $s, t : E \longrightarrow B$ are functions assigning to edges source and target bond nodes, respectively, in such a way that $\forall e \in E\ \exists x, y \in O : s(e) \in bd(x) \wedge t(e) \in bd(y) \wedge x \neq y$;
- $ch : O \cup B \cup E \longrightarrow 2^{O \cup B \cup E}$ is a child nesting function such that:
  - $\forall x, y, z \in O \cup B \cup E : x \in ch(y) \wedge x \in ch(z) \Rightarrow y = z$, i.e., a graph element cannot be nested in two different places;

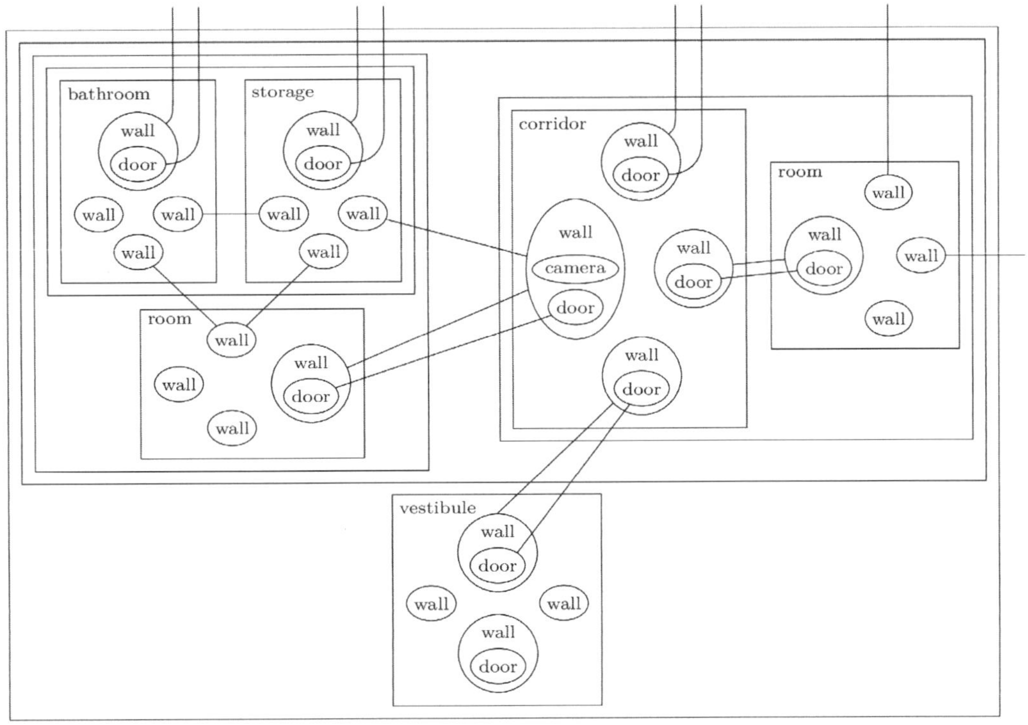

Figure 4 A part of a graph model corresponding to the layout displayed in Figure 3. Attributes and their values were omitted for brevity's sake.

- $\forall x \in O \cup B \cup E : x \notin ch^{+}(x)$, i.e., a graph element cannot be its own descendant;
- $\forall x \in B \ \ \forall y \in O \ : \ x \in bd(y) \Rightarrow x \in ch(y) \vee (\exists z \in B \ : \ x \in ch(z) \wedge z \in bd(y))$, i.e., a bond must be nested either in its object, or in some other bond belonging to this object.

- $lab : O \cup B \cup E \longrightarrow \Sigma$ is a labeling function;
- $atr : O \cup B \cup E \longrightarrow 2^{A}$ is an attributing function.

A part of B-graph being internal representation of the layout shown in Figure 3 is presented in Figure 4. Some bonds in Figure 4 are free. They are represented by bonds with the outgoing edges.

Adding information about attribute values to a B-graph produces a graph instance. Obviously, a single B-graph can be used as a base for many instances which differ in attribute values.

An instance I of a B-graph G is a pair $I = (G, val)$ where $val : (O_G \cup B_G \cup E_G) \times A \longrightarrow D$, with $D = \bigcup_{a \in A} D_a$, is a partial function assigning attribute values such that:

- $val(x, a)$ is defined if and only if $a \in atr_G(x)$;
- $val(x, a) \in D_a$ if defined.

HSSDR's main data structure is a graph instance.

Many-Sorted First-Order Logic

Since HSSDR system deals with computer representation of drawings in the form of B-graphs instances, the explicit specification related to the reasoning mechanism must be formal, i.e., the expressions must be defined in a formal language. We assume that our language is a many-sorted first-order logical language.

Many-sorted first-order logic introduces sorts, which represent distinct kinds of objects to reason about (Manzano 1993). Functions and predicates specify what sort of arguments they require.

Let us consider the following requirement that all rooms are to be at least one and a half meter wide formalized as follows:

$$\forall x : width(x) > 1.5$$

In our case, the "width" function takes a single argument of the "areas" sort and returns a result belonging to the "numbers" sort.

This paper extends the classical first-order logic to many-sorted first-order logic because in CAD applications domains and ranges of functions need various sorts of elements, for instance real numbers and set of sensors. The concept of sort allows one to specify for each function its domain and range.

The formal definition of many-sorted first-order logic formulas starts with the definition of sorts.

Let $S = \{ s_1, s_2, ..., s_k \}$ be a set of sorts.

Let X be a set of variables. Each variable is associated to a single sort. Thus X can be partitioned into subsets $X_1 ... X_k$ with each X_i containing variables of sort s_i.

Let C be a set of constant symbols. Again, each constant symbol is associated to a sort, and C is partitioned into $C_1 ... C_k$.

Let F be a set of function symbols. Each symbol is associated to a tuple of natural numbers from the [1, k] range. Notation $f : s_{i_1} \times ... \times s_{i_n} \longrightarrow s_{i_{n+1}}$ will be used to denote a symbol f associated to $(i_1, ..., i_n, i_{n+1})$.

Let P be a set of predicate symbols associated to tuples. Notation $p : s_{i_1} \times ... \times s_{i_n}$ will be used to denote a symbol p associated to $(i_1, ..., i_n)$.

A signature σ is a tuple $\sigma = (S, X, C, F, P)$.

A set of σ-terms of sort s_t is defined as the smallest set containing all expressions of the following form:

- x, where $x \in X_t$;
- c, where $c \in C_t$;
- $f(t_1, ..., t_n)$, where $f : s_{i_1} \times ... \times s_{i_n} \longrightarrow s_t$ and every t_j is a σ-term of sort s_{i_j}.

A set of σ-formulas is the smallest set containing expressions of the form:

- $t_1 = t_2$, where t_1 and t_2 are σ-terms of the same sort;
- $p(t_1, ..., t_n)$, where $p : s_{i_1} \times ... \times s_{i_n}$ and every t_j is a σ-term of sort s_{i_j};
- $\varphi \wedge \psi$, $\varphi \vee \psi$, $\varphi \Longrightarrow \psi$, and $\varphi \Longleftrightarrow \psi$, where φ and ψ are σ-formulas;
- $\neg \varphi$, $\forall x \varphi$, and $\exists x \varphi$, where φ is a σ-formula and $x \in X$.

Having separate sets of variables used for different sorts is, in practice, inconvenient. A constraint writer should not be required to remember that x, y, and z can be used to refer to rooms, while a, b and c refer to doors. Therefore HSSDR has a single set of variables, and the reasoning module infers the sort of a variable from the context in which it was used.

A formula where all variables are bound by quantifiers is known as a sentence. Sentences are either true or false, but only after all symbols used in formulas are assigned a specific semantics. This semantic information is provided by a relational structure defined as σ-structure R in the following way:

For a signature σ, a σ-structure R is a map with the following properties:

- each sort s_i is mapped to a nonempty set A_i;
- each constant symbol $c \in C_i$ is mapped to an element of A_i;
- each function symbol $f : s_{i_1} \times ... \times s_{i_n} \longrightarrow s_{i_{n+1}}$ is mapped to a function $f^R : A_{i_1} \times ... \times A_{i_n} \longrightarrow A_{i_{n+1}}$;
- each predicate symbol $p : s_{i_1} \times ... \times s_{i_n}$ is mapped to a subset $p^R \subset A_{i_1} \times ... \times A_{i_n}$.

There can be many interpretations for a signature. HSSDR's reasoning module uses a single, unchangeable signature, and interprets its symbols on the base of the B-graphs instance representing a step of designing of the floor layout being a current observable world state. Every modification of the drawing results in a new B-graph structure leading to a new relation structure.

Vocabulary of the Reasoning Module

It is necessary to notice that in HSSDR system an ontological commitment between designer's worlds in the form of sequences drawings on the monitor screen and the signature σ is assumed. On the base of this the vocabulary of the reasoning module is defined.

HSSDR defines the following sorts:

- areas;
- walls;
- doors;
- sensors;
- area labels;
- real numbers.

There are constants representing:

- labels ("hall", "bathroom", etc.);
- numbers (17, -4, 2.50, etc.).

The functions are:

- type : areas $\longrightarrow$ labels;
- width : areas $\longrightarrow$ numbers;

- length : areas → numbers;
- doorsDist : doors × doors → numbers (returns a distance between two pairs of doors in a single room);
- standard arithmetic operators, either numbers × numbers → numbers or numbers → numbers.

Two-argument predicates:

- adjacent : areas × areas;
- accessible : areas × areas (returns true if you can walk from one area to the other through a directly connecting door);
- doorsInRoom : doors × areas (returns true if the doors are embedded in a wall of the room);
- sensorInRoom : sensors × areas;
- isPassageWatched : doors × doors (returns true if every path between two pairs of doors in a single room is watched by one or more sensors);
- standard arithmetic comparison operators : numbers × numbers.

One-argument predicates (i.e., sort subsets):

- Areas : areas;
- Rooms : areas;
- Walls : walls;
- Doors : doors;
- ExternalDoors : doors;
- Sensors : sensors.

Only Rooms and ExternalDoors define proper subsets of their sorts. Other predicates always return true, and thus define sets equal to their whole sorts. From the formal point of view these predicates are not necessary, and are provided only because constraint writers sometimes prefer to write constraints with explicitly specified quantifier ranges:

```
forall a in Rooms:
  type(a) = "bank vault" =>
  (exists s in Sensors:
    sensorInRoom(s, a))
```

HSSDR's Relational Structures

For a given graph instance I representing a layout, the corresponding relational structure R is constructed as follows:

- $A_{areas} = O_I$;
- $A_{walls} = \{ x \in B_I : lab_I(x) = \text{"wall"} \}$;
- $A_{doors} = \{ x \in B_I : lab_I(x) = \text{"door"} \}$;
- $A_{sensors} = \{ x \in B_I : lab_I(x) = \text{"sensor"} \}$;
- $A_{labels} = \Sigma$;
- $A_{numbers} = \mathbb{R}$;
- label and number constants are mapped to themselves;
- $type^R(x) = lab_I(x)$;
- $width^R(x) = val_I(x, \text{"width"})$;
- $length^R(x) = val_I(x, \text{"length"})$;
- $doorsDist^R(x, y)$ is implemented algorithmically;
- arithmetic operators are defined as themselves;
- $adjacent^R = \{ (x, y) \subset O_I \times O_I :$ exists $e \in E_I$ such that $s_I(e) \in bd_I(x)$, $t_I(e) \in bd_I(y)$, $lab_I(e) = \text{"adjacent"} \}$;
- $acessible^R = \{ (x, y) \subset O_I \times O_I :$ exists $e \in E_I$ such that $s_I(e) \in bd_I(x)$, $t_I(e) \in bd_I(y)$, $lab_I(e) = \text{"accessible"} \}$;
- $doorsInRoom^R = \{ (x, y) \subset B_I \times O_I : lab_I(x) = \text{"door"}, x \in bd_I(y) \}$;
- $sensorInRoom^R = \{ (x, y) \subset B_I \times O_I : lab_I(x) = \text{"sensor"}, x \in bd_I(y) \}$;
- $isPassageWatched^R \subset B_I \times B_I$ is calculated by Java code;
- arithmetic comparisons are defined as themselves;
- $Areas^R = A_{areas}$;
- $Rooms^R = \{ x \in O_I : ch_I(x) \cap O_I = \emptyset \}$;
- $Walls^R = A_{walls}$;
- $Doors^R = A_{doors}$;
- $ExternalDoors^R = \{ x \in A_{doors} :$ there is no $e \in E_I$ such that $s_I(e) = x \}$;
- $Sensors^R = A_{sensors}$.

It worth noticing that cameras added at an early design stage allow one to show possibilities both of the new graph representation and of many-sorted logics.

Examples

This section provides several examples of tests, written in a form acceptable to HSSDR.

The following constraint requires at least one bedroom present in the layout:

```
exists x : type(x) = "Bedroom";
```

HSSDR's reasoning module, when loading this formula, will recognize x as a variable of an unspecified sort and "Bedroom" as a constant of the labels sort. Since x is used as an argument of the "type" function, it apparently must be of the areas sort. This function produces results of the labels sort, which means that both sides of the equality sign are of the same sort. The formula is syntactically correct.

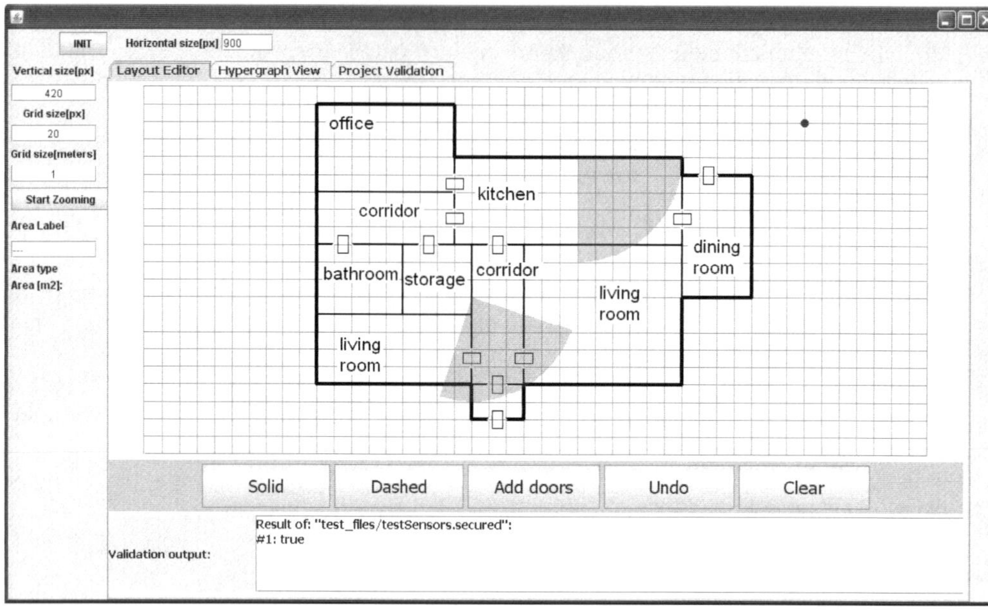

Figure 5 Corrected version of the layout from Figure 3.

The reasoning module uses exhaustive search when evaluating formulas with quantifiers. In this case, since x is of the areas sort, it will loop over all areas (and rooms) currently present in the layout – that is, over elements of the Areas^R set.

This constraint is syntactically invalid, because results of the "type" function belong to the labels sort, and cannot be compared with constants of the numbers sort:

```
exists r : type(r) > 42;
```

The last example is more complex. It checks if all path leading to secured areas are watched by sensors. To do that, it defines four auxiliary relations, which HSSDR adds to its vocabulary. Originally presented in (Palacz et al. 2011), here it was adapted to many-sorted logic.

```
SecuredArea(r) <=>
  type(r) = "Office"
  or type(r) = "Living_Room"
  or type(r) = "Garage";

UnwatchedPath(d1,d2) <=>
  d1 != d2 and (exists r:
    doorsInRoom(d1,r)
    and doorsInRoom(d2,r)
    and not isPathWatched(d1,d2));

UnwatchedPathInduction(d1,d2,n) <=>
  UnwatchedPath(d1,d2)
  or (n > 1 and exists d:
    UnwatchedPathInduction(d1,d,n-1)
    and UnwatchedPath(d,d2));

UnwatchedPathPlus(d1,d2) <=>
  UnwatchedPathInduction(d1,d2,99);

failure_msg "path leading to
  secured area is not surveiled"
not exists d1, d2: exists r:
  SecuredArea(r)
  and doorsInRoom(d2,r)
  and UnwatchedPathPlus(d1,d2);
```

Results produced by this test can be seen on screenshots in Figure 3 and Figure 5. At first, the test fails because a thief can enter through the doors in the dining room and walk unobserved through kitchen to the office. Adding a second sensor in the kitchen secures this path.

Conclusions

This paper presents how graph can be combined with the most logic-based knowledge representation techniques, where knowledge is represented explicitly by symbolic terms and reasoning is the manipulation of these terms. In the proposed approach the semantics of logical formulas uses relational structures based on B-graph instances.

It is known that the degree to which an ontology specifies a conceptualization depends on the richness both of the domain of discourse and the signature, and logic language expressiveness. In the considered paper many-sorted logic language is used.

The proposed approach provides insight in how humans aided by computer solve visual design problems. In our future research we shall focus attention on models for multi-storey buildings with multi-hierarchies graph representations with bonds.

References

Fagin, R., Halpern, J.Y., Moses, Y. & Vardi, M.Y. (2003). *Reasoning About Knowledge.* The MIT Press.

Grabska, E. (1993). *Graphs and Designing.* In: H.J. Schneider and H. Ehrig (Eds.), Graph Transformation in Computer Science, *Lecture Notes in Computer Science* 776, pp. 188-202.

Grabska, E., Borkowski, A., Palacz, W. & Gajek, Sz. (2009). *Hypergraph System Supporting Design and Reasoning.* In: Wolfgang Huhnt (Ed.), Computing in Engineering EG-ICE Conference 2009, Shaker Verlag, pp. 134-141.

Grabska, E., Łachwa, A. & Ślusarczyk, G. (2012). *New Visual Languages Supporting Design of Multi-Storey Buildings.* In: *Advanced Engineering Informatics* 26, pp. 681-690.

Goldschmidt, G. (1994). *On visual design thinking.* In: *Design Studies* 15, pp. 158-174.

Guarino, N. et al. (2009). *What Is an Ontology.* Handbook on Ontologies. Springer, Heidelberg.

Lawson, B. (1997). *How designers think.* Architectural Press.

Lifschitz, V., Morgenstern, L. & Plaisted, D. (2008). *Knowledge Representation and Classical Logic.* In: van Harmelen, F., Lifschitz, V., Porter, B. (Eds.), *Handbook of Knowledge Representation,* Elsevier, pp. 3-88.

Manzano, M. (1993). *Introduction to Many-Sorted Logic.* In: Meinke, K. & Tucker, J.V. (Eds.), *Many-Sorted Logic and Its Applications,* Wiley, pp. 3-86.

Palacz, W. (2004). *Algebraic Hierarchical Graph Transformation.* In: *Journal of Computer and System Sciences* 68(3), Elsevier, pp. 497-520.

Palacz, W., Grabska, G. & Gajek. Sz. (2011). *Conceptual Designing Supported by Automated Checking of Design Requirements and Constraints.* In: Frey, D. D. et al. (Eds.), *Improving Complex Systems Today,* Springer-Verlag, pp. 257-265.

Ślusarczyk, G. et al. (2015). *An Extended Hierarchical Graph-Based Building Model for Engineering Problems.* Submitted to *International Journal of Applied Mathematics and Computer Science.*

Tversky, B. & Suwa, M. (2009). *Thinking with Sketches.* In: *Tools for Innovation.* Oxford University Press.

Detection of Multiple Road Defects for Pavement Condition Assessment

Stefania C. Radopoulou, scr58@cam.ac.uk
University of Cambridge, Cambridge, UK

Ioannis Brilakis, ib340@cam.ac.uk
University of Cambridge, Cambridge, UK

Abstract
Pavement condition assessment is a prerequisite for pavement maintenance. State of the art practices are mainly manual, with only 0.8% of inspections using expensive specialized vehicles that automate data collection. This expensive and time-intensive task could be crowdsourced by transforming every day road users into omnipresent pavement inspectors using pre-existing car sensors. The objective is to automate the detection of pavement defects. This paper presents an application of the Semantic Texton Forests (STF) algorithm for automatically detecting patches, potholes and three types of cracks in video frames captured by a common parking camera. The prototype has been implemented in C# and validated using real data collected from local roads in the city of Cambridge, United Kingdom. Preliminary results demonstrate the successful application of STF in the context of pavements with over 70% accuracy in all of the tests performed, and over 75% precision for most of the defects.

Keywords: Road defects, automatic detection, road monitoring

1 Introduction

Roads are vital not only for economic prosperity, but for social and environmental well-being as well, since it is one of the means of connecting businesses and communities. Road maintenance is a very important and critical challenge for local councils due to a two-fold reason. On one hand, the road network is ageing and on the other, users expectations demand high-quality roads (UK Roads Liaison Group 2013). As an example, 61% of the UK's business leaders compare the country's road network unfavourably to international benchmarks, and 50% complain about its deterioration during the past five years (CBI and KPMG 2011).

Accurate pavement condition data is essential for efficiently designing, planning and decision-making of road maintenance programs. Pavement condition assessment aims at detecting and identifying the severity of defects. The current process comprises of three steps: (a) data collection, (b) detection of defects and (c) defects' severity assessment.

Step (a) is performed either with specialized vehicles or by manual visual surveys. For the latter, step (b) is performed simultaneously. Specialized vehicles are equipped with several sensors such as laser scanners, road profilers and cameras. The aims are to acquire the longitudinal and transversal profiles of the road and capture images of all highway assets (Fugro Roadware 2010; Highways Agency 2008; UKPMS 2005). However, such vehicles are expensive, both to purchase (approximately £500,000 depending on the sensors included) and operate (between £20 and £40 per kilometre) (Werro 2013). Hence, they are typically used only once a year (MnDOT 2009) and only on the primary road network.

In the UK, the primary road network (class 'A' roads) represent 9.6% of the country's entire network (Williams 2013). The remaining 90.4% is inspected with manual visual surveys (UKPMS 2005). Such surveys are also conducted on class 'A' roads, where the inspector is driven through the network at low speeds (SDDOT 2009) to enable visual detection of defects. Moreover, handheld equipment is also used to collect data while walking along the pavement (UKPMS 2005).

When data is collected using a specialized vehicle, steps (b) and (c) are performed by technicians who use multiple screens to view and analyse the collected video, images and sensor data to identify areas that have defects and assess the condition of the road (FHWA 2003; MnDOT 2003). In the case of manual visual surveys, inspectors need to upload all gathered information to databases to digitize it. This includes not only images of the defect, but also detailed descriptions of the situations encountered during the survey (e.g. type of defect, geographical location, urgency for maintenance, etc.). Although the guides and manuals that are used for the assessment of defects are well-written and reliable, technicians' subjectivity is inevitably introduced due to their varying level of experience (Bianchini et al. 2010).

When specialized vehicles are used, it is almost impossible to analyse the entire amount of collected data. Usually, only 10% of the data of each road is used for post-processing (MnDOT 2003). It is obvious that the current state of practice is tedious, laborious and quite time-consuming.

This paper focuses on automating step (b) and proposing an approach that will detect several defects simultaneously. It is part of a greater project on developing an affordable and automated pavement condition monitoring process based on the idea of crowdsourcing the task to everyday road users and effectively transforming them into ubiquitous pavement inspectors. The idea is to achieve this with sensors that already exist in vehicles, such as the parking camera, to keep the costs low. Many cars have such cameras, which only operate when the car is being driven in reverse gear. If these cameras are operating at all times they can be used for road monitoring.

It is hypothesized that the application of a supervised learning algorithm such as the Semantic Texton Forests (Shotton et al. 2008) can simultaneously detect a range of defects occurring in video frames more effectively than standalone algorithms. The scope of the paper is restricted to the following defects: alligator cracks, transversal cracks, longitudinal cracks, patches and potholes

2 State of research in road defect detection and classification

Many research methods have been proposed for crack detection (Gavilán et al. 2011; Ghanta et al. 2012; Jing and Aiqin 2010), real-time crack analysis (Huang and Xu 2006; Maode et al. 2007; Sy et al. 2008), crack classification (Moghadas Nejad and Zakeri 2011; Salari and Bao 2011; Ying and Salari 2010) and crack sealing (Haas 1996; Kim et al. 2009). Other methods have focused on detecting potholes (Koch and Brilakis 2011; Lin and Liu 2010), tracking them in videos (Koch et al. 2012b) and measuring their properties (Koch et al. 2012a). The same applies to methods for road patches (Radopoulou and Brilakis 2015; Battiato et al. 2007; Cafiso et al. 2006; Yao et al. 2008).

One method was proposed for detecting a range of defects at the same time (Zhou et al. 2006). This method only identifies the existence of a defect in an image; it cannot identify the location of the defect within the image or its type. There are no methods in the literature that are able to detect both the type and location of road defects with a single approach. Such methods are necessary, as many road defects share similarities and it is very common for manual inspectors, and even more so for vision-based inspection algorithms, to mistake one for another. In essence, inter-class differences in the classification process are not taken into account.

Simultaneous segmentation (separation of an image into areas that include identical objects) and recognition (identification) of multiple object-types in images is possible (Shotton et al. 2009; Uijlings et al. 2010; Zhang et al. 2007) with machine learning multi-classifier algorithms. The algorithm is initially trained with as many images of the object-types of interest as possible. Training images include a variety of the objects' poses to cover all possible appearances and allow the algorithm to be correctly trained. During this stage, feature descriptors such as SIFT (Scale Invariant Feature Transform) (Lowe 2004) and SURF (Speed-Up Robust Features) (Bay et al. 2008) are extracted from small regions of the image to create a codebook of visual words. A word in a codebook corresponds to an image region. While testing, images are segmented and categorized into pre-defined classes of object-types.

Semantic Texton Forests (STFs) is one such algorithm (Johnson and Shotton 2010). However, it uses kernel features instead of feature points. STFs are randomized decision forests (figure 1a), which are classifiers consisting of multiple decision trees (Geurts et al. 2006). They are trained with the bag of semantic textons (figure 1c). Given a patch of pixels with a fixed size (figure 1b), image features are extracted during training to form the bag of semantic textons. Each node of a tree is assigned a class distribution that represents its probability, and a binary function which is created using the raw pixel values in the semantic textons. Those are learned during the training process by being randomly selected from a small subset of the features that were extracted from the training images. This tactic ensures greater speed and avoids over-fitting (Johnson and Shotton 2010). Besides the pixel-level features, the context information is also involved in the classification. Therefore, STFs are using localized semantic textons as a feature descriptor and randomized decision forests as a classifier.

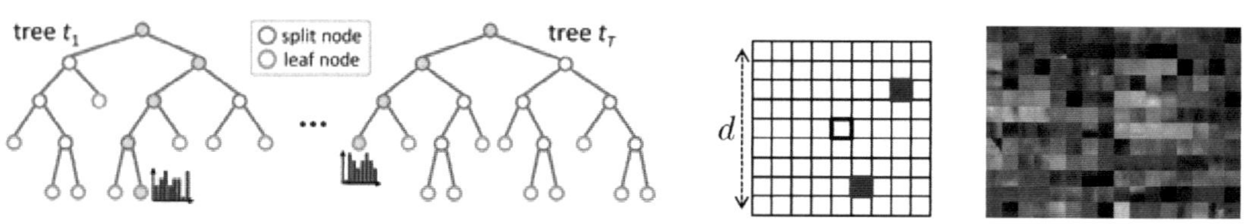

(a) (b) (c)

Figure 1 (a) Randomized decision forests, (b) a specified size pixel patch, and (c) Semantic Textons (Shotton et al. 2008)

For meeting this paper's objective, which is to automate the detection of road defects, we test whether it is possible to effectively detect the type and location of a range of defects using STFs. The scope is restricted to the defects of alligator, longitudinal and transverse cracks, potholes and patches. The databases used for training and testing the algorithm were formed from videos collected using a camera with the same standards as parking cameras; both in regards to its specifications and its position at the rear of the vehicle.

3 Research methodology

The research activities for testing the above hypothesis are presented in figure 2. Initially, road video data is processed frame-by-frame to prepare the ground truth data. During this step, each video frame is assigned the following metadata: 1) whether it includes a road defect, 2) the type(s) of defect(s) it includes, (if it does) and 3) the area/location of each defect. Two copies of video frames that depict defects are saved separately to form the database for training and testing the STFs. One copy is the actual image of the video frame and the other is the segmented ground truth. Segmentation is performed manually to mark the areas of the video frame that depict a defect from those that do not. Each road defect is represented with a different colour (table 1). Some examples of video frames depicting road defects and their ground truth copy can be seen in figure 3. The parts of the video frame that do not represent any category of interest are marked in black.

Video frames stored in the previously created database are randomly selected for training purposes. The ground truth copy is used to identify where the defective area is within the video frame, and the actual image is used to "learn" the characteristic features of each defect. When the algorithm finishes training, the semantic texton forest is ready to be tested. At this stage, randomly selected video frames from the same database are used to evaluate the forest. In this case, the ground truth of those frames is used for validation. The final output of the algorithm is the segmented version of video frames produced by the forest that was formed during training.

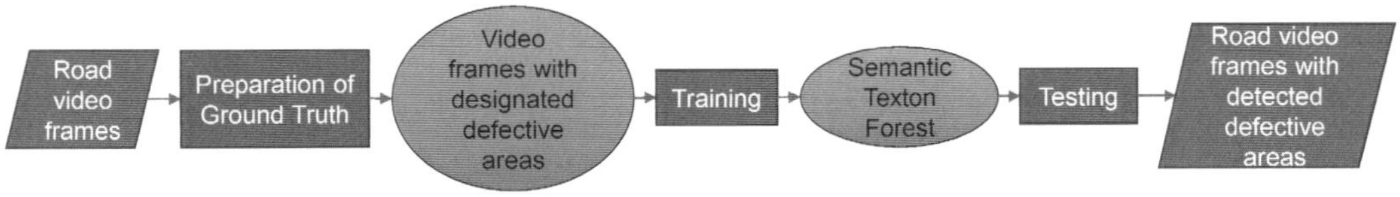

Figure 2 Research activities to test the applicability of STFs for detecting the type and location of road defects

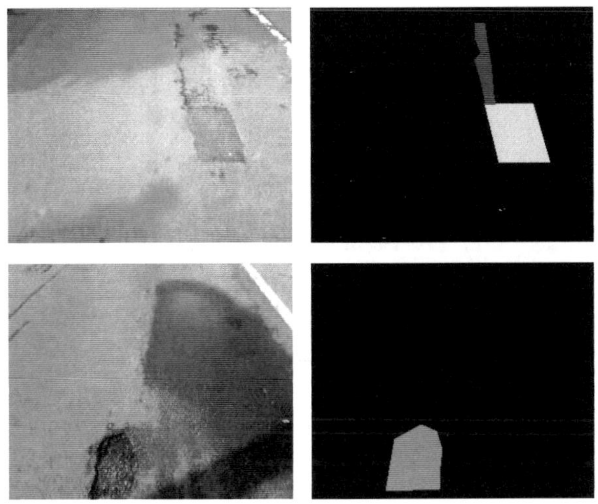

Figure 3 Examples of video frames depicting road defects (left column) and their ground truth (right column)

Table 1 Type of road defect and its representative colour in the ground truth

Type of defect	Colour
Alligator crack	Green
Longitudinal crack	Red
Transverse crack	Blue
Patch	Yellow
Pothole	Pink
Void	Black

4 Experimental Design, Implementation and Results

Initially, an HP Elite Webcam was used to simulate a low resolution parking camera. It was positioned on the rear of a car (figure 4) and data was collected from local streets in Cambridge, UK. The characteristics of the camera can be found in table 2. A database of 230 video frames was formed during the step of preparing the ground truth.

For validating the algorithms' performance, four metrics are used; two for measuring the performance of STFs in total,

Table 2 Characteristics of cameras used for data collection

	HP Elite Autofocus Webcam	Point Grey Blackfly 05S2M-CS
Image resolution	640 x 480	800 x 500
Horizontal angle of view	~50°	133°
Frame rate per second	30	50
Colour	RGB	Monochrome (grey)

which are the overall accuracy and the average accuracy and two for measuring how STFs are performing in regards to each defect separately, which are average precision and area under curve. Overall accuracy is the total proportion of pixels that were correctly segmented. Average accuracy is the average proportion of correctly detected pixels in each category. Average precision is the fraction of correctly detected pixels (True Positive, TP) over the sum of correctly and incorrectly (False Positive, FP) detected pixels. Finally, area under curve (AuC) is the area covered when TP is plotted versus FP; large AuC indicates better performance.

Several combinations of different parameters that affect the performance of the STF algorithm were tested. Specifically, 5 patch sizes and 4 sets of maximum tree depths were tested. The specific combinations and the accuracies they provided are summarized in table 3. The results regarding each defect separately are summarized in table 4.

The experiments continued, utilizing a Point Grey Blackfly 0.5 MP (PG camera) camera (see table 2 for more specifications). This camera has similar specifications to a typical car parking camera, which were defined after researching the corresponding market and car manufacturers' websites. The main differences when compared to the camera used previously are: 1) higher resolution, 2) wider angle of view and 3) higher frame rate. After capturing road videos from Cambridge's local streets, a database of 517 video frames was formed.

This time, one additional category was added; this is the category of healthy pavement. The colour that was used for marking such areas when preparing the ground truth is grey. The combination of different parameters of STFs tested on this database along with their overall performance can be seen in table 5. Their individual performance on each defect are summarized in table 6. A typical example of the STFs' performance can be found in figure 5.

For both of the above experiments, the car's speed was 15km/hr during data collection. This information along with the frame rate of the camera defines the frame/meter ratio. In the first set of experiments this was ~7fr/m, which translates to 7,000fr/km. In the second, it was ~11fr/m, meaning 11,000fr/km.

Video data was saved locally and post-processed using a desktop computer (Intel Core i7 @ 3.4 GHz, 8GB Ram). Due to the low image resolution of the camera, the video files stored are of small size. The ones collected varied from 155MB to 1GB depending on the time duration of each.

5 Conclusions

Current research has been focusing on automating the process of not only collecting road data, but also detecting and assessing road defects. The goal is to overcome the limitations of current methods, which are mainly manual and depend heavily on the inspectors' level of experience. In regard to detecting several road defects at once, no method has been proposed to date.

The research covered in this paper tested the use of Semantic Texton Forests for detecting a range of road defects in video frames. The goal is to automatically detect several road defects at the same time.

Experiments were performed with two different databases. The first was produced from colour videos with 640 x 320 image resolution, to test the use of a parking camera for road condition monitoring. The second database was created from monochrome videos with 800 x 400 image resolution, which are typical characteristics of car parking cameras. Several combinations of parameters were tested to identify those that provide the most accurate results.

For the first set of experiments, the performance of STFs for detecting transverse cracks was quite low. This is probably because the total number of video frames in the training database depicting this defect was smaller than for the other defects. Hence, the model created by the algorithm for detecting transverse cracks might not be sufficient. Another reason might be the low image resolution. This can be explained by the better results obtained for this type of defect in the second set of experiments.

In general, STFs performed better with the second database. The addition of the healthy pavement category in the ground truth data could explain the improvement in performance. In regard to computational time, STFs needed 20 minutes for training and testing the first database, and almost 3 hours for the second. The difference in computational time can be explained by the following differences between the two databases; 1) the larger number of data and 2) the higher image resolution of the second one.

STFs performed well for the detection of road defects, however one limitation is that all pixels of the image are categorized in one of the given classes. In the case of road video frames, images cover the road and part of the surrounding environment such as the sky, curb, passing cars etc., and this leads to incorrect detections. For future work, it is envisaged to incorporate these categories during the training phase and test whether STFs' performance improves. Moreover, this paper tested the scenario of saving data and post-processing it. The next step is to test real-time processing and transfer of semantic information only.

Figure 4 Point Grey camera positioned at the rear of the car to simulate the parking camera for data collection.

Table 3 Sets of parameters used for testing and overall performance results of STFs (data captured by HP Webcam)

	Test 1	Test 2	Test 3	Test 4	Test 5	Test 6	Test 7	Test 8
Patch size	15	11	13	9	17	15	15	15
Max tree depth	10 & 14	10 & 14	10 & 14	10 & 14	10 & 14	11 & 13	12 & 16	15 & 16
Overall accuracy	0.78	0.69	0.73	0.78	0.76	0.78	0.78	0.79
Average accuracy	0.64	0.55	0.73	0.62	0.6	0.6	0.64	0.65

Table 4 Average precision and Area under Curve for each defect (data captured by HP Webcam)

		Test 1	Test 2	Test 3	Test 4	Test 5	Test 6	Test 7	Test 8
Alligator crack	Av.Pr.	0.94	0.94	0.74	0.81	0.78	1	0.67	0.74
	AuC	0.99	0.93	0.98	0.94	0.99	1	0.96	0.97
Longitu-dinal crack	Av.Pr.	0.95	0.95	0.92	0.97	0.96	0.96	0.9	0.96
	AuC	0.86	0.88	0.8	0.9	0.9	0.9	0.9	0.89
Transver-se crack	Av.Pr.	0.2	0.04	0.009	0.28	0.02	0.27	0.35	0.01
	AuC	0.85	0.76	0.26	0.73	0.68	0.93	0.75	0.29
Patch	Av.Pr.	0.75	0.86	0.68	0.81	0.8	0.69	0.62	0.84
	AuC	0.88	0.91	0.81	0.92	0.88	0.86	0.8	0.92
Pothole	Av.Pr.	0.89	0.99	0.84	0.9	0.82	0.82	0.81	0.92
	AuC	0.96	0.99	0.95	0.96	0.9	0.9	0.96	0.96

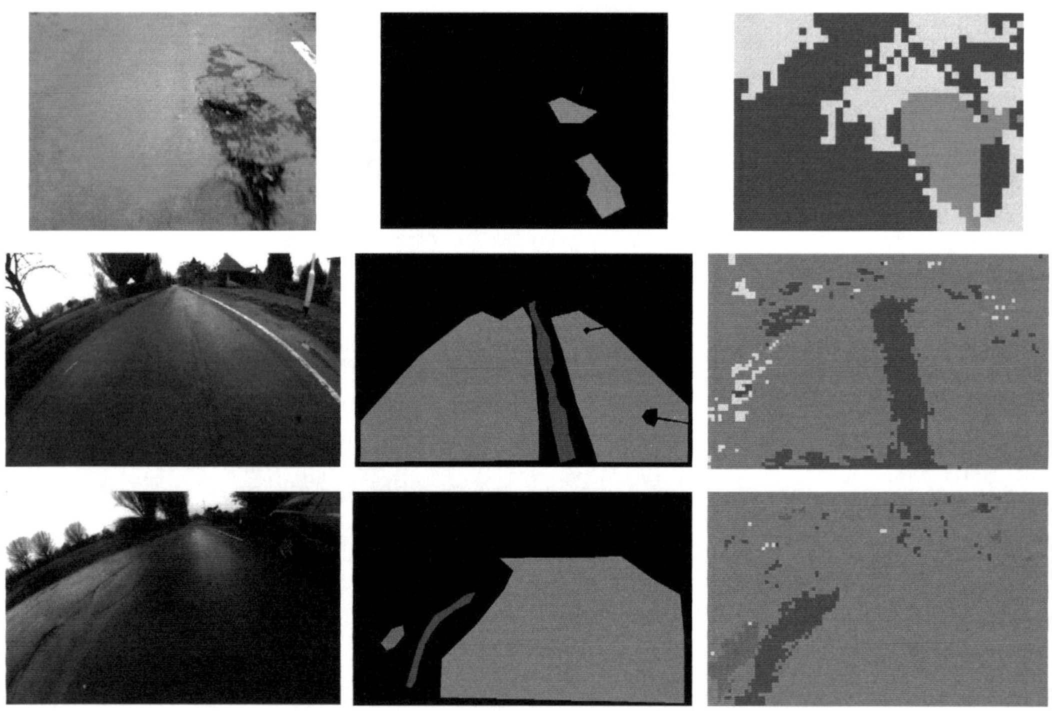

Figure 5 Examples of STFs performance. Row 1- acquired from the segmentations of test 5 of the coloured database. Rows 2 & 3 – acquired from the segmentations of the tests 4 and 5 of the monochrome database.

Table 5 Sets of parameters used for testing and overall performance results of STFs (data captured by PG camera)

	Test 1	Test 2	Test 3	Test 4	Test 5	Test 6	Test 7	Test 8
Patch size	15	11	13	9	17	13	13	13
Max tree depth	10 & 14	10 & 14	10 & 14	10 & 14	10 & 14	11 & 13	12 & 16	15 & 16
Overall accuracy	0.85	0.86	0.87	0.82	0.86	0.84	0.81	0.83
Average accuracy	0.83	0.79	0.8	0.75	0.81	0.74	0.78	0.71

Table 6 Average precision and Area under Curve for each defect (data captured by PG camera)

		Test 1	Test 2	Test 3	Test 4	Test 5	Test 6	Test 7	Test 8
Alligator crack	Av.Pr.	1	0.76	0.76	0.75	1	0.76	0.75	0.76
	AuC	1	0.96	0.97	0.9	1	0.95	0.93	0.95
Longitu-dinal crack	Av.Pr.	0.94	0.95	0.94	0.93	0.95	0.89	0.97	0.94
	AuC	0.97	0.96	0.97	0.93	0.97	0.95	0.98	0.96
Patch	Av.Pr.	0.96	0.96	0.98	0.96	0.94	0.95	0.97	0.9
	AuC	0.94	0.96	0.96	0.94	0.92	0.93	0.95	0.89
Pothole	Av.Pr.	0.8	0.63	0.84	0.81	0.82	0.63	0.85	0.8
	AuC	0.88	0.91	0.9	0.92	0.95	0.82	0.9	0.94
Healthy Pavement	Av.Pr.	0.96	0.99	0.95	0.97	0.97	0.99	0.98	0.98
	AuC	0.53	0.79	0.45	0.53	0.56	0.84	0.64	0.76

6 References

Battiato, S. et al. 2007. Adaptive Imaging Techniques for Pavement Surface Distress Analysis. In: *Communications to SIMAI Congress.*

Bay, H. et al. 2008. Speeded-Up Robust Features (SURF). *Computer Vision and Image Understanding* 110(3), pp. 346–359.

Bianchini, A. et al. 2010. Interrater reliability of manual pavement distress evaluations. *Journal of Transportation Engineering* 136(2), pp. 165–172.

Cafiso, S. et al. 2006. Evaluation of pavement surface distress using digital image collection and analysis. In: *Seventh International Congress on Advances in Civil Engineering.*

CBI and KPMG 2011. Making the right connections: CBI/KPMG infrastructure survey 2011. . Available at: http://www.cbi.org.uk/media/1052324/2011.09-cbi-kpmg-infrastructure-report.pdf [Accessed: 10 July 2013].

FHWA 2003. *Distress Identification Manual for the Long-Term Pavement Performance Program.* Federal Highway Administration.

Fugro Roadware 2010. Pavement Condition Assessment, Data sheets [Online] Available at: http://www.fugroroadware.com/related/english-alldatasheets [Accessed: 1 June 2013].

Gavilán, M. et al. 2011. Adaptive road crack detection system by pavement classification. *Sensors* 11(10), pp. 9628–9657.

Geurts, P. et al. 2006. Extremely randomized trees. *Machine learning* 63(1), pp. 3–42.

Ghanta, S. et al. 2012. Automatic road surface defect detection from grayscale images. In: *SPIE Smart Structures and Materials+ Nondestructive Evaluation and Health Monitoring.* p. 83471E–83471E.

Haas, C. 1996. Evolution of an automated crack sealer: a study in construction technology development. *Automation in construction* 4(4), pp. 293–305.

Highways Agency 2008. *Design Manual for Roads and Bridges: Volume 7 Section 3 Part 2.* Department for Transport, UK.

Huang, Y. and Xu, B. 2006. Automatic inspection of pavement cracking distress. *Journal of Electronic Imaging* 15(1), pp. 013017–013017.

Jing, L. and Aiqin, Z. 2010. Pavement crack distress detection based on image analysis. In: *Machine Vision and Human-Machine Interface (MVHI), 2010 International Conference on.* pp. 576–579.

Johnson, M. and Shotton, J. 2010. Semantic texton forests. In: *Computer Vision.* Springer, pp. 173–203.

Kim, Y.S. et al. 2009. Chronological development history of X–Y table based pavement crack sealers and research findings for practical use in the field. *Automation in Construction* 18(5), pp. 513–524.

Koch, C. et al. 2012a. Automated Pothole Distress Assessment Using Asphalt Pavement Video Data. *Journal of Computing in Civil Engineering* 27(4), pp. 370–378.

Koch, C. et al. 2012b. Towards automated pothole distress assessment using asphalt pavement video data. *Journal of Computing in Civil Engineering.* Available at: http://ascelibrary.org/doi/full/10.1061/(ASCE)CP.1943-5487.0000232 [Accessed: 17 August 2013].

Koch, C. and Brilakis, I. 2011. Pothole detection in asphalt pavement images. *Advanced Engineering Informatics* 25(3), pp. 507–515.

Lin, J. and Liu, Y. 2010. Potholes detection based on SVM in the pavement distress image. In: *Distributed Computing and Applications to Business Engineering and Science (DCABES), 2010 Ninth International Symposium on.* pp. 544–547.

Lowe, D.G. 2004. Distinctive image features from scale-invariant keypoints. *International journal of computer vision* 60(2), pp. 91–110.

Maode, Y. et al. 2007. Pavement crack detection and analysis for high-grade highway. In: *Electronic Measurement and Instruments, 2007. ICEMI'07. 8th International Conference on.* pp. 4–548.

MnDOT 2003. Mn/DOT Distress Identification Manual. . Available at: http://www.dot.state.mn.us/materials/manuals/pvmtmgmt/distressmanual.pdf [Accessed: 2 June 2013].

MnDOT 2009. *Pavement Condition Executive Summary.* Minnesota Department of Transportation.

Moghadas Nejad, F. and Zakeri, H. 2011. A comparison of multi-resolution methods for detection and isolation of pavement distress. *Expert Systems with Applications* 38(3), pp. 2857–2872.

Radopoulou, S.C. and Brilakis, I. 2015. Patch detection for pavement assessment. *Automation in Construction* 53, pp. 95–104.

Salari, E. and Bao, G. 2011. Pavement distress detection and severity analysis. In: *IS&T/SPIE Electronic Imaging.* p. 78770C–78770C.

SDDOT 2009. SDDOT'S Enhanced Pavement Management System - Visual Distress Survey Manual. . Available at: http://www.sddot.com/resources/Manuals/DistressManual.pdf [Accessed: 5 July 2013].

Shotton, J. et al. 2008. Semantic texton forests for image categorization and segmentation. In: *Computer vision and pattern recognition, 2008. CVPR 2008. IEEE Conference on.* IEEE, pp. 1–8.

Shotton, J. et al. 2009. Textonboost for image understanding: Multi-class object recognition and segmentation by jointly modeling texture, layout, and context. *International Journal of Computer Vision* 81(1), pp. 2–23.

Sy, N.T. et al. 2008. Detection of defects in road surface by a vision system. In: *Electrotechnical Conference, 2008. MELECON 2008. The 14th IEEE Mediterranean.* pp. 847–851.

Uijlings, J.R. et al. 2010. Real-time visual concept classification. *Multimedia, IEEE Transactions on* 12(7), pp. 665–681.

UKPMS 2005. The UKPMS user manual. Available at: http://www.pcis.org.uk/index.php?p=6/8/0/list,0,61 [Accessed: 15 June 2013].

UK Roads Liaison Group 2013. Highways - Maintaining a Vital Asset: What Should Councillors Know About Asset Management? Available at: http://www.ukroadsliaisongroup.org/en/UKRLG-and-boards/uk-roads-liaison-group/highways--maintaining-a-vital-asset.cfm [Accessed: 26 May 2014].

Werro, P. 2013. SCANNER surveys.

Williams, M. 2013. *Road lengths in Great Britain: 2012.* Department of Transport, UK.

Yao, X. et al. 2008. Automated Detection and Identification of Area-based Distress in Concrete Pavements. In: *Seventh International Conference on Managing Pavement Assets.*

Ying, L. and Salari, E. 2010. Beamlet Transform-Based Technique for Pavement Crack Detection and Classification. *Computer-Aided Civil and Infrastructure Engineering* 25(8), pp. 572–580.

Zhang, J. et al. 2007. Local features and kernels for classification of texture and object categories: A comprehensive study. *International journal of computer vision* 73(2), pp. 213–238.

Zhou, J. et al. 2006. Wavelet-based pavement distress detection and evaluation. *Optical Engineering* 45(2), pp. 027007–027007.

Automated assessment of members in meteorological ensemble forecasts based on supervised machine learning

Kristina Georgieva, kristina.georgieva@rub.de
Ruhr-University Bochum, Germany

Gordon Horn, gordon.horn@rub.de
Ruhr-University Bochum, Germany

Christian Koch, christian.koch@nottingham.ac.uk
University of Nottingham, United Kingdom

Andreas Schumann, andreas.schumann@rub.de
Ruhr-University Bochum, Germany

Markus König, koenig@inf.bi.rub.de
Ruhr-University Bochum, Germany

Abstract
Meteorological forecasts of precipitation are uncertain. This uncertainty depends on model physics, boundary and initial conditions. To consider the unavoidable uncertainties of flood forecasts, resulting from uncertainties of precipitation forecasts, which form the input into hydrological models, ensemble prediction systems are applied. These systems consist of several members simulated with varying conditions. The wide range of model-based flood forecasts derived from the meteorological ensembles has to be restricted by a weighting of ensemble members according to their performance.

In this paper, the performance of each ensemble member is evaluated by comparing the results of forecasts corresponding to this member with observed values in the past. With regard to the temporal resolution of forecasts (every 3 hours with a lead time of forecasts of 27 hours in an hourly time step), the evaluation of spatially distributed ensemble members is time-consuming and tedious if the evaluation is performed by one expert. Moreover, the evaluation is highly subjective, because the expert makes his decision based on his implicit knowledge.

Therefore, approaches for automated evaluation of such forecasts are required. Here, we present a semi-automated approach for the assessment of precipitation forecast ensemble members based on supervised machine learning. The approach is tested on ensemble precipitation forecasts for the area of the Mulde river basin in Germany.

Keywords: precipitation forecast, supervised machine learning, pattern recognition

1 Introduction

Flood forecasts in small and medium sized river basin is usually based on precipitation forecasts. These forecasts, however, are computed using numerical weather models. Therefore, the forecasts depend on model physics, boundary and initial conditions. Since the meteorological and hydrological processes are very complex, these forecasts come with a high level of uncertainty. Ensemble forecasting methods and ensemble prediction systems (EPS) are becoming more and more popular to frame the range of uncertainties (Schumann et al 2011). The ensemble forecasting process includes several simulation runs with one or multiple models with perturbed initial conditions or varied parameter sets or different model physics. Therefore an ensemble forecast predicts a vector of values for one time at one place. This group represents ideally the range of possible developments in the near future.

In this paper, a non-stochastic multi-model multi-analysis ensemble is used. This ensemble system keeps the type of perturbation of every single member constant for all forecasts. With regard to this fixation, it is useful to filter such ensemble members, which better performed in the past than others compared to observed precipitation.

To verify the quality of the ensemble members, the rainfall forecasts of the COSMO-DE-EPS-ensemble for the extreme flood in June 2013 in the River Mulde basin are compared with measured rainfall data. As observed rainfall data is normally point data only, the RADOLAN-rainfall estimations of the German Weather Service (calibrated radar-rainfall data) are applied. The assessment of the ensemble forecast is based on a supervised machine learning algorithm. Therefore data sets of every ensemble member are compared with radar images for the same time step. The performance of any meteorological ensemble member to represent the observed spatial distribution of rainfall is labeled as a good or bad prediction. The labeled forecast is then used to train an automatic classification tool based on specific features extracted from this data. Afterwards the classification model can be used to automatically classify forecast data depending on the learned information.

2 Background

2.1 Literature review

Garaud and Mallet (2011) measured the quality of an uncertainty estimation, and the reliability and the resolution of an ensemble using the Brier score, or scores derived from the rank histogram or the reliability diagram. Eckel and Walters (1998) used the verification rank histogram to interpret and adjust an ensemble probabilistic quantitative precipitation forecasts. Brochero et al (2011) applied backward greedy selection to assess the weight that each model within a subset of members. Williams et al (2008) proposed a technique based on a machine learning method that creates random forests to compare the utility of various predictors and identify a subset that may be used for storm prediction. Random forests are used to identify regimes representing different types of geographical locations. Gagne et al (2012) used machine learning algorithms to account for some of the spatial and temporal uncertainty in convective precipitation forecasts. Multiple approaches to post-processing storm-scale ensemble precipitation forecasts were evaluated. Mallet et al (2009) applied machine learning algorithms for sequential aggregation of ozone forecasts. Based on past observations weights for each model were produced by the learning algorithms. The performance of the individual models was measured with the root mean square error. Evans et al (2013) calculated the mean absolute error, the root mean square error, the spatial correlation and the fractional skill score for individual events to create subset ensembles, considering simulation performance. In Kou (2006), a recognition method for detecting abnormal patterns in spatial weather data, such as extreme precipitation events, is presented. The local outliers are identified with the help of graph based algorithms and a spatial neighborhood analysis. To model the spatial relationships, k-neighborhood based similarity graph applications are employed. With the aim of mapping different spatial scales, but keeping the complexity manageable, these graphs are constructed iteratively by means of wavelet transforms. However, the main focus is on the detection of abnormal conditions and tracking them over time. Wealands et al (2003) present methods available for the automatic comparison of spatial hydrological patterns, with the aim of evaluating hydrological models. The spatial similarity is identified and compared to that of predicted and observed patterns.

However, Hamill and Swinbank (2014) addressed the need of reducing systematic errors in numerical weather predictions. According to their work, statistical post-processing methods may be applied for this purpose, but continuous research into improved methods is still needed. Hamill and Juras (2006) also presented examples that demonstrate unexpected skill with common deterministic verification metrics, such as the Brier skill score or relative operating characteristic.

Therefore, methods not purely based on statistical measures need to be investigated.

2.2 Selected supervised machine learning methods

2.2.1 Support Vector Machine

Support vector machines are suitable for two-class datasets whose classes are linearly separable (Witten et al 2011). They combine linear modeling with instance-based learning.

Critical boundary instances, referred to as support vectors, are selected from each of the two classes by a support vector machine. Based on these instances, a linear discriminant function is built. This function defines a hyperplane which separates the support vectors as widely as possible. The hyperplane is called maximum-margin hyperplane, because it gives the greatest separation between the classes.

2.2.2 Multilayer Perceptron

There exist classifiers that can be applied also in cases when the data is not linearly separable (Witten et al 2011). For example, multilayer perceptrons are capable of coping with linearly non-separable problems. Multilayer perceptrons are feed-forward artificial neural networks (ANN). A perceptron is an online-learning algorithm, which means that it does not consider the entire dataset at the same time, but it processes the training instances one by one. Thereby, it generates a weights vector for the attributes of the training instances. The perceptron makes a prediction for the affiliation of a given instance to a certain class based on the weights learned so far and checks if this instance was classified correctly. If the instance was misclassified, the weights vector is updated. A multilayer perceptron is a neural network which consists of neurons aligned in layers (an input layer, one or several hidden layers, and an output layer). Given a fixed network structure, the weights can be determined using back-propagation.

2.2.3 Rotation Forest

Rotation Forest is a classifier ensemble method based on feature extraction (Rodriguez & Kuncheva 2006). The Rotation Forest employs the advantages of a combination of classifiers over the individual classifier models. Lately, multiple classifier systems consisting of classifiers trained on different data subsets or feature subsets have been designed. Commonly called classifier ensembles, these classifiers are constructed by taking bootstrap samples of objects and training a classifier on each sample. Then, the classifiers are combined using majority voting.

Specifically in Rotation Forest, the feature set is randomly split into subsets and Principal Component Analysis is applied to each subset. After that, a new extracted feature set is reassembled and the training data is transformed into the new features. The latter are used to train decision tree classifiers, whereby each split of the feature set leads to a different classifier. Each classifier calculates for a new instance the probability that the instance belongs to a certain class. Then, the outputs of the classifiers are combined and the probability assigned to an instance by the Rotation Forest is calculated using an average combination method.

2.3 COSMO-DE-Ensemble prediction system

The ensemble prediction system used in this study is named COSMO-DE-EPS (Consortium for Small Scale Modelling - Deutschland - Ensemble Prediction System) and it is provided by the German Weather Service (Baldauf et al 2011). In this study, we consider precipitation forecasts. Every ensemble member includes variations of lateral boundary conditions, initial conditions and model physics. The variations of the lateral boundary conditions and the initial conditions are based on forecasts of four different global models, which leads to a boundary condition ensemble prediction system (BCEPS). The perturbation of the model physics is based on different configurations of the COSMO-DE model, nested in the BCEPS. In every configuration only one parameter is modified. At the end 20 ensemble members are produced. They are released eight times a day providing 27 hours of forecast lead time (Theis et al 2012). Because of this non-stochastic approach, for every member the variation is kept constant over the entire lead time and for all forecast runs.

Based on these ensemble rainfall forecasts, the users in water management authorities can specify the uncertainties of their flood forecasts. To apply a probabilistic assessment of the meteorological ensemble members, an analysis of the forecasted precipitation with observed rainfall fields based on radar estimation is needed. To verify the quality of the COSMO-DE-EPS regarding to operational use in flood forecasting, ensembles of the flood event of May/June 2013 in the Mulde river basin are evaluated. For this purpose, the COSMO-DE-EPS is compared with RADOLAN data (Radar Online Adjustment Procedure) of the German Weather Service. The RADOLAN data combines a real-time precipitation analysis based on weather radar products with an online adjustment with rain gauges (Bartels 2004).

3 Methodology

The basic methodology of the proposed approach is depicted in **Figure 1**. A lagged

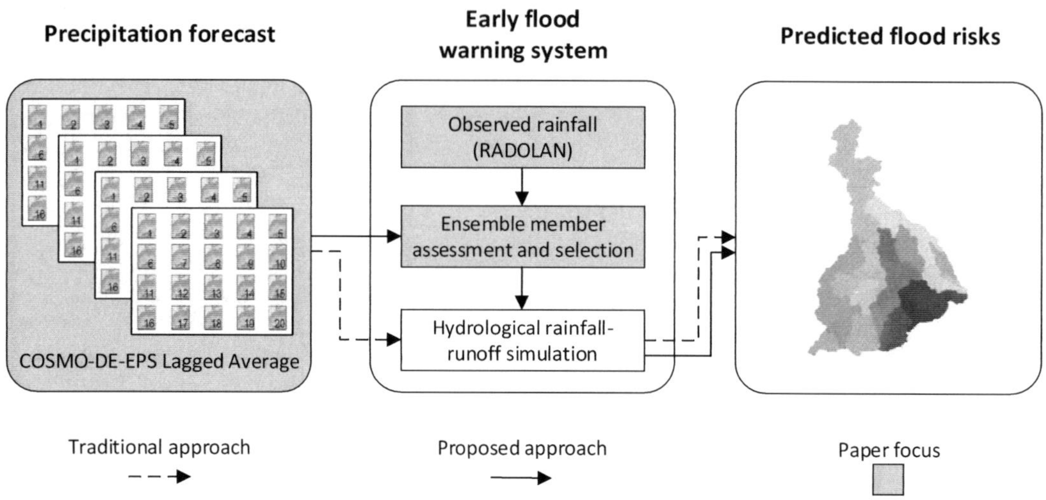

Figure 1 Overall research methodology

average of the ensemble prediction members is usually used as an input to hydrological rainfall-runoff simulations in order to predict flood risks. The objective of the approach proposed is to identify the members with poor prediction quality based on observed rainfall (RADOLAN) and to select and use only the best quality members for the rainfall-runoff simulation. As a result, the outcome of the simulation would be less uncertain or more accurate, respectively (**Figure 2**). This paper focuses on the estimation of forecasting skills of ensemble members based on supervised machine learning and historical forecast and observation data.

3.1 Framework

To automatically assess precipitation forecasts, a framework based on machine learning was devised. The framework consists of two tools – a training tool and an evaluation tool. The training tool offers experts the opportunity to manually label the prediction of an ensemble member at a certain point in time either as good or not. Thereby, corresponding EPS and RADOLAN data are mapped and converted to images to allow for a better representation, since the matrix format the data is usually saved in is not suitable for the direct evaluation by experts. Afterwards, the evaluation tool uses the labeled data to train a classifier using extracted features and to generate a classification model (**Figure 3**). Based on this model other predictions are automatically classified as good or bad. The overall capability of a certain member to accurately predict precipitation is calculated as the ratio of the good predictions to all predictions which belong to this member.

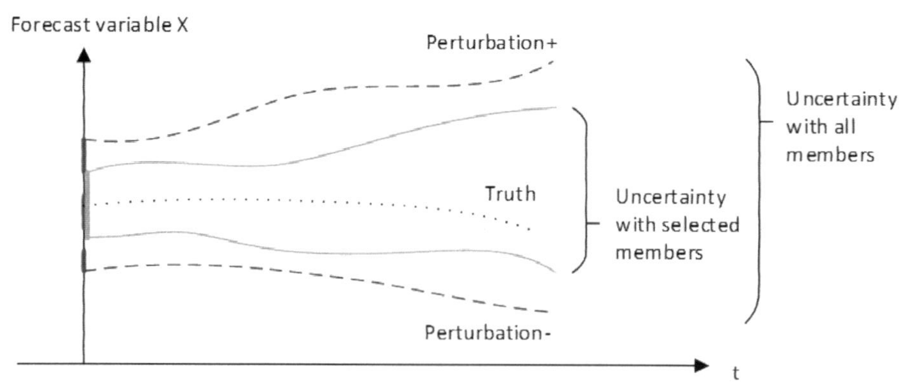

Figure 2 Forecast uncertainty using all ensemble members and selected best ensemble members

3.2 Feature extraction and classification

There exists a vast amount and range of statistical measures, which can be used to measure the similarity between two images (Mitchell 2010). However, when looking at precipitation maps, the landscape's topography (e.g. elevation and river layout) plays a significant role. Therefore, the features identified should not only be based on poor pixel values and local neighborhoods, they should also somehow encode semantic knowledge about the rainfall-runoff behavior of the entire area.

Commonly, precipitation forecast areas are subdivided into natural areas and sub-basins taking into account hydrologically relevant characteristics, such as altitudes, climate and river layout. Based on the precipitation values (forecast and measured data) and the defined areas, we propose the following similarity features that are computed per area and combined into the final feature vector. In the following equations, E is the COSMO-DE-EPS forecast, R represents RADOLAN data, and i,j decode the pixel position in the image.

- Difference of the mean values per area (md)

$$md = \left| \frac{1}{n}\sum_{j=1}^{n} E_{i,j} - \frac{1}{n}\sum_{j=1}^{n} R_{i,j} \right|$$

- Difference of the standard deviations per area (sdd)

$$sdd = \left| \sqrt{\frac{1}{n}\sum_{j=1}^{n}\left(E_{i,j} - \frac{1}{n}\sum_{j=1}^{n} E_{i,j}\right)^2} - \sqrt{\frac{1}{n}\sum_{j=1}^{n}\left(R_{i,j} - \frac{1}{n}\sum_{j=1}^{n} R_{i,j}\right)^2} \right|$$

- Root-mean-square error per area (rmse)

$$rmse = \sqrt{\frac{1}{n}\sum_{j=1}^{n}\left(E_{i,j} - R_{i,j}\right)^2}$$

- Bray-Curtis dissimilarity per area (bcd)

$$bcd = \frac{\sum_{j=1}^{n}\left|E_{i,j} - R_{i,j}\right|}{\sum_{j=1}^{n} E_{i,j} + \sum_{j=1}^{n} R_{i,j}}$$

4 Case study and results

4.1 Mulde basin

In this approach the study area is the Mulde River basin up to the gauge Bad Düben in Saxony, Germany. The catchment has an area of approx. 6170 km² and can be separated into three sub-basins. Shown in **Figure 4**, from west to east these are the basins of the tributaries Zwickauer Mulde, the rivers Zschopau and Flöha and the Freiberger Mulde. These rivers converge and form the Vereinigte Mulde. The

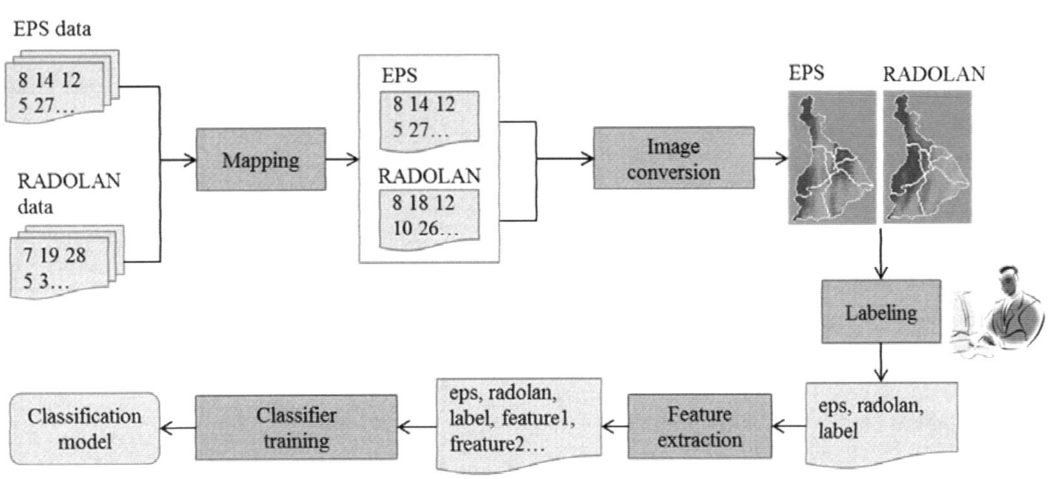

Figure 3 Framework to create a machine learning classifier to identify low quality ensemble members

topography of the catchment can be mainly subdivided into three natural spaces, which are different in their hydrological characteristics. From south to north these are the landscapes of the Ore Mountain, the Saxon Uplands and the Saxon Lowlands.

To maintain the hydrologic interactions between sub-basins (e.g. fallen precipitation in upstream areas have an impact on the downstream areas) and the climatological aspects (e.g. influence of the altitudes on the process of precipitation forming) of the different natural areas, the Mulde basin is divided into seven parts based on the intersection of the sub-basins and the borders of the natural areas. Under consideration of this division, the subsequent labeling between the RADOLAN and the COSMO-DE-EPS data is made.

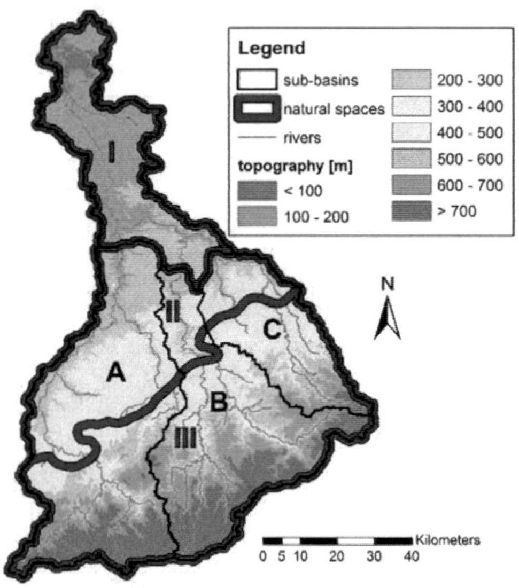

Figure 4 Mulde basin divided into sub-basins

4.2 Implementation

The forecast and the RADOLAN data are initially saved in text files. Each file contains the values predicted by the corresponding ensemble member or measured by the rain gauges and includes a header, which specifies the number of values saved in the file and the dimensions of the data grid.

The EPS and RADOLAN files need to be transformed in a form suitable for evaluation by experts. For this purpose, the files are converted to images, whereby different pixel colors indicate different precipitation values. The color scheme is chosen according to the suggestion of the experts so that relevant differences or dependences are visible. Moreover, for the case of the Mulde river basin, the borders of Mulde areas described in subsection 4.1 are drawn, because they are semantically important for the experts when evaluating the forecasts.

After that, a sample of EPS-RADOLAN pairs is chosen to train and evaluate a classifier. One or several experts label EPS-RADOLAN pairs either as similar or not. A similar pair indicates a COSMO-DE-EPS forecast that represents the actual RADOLAN data well, while COSMO-DE-EPS forecasts which are not labeled similar to a RADOLAN do not represent a good forecast and should not be considered for the flood forecasts.

A software tool was implemented to ease the process of labeling EPS-RADOLAN pairs. All COSMO-DE-EPS files which correspond to a particular RADOLAN file are found by the tool using information about the time of the forecast and the lead time of the COSMO-DE-EPS. This information is derived from the filenames of the COSMO-DE-EPS files. The latter procedure is denoted as Mapping in **Figure 3**.

After conversion to images, all COSMO-DE-EPS forecasts corresponding to the specified RADOLAN are visualized. The expert selects the COSMO-DE-EPS forecasts which are not similar to the RADOLAN (see **Figure 5**). When the expert clicks the "Save" button, a text file containing the COSMO-DE-EPS forecast and RADOLAN filenames as well as the label (similar, not_similar) is generated. The text file serves as a basis for the training of the classifier.

A second tool was developed for the evaluation. This tool reads the text file containing the labels, thereby loading the corresponding COSMO-DE-EPS forecast and RADOLAN files. Features required to classify the EPS-RADOLAN pairs as similar or not are calculated based on the precipitation values and the areas.

After feature extraction, the labeled EPS-RADOLAN pairs are submitted together with the calculated features to a machine learning workbench. The machine learning workbench creates a classification model based on this training data. The model can then be used to evaluate other not yet labeled EPS-RADOLAN pairs and asses the capability of a COSMO-DE-

EPS forecast to accurately predict the precipitation

In this study, the Waikato Environment for Knowledge Analysis (WEKA) was utilized as a machine-learning workbench (Witten et al 2011). WEKA offers a collection of state-of-the-art machine learning algorithms. In addition, a Java library is provided for embedded usage of the machine learning algorithms. WEKA provides an opportunity to test different machine classifiers on a dataset. Also, methods that evaluate the classifiers statistically and visualize the input data and the result of the learning are supported.

5 Results

There are several ways to evaluate the performance of machine learning classifiers. One commonly applied approach is to split labeled data into a training dataset and a test dataset. Two thirds of the data are used for training and the remaining one third is used for testing. However, the sample used for training may not be representative.

To mitigate any bias caused by the particular sample chosen for comparing the performance of the different classifiers, 10-fold cross-validation was applied. The cross-validation ensures that the results do not depend on chance effects. In case of limited training and test datasets, the cross-validation guarantees that the results obtained for the specified test set would be the same as results obtained by independent test sets. The main idea behind 10-fold cross-validation is to split the data into ten approximately equal partitions (10 folds). Then, one partition is used as test dataset and the other nine of the ten partitions are used as training dataset. An error rate is calculated for the particular combination. This process is repeated ten times with different partitions chosen as test dataset. At the end, the error estimates are averaged in order to calculate the overall error estimate.

The percentage of correctly classified instances, precision and recall were chosen to evaluate the capability of the classifiers to classify test instances accurately. 14400 pairs of COSMO-DE-EPS and RADOLAN files were converted to images and manually labeled by an expert. According to the expert's opinion 9778 COSMO-DE-EPS indicated good forecasts and 4622 COSMO-DE-EPS were significantly different from the RADOLANs in terms of assessing the precipitation forecast. The results of the 10-fold cross-validation are presented in **Table 1**. Compared to the Multilayer Perceptron (MP) and the Support Vector Machine (SVM), the Rotation Forest (RF) classifier achieved the

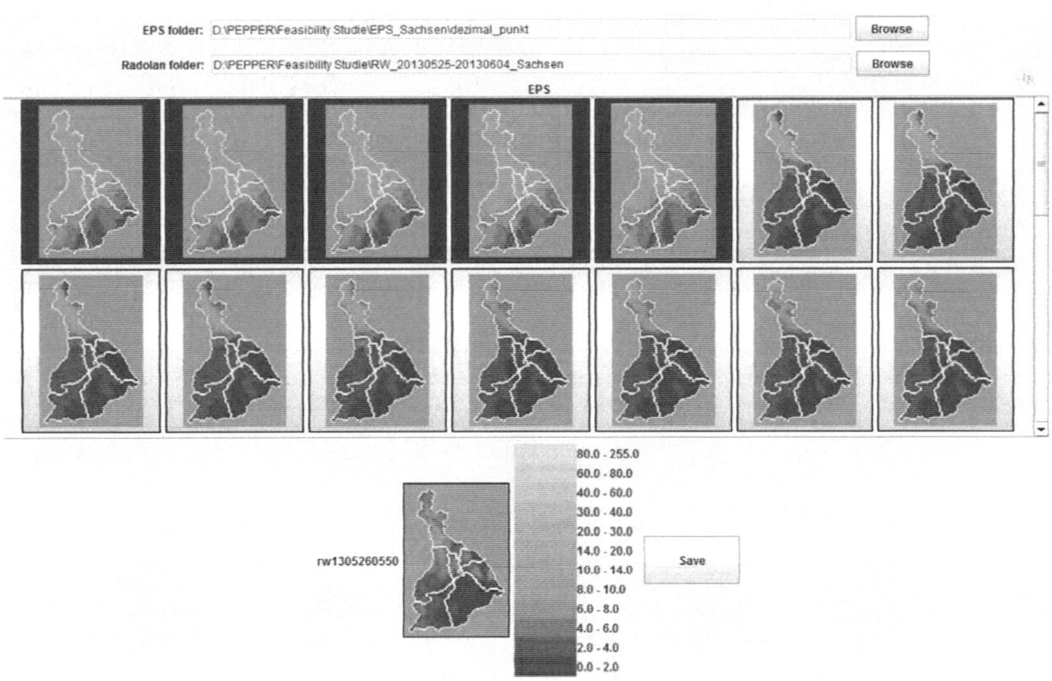

Figure 5 Screenshot of the training tool: Selection of EPS images (top, highlighted) not similar to the RADOLAN image (bottom)

best results. It classified correctly 94% of the EPS-RADOLAN pairs. The Rotation Forest reached a precision of 0.932 and a recall of 0.976. All three measures validate that most of the forecasts are classified correctly.

Table 1 Classification performance for different classifiers

Classifier	Precision	Recall	Correctly classified
MP	0.885	0.915	86.20
SVM	0.882	0.968	89.01
RF	0.932	0.976	93.54

6 Conclusions and future work

In recent years, ensemble prediction systems (EPS) have been applied to frame the uncertainties of hydrometeorological forecasts. An ensemble forecast represents a collection of two or more forecasts conducted using slightly different model components, model parameters or varying initial and boundary conditions. These forecasts are referred to as ensemble members.

Usually, the probability that an ensemble member leads to a reliable forecast is equal for all ensemble members and the diversity of the members compensates for errors due to lack of comprehensive initial data, accuracy and quality of the initial data, or model resolution not sufficient to capture all features of the observed event (WPC 2006).

However, in some cases the inclusion of less skillful members degrades the quality of the ensemble prediction. This could lead to underestimation or exaggeration of the risk of hazardous events, such as floods. For example, underrating the possibility of a flood due to considering too many "poor" ensemble members could result in a missing warning. Vice versa, overestimating the probability of a flood to occur would lead to many false alarms, which may encourage people to ignore warnings in the future (Dietrich et al 2009).

Therefore, ensemble prediction systems can be improved by introducing weights to the members or by reducing the number of members to a sub-ensemble sufficient to account for forecast uncertainties. Moreover, by reducing the number of ensemble members, the computational efficiency of meteorological systems can be enhanced.

To apply a probabilistic assessment of the meteorological ensemble members, their performance to describe an observed event in the past can be used. By post-processing such events, forecasters can assign smaller weights to members with a poor prediction quality or exclude such members from the ensemble. Yet, the assessment procedure is time-consuming, because numerous forecasts need to be considered.

The limitations of the manual assessment procedure can be compensated by utilizing automated approaches for forecast assessment. In this paper we presented an approach towards assessing precipitation forecasts based on supervised machine learning. The approach was validated against precipitation data of the Mulde river basin area in Germany. Future research may include the calibration of ensemble forecasts based on the assessment of the ensemble members.

References

Baldauf, M., Seifert, A., Förstner, J., Majewski, D., Raschendorfer, M. & Reinhardt, T. (2011). Operational convective-scale numerical weather prediction with the COSMO model: Description and sensitivities, *Monthly Weather Review* 139 (12), pp. 3887–3905

Bartels H. (2004). Projekt RADOLAN, Routineverfahren zur Online-Aneichung der Radarniederschlagsdaten mit Hilfe von automatischen Bodenniederschlagsstationen (Ombrometer), final report. *Offenbach: Deutscher Wetterdienst*

Brochero, D., Anctil, F. & Gagne, C. (2011) Simplifying a hydrological ensemble prediction system with a backward greedy selection of members – Part 1: Optimization criteria. *Hydrology and Earth System Sciences* 15, pp. 3307-3325

Dietrich, J., Schumann, A. H., Redetzky, M., Walther, J., Denhard, M., Wang, Y., Pfützner, B. & Büttner, U. (2009) Assessing uncertainties in flood forecasts for decision making: prototype of an operational flood management system integrating ensemble predictions. *Natural Hazards and Earth System Sciences* 9, pp. 1529-1540

Eckel, F. A. & Walters, M. K. (1998) Calibrated Probabilistic Quantitative Precipitation Forecasts Based on the MRF Ensemble. *Weather and Forecasting* 13, pp. 1132-1147

Evans, J. P., Ji, F., Abramowitz, G. & Ekström, M. (2013) Optimally choosing small ensemble members to produce robust climate simulations. *Environmental Research Letters* 8

Gagne II, D. J., McGovern, A. & Xue, M. (2012) Machine Learning Enhancement of Storm Scale Ensemble Precipitation Forecasts. *Conference on Intelligent Data Understanding (CIDU)*, pp. 39-46

Garaud, D. & Mallet, V. (2011) Automatic calibration of an ensemble for uncertainty estimation and probabilistic forecast: Application to air quality. *Journal of Geophysical Research* 116

Hamill, T. M. & Juras, J. (2006) Measuring forecast skill: is it real skill or is it the varying climatology? *Quarterly Journal of the Royal Meteorological Society* 132(621C), pp. 2905-2923

Hamill, T. M. & Swinbank, R. (2014) Stochastic forcing, ensemble prediction systems, and TIGGE. *World Weather Open Science Conference 2014*, Montreal, Canada

Kou, Y. (2006) Abnormal pattern recognition in spatial data, *Dissertation, Faculty of Virginia Poly-technic Institute and State University*, Falls Church, Virginia, USA

Mallet, V., Stoltz, G. & Mauricette, B. (2009) Ozone ensemble forecast with machine learning algorithms. *Journal of Geophysical Research* 114

Mitchell, H. (2010) Image Similarity Measures, *Image Fusion*, Springer Berlin Heidelberg, 167-185

National Weather Service, Weather prediction Center (WPC) (2006) Ensemble Prediction Systems: A basic training manual targeted for operational meteorologists. *Online*, available at: http://www.wpc.ncep.noaa.gov/ensembletraining/, accessed on 14.04.2015

Rodriguez, J. J. & Kuncheva, L. I. (2006) Rotation Forest: A New Classifier Ensemble Method. IEEE Transactions on Pattern Analysis and Machine Intelligence 28(10), pp. 1619-1630

Schumann, A.H., Wang, Y. & Dietrich, J. (2011) Framing uncertainties in flood forecasting with ensembles. *Hydrology for Flood Risk Assessments and Management*, Springer-Publishing Company

Theis, S., Gebhardt, C. & Bouallègue, Z. B. (2012) Beschreibung des COSMO-DE-EPS und seiner Ausgabe in die Datenbanken des DWD, Version 1.0. *Offenbach: Deutscher Wetterdienst*

Wealands, S.R., Grayson, R.B. & Walker, J.P. (2003) Hydrologic model assessment from automated spatial pattern comparison techniques, *Proceedings of the International Congress on Modelling and Simulation*, Australia, 2003, pp. 426-42

Williams, J. k., Ahijevych, D. A., Kessinger, C. J., Saxen, T. r., Steiner, M. & Dettling, S. (2008) A machine learning approach to finding weather regimes and skillful predictor combinations for short-term storm forecasting. *13th Conference on Aviation, Range and Aerospace Meteorology*, New Orleans, LA, American Meteorological Society

Witten, I. H., Frank, E. & Hall, M. A. (2011) *Data mining: practical machine learning tools and techniques*, Elsevier

Similarity estimation of BIM-based schedules

Kateryna Sigalov, kateryna.sigalov@rub.de
Ruhr-Universität Bochum, Bochum, Germany

Markus König, koenig@inf.bi.rub.de
Ruhr-Universität Bochum, Bochum, Germany

Abstract
Construction scheduling is a very demanding and time intensive process. Building information modelling (BIM) is becoming increasingly important for planning and scheduling, as it provides significant support for this challenging assignment. Further improvements can be achieved by applying predefined process templates for automatically generated BIM-based schedules. It can help reduce the planning time and thus increase the productivity. However, a manual definition of proper and application-specific process templates is very challenging. The automatic detection of recurring similar configurations of construction processes, called process patterns, would greatly support this complex task. This paper presents an overall concept for pattern recognition in BIM-based construction schedules by applying graph-based methods. Special attention is paid to the estimation of similarity in construction schedules, describing the selected methods and similarity measure definitions in detail. Finally, implementation results are evaluated on a comprehensive case study.

Keywords: BIM-based scheduling, process patterns, similarity estimation.

1 Introduction

The success of construction projects as well as their compliance with budgets and timelines are directly related to the quality of construction scheduling. Indeed, the determination of valid and efficient schedules is extremely challenging and time-consuming. Current software tools provide only partial support for this demanding assignment. For example, linking building elements of a 3D model with the corresponding construction processes, known as 4D Building Information Modelling (BIM), enables a visual analysis of construction schedules. Nevertheless, this alone does not sufficiently simplify the check for completeness and correctness of the schedules. Furthermore, the definition of construction processes and their dependencies are still performed manually. The possibility to automate construction scheduling has been recognized and addressed in only a few research projects in recent years (Huhnt & Enge 2006, Mikulakova et al. 2010, Hartmann et al. 2012, Kim et al. 2013, Liu et al. 2014 and Tauscher et al. 2014). Thereby, the required information is automatically extracted from a BIM-model to enable the generation of a schedule.

However, the choice of construction processes, their execution sequences, as well as decisions for one or another process alternative must be done by a responsible planner or a planning team and is based on their own knowledge and experiences. In many cases such decisions are not explicitly documented, which makes it difficult to verify them and to reuse the gained experience for future projects. This is due to the lack of the adequate support of commonly-used planning tools and the related high expenditure of time. The generation of schedules by applying predefined process templates can enormously reduce the planning time and thus increase the productivity. It can also help to understand the precedent decisions and improve the quality of schedules by reflecting previous knowledge and experience. Nevertheless, a manual definition of adequate process templates is also very challenging. They have to be designed application-specific and represent frequent or approved solutions. Certainly, the automatic detection of recurring similar configurations of construction processes would greatly support the creation of process templates. The search for the recurrences and regularities in general is known as pattern recognition and is widely used in many application areas.

In order to recognize process patterns in construction schedules it is appropriate to use graph-based methods, as schedules can be obviously represented in the form of precedence graphs. For this purpose, it is necessary to examine the given graphs for similarities with respect to the content information contained in the nodes (processes) and structural composition given by process interdependencies. The present paper provides the recent research on the pattern recognition methods in the domain of construction management as well as the state of the art techniques in this field. After the short description of the underlying BIM-based framework for the automatic generation of construction schedules, an overall developed concept for process pattern recognition is presented. The similarity estimation of construction schedules is discussed in detail, describing the defined similarity measures and the selected methods including the application specific adjustments. Finally, the achieved results of the implementation are evaluated on a considerable test database.

2 State of The Art

2.1 Construction Management and Pattern Recognition

The application and recognition of process patterns in the construction management has not yet been widely explored. In this context just several researches from Wu et al. (2010), Enge (2010), Enge et al. (2012), Sharmak (2011) and Benevolenskiy et al. (2012) can be mentioned. Almost all of them focus merely on the usage and the proper manual configuration of process templates. The automatic pattern recognition is addressed only in Enge (2010). Thereby, elements of a construction project are manually assigned to the corresponding process templates. However, construction schedules that were not generated from the manually predefined process templates cannot be analyzed. It should also be pointed out, that the researches listed above are only very marginally concerned with BIM-based scheduling, although the modelling method presented in Enge (2010) was kept consistent to the model-based methodology of BIM and the ontology concepts described in Benevolenskiy et al. (2012) are similar to the data model of Industry Foundation Classes (IFC).

2.2 Graph Matching and Indexing

The problem of automatic pattern recognition in graph structures is nevertheless not a new one and was widely investigated in other research domains due to its important role in many applications (Messmer & Bunke 2000). Searching for similar subschedules (subgraphs) in schedules (graphs) corresponds with the problem of subgraph isomorphism that can be solved by means of so-called matching algorithms. One of the most frequent formulated problems is searching for a single query graph (exact matching) or for graphs similar to the query (inexact matching) in the graph database. However, there is no algorithm that can solve this problem efficiently, as the problem of subgraph isomorphism is known to be *NP*-complete (Sakr & Al-Naymat 2012). Thus, matching algorithms are, in general, very time- and resource-consuming. Given the high time complexity a naive approach of the pairwise comparison of the graphs is unacceptable for the large databases, as it results in a directly dependence on the size of the database.

One of the most prevalent techniques for solving this problem efficiently is graph indexing. In recent years a wealth of graph indexing techniques have been presented (cf. Di Natale et al., Yan & Han 2010, Ferro et al. 2012 and Sakr & Al-Naymat 2012). The aim of this strategy is to reduce the search space and the time complexity, so that the problem becomes affordable. Most of the indexing techniques are carried out in three main steps: pre-processing, filtering and verification. As the construction of the index is a computationally intensive task, it usually takes place in the pre-processing phase. Graphs, which are clearly dissimilar to the query, are sorted out during the filtering step and only the remaining graphs have to be examined by the computational complex matching algorithms in the verification step.

2.3 Feature-Based Indexing

A great number of the recent graph indexing systems are based on features (cf. Ferro et al. 2012 and Sakr & Al-Naymat 2012). Features are small characteristic fragments of the graphs that can be defined as paths, trees or other subgraphs. The graphs in the database are decomposed into features during the pre-computing step, whereby the features serve as indices for building an inverted index. While query processing, features, which are extracted from the query graph in the same way, are compared to the features from the database. The set of the graphs that don't contain the same or similar enough features are obviously distinct to the query and can be discarded. The size and the number of features as well as the number of the remaining candidate graphs have a crucial impact on the effectiveness of the filtering. Consequently, a proper definition of features and a sufficient similarity approximation between the features and thus, between the graphs, represent major challenges for a good indexing technique. Yan et al. (2010) have presented a feature-based similarity search algorithm for business process graphs, which was later improved and extended in Yan et al. (2012). Thereby, features are determined as simple but representative fragments of a process model, e.g., processes and sequences of processes, with respect to their structural roles in the graph. The proposed feature definition and similarity estimation are tailored to the specific structure of process graphs. Therefore, they are particularly well suited for adoption and subsequent adaptation for the requirements of construction schedules.

3 Overall Approach

The initial situation for the recognition of process patterns is the availability of a 4D building information model. The concept presented in this paper is quite generic and can be easily adapted to suit specific applications. There are just a few requirements that must be fulfilled. Schedules should be given as directed graphs, whereby nodes correspond to the processes and directed edges correspond to their logical dependencies. Furthermore, in order to obtain a proper similarity estimation the processes should provide the information about the objects to be built and constraints to be fulfilled. The more information is given, the more exact the estimation can be made.

3.1 BIM-Based Scheduling Concept

The software framework used for the automatic generation of construction schedules is based on the modelling concept described by Huhnt & Enge (2006), König et al. (2006), Tauscher et al. (2009), Mikulakova et al. (2010) and Hartmann et al. (2012). BIM models are based on the Industry Foundation Classes (IFC) and serve as a source of information for creating a schedule. All construction processes are defined separately including relevant information about constraints to be fulfilled. Process constraints, representing prerequisites and results, are described by structural or non-structural elements in certain states (s. Fig. 1). In consequence, processes are directly linked with corresponding elements of the IFC-model. Construction schedules can be generated automatically by matching prerequisites of one process to corresponding results of another process. An object may be realized in several stages and thus undergoes different states during its realization. Therefore, several single processes can belong to one building object. Naturally, process constraints are expressed as objects with attributes. Such attributes as *state* and *progress* need to be additionally defined in the framework, whereas most of the properties, such as *name, type, material* etc., are provided for the structural elements directly by IFC.

Process flows that serve a clear purpose can be logically grouped to subprocesses, creating a hierarchical structure of processes. According to the Business Process Model and Notation (BPMN) an atomic process is called task and a compound process, which includes other processes, is called subprocess (s. Fig. 1).

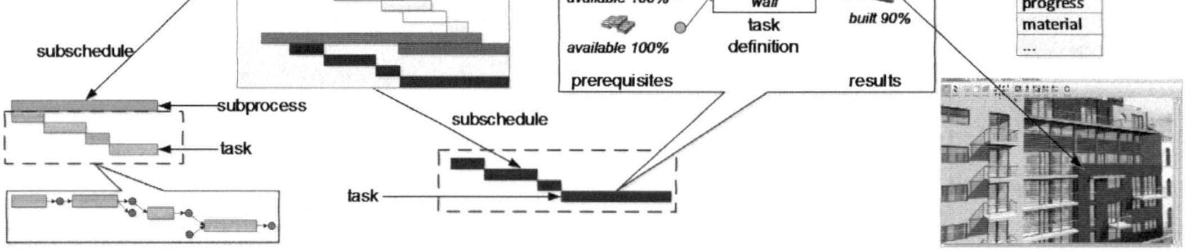

Figure 1 Internal structure of the BIM-based schedules

3.2 Process Pattern Recognition

For the purpose of detection of recurring process structures construction schedules have to be compared with each other. It is not feasible to compare whole schedules, as they are usually very complex, consisting of a great number of different processes. Thus, modeled schedules must be broken down into a set of logically related subschedules first (Fig. 2, step 1). The decomposition in subschedules can be realized manually or semi-automatically. Currently, only a manual decomposition is considered by grouping logically related tasks into subprocesses, e.g. all tasks for concrete column construction. Certainly, the semi-automatic decomposition is an area of future research.

The actual pattern recognition includes the search for recurring subschedules. After selecting one of the available subschedules as a query (Fig. 2, step 2) the similar subschedules are to be determined in the next step. During the preprocessing phase existing subschedules are decomposed into features and index structures are built. Thereafter, the feature-based similarity of the subschedules is estimated. Based on it the subschedules from the database are classified as *relevant* or *potentially relevant* to the query and the irrelevant are filtered out. The efficiency and the accuracy of this classification depend essentially on the choice of features as well as on the definition of the similarity measures for features and subschedules. This step is discussed in more detail in the next section. The *relevant* subschedules are similar to the query to a high degree and therefore may be used directly for the definition of a recurring process pattern.

However, it can be assumed that subschedules, classified as *potentially relevant*, are rarely structurally equal. Furthermore, complex subschedules, that contain a lot of tasks or subprocesses, can differ in their structures significantly. By determining the feature-based similarity of the subschedules it is not possible to declare which fragments of the subschedules actually match. For this reason, in the next step one of the inexact matching algorithms will be used to verify the similarity of the subschedules and to detect the actually similar fragments (s. Fig. 2). The selection of the matching algorithm is also of crucial importance and will be examined in future research. In the last step (s. Fig. 2) the recurring subschedules have to be verified and generalized by the user as a process pattern. The defined process pattern is then stored for reuse as a template.

4 Similarity Estimation of BIM-based Schedules

The initial decomposition into subschedules is essential for the subsequent applicability of the matching algorithms. At this point a set of different subschedules is assumed to be present. During the preprocessing, graphs from the database are normally broken down into features and index structures are built. A manually pre-classification of subschedules is considered to be given as well and only the subschedules, which are context similar to the query, are decomposed into features (s. Fig.3). This section focuses on the similarity estimation between the subschedules during the filtering step based on the approach of Yan et al. (2012). As soon as feature identification in the relevant subschedules is done, features of the query subschedule S_q are compared to the features of the context-relevant

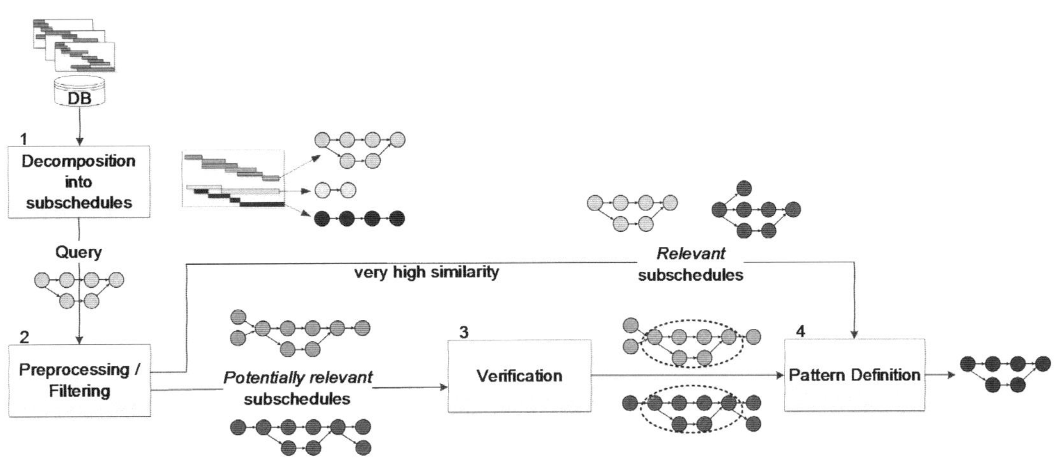

Figure 2 Concept overview

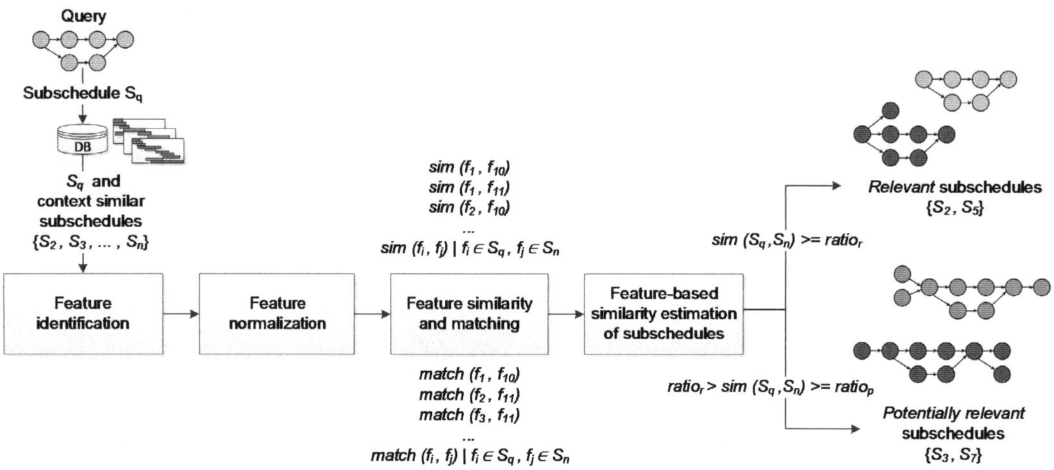

Figure 3 Feature-based similarity estimation of construction subschedules

subschedules from the database (s. Fig. 3) with the objective to find so-called matching features. Two features are matched if they are sufficiently similar. The fraction of matching features between two subschedules is then used to estimate their similarity. The adopted definition of features and adjusted metrics to quantify their similarity are presented below.

4.1 Feature Definition and Similarity

The appropriate definition of features is essential for the fast and accurate similarity estimation. Adequate features for construction schedules have to consider both the construction-related information and the specific structure of precedence graphs. For this purpose the definition of so-called *structural features* according to Yan et al. (2012) is particularly well suited. During the decomposition of subschedules a differentiation is made between *start*, *stop*, *split*, *join* and *sequence* features, consisting of one or more *node features* (s. an example in Figure 4a). Two structural features match "per definition", if their entire node features match. Besides the content similarity of node features (*csim*), the structural similarity (*rsim*) is taken into account by means of their roles in the precedence graph. The set of possible roles that may be assigned to one node $n \in N$ of the graph $G = (N, E)$ is $\mathcal{R} = \{start,\ stop,\ split,\ join,\ regular\}$. The definition of role features is given in Figure 4b.

Given two subschedules $G_1 = (N_1, E_1)$ and $G_2 = (N_2, E_2)$, the structural similarity between two nodes $n \in N_1$ and $m \in N_2$, denoted as *rsim(n, m)*, is determined as the role feature similarity according to Yan et al. (2012). The calculation of the content similarity measure between two nodes, i.e. construction processes, is not trivial. The developed metric considers the similarity of prerequisites and results of construction processes. It integrates the method presented in Mikulakova et al. (2010), where the process similarity is estimated based on the mutual comparison of the attributes of the building objects. The content feature similarity *csim* between two nodes *n* and *m* is calculated as

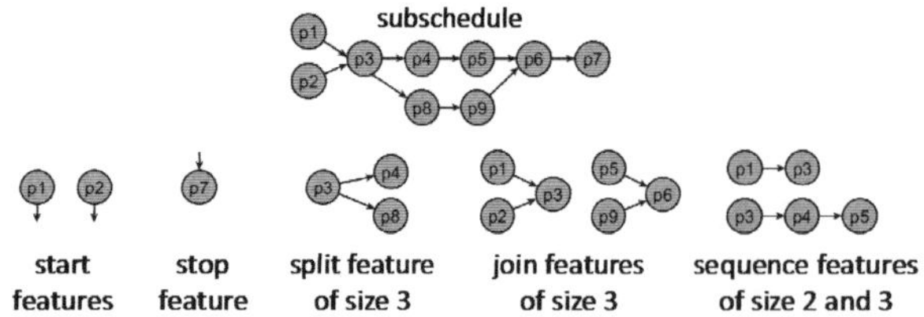

$$start \in \mathcal{R} \Leftrightarrow |\bullet n| = 0$$
$$stop \in \mathcal{R} \Leftrightarrow |n \bullet| = 0$$
$$split \in \mathcal{R} \Leftrightarrow |n \bullet| \geq 2$$
$$join \in \mathcal{R} \Leftrightarrow |\bullet n| \geq 2$$
$$regular \in \mathcal{R} \Leftrightarrow |\bullet n| = 1 \wedge |n \bullet| = 1$$

(a) (b)

Figure 4 Structural features (a) and Role Feature Definition (b) according to Yan et al. (2012)

$$csim(n,m) = w_p \cdot sim_p(n,m) + w_r \cdot sim_r(n,m), \quad (1)$$

where sim_p and sim_r are the similarities between the prerequisites and results, respectively, and w_p and w_r are the corresponding weights with $w_p + w_r = 1$. One process can have several prerequisite and result objects (hereinafter called events), as specified in section 3.1. Therefore, the sets of events of the compared processes can differ in their size. In order to reflect these differences, a structural similarity measure is calculated in addition to the content similarity measure with respect to appropriate weights, as proposed in Mikulakova et al. (2010):

$$sim_{p/r}(n,m) = w_{cont} \cdot sim_{cont}(E_n, E_m) + w_{struct} \cdot sim_{struct}(E_n, E_m), \quad (2)$$

where E_n and E_m are the sets of prerequisites and results of the compared processes n and m and $w_{struct} + w_{cont} = 1$. The structural similarity measure regards the number of matched events and is calculated using the Feature Contrast Model (FCM) from Tversky (1977):

$$sim_{FCM}(E_n, E_m) = \frac{\alpha \cdot |E_n \cap E_m| - \beta \cdot |E_n \backslash E_m| - \gamma \cdot |E_m \backslash E_n|}{|E_n \cup E_m|};$$

$$\text{with } \alpha + \beta + \gamma = 1, \quad (3)$$

$$sim_{struct}(E_n, E_m) = \frac{sim_{FCM}(E_n, E_m) + max(\alpha,\beta,\gamma)}{1 + max(\alpha,\beta,\gamma)} \quad (4)$$

More details for this similarity measure can be obtained from Mikulakova et al. (2010). For the determination of the overall content similarity the similarity values are calculated for each event separately. It considers the weighted similarity between the values of the attributes $a_{1,\cdots,}a_r$ of the corresponding objects (IFC-objects or abstract elements), such as *name, type, state, progress* etc. The similarity between two events $e_i \in E_n$ and $e_j \in E_m$ is calculated as follows:

$$sim_e(e_i, e_j) = \sum_{k=1}^{r} w_k \cdot sim_{a_k}(e_i, e_j) \quad (5)$$

where r = number of the relevant attributes; $sim_{a_k}(e_i, e_j)$ = similarity between the values of the corresponding attributes a_k; w_k = weights of the attribute a_k and $\sum_{k=1}^{r} w_k = 1$.

The overall content similarity of prerequisites or results is calculated as shown in the equation **(6)**. The proposed metric can be easily supplemented by any further attributes. All weighting parameters can be set as desired to get better results.

$$sim_{cont}(E_n, E_m) = \frac{\sum_{i=1}^{|E_n|} sim_e(e_i, e_j)}{|E_n|} \quad (6)$$

where $e_i \in E_n$, $e_j \in E_m$ and $|E_n|$ is the cardinality of the set E_n.

After the calculation of the role and the content similarity the matching is possible. Two features n and m are considered to be matched, if they are sufficiently similar, e.g. if $csim(n,m) \geq ccutoff_{high}$ or $csim(n,m) \geq ccutoff_{medium}$ and $rsim(n,m) \geq rcutoff$. The parameters $ccutoff_{high}$ and $ccutoff_{medium}$ determine the required degree of the context similarity between the nodes and the parameter *rcutoff* is the required degree of the role similarity (s. Yan et al. 2012).

Finally, the similarity between two subschedules S_n and S_m can be estimated according to the number of their matched features. It is defined similar to the structural similarity measure of the prerequisites or results using FCM (s. equations **(3)** and **(4)**):

$$sim_{FCM}(F_n, F_m) = \frac{\alpha \cdot |F_n \cap F_m| - \beta \cdot |F_n \backslash F_m| - \gamma \cdot |F_m \backslash F_n|}{|F_n \cup F_m|}, \quad (7)$$

$$sim_{struct}(F_n, F_m) = \frac{sim_{FCM}(F_n, F_m) + \max(\alpha,\beta,\gamma)}{1 + \max(\alpha,\beta,\gamma)}, \quad (8)$$

where F_n and F_m are feature sets derived from the subschedules S_n and S_m respectively. In contrast to Yan et al. (2012) this weighted calculation enables the differentiation between the missing features, which are quite important, and superfluous ones that can be almost ignored. Once the similarity degree between a query subschedule S_q and all relevant subschedules from the database is quantified, it is possible to identify *relevant* and *potentially relevant* subschedules. In the same way as in Yan et al. (2012) each subschedule S_n is classified as *relevant*, if $sim(S_q, S_n) \geq ratio_r$ and as *potentially relevant*, if $ratio_r > sim(S_q, S_n) \geq ratio_p$.

4.2 Feature Normalization

In many cases construction schedules have a crucial structural difference compared to business process models. The main reason is that similar building elements are frequently installed in the same way in parallel, which results in a distinct process pattern. In Figure 5a can be seen that schedules S_1 and S_2 are very similar, they only differ in the number of constructed columns. Due to the fact that the number of matched features is a crucial factor for

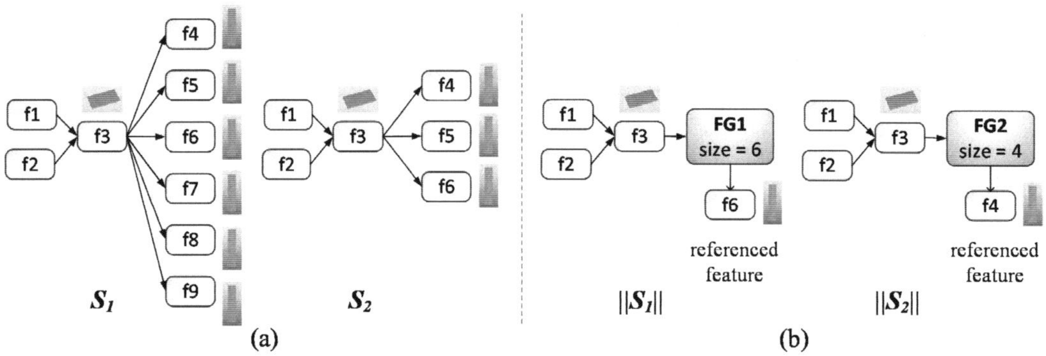

Figure 5 Subschedules *S1* and *S2* (a) and subschedules ||*S1*|| and ||*S2*|| with normalized features (b)

the similarity estimation, the similarity degree between such subschedules would be distorted. The greater the difference in number of similar processes is, the bigger the distortion of the result becomes. It can be reasonably assumed that such kind of disparity occurs quite often, particularly by projects of different scale.

As a solution to this problem, a kind of normalization for features is specified and implemented to make such differences negligible. If parallel construction processes are constructed identically (sc. have the same prerequisites and results that differ only in the object IDs), the related node features are grouped to so-called *grouping features.* In the example presented in Figure 5b, grouping feature *FG1* is composed of features *f4* – *f9* of subschedule S_1 and grouping feature *FG2* is composed of features *f4* – *f6* of subschedule S_2. Each split and join feature is examined to ascertain whether it contains such identical processes. One of the node features is then selected as a *referenced feature* (*f6* from S_1, and *f4* from S_2), which serves as a representative for the future similarity estimation. Additionally, the information about the grouped features and their number is also retained. The roles of the involved node features remain unchanged in order not to affect the structure of subschedules. The normalization of features is performed right after the decomposition step (s. Fig. 3). During the similarity estimation only the referenced features and, if applicable, the size of the groups have to be compared.

5 Case Study

The presented concept has been validated by synthetic data to ensure a high degree of similarity between the schedules. The case study has been implemented for an existing high-rise office building and comprises subschedules for the erection of concrete columns that can be made in different ways: as cast-in-place concrete or precast columns. The main five working steps

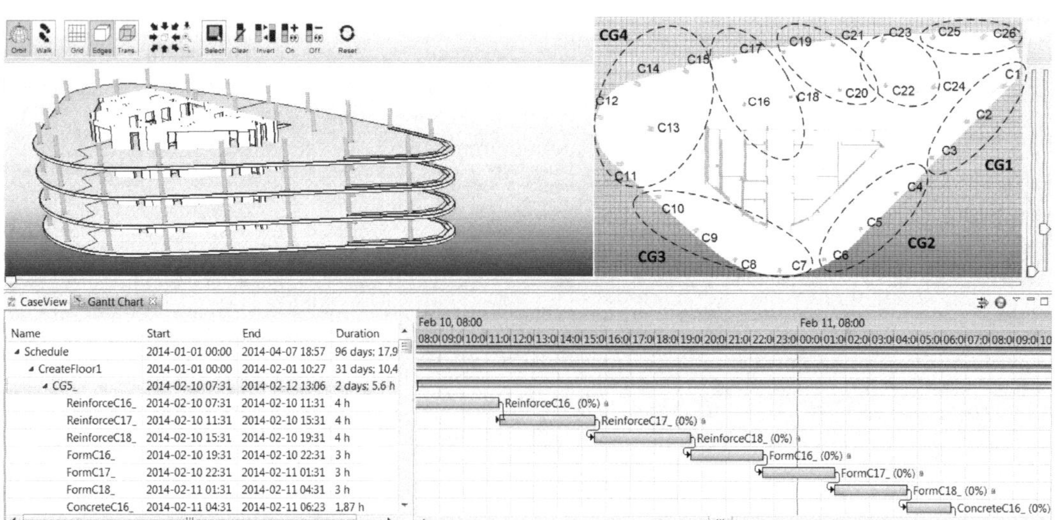

Figure 6 3D model, the top view of the building and an excerpt from the generated schedule

for the cast-in-place columns are: *reinforce (R) ⟶ form (F) ⟶ concrete (C) ⟶ cure (CU) ⟶ strip (S)*. The required tasks can be carried out for one or for a group of columns (s. Fig. 7). After each task the corresponding columns are in their respective states: *Cx_r* in Figure 7 means that the column with the ID x is in the state *reinforced*. The required tasks for the precast columns were designed in a similar manner. In total, 32 different subschedules were defined for four building storeys, containing from 5 up to 21 tasks per schedule. The subschedules differ in the arrangements of their tasks and in the number of grouped columns. The aggregation of columns is exemplarily shown in the top view of the ground floor (Fig. 6), where the abbreviation CG stands for column group. In order to achieve some recurrences, the ground floor and the first floor are built in the same way, so that the corresponding subschedules differ only in the IDs of the used columns.

During the validation all subschedules were decomposed into features and compared with each other to determine the similarities. Some examples for the designed subschedules are given in Figure 7. Similar to subschedule *CG3* of the ground floor, *CG3_1* is defined for the first floor. Further, subschedules *CG4* (ground floor) and *CG4_1* (first floor) have the same structure as *CG3*, but contain five instead of four columns. Choosing, for example, *CG3* as a query, subschedules *CG3_1, CG4* and *CG4_1* have been classified as *relevant*. Due to the introduced normalization of features, the number of grouped columns is irrelevant for proper results. Moreover, subschedule *CG2* (s. Fig. 7) and other subschedules defined in the same manner have been recognized as *potentially relevant*. Just as expected, no similarities have been detected by comparing, for example, *CG2_2* to all other subschedules (s. Fig. 7). Such proper results have been achieved in all tests, taking successively all subschedules as a query.

In this case study suitable values for all required parameters have been adjusted during the test phase. These settings provide adequate results, however they are not optimal. Certainly, the optimization of parameters is an objective of future research. To achieve this, in the first step a sensitivity analysis has to be provided for determining the parameters that affect the similarity results the most.

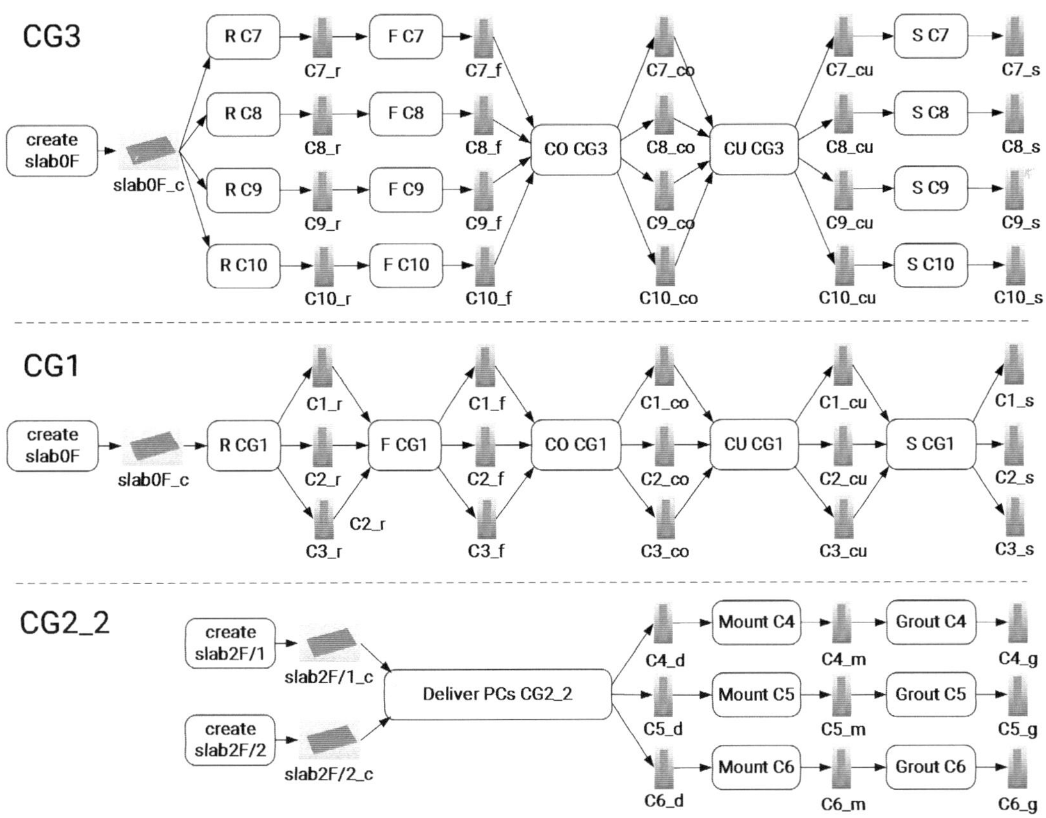

Figure 7 Defined subschedules CG3, CG1 and CG2_2

6 Conclusions and Future Work

A significant improvement in the efficiency of construction planning can be achieved by application of reusable process patterns during the generation of BIM-based schedules. Since the manual definition of valid process templates is a cumbersome and time-consuming procedure, an automated support for the recognition of process patterns would simplify that task a lot. However, the detection of similar construction subschedules is a complex, non-trivial task as well. For this purpose inexact graph matching algorithms can be used suitably. Due to their computationally intensity it is appropriate to apply feature-based indexing techniques, in order to preselect only similar candidate subschedules for the matching algorithms.

In this paper an intelligent concept for the recognition of process patterns in the construction schedules has been provided. For the determination of similar subschedules an existing feature-based similarity method was integrated and adapted. The approach and the defined similarity metrics for features and subschedules have been described in detail. The evaluation on the case study shows that the presented concept leads to the results desired and is very promising. Subsequently, the used parameters have to be optimized and evaluated on a larger database based on realistic projects. The examination and application of existing inexact matching algorithms for the verification step of the concept is an area for future work. Certainly, the performance improvement of the implementation will also need to be explored in further research.

References

Benevolenskiy, A., Roos, K., Katranuschkov, P. & Scherer, R. (2012). Construction processes configuration using process patterns. *Advanced Engineering Informatics* 26(4): 727–736.

Di Natale, R., Ferro, A., Giugno, R. et al. (2010). SING: Subgraph search. In *Non-homogeneous Graphs. BMC Bioinformatics 2010* 11:96.

Dijkman, R., Dumas, M., van Dongen, B. et al. (2011). Similarity of business process models: metrics and evaluation. *Information Systems* 36: 498–516.

Enge, F. (2010). *Muster in Prozessen der Bauablaufplanung*. Aachen: Shaker Verlag.

Enge, F., Olbrich, L. & Huhnt, W. (2012). Hierarchical Templates for the Design of Planning and Construction Processes. In: *Proceedings of the XIVth International Conference on Computing in Civil and Building Engineering*, 2012, Moscow, Russian Federation.

Ferro, A., Giugno, R., Pulvirenti, A. et al. (2012). Efficient Techniques for Graph Searching and Biological Network Mining. In Sakr, S. & Pardede, E. (eds) *Graph Data Management: Techniques and Applications.* USA: Information Science Reference (IGI Global), 89-111.

Hartmann, V., Beucke, K., Shapir, K. & König, M. (2012). Model-based Scheduling for Construction Planning. In: *Proceedings of the XIVth International Conference on Computing in Civil and Building Engineering*, 2012, Moscow, Russian Federation.

Huhnt, W. & Enge, F. (2006). Can algorithms support the specification of construction schedules? *ITcon*, 11, pp. 547-564.

Kim, H., Anderson, K., Lee, S. & Hildreth, J. (2013). Generating Construction Schedules through Automatic Data Extraction Using Open BIM Technology. *Automation in Construction*, 35, 285-295.

König, M., Beucke, K. & Tauscher, E. (2006). Management and Evaluation of Alternative Construction Tasks, *XIth International Conference on Computing in Civil and Building Engineering*, Montreal.

Liu, H., Lei, Z., Li, H. & Al-Hussein, M. (2014). An Automatic Scheduling Approach: Building Information Modeling-based Onsite Scheduling for Panelized Construction. *Construction Research Congress 2014*: pp. 1666-1675.

Messmer, B.T. & Bunke, H. (2000). Efficient subgraph isomorphism detection: a decomposition approach, *IEEE Transactions on Knowledge and Data Engineering* 12(2): 307-323.

Mikulakova, E., König, M., Tauscher, E. & Beucke, K. (2010). Knowledge-based schedule generation and evaluation. *Advanced Engineering Informatics* 24(4): 389-403

Sakr, S. & Al-Naymat, G. (2012). An Overview of Graph Indexing and Querying Techniques. In: Sakr, S. & Pardede, E. (eds) *Graph Data Management: Techniques and Applications.* USA: Information Science Reference (IGI Global), 89-111.

Sharmak, W. (2011). *Dynamic Network Planning in Construction Projects using Configurable Reference Process Models.* Dissertation. In Schriftenreihe des Instituts für Bauinformatik, TU Dresden.

Tversky, A. (1977). Features of similarity, *Psychol. Rev.* 84 (2): 327–352.

Tauscher, E., Smarsly, K., König, M. & Beucke, K. (2014). Automated Generation of Construction Sequences using Building Information Models. *Computing in Civil and Building Engineering.* June 2014, 745-752

Yan, Z., Dijkman, R., & Grefen, P. (2010). Fast business process similarity search with feature-based similarity estimation. In *On the Move to Meaningful Internet Systems: OTM 2010*, Springer Berlin Heidelberg, 60-77.
Yan, Z., Dijkman, R.M. & Grefen, P.W.P.J. (2012). Fast business process similarity search. *Distributed and Parallel Databases* 30(2): 105-144
Yan, X. & Han, J. (2010). Graph Indexing. In: Aggarwal C. and Wang H. (eds), *Managing and Mining Graph Data*, Springer US, 161-180.
Wu, I-C., Borrmann, A., Beissert, U., König, M. & Rank, E. (2010) Bridge Construction Schedule Generation with Pattern-based Construction Models and Constraint-based Simulation, *Advanced Engineering Informatics* 24(4), 379-388.

Integrating visual state recognition with 4D BIM for indoor progress monitoring

Christopher Kropp, christopher.kropp@rub.de
Ruhr-Universität Bochum, Germany

Christian Koch, christian.koch@nottingham.ac.uk
The University of Nottingham, United Kingdom

Markus König, koenig@inf.bi.rub.de
Ruhr-Universität Bochum, Germany

Abstract

The need for a higher degree of automation in progress monitoring has spurred research in recent years. Leveraging existent 4D BIM models for progress monitoring appears to represent the appropriate means in order to achieve activity state recognition. However, BIM based progress monitoring approaches currently target only a small quantity of activities and are not applicable indoors. Nevertheless, there exists an abundance of vision based state recognition methods that are not currently being considered in progress monitoring. Within this paper, a generic framework that links vision based state recognition methods with BIM based progress monitoring is developed. The integration of the framework into BIM based progress monitoring as well as the implementation of state recognition workflows are elaborated. Case studies show the ability of these new state recognition methods within this framework as well as the assimilation of an existing image retrieval method as an additional state recognition method.

Keywords: Progress monitoring, 4D BIM, computer vision, state recognition, framework

1 Introduction

With the introduction of Building Information Modelling (BIM) in research and recently also in practice, the management of construction projects has been enabled for the whole lifecycle of a building. One of the big advantages of BIM is the object-oriented collection and provision of data for each phase during the lifecycle by a single concept. There is common data that is necessary in almost each phase, yet, every phase and each application (e.g.: maintenance, cost assessment) may require additional or more detailed data. During the phase of planning, building models and schedules are created and linked within the so-called 4D BIM model. The construction phase takes these schedule-loaded BIM models as key data and reference for execution. While the building model is mainly divided into groups of three-dimensional spatial objects, the schedule adds an additional temporal dimension of change over time for constructional objects.

Delays during the phase of construction lead to high financial penalties (Trauner et al. 2009). Although risks are often regarded in schedules in terms of probability and uncertainties, they cannot be predicted accurately. Therefore, deviations are of unavoidable and unpredictable nature in every construction project and resulting financial and temporal costs can often only be minimized by immediate decision making and counteraction handling. In current practice, inspections are mainly performed manually. Thus, weekly or daily paper-based progress reports are collected manually by field personnel (Roh et al. 2011). This procedure leads to a high workload of the field personnel in order to fulfil the need for a reasonable frequency of inspections. Hence, manual progress monitoring involves either a massive amount of human

Figure 1 Relation between existing approaches using 4D BIM or vision based state recognition and progress monitoring

intervention or inspection updates cannot be performed as frequently as required. Thus, there is a need for a higher degree of automation in progress monitoring. This requires for the automatic comparison of the as-planned information that is present in BIM with the actual as-built state of the building.

Recently, the research community has been investigating methods that aim to achieve a higher degree of automation in progress monitoring. In this context, vision-based methods appear to represent the appropriate means to target construction state recognition. However, current methods for indoor construction state recognition are independent of, and not associated with 4D BIM. This paper presents a generic framework to link vision based state recognition methods to 4D BIM based progress monitoring.

2 Background

In this section, a review on the current state of research is given regarding BIM based progress monitoring and vision based state recognition. Moreover, the problem statement that is derived from the gap in the current state of research and forms the objective of this paper is presented.

2.1 BIM-based Progress Monitoring

In case of automated progress monitoring, 4D BIM data provides the as-planned foundation for comparison with an as-built status. Since a direct comparison of 4D BIM and imagery is not possible, intelligent comparison approaches are to be developed. 4D BIM offers different information resources, e.g. the building model offers geometry; from the schedule, a timely order of construction activities can be derived; and from object-related attributes, the appearance of construction components can be extracted. Only relevant data needs to be selected from the 4D BIM model according to the chosen approach.

Several research groups have investigated BIM-based progress monitoring on the basis of imagery acquired on the construction site, each using specific BIM resources for their purpose. Lee & Pena-Mora (2006) investigate visualization methods and discusses their application in the context of progress monitoring. By linking images to the schedule, deviations within the schedule are proposed to be quantified and visualized by superimposing the colorized building model. Podbreznik & Rebolj (2005) present a global concept to control building activities. A reconstruction of building model objects from images of fixed cameras is performed. The building model is used to extract model components according to the current schedule state for comparison aims. Rebolj et al. (2008) use the images of a single pre-calibrated camera and performs image segmentation by color and texture on basis of a manually initiated region growing algorithm. A comparison with a rendered image extracted from the building model is conducted and the minimal difference associates building elements to image regions. The progress is stated by the recognition of present and missing elements. Son & Kim (2010) create 3D data of the construction scene with stereo cameras. The structure is recognized in terms of a color-based object segmentation to structural components and 3D data. Kim et al. (2011) reconstruct the building from images of multiple views. Thereby, a selection of concrete components by color is made and a manual comparison between the building model view and the real image is performed. The approach presented in Golparvar-Fard et al. (2009) performs a manual selection of correspondences between a schedule respective building model and an image. Deviations are visualized and depicted manually. Golparvar-Fard et al. (2010) obtain a point cloud by reconstruction of the scene of unordered construction photos. A registration of the point cloud with the building model is performed to assure comparison abilities in further steps. Occupancy of the points in the model determines the current state. In Ibrahim et al. (2009), a visual comparison of workpackage components with a fixed camera is conducted. The building model is subdivided into workpackages regarding the schedule and is superimposed on the time-lapsed images of the single camera appointed. The change of the pixels covered by the workpackages over the lapse of time indicates the construction progress. In Golparvar-Fard et al. (2010), a complex system for progress monitoring under the use of 3D reconstructions is developed. Unordered daily images are used to reconstruct the building as a point cloud representation. This point cloud is registered with the building model and the basis for occupancy-based derivation of the current state of the construction progress. Han & Golparvar-Fard (2014a; 2014b) extend this system with an appearance-based material classification method for monitoring construction progress.

The listed approaches consider the building shell, mainly consisting of columns and beams, or outer surfaces in their concept. Furthermore, case studies or experiments are limited to outdoor applications by the nature of their corresponding approaches' methods of creating comparable models. However, approaches with fixed cameras (Lee & Pena-Mora 2006; Rebolj et al. 2008; Kim & Kano 2008; Ibrahim et al. 2009; Zhang et al. 2009) are only applicable when they oversee the major construction site with a limited number of observable objects. An application in the interior of a building is feasible, but the effort/effectiveness relationship for installing fixed cameras makes these approaches impossible to realize indoors. Approaches that perform visual reconstruction through Structure-from-Motion methods (Kim et al. 2011; Golparvar-Fard, Pena-Mora, et al. 2009; Golparvar-Fard et al. 2010; Han & Golparvar-Fard 2014a; Han & Golparvar-Fard 2014b) cannot easily be shifted to interior finishing, due to the lack of motion combined with the problem of simultaneously keeping the reconstructed objects in focus of the camera. Hence, none of the existing approaches regarding BIM-based progress monitoring shows reasonable applicability indoors.

2.2 Vision based State Recognition

The research community has shown the promising applicability of vision based recognition and developed a number of approaches that focus on the vision-based recognition of construction components and activities.

Several approaches were presented that aim for the recognition of materials in construction. In Brilakis et al. (2006), an automated and content based construction site image retrieval method is proposed, which is based on image retrieval techniques that are related to material and object identification. The method performs matching of known material samples with material clusters. Thereby, vectors with values of several filter responses and colors are compared with each other. This approach is extended to the automatic distinction between linear and nonlinear construction objects with additional feature values from edge descriptors in Brilakis & Soibelman (2008). In Dimitrov & Golparvar-Fard (2014), a similar approach to material recognition is used for segmentation of 3D point clouds of outdoor construction sites. This is done to achieve semantic knowledge about the 3D point clouds. In Han & Golparvar-Fard (2014a), a detection method for determining the construction progress at the operation-level in the context of 4D BIM is proposed. This represents an appearance-based approach recognizing construction material from site image data. It includes extracting patches in the first stage. For the recognition, a one-vs-all approach is deployed, which tests an extracted patch against all possible materials. In Zhu et al. (2010), a material detection of concrete in a cluttered construction environment was proposed. The method separates the characteristic color of concrete from differently colored image parts. In Zhu & Brilakis (2010), the approach of detecting concrete is extended to the detection of concrete columns. In Kropp et al. (2014), a cascaded multi-step approach is developed in order to determine the different stages of a drywall installation activity.

Only a few approaches are presented, that consider the detection or recognition of construction components. In Roh et al. (2011), object detection is considered especially for indoor purposes of progress monitoring. The approach detects air condition equipment and is in general only applicable for small objects with distinct characteristics. Kropp et al. (2013) presents an approach that aims to recognize structural finishing components. The approach is evaluated with the recognition of heating devices.

Although 4D BIM offers sources of rich information that may support the recognition of the current state of a building component or activity, research efforts in vision-based state recognition are mainly independent of 4D BIM. This particularly affects the recognition of objects and materials. Hence, their association to further information accessible by the link to 4D BIM and its objects and tasks is not considered and is insufficiently investigated in research. Furthermore, a wide range of materials and structural objects needs to be recognized for indoor progress monitoring, which is not covered by just a single recognition method.

2.3 Problem statement and objectives

On the one hand, BIM-based progress monitoring in research does not currently perform satisfactorily for a variety of construction activities so far. Approaches are

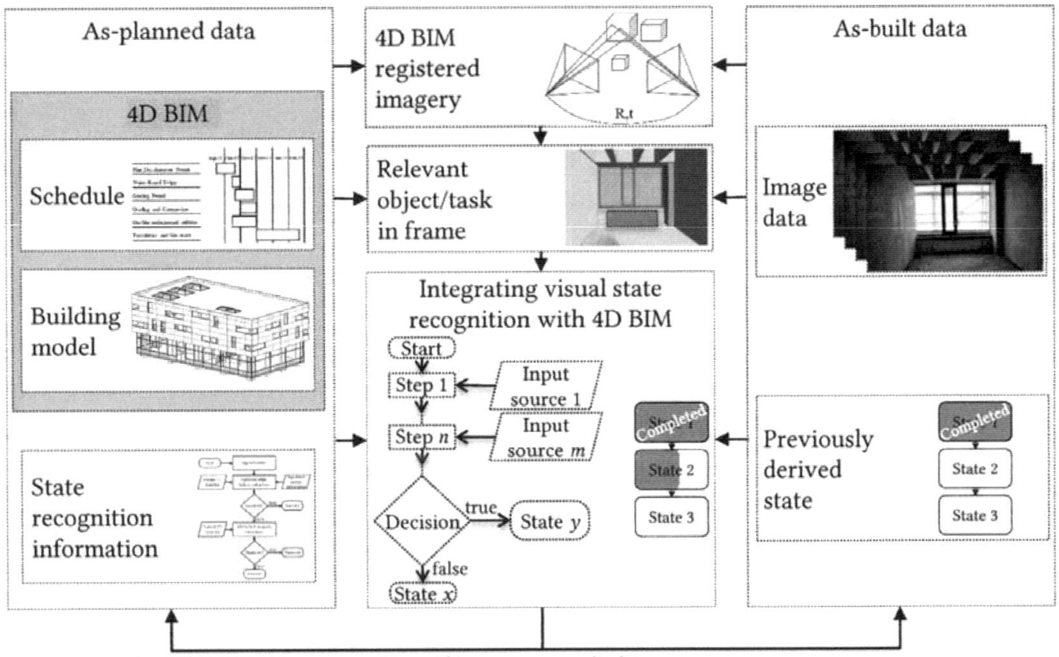

Figure 2 Integration of the visual state recognition within progress monitoring

presented that mainly target the recognition of the progress of the wall, column and beam dominated building shell. Thereby, time-lapse photos reveal progress by changes in appearance, or structural changes are derived by occupancy-based approaches that access models of the reconstructed as-built project. In the end, current research does not target the assessment of all activities that are performed on a construction site, particularly no interior finishing activities.

On the other hand, vision-based state recognition methods are currently not able to determine the state of particular activities that have to be observed according to the schedule of the 4D BIM model. The recognition of states is not a simple task. Each state of activity that needs to be distinguished induces a specialized recognition strategy, regarding the objects involved, the chronology, the geometry and other particularities. According to the applied recognition strategy, the activity needs to be both recognized in imagery and associated to the 4D BIM in order to derive progress statements for the planned activities. Current methods do not provide these features. Hence, the actual state of research does not meet the conditions for a holistic and automatic indoor progress monitoring.

Thus, the present state of research lacks a formalized and generic framework that links vision-based state recognition with 4D BIM progress monitoring. As illustrated in Figure 1, there exists a gap between those approaches related to progress monitoring. In order to design such a framework, the following research question need to be considered: How can 4D BIM information be linked and integrated with a diversity of vision based object, state and activity recognition through a generic framework for indoor progress monitoring?

3 Methodology

Within this paper, the previously defined research question is addressed. A method that represents a formalized and generic framework linking vision-based state recognition with 4D BIM progress monitoring is developed. This method is embedded within automatic indoor progress monitoring. The framework is based on the assumption that the imagery is registered with the 4D BIM. This framework states the foundation for a possible improvement of many present recognition methods.

First, the relation of the developed state recognition framework within progress monitoring is described (see Figure 2). The new state recognition framework is placed in-between present as-planned data and newly acquired or previously derived as-built data within the process of state recognition. In order to provide additional as-planned data for state recognition, the 4D BIM model (schedule and

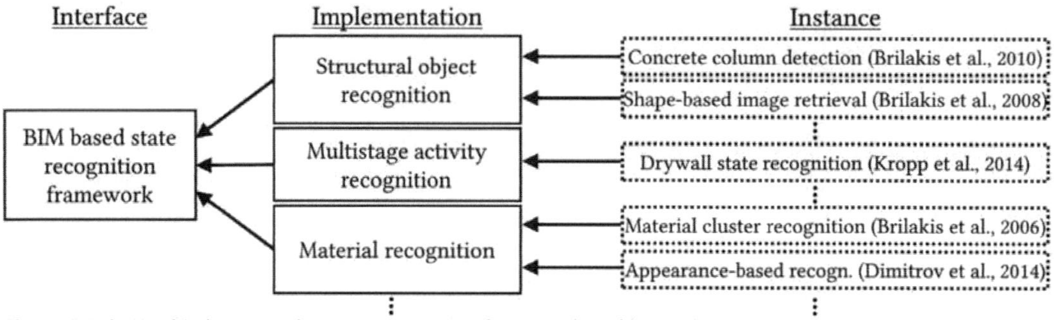

Figure 3 Relationship between the state recognition framework and its implementations

building model) is extended with visual state recognition workflows.

There are several information resources that are used in this framework. The information resources are either present from planning (as-planned); acquired during inspections or present from former inspections (as-built); or derived by processing the previously named information resources algorithmically. Within the as-planned information resources, the 4D BIM model is the main source for information containing the building model and the schedule. The building model contains object-related information about the extents, the geometry and the parts of objects, whereas the schedule contains information about the activities concerning the objects and temporal order and dependencies. Furthermore, the classification workflow and classification information represents the information that is needed to distinguish between different states of the activities in an image-based manner. The as-built information resources consist of the image data that is taken during inspections and previously derived states from earlier inspections, whereby this data is not always available, particularly not during the first inspection of a construction site.

Derived from the 4D BIM registered imagery with pose, orientation and time, it is possible to determine a region of interest (ROI) in the images of observable objects and tasks. With the image data that is prepared in this way, the state recognition framework is used to retrieve statements about the actual state of the activity based on the image patches defined by the ROI. As the outcome of the state recognition framework, the actual state of an activity is expected. This state is then recursively affects the schedule by reactive re-scheduling of the constructional dependencies and is additionally available as data for future inspections with information that was previously obtained. The state recognition framework has several input sources that can be considered during implementation.

Furthermore, the framework is designed as a generic framework to process the filtered image data that is expected to contain the desired object and delivers the state of the analyzed task after processing. It offers different types of input sources which are partly mandatory for every state recognition process. A descriptive part explains the workflow of process steps in detail and depicts further resources that are necessary to obtain a statement about the current state of the activity results. The single steps within the workflow are describing pre-processing, feature extraction from the input image and classification of the input image. It is manually predefined for every activity that needs to be investigated due to the complexity and diversity of activities associated with interior finishing. The definitions of the workflows can be stored in a database and obtained when needed. Moreover, the content related part is filled with the input image and the expected ROI of the desired activity in it. Additional information that is concomitant with the needs of the considered activity can be integrated into the state recognition process. The different elements of a flow chart for a classification workflow are displayed. Each implementation of the state recognition framework requires a workflow for completion. The flow chart describes the inner processes that lead from the entry of the input data in the first processing step until a state is determined. The structure of the workflow is modular and single steps can easily be interchanged. This representation of the inner processes of an implementation of the framework is on a low level and close to the actual realization.

The workflow is initialized with a *start* token. From there, different processing *steps* lead to a set of output *states*. *Decisions* on the results of single steps allow for differentiating cases, e.g. to decide if the queried image shows a certain state

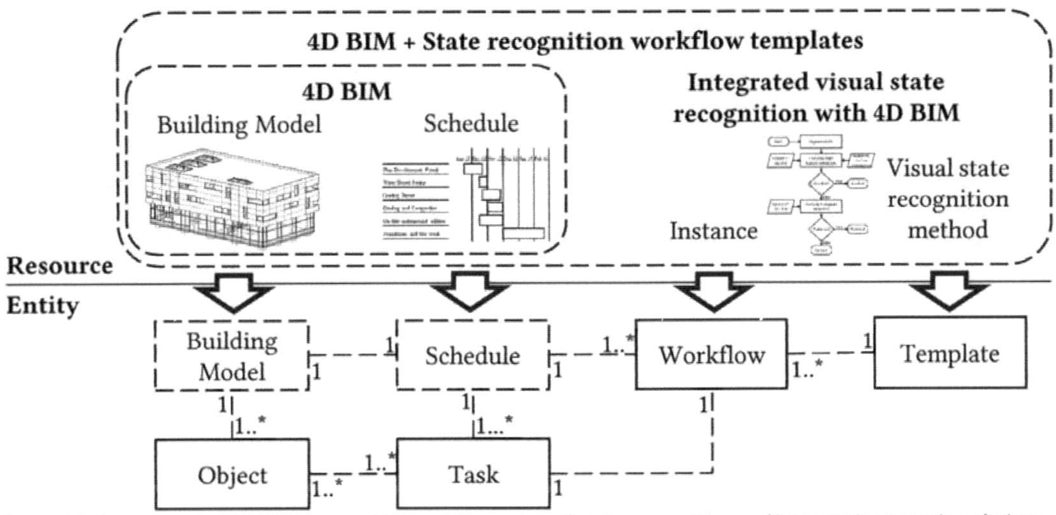

Figure 4 Enhancement of 4D BIM to an additional dimension of state recognition and its mapping to entity relations

of an activity. The nature of the decision is binary, such that only *true* or *false* statements lead to different branches. The sundry processing steps receive data input sources in order to refine the incoming input from a previous step. Finally, the output of the state recognition framework is the actual state of completion of the activity.

The state recognition framework serves as an interface for the actual implementations of visual recognition methods. Figure 3 illustrates the relationship of possible implementations of the framework. Thereby, each implementation references to the state recognition framework. They are able to utilize the available input sources and must meet the requirements for the output specifications. The state recognition framework has no pre-sets for the inner choice and order of the processing steps.

Finally, it requires explanation how to integrate the state recognition into the existing 4D BIM structure (see Figure 4). By adding information about the state recognition framework, the schedule loaded BIM is expanded to an additional dimension. The activity state recognition extends the existing 4D BIM with the ability of integrating resources of as-built acquisition and analysis information. Figure 4 shows an illustration of the resources of the state recognition workflow extended 4D BIM. In the data point of view, a connection needs to be established between the existing and the extended parts by means of entities and multiplicities. This mapping is displayed in the lower half of Figure 4. In this context, a recognition method represents a template that can be instantiated by several workflows for the identification of specific tasks from the schedule.

4 Case studies

Three case studies are presented that underline the versatility of the presented state recognition framework for state recognition. Two implementations of the state recognition framework were developed that show the successful recognition of drywall states, where mostly the surface of a present object changes. A

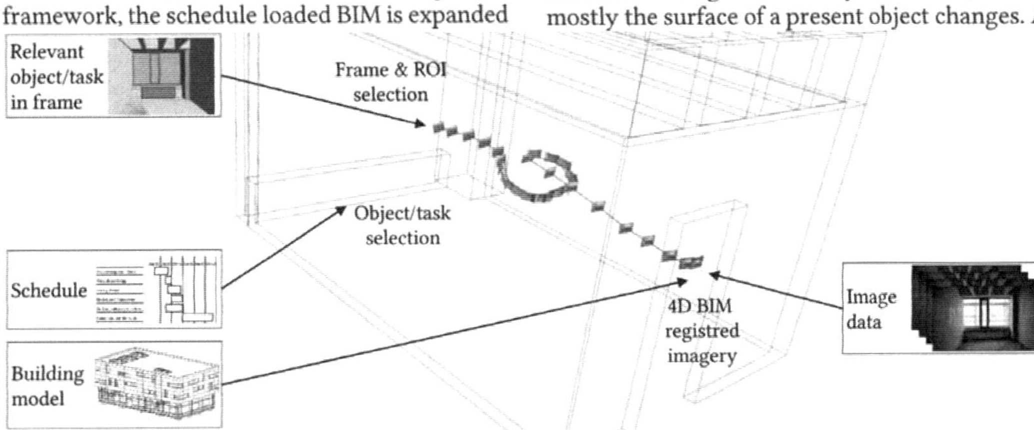

Figure 5 Overview of the basis for the state recognition by the example of a heating device installation

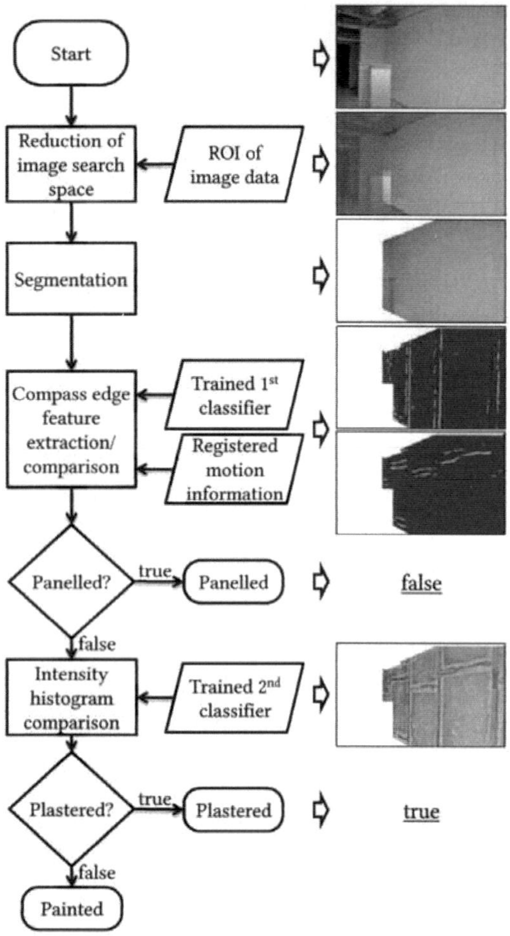

Figure 6 Workflow for the classification of the drywall installation completion state with the example of a plastered wall

third implementations recognizes the state of the mounting of radiators that includes structural changes. Figure 5 illustrates how input sources are conducted to provide the relevant object or task within the frames from the 4D BIM registered imagery.

4.1 Drywall state recognition

The different states of drywall installation activities are characterized by different visual features that result in a challenging recognition. The main challenges for determining the state of the drywall are the low structure and the homogeneous color distribution over the wall. Furthermore, in indoor environments, walls may not be completely visible if no special lens is applied. Drywall installation activities are usually finished after completing three states: a) the installation of panels, b) the plastering of the drywall and c) the painting of the drywall.

According to the description of the introduced state recognition framework, the method is explained as a workflow to achieve state differentiation. The classification workflow is illustrated as a flow chart in Figure 6. In the first step, the image is loaded and cut according to the re-projection of the object to the current video frame in order to reduce the search space for the activity to the relevant image region. The second step includes segmentation that prevents the inclusion of unexpected objects, like ladders, painting pots or cables that may occlude the desired drywall and thus disturb a clear view on the expected texture characteristics and influence results. After these preparatory steps, the sheer drywall can be investigated. Therefore, the subsequent step performs a compass edge feature extraction and comparison. The compass edge features are extracted with the information from the registered motion information that provides the camera view and rotation relative to the wall. With that information, an edge filter can be adapted in order to find the horizontal and vertical gaps as well as the round screw spots at the drywall. Also within this step, a preliminarily trained classifier with the ability to decide between paneled drywalls and the other two stages pursuant to the extracted edge features is applied. The paneled state is the earliest outcome state in this classification workflow, which exits if this state is reached. For the purpose of differentiation between the remaining states, further steps within the workflow are necessary. The further state distinction is focused on increasing the contrast of the areas that are painted to the plastered panels. Histogram based adaptive contrast normalization is used to expose the contrast at the plastered areas of the wall. Afterwards, a histogram considering the pixel intensity is used as a feature vector for classification. A deeper insight into the method is given in (Kropp et al. 2014).

4.2 Recognition of heating device installation state

The second investigated case for the integration of a classification approach into the framework as an implementation of the proposed framework is based on the method presented in Kropp et al. (2013). The approach is intended to derive the current state of an activity by recognizing the presence of structural objects with changing appearance from different views by making an approximation of its real perspective transform. It assumes that views onto an object from a certain similar spatial

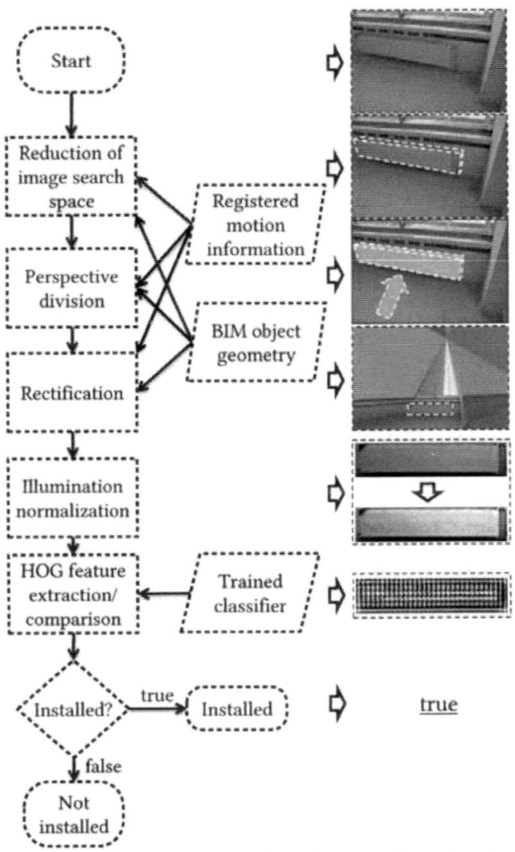

Figure 7 Workflow for the classification of the heating installation completion state with example image data

region result in comparable object appearances, such that it is sufficient to train a classifier for achieving good recognition results. It takes into account knowledge about the object from BIM, as well as motion information to reduce the complex three dimensional recognition problem into a simple two dimensional recognition problem. The method was evaluated on the example of the recognition of heating devices.

The workflow that is related to the current approach is displayed in the flow chart in Figure 7. As the first step within this flow chart, the large quantity of image data is scaled down to a degree that enables treatment of only necessary data portions. This is done by the projection of the minimal enclosing cuboid of the geometry of the expected object onto the image plane. In the second step, the view onto the object is classified. With the classification, an association of the view into a perspective bin is carried out. The association to a bin is performed according to the available surfaces of the object within the current view. Hereby, information from the BIM object geometry and the registered motion information is used in order to obtain the relative pose of the object to the camera. Exactly this data is applied in the third step again to perform a rectification of the visual appearance of the object. The rectification is intended to reduce the three dimensional appearance into a normalized two dimensional representation of all views in a bin. In doing so, the pixels of the object's 2D extent are transformed by the frontal plane of the minimal enclosing cuboid in Euclidean space to a rectangle in the image plane. Before visual features are extracted, this rectangle is illuminated to remove illumination inequalities. Finally, the method of Histogram of Oriented Gradients is applied to extract information about visual characteristics and compared to a trained classifier. This enables the derivation of the presence of the object and hence, for this special class of activities, a state of the activity. Kropp et al. (2013) contains a detailed description of the explained steps.

4.3 Adoption of material recognition from Brilakis et al. (2006)

The third case study shows adoption abilities of the framework for present visual recognition methods. For this reason, the very innovative approach presented in (Brilakis et al. 2006) is adapted as an implementation of the state recognition framework. The original method targets the recognition of specific materials in construction to perform image retrieval in order to gain knowledge about the image content for documentary reasons. In this case study, the method is adopted for the material identification to achieve activity state recognition.

The original method consists of four significant steps. In the first step, an extraction of basic features (e.g. color, texture, or structure) by applying filtering techniques to target the decomposition of the images is deployed. Then, the images are divided into regions by clustering using a combination of the extracted features. The third step consists of the computation of the feature signatures of each obtained cluster. In the final step, a matching of the feature signatures acquired from a queried image is compared to a present material knowledge base.

The four original steps that are described by this method are extended by additional information that results in the restriction and reduction of input data. The nature of the framework within the framework containing rich information from several data sources may not only allow for successful integration, but also for the improvement by means of accuracy and computational effort.

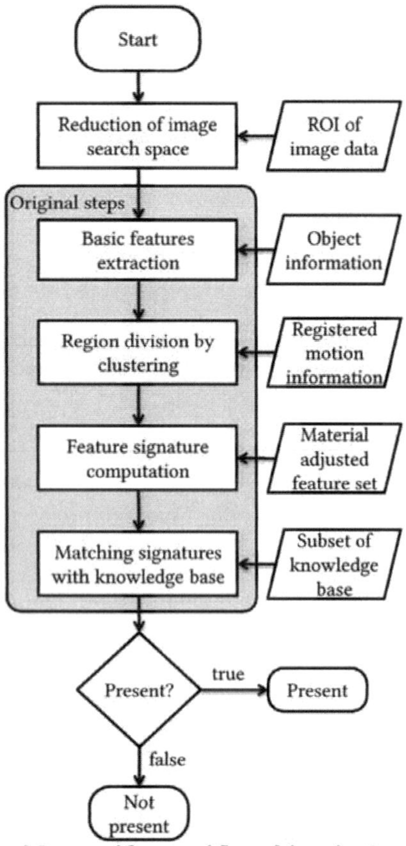

Figure 8 Proposal for a workflow of the adaption of the visual recognition method presented in Brilakis et al. (2006)

Following, it is described how the present method is successfully embedded into an implementation of the state recognition framework. As displayed in Figure 8, the processing of the classification workflow begins with the reduction of the image to the expected ROI. Consequently, the processing enters the modification of the original method. With the ROI, the basic feature extraction receives solely a fracture of the image it originally would receive. This reduces the area to investigate and decreases the possibility of false detections in irrelevant space compared to the original method. Furthermore, the information about the object can be leveraged to reduce the set of features that need to be extracted, since some features are of no significance when separating material. Since fewer features need to be extracted from the image, the risk of misinterpretation, as well as the computational demand is decreased. In the next step, the region division can be improved by knowledge of the structure, texture, and color that is expected by the camera view delivered by motion information and object information from BIM. Adopted filtering techniques can result in limited computational demand and avoid the application of filters that deliver redundant information. Finally, the reduced feature signatures set only needs to be compared to signatures from the knowledge base that are expected to be present in the image. By adopting the original method, the modified and improved version of the material recognition is embedded and states if the expected material is present in the image and, thus, if the activity is at a certain state. Another achievement by the adoption of the existing method is the material association to BIM.

5 Conclusion

In order to determine the actual state of buildings under construction, research delivered promising outcomes using vision based methods. On the one hand, many approaches for automatic progress monitoring are mainly BIM based and do not support a sufficient set of objects or tasks. On the other hand, current visual state recognition methods do not consider the rich data sources provided by 4D BIM.

The presented state recognition framework fills the gap between these two aspects of automatic progress monitoring and is able to link a majority of existing recognition methods in construction beneath a single roof of visual state recognition. The framework targets the provision of a common method for the integration of a diverse set of recognition algorithms supported by 4D BIM data. Implementations of this framework can either be adopted from existing visual recognition methods, or directly developed regarding the specifications and considering the great advantages of the framework. Adaptations do not solely transform existing methods to fit into the framework. They can benefit by applying additional information provided by 4D BIM data and registered motion information. Thus, there is potential for enhancement in terms of accuracy and computational effort by binding existing methods to a higher level of processing.

The paper includes three case studies concerning implementations of the framework for visual recognition methods by the presence of structural objects, a complex multiple state activity, and the activity state derivation by material recognition. Two of them state a direct development within the framework that immediately takes all advantages and offerings of the available data sources. Within the third case study, an existing visual recognition method is successfully implemented into the framework. Thereby, an adoption is performed from the original objective of image annotation to activity state recognition to fit into framework specifications. Future work will focus on the establishment of a database which associates classification methods with certain activities according to the presented framework. This will allow for a vast step into the direction of achieving a higher degree of automation in progress monitoring.

References

Brilakis, I.K. & Soibelman, L., 2008. Shape-Based Retrieval of Construction Site Photographs. *Journal of Computing in Civil Engineering*, 22, pp.14–20.

Brilakis, I.K., Soibelman, L. & Shinagawa, Y., 2006. Construction site image retrieval based on material cluster recognition. *Advanced Engineering Informatics*, 20(4), pp.443–452.

Dimitrov, A. & Golparvar-Fard, M., 2014. Vision-based material recognition for automated monitoring of construction progress and generating building information modeling from unordered site image collections. *Advanced Engineering Informatics*, 28(1), pp.37–49.

Golparvar-Fard, M., Peña-Mora, F., et al., 2009. Visualization of Construction Progress Monitoring with 4D Simulation Model Overlaid on Time-Lapsed Photographs. *Journal of Computing in Civil Engineering*, 23, pp.391–404.

Golparvar-Fard, M., Pena-Mora, F. & Savarese, S., 2009. D4AR - A 4-Dimensional augmented reality model for automating construction progress monitoring data collection, processing, and communication. *Journal of Information Technology in Construction*, 14, pp.129–153.

Golparvar-Fard, M., Savarese, S. & Peña-Mora, F., 2010. Automated Model-Based Recognition of Progress Using Daily Construction Photographs and IFC-Based 4D Models. In *Construction Research Congress 2010*. pp. 51–60.

Han, K. & Golparvar-Fard, M., 2014a. Automated Monitoring of Operation-level Construction Progress Using 4D BIM and Daily Site Photologs. In D. Castro-Lacouture, J. Irizarry, & B. Ashuri, eds. *Construction Research Congress 2014*. Atlanta, Georgia: American Society of Civil Engineers, pp. 1033–1042.

Han, K. & Golparvar-Fard, M., 2014b. Multi-Sample Image-Based Material Recognition and Formalized Sequencing Knowledge for Operation-Level Construction Progress Monitoring. In I. Raymond & I. Flood, eds. *Computing in Civil and Building Engineering*. Orlando, Florida, United States: American Society of Civil Engineers, pp. 364–372.

Ibrahim, Y.M. et al., 2009. Towards Automated Progress Assessment of Workpackage Components in Construction Projects Using Computer Vision. *Adv. Eng. Inform.*, 23(1), pp.93–103.

Kim, C., Son, H. & Kim, C., 2011. The Effective Acquisition and Processing of 3D Photogrammetric Data from Digital Photogrammetry for Construction Progress Measurement. *Computing in Civil Engineering*, pp.178–185.

Kim, H. & Kano, N., 2008. Comparison of construction photograph and VR image in construction progress. *Automation in Construction*, 17, pp.137–143.

Kropp, C., König, M. & Koch, C., 2014. Drywall state detection in image data for automatic indoor progress monitoring. In R. Issa & I. Flood, eds. *Proceedings of the 2014 International Conference on Computing in Civil and Building Engineering (ICCCBE 2014)*. Orlando, Florida, United States: ASCE, pp. 347–354.

Kropp, C., König, M. & Koch, C., 2013. Object recognition in BIM registered videos for indoor progress monitoring. In *European Group for Intelligent Computing in Engineering: EG-ICE Workshop: Intelligent Computing in Engineering*. Vienna, Austria.

Lee, S. & Pena-Mora, F., 2006. Visualization of construction progress monitoring. In *Joint International Conference on Computing and Decision Making in Civil and Building Engineering*. pp. 2527–2533.

Podbreznik, P. & Rebolj, D., 2005. Automatic comparison of site images and the 4D model of the building. In *Conference on Information Technology in Construction,)*.

Rebolj, D. et al., 2008. Automated construction activity monitoring system. *Advanced Engineering Informatics*, 22, pp.493–503.

Roh, S., Aziz, Z. & Peña-Mora, F., 2011. An object-based 3D walk-through model for interior construction progress monitoring. *Automation in Construction*, 20(1), pp.66–75.

Son, H. & Kim, C., 2010. 3D structural component recognition and modeling method using color and 3D data for construction progress monitoring. *Automation in Construction*, 19, pp.844–854.

Trauner, T.J.J. et al., 2009. Project Scheduling. In *Construction Delays, Second Edition: Understanding Them Clearly, Analyzing Them Correctly*. Butterworth-Heinemann, pp. 1–22.

Zhang, X. et al., 2009. Automating progress measurement of construction projects. *Automation in Construction*, 18, pp.294–301.

Zhu, Z. & Brilakis, I., 2010. Parameter optimization for automated concrete detection in image data. *Automation in Construction*, 19(7), pp.944–953.

Zhu, Z., German, S. & Brilakis, I., 2010. Detection of large-scale concrete columns for automated bridge inspection. *Automation in Construction*, 19(8), pp.1047–1055.

Assessment and optimization of the robustness of construction schedules

Veronika Hartmann, veronika.hartmann@uni-weimar.de
Computing in Civil Engineering, Bauhaus-Universität Weimar, Germany

Tom Lahmer, tom.lahmer@uni-weimar.de
Optimization and Stochastics, Bauhaus-Universität Weimar, Germany

Kay Smarsly, kay.smarsly@uni-weimar.de
Computing in Civil Engineering, Bauhaus-Universität Weimar, Germany

Abstract

Construction schedules are known to be unreliable. Deadlines are passed, because a schedule's input data, which is usually not exactly known in the planning phase, is considered deterministic when generating the schedule. This paper discusses the effects of uncertainties inherent in input data of construction schedules. It further discusses models that take into account these uncertainties and presents a method for optimizing the robustness of construction schedules by identifying the most robust combination of alternative processes. In this study, uncertainties are considered by describing the process durations with distribution functions instead of discrete values. The project makespan, based on stochastic process durations, is determined with a Monte Carlo simulation. To assess the robustness, a criterion is defined, which relates the makespan considering uncertainties to the makespan assuming deterministic process durations. With an adapted genetic optimization algorithm, the most robust combination of alternative processes is determined. A case study shows the effectiveness of the method.

Keywords: Construction scheduling, uncertainties, robustness, optimization

1 Introduction

Construction schedules provide information about all processes necessary to realize a project. A large amount of data is extracted from different sources to gain knowledge about the processes, such as durations, construction methods, required resources, dependencies, and boundary conditions. The compliance with dependencies and boundary conditions is ensured by defining appropriate relations between the respective processes. Based on the knowledge about the processes and their relations, a network plan is determined. By assigning a value to each process, which defines the process duration, a schedule can be created from the network plan, and start and end dates for the processes as well as the makespan of the project can be calculated.

Since construction projects involve many different stakeholders depending on each other, a reliable schedule is of great importance. Typically, deadlines and makespans are determined using the Critical Path Method (CPM), a method developed in the 1950s. Although this method is well-established, construction schedules are known to be unreliable. The reason why deadlines and makespans determined with CPM are often passed is, that CPM assumes the input data, particularly the process durations, to be deterministic. However, only little of the input data is exactly known during the planning phase and, in fact, most values are based on estimation, which may result in a deviation during the construction phase from the initial schedule. Assessing the reliability of a schedule requires considering the uncertainties inherent in the input data. These uncertainties have different reasons, such as unpredictable weather conditions, inaccurate estimations of process durations, machine failure etc. Although these uncertainties cause, depending on their nature, different types of deviations, most deviations can well be modeled by variable instead of discrete process durations.

The objective of this work is not only to take into account uncertainties in the input data of construction schedules, but also to improve the robustness and thus the reliability of schedules. Robustness, in the broadest sense, is insensitiveness against adverse conditions. There is no universal and at the same time more precise definition of robustness, because the definition can only be specified depending on the context. In this work, investigating the reliability of construction schedules, *insensitiveness* of schedules concerns the deadlines, whereas *adverse conditions* are the process durations that might, in the construction phase, deviate from the values estimated during the planning phase. A schedule is robust and thus reliable when deadlines are insensitive against changes in the input data, i.e., if deadlines only change insignificantly even if the input data undergoes major changes.

Robustness of schedules has been investigated in different domains, e.g. in machine scheduling and in vehicle routing. Schedule robustness in these domains is usually improved by varying the order of tasks. However, this strategy cannot be used in construction industry, because the order of tasks is fixed due to the dependencies and boundary conditions. Although there is no freedom in the order of tasks, there often is freedom in the choice among alternative processes. If different construction methods exist for one task, the methods can be considered alternative processes. To give an example, a column can be realized as prefabricated column or it can be concreted in situ. In addition, alternative processes can be provided by different options for the distribution of resources. Common schedules only consider one process per task and do not provide information about alternative processes or about the reasons for having chosen the specific process. As a result, consideration of alternative processes is usually not focused when improving schedules. This paper investigates the potential of improving schedule robustness by varying the choice of processes for tasks that offer alternative processes. For this purpose, it is not sufficient to assess and compare separate processes without regarding the context of a schedule. It is rather of interest to investigate the impact of different combinations of alternative processes in the context of the considered schedule. Robustness of a schedule can be improved by identifying the combination of alternative processes that shows the least sensitiveness against changes in the input data.

This paper describes a method to optimize the robustness of construction schedules with respect to deadlines and makespans by varying the combination of alternative processes. Uncertainties are taken into account by using random instead of deterministic process durations. In the next section, a short summary of related research is given. In section 3, the method developed for the optimization is presented and further illustrated by a case study described in section 4. Finally, in section 5 conclusions are drawn and an outlook on future work is given.

2 Robustness in scheduling

In this work, robustness of schedules with respect to the makespan is investigated. Uncertainties inherent in the input data should affect the makspan as little as possible. Therefore, two different aspects will be examined. First, a model is to be identified to adequately consider uncertainties. Second, a criterion has to be defined for quantifying the schedule robustness, and a method has to be developed for optimizing the schedule robustness with respect to the defined criterion. The following subsections provide a short overview of research work related to scheduling under uncertainties and schedule robustness.

2.1 Consideration of uncertainties

The Critical Path Method (CPM), developed in the 1950s, is a common method in construction scheduling for determining deadlines and makespans of projects (Winch et al. 2005, Besner et al. 2008). Based on a network plan and on durations defined for all processes, the makespan is calculated as the longest path in the network. For these calculations, the input data is assumed to be deterministic. The shortcomings of using deterministic data are obvious: Schedules not taking into account the uncertainties inherent in the input data are not fully reliable, because deviations from the initial schedule usually occur during the construction phase. Although the reasons for such deviations are manifold, their consequence is generally a change in process durations. Variable instead of discrete process durations are hence an adequate way of considering uncertainties.

Almost at the same time as CPM, the so called Program Evaluation and Review Technique (PERT) has been developed (Malcolm et al. 1959). In PERT, a stochastic approach is chosen and process durations are defined by distribution functions. For computing critical paths and makespans of projects, simplifying assumptions are made. The two most relevant simplifications are

(i) the assumption of independence of all processes and
(ii) the definition that the maximum of two stochastic distributions is determined solely by the maximum of their expected values without considering the standard deviations.

The computed makespan, based on the law of large numbers, is described by a normal distribution with a mean value μ and a standard deviation σ. The simplifications entail an underestimation of the mean value and the standard deviation. Therefore, although considering uncertainties, PERT does not result in more reliable schedules than the purely deterministic CPM. Therefore, the idea of stochastic scheduling has been further investigated. The main focus lies on the so called stochastic resource-constrained project scheduling. Taking into account resource constraints as well as variable process durations described by distribution functions, schedule policies are investigated that generate schedules that are usually optimized for a minimum makespan (Storck 2000, Liu and Sanlaville 1997, Herroelen and Leus 2005).

Soon after the concept of fuzzy numbers became popular through the work of Zadeh (1965) and later Dubois and Prade (1978), it was applied to scheduling problems under uncertainty (Lootsma 1989). In fuzzy PERT, process durations are defined as fuzzy numbers, usually of triangular or trapezoidal shape. Makespan and process start times are determined using the operators addition, subtraction, maximum, and minimum. The approach leads to an inappropriate accumulation of vagueness for the result, i.e. makespan and start times. Hsiu and Liu (2009) have proposed an extended fuzzy PERT approach. Among other adaptions, Hsiu and Liu introduce a α_i-level cut method for the determination of the earliest start times, thus avoiding the inappropriate accumulation of vagueness.

An overview of scheduling under uncertainties can be found in Herroelen and Leus (2005). In summary, stochastic as well as fuzzy approaches are investigated under different objectives. It can be concluded that, although minimizing the makespan of schedules is a common objective, increasing attention is paid to the optimization of the schedule robustness.

2.2 Robust scheduling

The term *robustness* is used in many areas and in different respects. In the context of scheduling, Sörensen (2001) distinguishes between solution and quality robustness. Solution robustness implies that the structure of the schedule itself is insensitive against deviations from the initial input data, whereas for a quality robust schedule the impact of changes on a certain quality of the schedule is considered; such quality can, e.g., be the makespan or the costs of a project. In literature, different methods and criteria for measuring the robustness of a schedule have been proposed, some of which being discussed in the following paragraphs.

Van de Vonder et al. (2006) use the sum of weighted differences between actual and planned process start times based on process durations defined by distribution functions. Policella (2005) inserts time slacks to simulate prolongations of processes. Policella defines a criterion labeled *disruptibility*, which is the sum of the number of changes triggered by a prolongation in relation to the length of the inserted time slack. The smaller the sum, the less processes are disrupted by the considered prolongation. Chanas und Zielinski (2001) define a criticality index based on fuzzy process durations. The index measures the probability for a path to become the critical path.

The above described criteria illustrate that robustness has manifold aspects. The sum of weighted differences between actual and planned start times gives an idea of the reliability of start times, which is important for reliable scheduling, but does not necessarily provide conclusions on deadlines and makespans. The *disruptibility* proposed by Policella reflects the problem of chain reactions caused by the prolongation of one process, but does not give any information about the timely shift caused by the prolongation considered.

Therefore, robustness cannot be assessed by one general criterion; rather, a specific criterion must be defined for a specific aspect of robustness. The criterion, which allows quantifying schedule robustness, can be used to optimize schedule robustness. For example, Seveaux and Sörensen (2002) and Sörensen and Seveaux (2009) use such a criterion as robust evaluation function within a genetic algorithm and apply the optimization algorithm to a single machine problem and a vehicle routing problem. Both problems require the identification of the optimal order of processes without processes running in parallel. However, in construction scheduling the order of processes is mainly predefined and many processes are running in parallel. König (2011) combines three different criteria to assess the robustness of construction schedules calculated by a constraint-based simulation approach. A set of Pareto optimal solutions is determined by applying the evolution strategy optimization technique.

From the different approaches found in the literature, it can be concluded that robust scheduling requires a specific robustness criterion and, depending on the context, a specifically adapted optimization method. Whereas robust scheduling usually searches for the optimal order of processes, the presented work investigates the potential of alternatives of processes and their combinations to improve the robustness of a schedule.

3 Assessment and optimization of construction schedules

This work investigates the assessment and optimization of the robustness of construction schedules. Herein, schedule robustness is defined as insensitiveness of deadlines and makespans against the impact of variable process durations. It is assumed that

(i) the order of tasks is fixed and

(ii) for some tasks there is an option to choose between two or more alternative processes.

The improvement of the robustness is achieved by calculating the most robust combination of processes among the alternative processes. In this study, a model is developed that represents a schedule with alternative processes and variable process durations. Furthermore, a criterion is defined that quantifies the impact of variable process durations on deadlines and makespans. The most robust combination of processes is then determined through an optimization algorithm.

3.1 Modelling a schedule with uncertainties and alternative processes

The schedule is represented by a simple, directed graph

$$G^{task} = (E, T) \tag{1}$$

where the set of vertices E is a set of k events

$$E = \{e_1, e_2, \dots e_k\} \tag{2}$$

and the set of edges T is a set of n tasks

$$T = \{t_1, t_2, \dots t_n\} \tag{3}$$

The tasks describe the process transforming the as-is state, described in the corresponding start event, into a target state, described in the corresponding end event. For a task t_i, two or more alternative processes may exist, resulting in a set of processes P for each task t_i:

$$P(t_i) = \{p_{i1}, p_{i2}, \dots p_{im}\} \tag{4}$$

The graph G^{task} therefore represents a set of graphs $G_j^{process}$

$$G_j^{process} = (E, P(\boldsymbol{c}_j)) \tag{5}$$

where $P(\boldsymbol{c}_j)$ is a set of processes containing one process for each task and therefore representing one possible combination of processes chosen from the sets $P(t_i)$. The vector $\mathbf{c}_j$ includes the indices c_{ij} identifying the specific process $p_{ic_{ij}}$ for each task t_i chosen from its set of alternatives processes $P(t_i)$.

$$\boldsymbol{c}_j = \{c_{1j}, c_{2j}, \dots c_{nj}\}, \quad c_{ij} \in \{1, 2 \dots m\} \tag{6}$$

$$P(\boldsymbol{c}_j) = \{p_{1c_{1j}}, p_{2c_{2j}}, \dots p_{nc_{nj}}\} \tag{7}$$

Assuming that each of the n tasks has m alternative processes, the durations d_{ij} of all processes can be defined in a matrix D.

$$D = \begin{bmatrix} d_{11} & \cdots & d_{1m} \\ \vdots & \ddots & \vdots \\ d_{n1} & \cdots & d_{nm} \end{bmatrix} \tag{8}$$

To take into account uncertainties, all d_{ij} are assumed to be normally distributed random variables. Each edge of a graph $G_j^{process}$ is weighted by the duration of the represented process.

3.2 Assessing the effect of variable process durations

As has been elucidated in the previous section, the consequences of uncertainties in scheduling can be investigated in different respects. In this work, the focus is set on the impact of uncertainties on deadlines and makespans, because due dates are of high economic relevance in construction industry. To assess this effect, the makespan reflecting uncertainties, in the following labeled M^{unc}, is compared with the makespan determined by assuming all input data being deterministic, in the following labeled reference makespan m^{ref}. The reference makespan m^{ref} is a discrete value, determined using process durations discretely defined by their most probable values, that corresponds to the makespan usually calculated in traditional approaches. For the computation of the distribution describing M^{unc}, the model developed in this study considers uncertainties through variable process durations that are defined by normal distributions. The mean value μ of a distribution is set to the most probable value of the process duration. The standard deviation σ, defined by the project manager, reflects the magnitude of the risk of the process duration differing from its estimated value. M^{unc} and m^{ref} are illustrated in **Figure 1**.

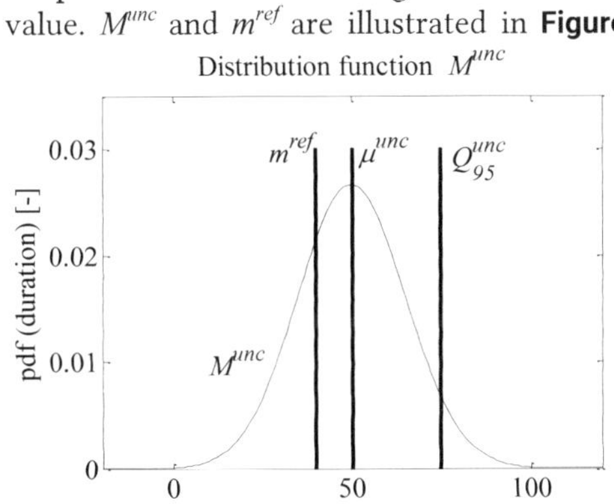

Figure 1: Distribution function of M^{unc}

It should be mentioned that only for schedules with a dominant critical path, the makespan m^{ref} is equal to the mean value μ^{unc} of M^{unc}. As soon as changes in process durations trigger changes of the critical path, μ^{unc} will become larger than m^{ref}. The more susceptible a schedule is for changes in the critical path due to changes in process durations, the larger is the difference between μ^{unc} and m^{ref}, and the less robust is the schedule.

As discussed previously, calculating the makespan of a project based on stochastic process durations is not trivial. Common methods underestimate the mean value μ as well as the standard deviation σ of the distribution describing the makespan. These methods are therefore not appropriate for assessing the effect of uncertainties on the makespan. Hence, in this study a Monte Carlo simulation is used to determine the makespan. By randomly choosing discrete values for any process duration from the corresponding distribution, a certain number of possible scenarios is generated. Each scenario represents a discrete problem, for which the makespan is computed as the length of the longest path in the network plan. From a sufficiently large number of makespans, the distribution of M^{unc} is calculated.

With M^{unc} and m^{ref} being determined, a criterion is defined to relate the value of m^{ref} to the distribution function describing M^{unc}. The coefficient of variance σ^{unc}/μ^{unc} as a common expression of robustness is not suitable, because it would only involve m^{ref} in case m^{ref} is equal to μ^{unc}. As the equality of m^{ref} and μ^{unc} can generally not be expected, the value of the 95% quantile of M^{unc}, Q_{95}^{unc}, is calculated instead. The difference

$$R = Q_{95}^{unc} - m^{ref} \qquad (9)$$

quantifies the schedule robustness, as illustrated in **Figure 1** and serves as the objective function in the optimization process.

3.3 Optimization of schedule robustness

Schedules with alternative processes for a certain number of tasks are optimized with respect to the robustness criterion developed above. Assuming that each of n tasks has m alternative processes results in m^n possible combinations of processes. Although in construction industry it is unrealistic that each task has two or more alternative processes, it would still be too time consuming to compute each possible combination in order to identify the most robust solution. Therefore, an optimization algorithm, more precisely a genetic algorithm, is applied to the problem of identifying the most robust combination of processes. A combination, defined in Eq. 7, contains one process for each task, each process being chosen from the set of alternative processes available for the respective task. The n-dimensional vector $\boldsymbol{c}$ defined in Eq. 6 contains the indices of the chosen processes only. The *i-th* element of $\boldsymbol{c}$ contains the index of the process chosen for task t_i out of its set of alternative processes. In the context of a genetic algorithm, the vector $\boldsymbol{c}$ is an individual, the elements being its genes. A set of these vectors, generated by randomly choosing a process for each task, composes the initial population for the genetic algorithm. During the optimization, the robustness criterion defined in the previous section in Eq. (9) is used to evaluate the fitness of the individuals. The two fittest individuals are taken over to the next generation unchanged. Parents are chosen from the current generation to form the next generation by crossover and mutation processes. The selection of parents is random, but the fitter an individual is, the higher is its chance to be chosen as parent. In the crossover process, the decision, which gene is copied from which parent, is made randomly without changing their order. In the mutation process, the selection of genes that are mutated, is also made randomly. For each individual, the determination of the fitness value requires the computation of m^{ref} and M^{unc} involving a Monte Carlo simulation for the calculation of M^{unc}.

Due to the characteristic of the problem, there can be several combinations of processes with rather similar robustness. Only the processes lying on the critical path affect the makespan and thus the robustness defined by the chosen criterion. However, vice versa it cannot be concluded that all processes not lying on a critical path can be exchanged by their alternative processes without changing the robustness, because processes, which have not been critical earlier, may become critical after change. Nevertheless, there might be certain constellations of processes, which result for some processes in a very low probability of lying on the critical path and influencing the robustness, regardless of the alternative processes chosen. As a consequence, consecutive optimization runs can result in different solutions with very similar fitness values. A set of these solutions can be determined through a repetitive application of the optimization algorithm when excluding in each run the solutions identified in the previous optimization runs.

4 Case study

To validate the method proposed in this work, several network plans have been tested within a case study. In the network plans, the order of tasks is predefined. For each task, alternative processes are available. The most robust combination of processes with respect to the robustness criterion defined in the previous section is identified. In this case study, the following simplifications are made:

(i) the processes are assumed to be independent,
(ii) the process durations are normally distributed, and
(iii) each task has two alternative processes.

Exemplarily, a network plan consisting of a set of tasks $T = \{t_1,..., t_{12}\}$ and a set of events $E = \{e_1,..., e_9\}$ is shown in Figure 2.

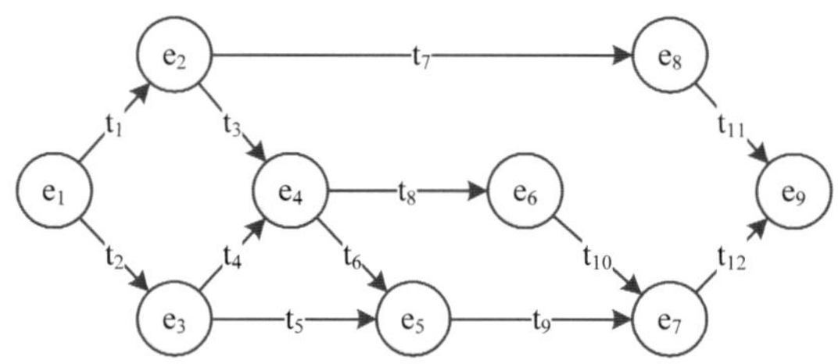

Figure 2: Example network plan

In the given example, only two different distribution functions are provided for a total of 24 different processes. All processes p_{i1} have a distribution function defined by μ_1 and σ_1, and all processes p_{i2} have a distribution function defined by μ_2 and σ_2, respectively. The values are given in **Table 1**. With $\sigma_2 < \sigma_1$, all p_{i2} are more robust than all p_{i1}. The characteristics of the processes have been kept simple to demonstrate the importance of investigating not the robustness of separate processes but of their combination in the context of the considered schedule.

Table 1: Mean values and standard deviations of process durations

	Task	t_1	t_2	....	t_{12}
P_{i1}	μ_1 in days	50	50	50	50
	σ_1 in days	12	12	12	12
P_{i2}	μ_2 in days	80	80	80	80
	σ_2 in days	8	8	8	8

Random combinations of processes are generated by randomly choosing one of the two alternative processes for each task. As described in the previous section, each combination is decoded by a vector. A set of such vectors defines the initial population for the genetic algorithm. As can be seen from the diagram in **Figure 3**, the genetic algorithm rather quickly reduces the value of the cost function.

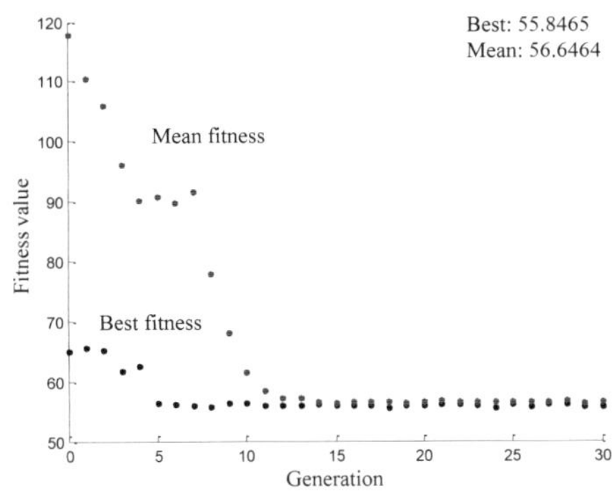

Figure 3: Development of best and mean fitness value over number of generations

The best solution found for the example shown in Figure 2 is given by the vector $\boldsymbol{c}$ = (1, 2, 1, 1, 2, 1, 1, 1, 2, 1, 2, 2, 2), denoting that for the tasks t_1, t_3, t_4, t_6, t_7, t_8 and t_{10} processes p_{i1} are chosen, and that for the tasks t_2, t_5, t_9, t_{11} and t_{12} processes p_{i2} are chosen. The fitness value of the solution is 56 days, the reference makespan m^{ref} = 320 days, the mean value μ^{unc} = 343 days, and the standard deviation σ^{unc} = 20 days. In **Figure 4**, the probability density functions of M^{unc}, gained from Monte Carlo simulations, are depicted for three different combinations and the values m^{ref}, μ^{unc} and $Q_{95}{}^{unc}$ are highlighted. The first two combinations are calculated choosing for all processes the variant p_{i1}, p_{i2} respectively. The third combination is the most robust solution found by the described algorithm.

As discussed in the previous section, the defined robustness criterion takes into account the susceptibility of the schedule for changes in the critical path reflected by the difference between m^{ref} and μ^{unc}. The effect can be seen in the result, as the most robust combination is not generated by simply choosing for each task the most robust process from its set of alternative processes – in the example, this would be p_{i2} for all tasks, because all p_{i2} have a smaller standard deviation than their related p_{i1}.

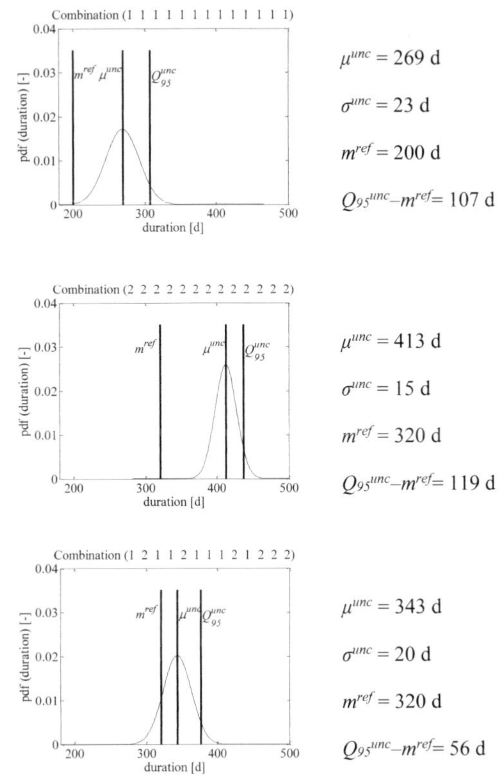

Figure 4: Results for three different combinations

In summary, the optimization algorithm with the defined criterion leads to the desired result. It identifies the combination of processes whose stochastically determined makespan shows the smallest deviation from the deterministically determined makespan.

5 Conclusions and outlook

The paper has discussed the effects of uncertainties inherent in input data of construction schedules. A model, which takes into account uncertainties as well as alternative processes, has been developed as a basis for optimizing the schedule robustness by determining the most robust combination of alternative processes. By describing the process durations with distribution functions instead of discrete values, the uncertainties inherent in the input data are considered. For the determination of a project makespan based on stochastic process durations, a Monte Carlo simulation has been used. To assess the robustness, a criterion has been defined, which compares the makespan considering uncertainties with the makespan assuming deterministic process durations. With a genetic algorithm, the most robust combination of alternative processes could be determined, as shown in a case study.

In conclusion, the case study has demonstrated the effectiveness of the proposed method. In future work, the method may be extended towards more general cases. Furthermore, the effect of correlations of processes as well as the effect of different stochastic distributions may be investigated. Additional attention should also be paid to the total length of the planned makespan m^{ref}, aiming at a reasonable trade-off between minimizing m^{ref} and maximizing the schedule robustness, because both criteria may be in conflict.

Acknowledgements

This work has been funded by the *Thüringer Graduiertenförderung*, a program of the Free State of Thuringia, Germany, supporting graduate students.

References

Besner, C. & Hobbs, B. (2008). Project Management Practice, Generic or Contextual: A Reality Check. *Project Management Journal*. 39(1). pp. 16-33.

Chanas, S. & Zielinski, P. (2001). Critical path analysis in the network with fuzzy activity times. *Fuzzy Sets and Systems*. 122. pp. 195-204.

Dubois, D. & Prade, H. (1978). Operations on fuzzy numbers. *International Journal for System Sciences*. 9. pp. 613-626.

Herroelen, W. & Leus, R. (2005). Project Scheduling Under Uncertainty. Survey and Research Potential. *European Journal of Operational Research*. 165(2). pp. 289-306.

Hsiau, H.J. & Lin, C.W. (2009). A fuzzy pert approach to evaluate plant construction project scheduling risk under uncertain resource capacity. *Journal of Industrial Engineering and Management*. 2(1). pp. 31-47.

König, M. (2011). Generation of robust construction schedules using evolution strategies. *Proceedings of the 2011 eg-ice Workshop*. University of Twente, Twente, The Netherlans, July 6th-8th 2011.

Liu, Z. & Sanlaville, E. (1997). Stochastic Scheduling with Variable Profile and Precedence Constraints. *SIAM Journal of Computing*. 26(1). pp. 173-187.

Lootsma, F.A. (1989). Stochastic and fuzzy PERT. *European Journal of Operational Research*. 43. pp. 174-183.

Malcolm, D.G., Roseboom, J.H., Clark, C.E. and Fazar, W. (1959). Application of a technique for research and development program evaluation. *Operations Research*. 7. pp. 646-669.

Policella, N. (2005). Scheduling with Uncertainty - A Proactive Approach using Partial Order Schedules. Ph. D. Thesis. Rome, Italy: Università degli Studi di Roma La Sapienza.

Seveaux, M. & Sörensen, K. (2002). A genetic algorithm for robust schedules in a just-in-time environment. Research Report LAMIH/SP-2003-1. University of Valenciennes, France.

Sörensen, K. (2001). Tabu Searching for Robust Solutions. *4th Metaheuristics International Conference*. Porto, Portugal, July 16th 2001.

Sörensen, K. & Seveaux, M. (2009). A practical approach for robust and flexible vehicle routing using metaheuristics and Monte Carlos sampling. *Journal of Mathematical Modelling and Algorithms*. 8(4). pp. 387-407.

Stork F., 2001. Stochastic resource-constrained project scheduling. Ph.D. Thesis. Berlin, Germany: Technische Universität Berlin.

Van de Vonder, S., Ballestin, F., Demeulemeester, E. & Herroelen, W. (2007). Heuristic procedures for reactive project scheduling. *Computers and Industrial Engineering*. 52(1). pp. 11-18.

Winch, G.M. & Kelsey, J. (2005). What do construction project planners do? *International Journal of Project Management*. 23(2). pp. 141-149.

Zadeh, L.A. (1965). Fuzzy sets. *Information and Control*. 8. pp. 338-353.

Definition of views to generate, visualize, and evaluate multi-view space models of schematic building designs

Georg Suter, georg.suter@tuwien.ac.at
Design Computing Group, Center for Geometry and Computational Design, TU Wien, Vienna, Austria

Abstract

Modeling of spaces is a relevant aspect of architectural and building services design. A particular challenge concerns the modeling of multiple, domain-specific space views. While existing building information modeling (BIM) systems provide basic space modeling capabilities, computational support for modeling multiple space views is limited. In previous work, a space modeling system has been developed by the author that generates multi-view space models from space data created in a BIM system. A multi-view space model consists of one or more space layouts. Each layout has a spatial relation network (SRN) which may be visualized to reveal a layout's spatial structure. Moreover, designers may evaluate the spatial performance of a layout based on SRN metrics. Evaluation examples include determining walking distances between spaces, or access of spaces to natural light. In this paper, a set of space views are defined that appear useful to generate, visualize, and evaluate multi-view space models of schematic building designs. Each view corresponds to an operation sequence that is processed to derive a view-specific layout from a given source layout. Views cover aspects of architectural, pedestrian circulation, natural lighting, natural ventilation, and functional organization domains. The application potential of these views is demonstrated with a housing design example.

Keywords: Building information modeling, Space modeling, Collaborative design

1 Introduction

Supporting effective information sharing and decision making in multi-disciplinary design teams remains a significant challenge in building information modeling (BIM). According to a survey, improved interoperability and functionality are seen by practitioners as critical for increased benefits from BIM (Bernstein 2012, p.22). In construction projects, multiple partial building models must be maintained that correspond to domain-specific views and are consistent with each other (see, for example, Nederveen 1992; Rosenman and Gero 1996). Modeling multiple views of spaces is a sub-problem of this general problem. Space modeling is a relevant aspect of architectural and building services design. This is because indoor activities of users are enabled by spaces that must be configured and conditioned to ensure user comfort as well as security and safety. Consequently, architectural and building services designers model domain-specific spaces and objects. For example, a lighting designer may model spaces that correspond to rooms, as well as windows and luminaires. Moreover, partial spaces near luminaires or windows may need to be included. Conversely, a heating, ventilation, and air conditioning system designer may group rooms with similar orientation, function, or indoor climate requirements into larger thermal zones.

2 Related work

Several view definition methods exist for the Industry Foundation Classes (IFC) model. An IFC model view definition is a subset of the original IFC schema that is relevant for specific applications and life-cycle phases (BuildingSmart 2013a). The IFC Coordination View defines a view for architectural, mechanical, and structural design coordination

(BuildingSmart 2013b). Weise et al. (2003) describe a schema for the definition of arbitrary IFC model views. Objects may be selected from an original model by user-defined filters. Unnecessary attributes or object references may be removed from the model based on a static model view. Existing model view definition methods as well as building model query languages (Adachi 2002; You 2004, Borrmann and Rank 2009a; Eurostep 2013; Mazairac and Beetz 2013) are general purpose and flexible. However, their support for building model transformation operations is currently limited (Eastman and Siabiris 1995; Fischer et al. 1998). In space modeling, an example for a desirable model transformation operation is the merging of sets of adjacent rooms with the same function into larger zones.

Modeling of domain-specific space views has been explored, for example, in evacuation code checking (Lee et al. 2010; Choi et al. 2014). The BERA language provides high-level constructs to check building models against pedestrian circulation or space requirements (Lee 2011). Views may include space groups or paths of connected spaces. Pedestrian circulation networks are generated automatically from door, vertical access, and concave points that lie on buffered space boundary polygons. The latter are offset from space boundaries towards space interiors. The extension of these space views beyond specific domains is currently an unresolved issue.

3 System overview

A space modeling system has been developed by the author in previous work that supports the generation, visualization, and spatial evaluation of multi-view space models of schematic building designs (Suter 2013, Suter et al. 2014). A multi-view space model consists of one or more space layouts, where each layout models a specific space view. Each layout has a spatial relation network (SRN), in which selected spatial relations between objects are explicitly modeled. The adjacency relation between spaces and the enclosure relation between physical objects (such as windows or walls) and spaces are examples for relations that are modeled in an SRN. Visualizations of SRNs reveal the spatial structure of layouts to designers. Spatial evaluation of layouts is based on SRN metrics. As an example for spatial evaluation supported by the system, a designer may estimate walking distances from spaces to their nearest building exit in a layout that models a pedestrian circulation view. Similarly, he may determine the number of unlit spaces in a layout that models a natural lighting view.

The workflow in the space modeling system involves three steps. At first, a designer creates one or more source layouts in an existing BIM system (Autodesk 2011). In the second step, source layouts and view definitions are passed to the system to generate a multi-view space model. In the third step, the generated space model is visualized in the BIM system, and the designer evaluates its spatial performance based on SRN metrics.

4 Space view definition method

Views are defined in the space modeling system by layout operation expressions. Fundamental operations on space layouts have been introduced in previous work (Suter 2014). Examples include selection, aggregation, and decomposition operations In each operation, objects in a layout, such as spaces, doors, or windows, may be inserted, removed, or modified. Operations may be composed into expressions to achieve elaborate layout transformations. Selection, aggregation, and update operations are used to define views that are described in Section 5. Whereas selection and aggregation determine the structure of generated layouts, updates are relevant in particular for visualization and evaluation. These operations are briefly reviewed in the following; for detailed descriptions see (Suter 2014).

In the *select* operation, objects are selected from an argument layout based on a given filter on object attributes. In the *aggregate* operation, spaces in an argument layout that belong to the same group of spaces, as defined by a given grouping criterion, and are connected in a subnetwork of the SRN, as defined by a given SRN filter, are merged into larger spaces. For example, spaces that have the same function (grouping criterion) and are connected in an argument layout's space adjacency network (SRN filter) may be merged. Objects in the argument layout that are contained in or enclose merged spaces are also included in a result layout. In both *select* and *aggregate* operations, the SRNs of result layouts are derived automatically by geometric and solid model processing (Suter 2013).

The $update_{degree}$ operation derives the *degree* attribute of objects based on a given SRN filter. Objects that pass the SRN filter are updated. The degree of an object corresponds to the number of incident spatial relation edges that pass the filter.

For example, the number of windows in each space in an argument layout may be determined with $update_{degree}$ based on the space enclosure network whose nodes are restricted to spaces and windows (SRN filter). The number of windows that enclose a space correspond to the space's degree.

The $update_{distance\_nearest}$ operation derives the *distance* attribute of objects based on given source object, destination object, and SRN filters. The distance of each object that passes the source object filter is updated. It corresponds to the shortest path to the nearest object that passes the destination object filter. Only those nodes and edges in an argument layout's SRN are considered to determine shortest paths that pass the SRN filter. For example, distances of all spaces (source object filter) in an argument layout may be updated with respect to external spaces (destination object filter) and the space adjacency network (SRN filter).

The $update_{distance\_must\_pass}$ operation is similar to $update_{distance\_nearest}$. In this operation *distance* attributes of must-pass objects, which are specified by a must-pass filter, are updated. An object's distance corresponds to the shortest path between the nearest source and nearest destination object (both chosen from source and destination object sets, as specified by respective filters) that passes through the must-pass object. For example, distances of all internal spaces (must-pass object filter) in an argument layout may be updated with respect to external spaces (source and destination object filters) and the space adjacency network (SRN filter).

5 Views

5.1 Introduction

Views presented in this section cover architectural, pedestrian circulation, natural lighting, natural ventilation, and functional organization domains. The generation, visualization, and evaluation of space models that are based on these views is illustrated with a housing design by Kaden Klingbeil Architects (Heckmann 2011). Housing has rich spatial requirements, which are already evident in small floor plans.

Layouts that model targeted views are generated from a single source layout (Figure 1, 2a). The example features an apartment that is accessed from a detached stair case and an elevator. The source layout includes spaces and physical objects, such as windows, openings, and furnishing elements. Walls are not modeled since they are not required by targeted views. Windows or doors may exist without related walls to ensure modeling flexibility. The distinction of external and internal spaces is critical for most views. Therefore external spaces are modeled explicitly. The source layout does not have an SRN. This minimizes data entry by designers in the BIM system. SRNs are derived automatically for each generated layout (Figure 2b, 3).

5.2 'Architectural' view

Spaces and architectural objects, such as windows or furnishing elements, are selected from the source layout for this view (Figure 2b). The view is defined in Table 1 together with other views. Each object has a property set which carries required properties for view generation. Space connectivity is evaluated in the 'Architectural' view based on the space enclosure network and the *degree* attribute. A text-based summary of respective attribute and network metrics complements the layout visualization in Figure 2b.

In the example, the living room is the space with maximum degree 9. On average, the degree of spaces is 2.7. That is, the connectivity of other spaces is significantly lower than the living room's connectivity. Two duct spaces have minimum degree 0. They are individual, disconnected components in the space enclosure network.

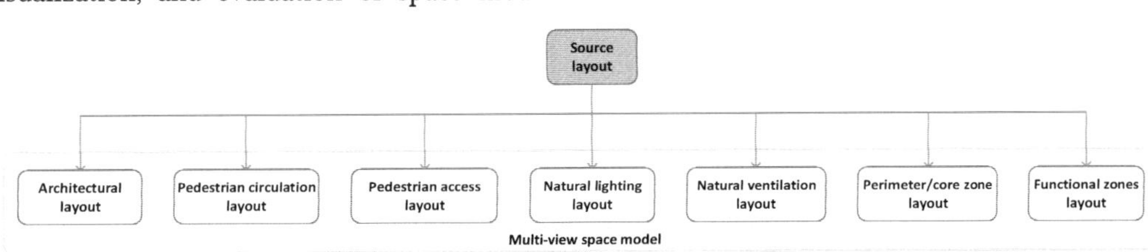

Figure 1 Multi-view space model generated from a source layout. Each targeted view is modeled by a space layout. Views are defined in Table 1.

5.3 'Pedestrian Circulation' view

Spaces and objects that enable pedestrian circulation, such as doors or openings, are selected from the source layout (Figure 3a, Table 1). Walking distances are estimated and evaluated in this view. This is done by determining distances from spaces to their nearest unit doors based on the space enclosure network. A unit door controls access to spaces in a unit (e.g. spaces in an apartment or a group of office spaces) from a circulation space (e.g. hallway or stair case).

The apartment entrance door is the only unit door in the example. Path weight is used as a distance metric. Weights of edges in an SRN correspond to the Euclidean distance between related nodes. Space nodes are located at the centroid of space volumes. The maximum distance is 12.48m from the bathroom to the unit door. There are no cycles in the space enclosure network. The entrance and the living room control access to bedrooms and service rooms. Such non-cyclical space access structures are common for spaces with private functions (Steadman 1983, Hillier 1989). Duct spaces are selected from the source layout but are inaccessible.

5.4 'Pedestrian Access Zones' view

Spaces and pedestrian circulation objects are selected from the source layout (Figure 3b, Table 1). Spaces are merged into access zones. Classification of access systems according to the number of units served by main circulation spaces, which include stair cases and shared hallways, is supported by this view.

In the example, a main circulation zone is generated by merging stair case, elevator, and other external circulation spaces, and an apartment zone by merging all accessible spaces in the apartment. Both zones are (partially) enclosed by the unit door. Access system classification is done based on the space enclosure network and the *degree* attributes of main circulation zones. In the example, this zone has degree 1, and hence the access system is single-loaded.

5.5 'Natural Lighting' view

Spaces and objects that transmit light are selected from the source layout (Figure 3c, Table 1). Access to daylight is evaluated in this view. This is done by determining the distance of internal spaces to the nearest external spaces based on the space enclosure network. Path length (that is, the number of edges in a path) is used as a distance metric. Spaces with distance 2 have direct access to natural light, whereas those with distance greater than 2 receive indirect natural light via other spaces.

In the example, spaces have either direct or no access to natural light. The space enclosure network has seven components. Five spaces, including a bathroom and a laundry room, are disconnected and hence are not lit naturally. There are two components with, respectively, three and four internal spaces. From this follows that each group of spaces receives natural light from different external spaces (that is, street and courtyard spaces).

5.6 'Natural Ventilation' view

Spaces and objects that transmit air are selected from the source layout (Figure 3d, Table 1). Natural ventilation potential is evaluated. This is done by determining must-pass distances of internal spaces based on the space enclosure network. External spaces are source and destination spaces of shortest paths that pass through internal spaces. Path weight is used as a distance metric. The first and last edge in a path is

Table 1 View definitions.

View	Operation	Filter
Architectural (Fig. 2b)	$select$	Spaces and objects o where $architectural \in o.property\_set$
	$update_{degree}$	Network: space enclosure relation
Pedestrian Circulation (Fig. 3a)	$select$	Spaces and objects o where $pedestrian\_circulation \in o.property\_set$
	$update_{distance\_nearest}$	Source nodes: spaces; Destination nodes: objects o where $unit\_door \in o.property\_set$; Network: space enclosure relation; Distance metric: path weight
Pedestrian Access Zones (Fig. 3b)	$select$	See 'Pedestrian Circulation' view
	$aggregate$	Grouping criterion: none; Network: space enclosure relation except objects o where $(unit\_door \vee building\_entrance) \in o.property\_set$,
	$select$	Objects o where $unit\_door \in o.property\_set$
	$update_{degree}$	Network: space enclosure relation
Natural Lighting (Fig. 3c)	$select$	Spaces and objects o where $transmits\_light \in o.property\_set$
	$update_{distance\_nearest}$	Source nodes: spaces; Destination nodes: spaces s where $external \in s.property\_set$; Network: space enclosure relation; Distance metric: path length
Natural Ventilation (Fig. 3d)	$select$	Spaces and objects o where $transmits\_air \in o.property\_set$
	$update_{distance\_must\_pass}$	Must-pass nodes: spaces s where $internal \in s.property\_set$; Source/destination nodes: spaces s where $external \in s.property\_set$; Network: space enclosure relation; Distance metric: path weight
Perimeter/Core Zones (Fig. 3e)	$select$	See 'Architectural' view
	$update_{distance\_nearest}$	Source nodes: spaces; Destination nodes: spaces s where $external \in s.property\_set$; Network: space adjacency relation; Distance metric: path length
	$aggregate$	Grouping criterion: same $distance$; Network: space adjacency relation
Functional Zones (Fig. 3f)	$select$	See 'Architectural' view
	$aggregate$	Grouping criterion: $property\_set$ includes same items from $(hallway, hallway\_unit, bedroom, service\_space, elevator, external)$; Network: space adjacency relation
	$update_{distance\_must\_pass}$	See 'Natural Ventilation' view, except Distance metric: path length

Figure 2 a) Source layout of the housing design example. b) 'Architectural' view. Non-shaded spaces are external spaces.

ignored to determine distances. This is because these edges enclose external spaces. Shorter paths are associated with higher natural ventilation potential than longer ones.

In the example, the space with the minimum must-pass distance of 4.88m is the only space which is oriented to two different external spaces. Cross ventilation may be feasible in this space. The laundry room has the maximum must-pass distance of 21.26m. In this room as well as the bathroom, two edges are traversed twice to derive the shortest path. Natural ventilation potential of these spaces appears limited. Must-pass distances for the other spaces are between 10.58 and 13.13m.

5.7 'Perimeter/Core Zones' view

Spaces and architectural objects are selected from the source layout (Figure 3e, Table 1). Perimeter and core zones are distinguished in this view. A perimeter zone is adjacent to an external zone. Conversely, a core zone is adjacent to a perimeter zone or another perimeter zone. This distinction is relevant e.g. for lighting, air circulation, and thermal design. For example, core zones may need to be lit artificially. Perimeter and core zones are generated by merging spaces with the same distance to the nearest external space based on the space adjacency network. Path length is used as a distance metric. Spaces with distance 1 are perimeter zones, while spaces with distance 2 or greater are core zones.

In the example, the perimeter/core zone structure is shallow because the maximum distance (or depth) is 2. Deeper core zones with distance 3 or greater are common in spatially complex housing plans. Core zones in the example are small, with their combined areas making up only 7.3% of the gross area of internal spaces.

5.8 'Functional Zones' view

Spaces and architectural objects are selected from the source layout (Figure 3f, Table 1). Spaces that are connected in the space adjacency network and have similar functional properties are merged into zones. For example, bedrooms are merged into bedroom zones, or bathrooms and storage spaces into service zones. The orientation of functional zones to external spaces is determined based on the space enclosure network. Orientation affects, among other things, views or solar gains. Orientation is inferred from must-pass distances, which are computed similar to those in the 'Natural Ventilation' view (Section 5.6), except that path length is used as distance metric. Zones with must-pass distance 2 are oriented to at least two external spaces. Zones with must-pass distance 4 are oriented to one external space. Zones with must-pass distance of 6 or greater may be either core zones or perimeter zones that are oriented to a single external space. The distinction of perimeter and core zones in turn is based on the distance to nearest external spaces (Section 5.7).

Figure 3 Views of the source layout. Text summaries include object (element) and spatial relation network properties/metrics. a) 'Pedestrian Circulation' view. b) 'Pedestrian Access Zones' view. c) 'Natural Lighting' view. d) 'Natural Ventilation' view. e) 'Perimeter/Core Zones' view. f) 'Functional Zones' view.

In the example, there is a zone that consists of a single space and is oriented to two external spaces. Internal unit circulation, bedroom and service zones are oriented to, respectively, the courtyard and the street. Must-pass distances of elevator and duct spaces are undefined. Hence their orientation may not be determined by this metric.

6 Discussion

Results from the housing design example suggest that spatial evaluation enabled by these views supports the detection of design issues in multiple domains. In the housing example, spatial evaluation revealed, for instance, that certain service rooms have a lack of daylighting and limited natural ventilation potential. Moreover, detailed distance metrics e.g. for pedestrian circulation and natural ventilation are available to support design evaluation. Classification of spaces as perimeter or core spaces, or as naturally lit is straightforward and may be done either automatically or by inspection of SRN network visualizations by designers. This may be particularly useful in large and spatially complex designs in which the manual identification of design issues and space classification is more time-consuming and prone to errors.

Multi-view space models and their spatial evaluation, as described in this paper, may complement existing performance simulation tools in two ways. First, certain views could be reused as input data for specialized simulation tools with more detailed analysis capabilities. For example, the 'Natural ventilation' view includes an SRN that could be used for multi-zone air flow analysis (Feustel 1999). Second, multi-view space models could be used to locate problematic areas, rooms or zones in a design that may be examined subsequently in more detail with dedicated physical simulation tools e.g. for lighting, energy, and air flow analysis. As the preparation of input models for physical simulations is time-consuming, it is common to limit the scope for analysis to typical floors, spaces, or construction details.

The housing design example is an initial test to explore the application potential of presented views and spatial evaluation metrics. Further tests with larger and different types of buildings are necessary. As mentioned in Section 5.8, certain update operations could be reused for spatial evaluation in other views. For example, the method for determining the orientation of functional zones may be applied to spaces in 'Architectural' or 'Natural ventilation' views. It is desirable to define additional, possibly more specialized views. Fire or thermal zone views are examples of such views. Shading or artificial lighting views could extend or complement the 'Natural Lighting' view. Such views could be useful in the design of lighting automation systems e.g. in office buildings (Suter et al. 2012).

The current implementation of the spatial evaluation method is limited in important ways. For example, in case of concave space volumes, space nodes may not lie on the volume interior. Consequently, distance estimates (e.g. of walking distances) may be incorrect because obstructing space boundaries are not considered. As a workaround, such spaces may be decomposed into smaller convex spaces that are connected by openings. However, this requires additional modeling effort by users. Instead, it is preferable for the space modeling system to generate these spaces and openings automatically.

7 Conclusion

This paper has shown how multi-view space models of schematic building designs may be generated, visualized, and evaluated based on a set of formally defined views. These views may be modified and extended to address spatial evaluation needs of other and more specific domains.

Reuse of existing space data will be essential to achieve seamless integration with designers' existing workflows across BIM platforms. Therefore the exchange of multi-view space model data to and from IFC is an important area of future work.

An interesting empirical research issue concerns the correlation of spatial evaluation metrics with results from physical performance simulation tools. This would require the compilation of possibly large building repositories for benchmarking and comparative analysis. Such repositories would facilitate a more systematic assessment of the utility of views and spatial evaluation metrics presented in this paper.

References

Adachi, Y. (2002), Overview of partial model query language, Technical report, SECOM Co.
Autodesk, Inc. (2011), 'AutoCAD Architecture 2012 user's guide'. [Accessed 20 January

2015]. URL: http://www.autodesk.com
Bernstein, H., Jones, S., Russo, M., Laquidara-Carr, D. & Fitch, E. (2012), 'The business value of BIM in North America', Smart Markets Report, McGraw-Hill Construction.
Borrmann, A. & Rank, E. (2009), 'Topological analysis of 3d building models using a spatial query language', Adv. Eng. Inform. 23(4), 370–385.
buildingSMART International (2013a), 'Coordination View Version 2.0'. [Accessed 18 October 2013]. URL: http://www.buildingsmart-tech.org/specifications/ifc-view-definition/coordinationview-v2.0
buildingSMART International (2013b), 'MVD process'. [Accessed 20 October 2013]. URL: http://www.buildingsmart.org/standards/mvd/mvd-process
Choi, J., Choi, J. & Kim, I. (2014), 'Development of BIM-based evacuation regulation checking system for high-rise and complex buildings', Automation in Construction 46, 38 – 49.
Eastman, C. & Siabiris, A. (1995), 'A generic building product model incorporating building type information', Automation in Construction 3 (1), 283–304.
Eurostep (2013), 'Product model query language'. URL: http://www.eurostep.com/products/share-a-space-features.aspx
Feustel H.E. (1999), COMIS—an international multizone air-flow and contaminant transport model, Energy and Buildings, 30(1):3–18.
Fischer, M., Aalami, F. & Akbas, R. (1998), Formalizing product model transformations: Case examples and applications, in 'Artificial Intelligence in Structural Engineering, Information Technology for Design, Collaboration, Maintenance, and Monitoring.', pp. 113–132.
Heckmann, O. & Schneider, F. (2011), Grundrissatlas Wohnungsbau, 4th edn, Birkhäuser, Basel, Switzerland.
Hillier, B. & Hanson, J. (1989), The Social Logic of Space, Cambridge University Press.
Lee, J. (2011), Building Environment Rule and Analysis (BERA) Language And its Application for Evaluating Building Circulation and Spatial Program, PhD thesis, Georgia Institute of Technology.
Lee, J., Eastman, C., Lee, J., Kannala, M. & Jeong, Y. (2010), 'Computing walking distances within buildings using the universal circulation network', Environment and Planning B 37(4), 628 – 645.
Mazairac, W. & Beetz, J. (2013), 'BIMQL - an open query language for building information models', Advanced Engineering Informatics 27(4), 444–456.
Rosenman, M. & Gero, J. (1996), 'Modelling multiple views of design objects in a collaborative environment', Computer-Aided Design 28(3), 193–205.
Steadman, P. (1983), Architectural morphology, Pion.
Suter, G. (2013), 'Structure and spatial consistency of network-based space layouts for building and product design', Computer-Aided Design 45(8 - 9), 1108 – 1127.
Suter, G., Petrushevski, F. & Sipetic, M. (2012), A space model for personal lighting control, in '12th Conference on Construction Applications of Virtual Reality', National Taiwan University, Taipei, Taiwan.
Suter, G., Petrushevski, F. & Sipetic,M. (2014), 'Operations on network-based space layouts for modeling multiple space views of buildings', Advanced Engineering Informatics 28(4), 395 – 411.
van Nederveen, G. & Tolman, F. (1992), 'Modelling multiple views on buildings', Automation in Construction 1(3), 215–224

Conflict Analysis Using BIM Tools

Alcinia Z. Sampaio, zita.sampaio@tecnico.ulisboa.pt
Dep. Civil Engineering and Architecture, University of Lisbon, Lisbon, Portugal

Edgar Berdeja, edberdeja@sapo.pt
Dep. Civil Engineering and Architecture, University of Lisbon, Lisbon, Portugal

Abstract

The development of a building design requires the participation of several parties involved in different disciplines, where each discipline conducts its own project in a somewhat disconnected manner from the remaining, therefore requiring project compatibility. In this context, an efficient conflict analysis between disciplines is essential to guarantee a well-developed design. The Building Information Modelling (BIM) methodology and tools associated with it present themselves as an excellent asset to support the process of conflict analysis, as they make it possible to merge all disciplines in an integrated virtual environment. The high level of detail and visualization provided by a BIM model leads to better collaboration between those involved throughout the design, hence resulting in a significant reduction of potential errors during the construction phase. The aim of the present study was to evaluate the practical capabilities of the BIM concept in the conflict analysis between building services, namely, the water supply and drainage systems design, and the architectural and structural design. As such, it was case study the development of an architectural, structural and building service (Mechanical, Electrical and Plumbing, MEP) BIM models and their subsequent conciliation and clash detection. In this work, commercial software such as Revit 2014, Tekla BIMsight and Navisworks Manage were used, the latter two providing features for automatic collision detection. This work contributes to demonstrate the advantages of BIM in the conciliation and coordination between different specialties, as well as the benefits of its application in conflict analysis in an engineering design.

Keywords: BIM methodology; BIM software; MEP; Clash detection; Conflict analysis.

1 Introduction

Jung and Joo (2010) claims Building Information Modelling (BIM) as the process of generating, storing, managing, exchanging, and sharing building information in an interoperable and reusable way. In addition, Kymmell (2008) defines Building Information Model (BIM) as a virtual representation of a building, containing all the necessary information for its construction, supported by the use of the appropriate hardware and software. Similarly, Ju and Seo (2012) describes BIM as a technology supported in BIM based tools that allows the user to go beyond the geometrical representation, placing him in a simulated construction process, that is, the development of a prototype of the final product. These three main concepts together complement each other: process, model and tools. Remarking this notion Barlish and Sullivan refer that for some stakeholders, BIM is a software application; for others it is a process for designing and documenting building information; for others it is a whole new approach to practice and advancing the profession which requires the implementation of new policies, contracts and relationships amongst project stakeholders. Following this last aspect Gu and London (2010) increments these topics with the need of changing the mentality of people involved, to position BIM adoption in terms of current status and expectations across disciplines. Both technical and non-technical issues that need consideration on the implementation of BIM and they also suggest that there are varying levels of adoption and therefore the need for a specific tool to facilitate BIM adoption.

Although BIM implementation requires profound process changes of the involved parties, the benefits in new construction projects both of private and institutional owners are manifold and often confirmed by involved stakeholders (Zhanga and Hub, 2011). This integration is not so apparent in current building projects, where designers start employing advanced visualization and modelling technologies only at the very late design stages and consequently the design knowledge is mainly not captured (and lost) during early conceptual phase, where the most vital decisions are made (Abrishami et al., 2014). Major benefits consist in design consistency and improved stakeholder collaboration. In addition, professional and educational institutions have started to adopt BIM software tools and adapt their existing delivery systems to satisfy evolving market requirements (Succar and Sher, 2013). In a school context the development of research works as described here, contribute to improve student skills and better prepare them to their future challenges as civil engineers. Teaching BIM issue in technical schools is then a very important way of disseminate BIM in the AEC industry.

Volk et al. (2013) mention that BIM can be seen from a narrow perspective, comprising solely the digital building model itself in the sense of a central information management hub or repository, and its model creation issues, and from a broader sense, concerning interrelated functional, informational, technical and organizational/legal issues. Therefore, two types of expert software might interact with a BIM model: data input applications providing services of import, data capture and monitoring, data processing or transformation of captured data into BIM or data output applications providing reports or technical analyses such as structural and energy analyses or clash detections. Currently, major research trends focused on the improvement of preplanning and design, clash detection, visualization, quantification, costing and data management. The aim of this paper concerns the use of BIM software capacities on the analyses of clash detection.

The manuscript presents a section concerning BIM/MEP issue. It is followed by the generation of the architectural and structural components of the BIM model. The MEP component is then created over the architectural part. For the analyses of conflicts between elements three distinct software of collision analyses capacity were applied. Finally some conclusions and recommendations are then carried out.

2 BIM/MEP Design

As conducted in the field of construction, the utilization of BIM is becoming a hot issue for many public work projects (Ju and Seo, 2012). Resource scarcity, sustainability challenges and stricter decrees for recycling and resource efficiency in buildings motivate the Architecture, Engineering and Construction industry (AEC), and also Facility Management (FM) to manage resources efficiently. Development of 3D modeling started in the 1970s, based on the early computer-aided design (CAD) efforts in several industries (Jung and Joo, 2010). BIM modeling was introduced in pilot projects in the early 2000s to support building design of architects and engineers. The focus of contemporary AEC design projects is increasingly moving from an architecture with aesthetical emphasis towards performance (structure, construction, environment, socio-economically and cultural, etc.) based architecture. This shift in design attitude is inviting architecture to adopt new technologies that can support this transition. The AEC designers started adopting technology from industrial design, mechanical engineering and product developments, where performance tends to play a crucial role, as well as adopting new computational design methods such as parametric approach and topological space are also being engaged (Abrishami et al., 2014).

BIM requires the development and use of a computer generated model to simulate the planning, design, construction and operational phases of a project. BIM user finds many benefits and resource savings during design, planning, and construction of new buildings (Eadie et al., 2014). However, Ju and Seo (2012) examined the BIM technology regarding its application and find that BIM data in each construction stage, lack of cooperative system, insufficient standard library and guideline. Actually BIM developments suggest that not only is it useful for geometric modelling of a building's performance but also that it can assist in the management of the integration of several components in a building design placed in a unique virtual building model. Following this many industries developed integrated analysis tools and object-based parametric modeling, being the basic concept of BIM. Consequently, major research trends focused on the improvement of preplanning and design, clash detection, visualization, quantification, costing and data management (Porwal and Hewage, 2012)

Coordination of Mechanical, Electrical and Plumbing (MEP) systems is a huge challenge for many technical projects. The use of BIM tools and processes promises to address the challenges of the MEP coordination process. Khanzode et al. (2008) present a case study supported on the use of BIM tools and discuss the challenges project team members faced in implementing the BIM tools, processes for MEP coordination, and the specific quantitative and qualitative benefits from the use of BIM tools. The MEP design is critical for decision making, accurate documentation, budgeting, performance forecasting, construction planning and management and, eventually, facility maintenance. However, the design of MEP systems has proven to be a huge challenge in many projects, namely in the technically more complex ones, such as those focused on the high technology, healthcare and biotech industries. In such cases, the MEP systems could comprise as much as 50% of the total project value. Therefore, the coordination and routing of these kinds of systems is of great importance. Following Olofsson et al. (2008) these systems need to be routed on limited spaces under the design, construction and maintenance criteria established for them.

In this area, the success of BIM technology in construction projects shown by the rapid adoption of its associated tools, have redefined the expectation of clients by MEP consultants. Just as for the structural conception and construction projects, BIM applied to MEP is a project methodology characterized by the creation and use of consistent, coordinated and computable information for the MEP design of a building. Although it is still in a growing stage, BIM technology has revealed itself as a key factor to keep market competitiveness. These are some of the main advantages provided by BIM for the users of the MEP domain (Revit, 2014):

- By enabling a holistic approach in the modeling of building service systems, BIM technology can be used to unify all the MEP disciplines within an integrated digital environment for the purpose of design, analysis and documentation;
- The accuracy and, consequently, the reliability factor with MEP engineering designs is higher, due to the fact that BIM offers a higher visibility level which translates to better coordination among engineers and architects, and therefore leading to a significant decrease in errors;
- BIM technology provides automatic clash detection during the development of the building design;
- It bestows the MEP engineers the ability to foresee the end results of their work with a higher precision before the project completion, allowing therefore the development of sophisticated and sustainable buildings within a shorter period of time and comparatively economically.

3 Generating Architectural and Structural Components

The case study used for the development of this work, refers to a single family house located in the northern part of Portugal. The available documentation of the real project that was consulted to define the main disciplines BIM components was a set of drawings. The house consists of two floors, with the ground floor comprising the garage and entrance hall and, the first floor containing the living room, kitchen, three bedrooms, two bathrooms, one utility room and hallways.

In the generation process of the BIM model's architectural and structural components, all represented elements, such as walls, windows, doors, floors, columns, roofs and footings, were created by adapting the 3D parametric objects existing in the Revit library, in order to resemble closely the real case. When comparing with the initial project, some details where purposely left aside because they are of no relevance for this work, namely, in the structural model of this house the rebars were not included, as only the geometrical shape of the concrete elements will be required for conflict checking in this work. The sequence of steps taken in the modeling of the structural and architectural components of the BIM model is: Initial settings (setting the project units and the levels, project browser organization and adding grids); Architectural component (creating and adding walls, doors and windows, floor coverings, roofs, stairs and adding equipment); Structural component (Creating and adding structural columns, footing, beams, concrete slabs). For modeling purposes, Revit

2014 software was used. Figures 1 and 2 illustrate the house after the modeling of said components.

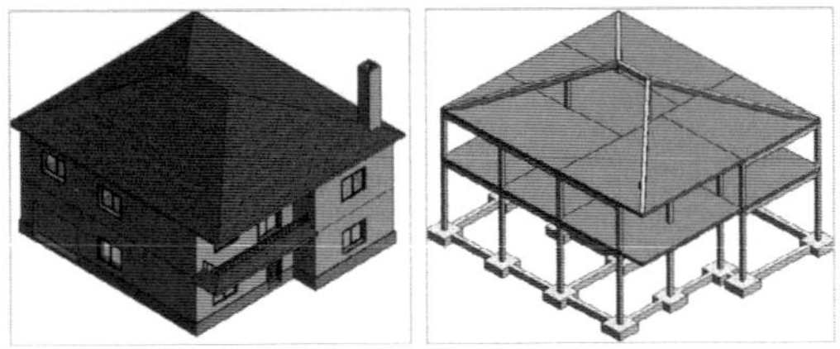

Figure 1 Architectural component and structural component.

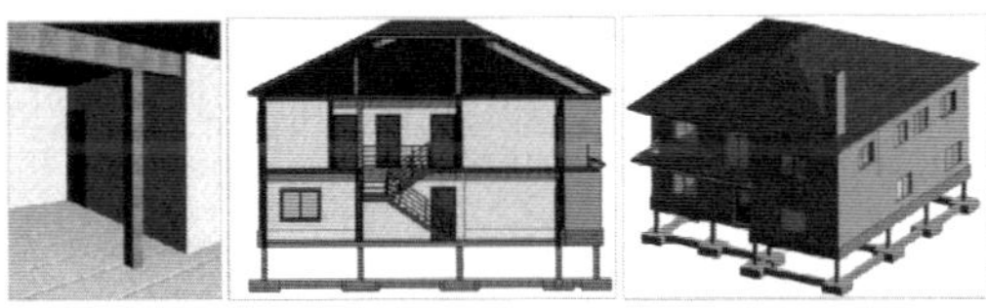

Figure 2 Overlapping disciplines: 3D interior view (left), vertical section (center) and general perspective (right).

4 Generating MEP Component of the BIM model

This section describes the modelling in Revit 2014 of the MEP component of the BIM model, namely, the domestic hot and cold water supply system, the domestic wastewater system and the rain water drainage system. The Revit MEP is steel a component of Revit in development in order enhance better performance.

Actually Revit 2014 version has an intuitive modeling, sufficient and well-conceived design features, direct integration with architectural and structural Revit software tools, and a good drawing sheet management. Revit is capable and popular software, but an initial expensive investment in heavy training or hire people is needed. In school the Autodesk software can be freely downloaded for students and teachers. That's the reason of the choice for the development of this work within a MSc thesis research.

The modeling was initially performed solely based on the architectural component of the house, with no visual guidance from the structural component. The architectural model was then supplemented with the plumbing fixtures. For the routing of these systems, the fundamentals of "Handbook for the building distribution systems and drainage" (Pedroso, 2008) were taken into consideration. The piping diameters used in this work are approximate values of those present in the real design, for it was decided that the predefined nominal diameters from Revit were to be used.

The setting of the mechanical properties of the model elements was not taken into consideration, as this aspect is not relevant to the conflict analysis carried out in this work. The sequence of steps taken for the modeling of the MEP component is: hot and cold water supply system (adding plumbing fixtures, creating and adding water supply pipes, adding pipe accessories and insulation); domestic wastewater drainage system (adding floor siphons, creating and adding plumbing fixture drainage pipes and discharge stacks, adding access chambers); rain water drainage system (adding rain gutters, downspouts, and access chambers). Figure 3 illustrates some of the end results.

5 Clash Detection

Conflict analysis is an integral and very important part in the development process of a three-dimensional BIM model.

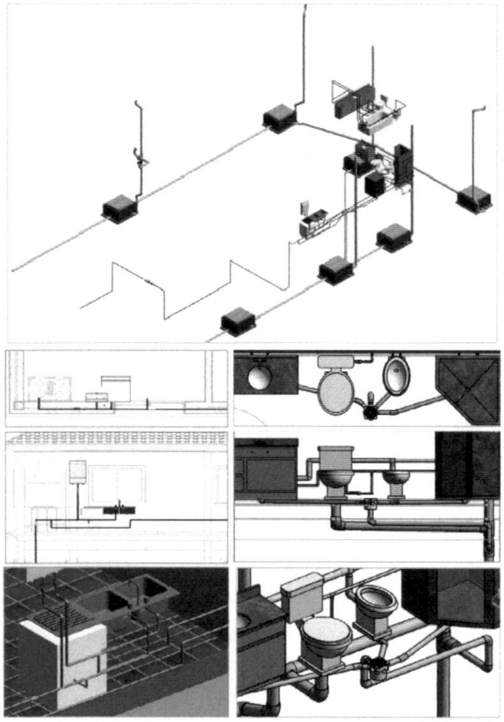

Figure 3 General perspective of the MEP component and orthogonal views (top), 3D views of the water supply system in the kitchen (bottom left) and the wastewater drainage system in one of the bathrooms (bottom right).

The BIM tool in use allows the overlapping of multiple disciplines that coexist in an integrated manner, forming a complete model of the design. Each discipline (structural engineering, MEP engineering, environmental engineering, etc.) creates an independent model using objects, specific to each component, using the architectural BIM model as basis for the development. After each discipline has made its contribution for the BIM model the collision detection can be performed. This process consists in searching objects belonging to different disciplines that conflict with each other, that is, elements that are using the same physical space or that have incompatible parameters or even, in the case of 4D modeling, calendar conflicts (BIM Journal, 2014). The analysis of these inconsistencies is a critical task, especially regarding MEP and fire protection (FP) designs Kymmell (2008), since they could eventually severely impact the construction process, causing delays, design changes and increased expenses in materials and surpluses in the budget (BIM Journal, 2014).

The conflict analysis should be an iterative process in which every notable design incompatibility must be addressed and reassessed, changing and updating solutions to achieve the desired level of coordination Kymmell (2008). If conflicts revealed in 2D, 3D and 4D formats are not thoroughly studied during the discipline coordination, it could lead to an endless cycle of corrections because some times when fixing something in a place may result in another conflict in another.

The modeling of the structural and MEP components were carried out using only the architectural component as guidance, that is, the structural component was not visible during the MEP modeling and vice versa. However, Revit, allows simultaneous viewing of all modeled components. This can be done by using the coordination view, one of Revit's features that aids in the coordination of the various building disciplines. Figure 5 shows the structural and the MEP components as seen in a Revit 3D coordination view (Figure 4).

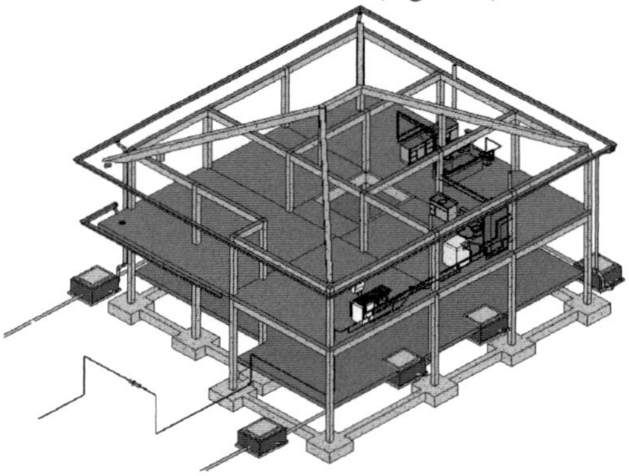

Figure 4 Structural and MEP disciplines as seen in a Revit 3D coordination view.

6 Revit software

According to Benning et al. (2010), there are three types of clashes: hard clash, soft clash and near misses clash, the latter of which also referred to in some sources as being a clearance clash. The hard clash consists in two objects occupying the same space. The soft clash refers to objects that occupy a space that can affect the movement of another object or person. The near misses clash is a conflict that occurs when a regulation or building code, such as the minimum distance between gas and water pipes, is not met. Various sources group together the definitions of soft and near misses clashes, designating them solely as soft clashes. That being said, for the purposes of clash detection, this work will take that grouping into consideration. Through the handling of the view plan of Revit, the clashes shown in Table 1 were detected. Figures 5, 6 and 7 illustrate some of these clashes.

Table 1 A table demonstrating the use of tables

Description	Type	Number	Figure
Column vs. Pipe	Hard clash	9	Figure 6
Beam vs. Pipe	Hard clash	5	Figure 7
Usable space v Pipe	Soft clash	2	Figure 8
	Total	**16**	

7 Tekla BIMsight software

Tekla BIMsight is a project review software that enables the coordination of the different disciplines of a building, making the clash detection possible and therefore aiding in finding a solution. It is a program that has become especially useful in coordinating disciplines modeled by different software using the Industry Foundation Classes (IFC) format to allow their integration.

In this work, the various disciplines were modeled always using the same Revit document. Nevertheless, in order to demonstrate Tekla BIMsight's clash detection capabilities, the MEP and structural components where saved in separate documents. After integrating the two disciplines, clash detection can be conducted by using the Conflict Checking function. But first, it is necessary to establish a rule that makes clash detection possible between the two disciplines. This new rule was designated "MEP vs. Structure" and the files to clash are selected. An overlap tolerance value between objects can be defined as well as minimum distance value and also to check for clashes between rebars (Figure 8).

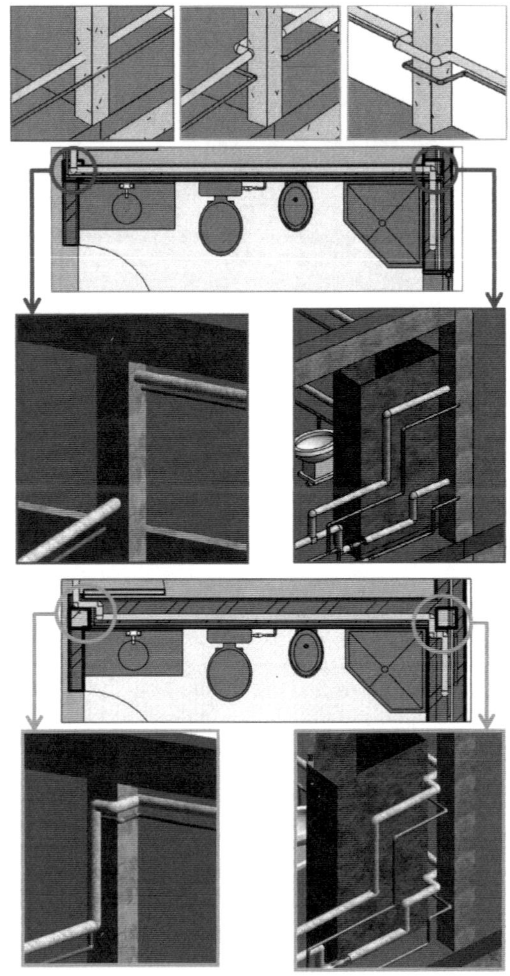

Figure 5 Hard clash between column and water supply pipes and suggested correction.

Figure 6 Hard clash between beam and ventilation pipe and suggested correction

Figure 7 Soft clash consisting of a visible ventilation pipe in a bedroom and suggested correction.

After running the new rule the detected clashes are listed and pinpointed on the model (Figure 8).

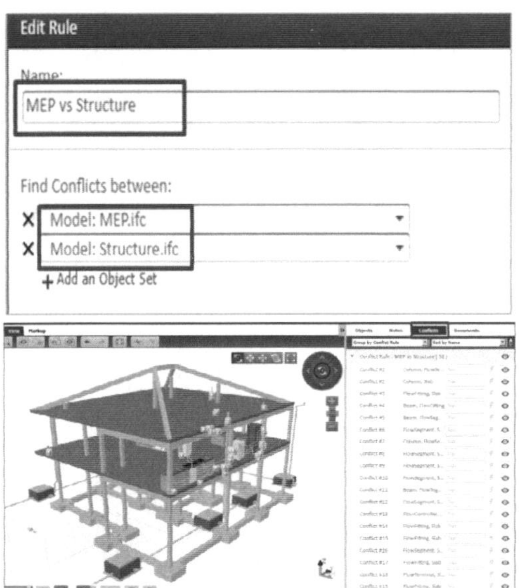

Figure 8 Creating a rule to check for clashes between the MEP and structural models and detected clashes are listed and pinpointed in the model

8 Navisworks software

Navisworks is also a coordination software from Autodesk and frequently used in project as a review software amongst BIM users. The existing Clash Detective function is of great help in conflict analysis and project coordination, especially if the used BIM modeler is Revit. Contrary to Tekla BIMsight, Navisworks allows the clashing of different disciplines within the same model and, therefore, there is no need to save them as separate files. In addition, the viewing of the case study model doesn't require exporting it to the IFC format, because Revit produces files in a readable format by Navisworks, as they are both Autodesk products (Figure 9).

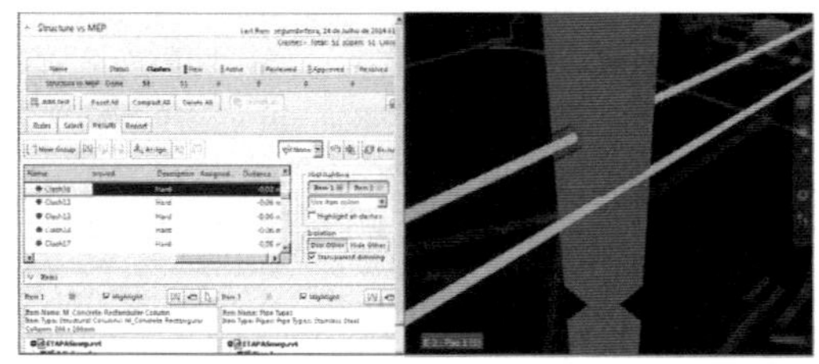

Figure 9 Clash detective tool.

Be it Navisworks or Tekla BIMsight, the conflict resolution must be conducted in the modeler, Revit. However, Navisworks features the Switchback function that, when enabled, opens the Revit model immediately focusing the conflicted elements, thus allowing to quickly fixing the problem. Afterwards, the updated Revit file is saved, taking into account that the previous file must be overwritten. This way, it is only necessary to refresh the model in Navisworks for it to update the changes. This ability to add and update information between Revit and Navisworks with the Switchback function is one of the greatest advantages when using these BIM tools together, for it provides an iterative and efficient workflow that comes a few steps closer to resembling what the BIM methodology really is about.

9 Conclusions

An efficient conflict analysis depends mainly on the level of detail of the projects involved, which can currently be attained through the use of BIM modeling software. In this work, the BIM tool Revit 2014 was used to model the architectural, structural and MEP disciplines. It was noted that when compared with more traditional AutoCAD usage, the representation of elements is more complete (non-geometrical information associated) and its 3D viewing is immediate. In addition, the ability to simultaneously conciliate the architectural component with the structural component through the coordination view aids with obvious advantages the process of establishing a structural solution. On the other hand, the complete composition of elements, such as walls, still reveals itself as quite a limiting aspect, as it requires knowing beforehand the main features of the wall's composition.

Naturally, afterwards, it is possible to update its composition, while preserving the bonding relations to the neighboring elements that were already established during the modeling, thus reflecting a great advantage when compared to traditional AutoCad modeling. Regarding the modeling of the MEP discipline, the draining and water supply systems were modeled. The entire pipe and complementary accessories modeling process was performed in order to accommodate them to architectural elements, especially walls and pavements. When comparing the applied process with the traditional AutoCad methods, a big difference can be noted, with great benefits for the designer. Even when it was necessary to use non-existing components, the operation did not prove itself too complicated.

The use of BIM tools as a means of conflict analysis presents an irrefutable advantage over traditional methods. The use of modelers, such as Revit, for this purpose enables a virtual visualization of conflicts with a very high level of detail. Solving the problem is immediate because the analysis is being made in the modeling software. However, the use of project review software must be emphasized, for they have functions targeted specifically to conflict analysis, like Conflict checking, from Tekla BIMsight, and Clash Detective, from Navisworks Manage. To emphasize the latter, which due to the Switchback feature, enables a workflow that tends to resemble the BIM ideology.

The advantages of BIM in the construction domain are more than evident, especially when related to conflict analysis. This will never be a 100% automated process, because the coordination of different disciplines requires more than just the push of a button and waiting for the problems to get solved. Conflict analysis is an iterative process that requires a joint approach by everybody involved in order to reach and make a final decision. The conflict detection software are only a tool to help in the decision making process.

References

Abrishami, S., Goulding, J.S., Rahimian, F.P., Ganah, A. (2014) Integration of BIM and Generative Design to Exploit AEC Conceptual Design Innovation, *Journal of Information Technology in Construction, (ITcon)*, Special Issue BIM Cloud-Based Technology in the AEC Sector: Present Status and Future Trends, 19 (2014), pp. 350-359, http://www.itcon.org/2014/21

Barlish, K., Sullivan, K. (2012) How to Measure the Benefits of BIM — A Case Study Approach, *Automation in Construction*, Ed. Elsevier Science, 24 (2012), pp. 129–159, doi:10.1016/j.autcon.2012.02.008.

BIM Journal (2014) http://www.bimjournal.com/2012/03/clash-detection-in-bim-modeling/

Eadie, R., Odeyinka, H., Browne, M., McKeown, C., Yohanis, M. (2014) Building Information Modelling Adoption: An Analysis of the Barriers to Implementation, *Journal of Engineering and Architecture*, 2 (2014), pp. 77-101, No. 1, ISSN: 2334-2986 (Print), http://aripd.org/journals/jea/Vol_2_No_1_March_2014/7.pdf

Gu, N., London, K. (2010) Understanding and Facilitating BIM Adoption in the AEC Industry, *Automation in Construction*, 19(2010), pp. 988–999, doi:10.1016/j.autcon.2010.09.002

Ju, K.B., Seo, M.B. (2012), A Study on the Issue Analysis for the Application of BIM Technology to Civil Engineering in Korea, *Creative Education journal*, Copyright © 2012 SciRes. 21, 2012. Vol.3, Supplement, pp. 21-24, doi: 10.4236/ce.2012.37B005.

Jung, Y., Joo, M. (2011), Building Information Modelling (BIM) Framework for Practical Implementation, issue: Building Information Modeling and Changing Construction Practices, *Automation in Construction*, Ed. Elsevier Science, 20 (2011), pp. 126–133, Issue 2, doi:10.1016/j.autcon.2010.09.010.

Khanzode, A., Fischer, M., Reed, D. (2008) Virtual design and construction (vdc) technologies for coordination of mechanical, electrical, and plumbing (MEP) systems on a large healthcare project ed. T. Olofsson, G. Lee & C. Eastman, *Journal of Information Technology in Construction, (ITcon)*, Special Issue: Case studies of BIM use, 13 (2008), pp. 324-342, http://www.itcon.org/2008/22

Kymmell, W. (2008), Building Information Modeling: Planning and Managing Construction Projects with 4D CAD and Simulations, *McGraw-Hill Construction Series*, ISBN-13: 978-0071494533, Ed: 1st, New York, 2008.

Olofsson, T., Lee, G., Eastman, C. (2008) Benefits and Lessons Learned of Implementing Building Virtual Design and Construction Technologies for Coordination of Mechanical, Electrical, and Plumbing (MEP) Systems on a Large Healthcare Project. USA. (2008).

Pedroso, V. (2008) Handbook for the Building Distribution Systems and Drainage (in portuguese) . 4th ed., *National Laboratory of Civil Engineering*, Lisbon, Portugal, 2008.

Porwal, A., Hewage, K.N. (2013) Building Information Modeling (BIM) Partnering Framework for Public Construction Projects, *Automation in Construction*, 31 (2013), pp. 204–214, doi:10.1016/j.autcon.2012.12.004

RevitMEP (2014) http://download.autodesk.com/us/interactiveoverviews/export_web_ARS/pdf/Whitepaper_Revit_Systems_BIM_for_MEP_Engineering.swf

Succar, B., Sher, W., Williams, A. (2013) An Integrated Approach to BIM Competency Assessment, Acquisition and Application, *Automation in Construction*, 35 (2013), pp. 174–189, doi:10.1016/j.autcon.2013.05.016

Volk, R., Stengel, J., Schultmann, F. (2014) Building Information Modelling (BIM) for existing buildings: Literature review and future needs, *Automation in Construction*, 38 (2014), pp. 109–127, doi:10.1016/j.autcon.2013.10.023

Zhanga, J.P., Hub, Z.Z. (2011) BIM- and 4D-based Integrated Solution of Analysis and Management for Conflicts and Structural Safety Problems During Construction: 1. Principles and Methodologies, Special issue: Building Information Modelling and Changing Construction Practices, *Automation in Construction*, 20 (2011), pp. 155–166, Issue 2, doi:10.1016/j.autcon.2010.09.013

Dimensional Quality Assessment of Atypical Precast Elements using Laser Scanning and BIM

Min-Koo Kim, kmk0125@kaist.ac.kr
Korea Advanced Institute of Science and Technology, Republic of Korea

JoonWoo Park, joonwoonpark@kaist.ac.kr
Korea Advanced Institute of Science and Technology, Republic of Korea

Qian Wang, wangqian@kaist.ac.kr
Korea Advanced Institute of Science and Technology, Republic of Korea

Hoon Sohn, hoonsohn@kaist.ac.kr
Korea Advanced Institute of Science and Technology, Republic of Korea

Abstract
Over the last few decades, precast concrete elements have become a popular component for construction projects. Since success of the precast concrete based construction comes from the dimensional conformability of individual precast concrete elements to their design specifications, checking the dimensional qualities of individual precast concrete element is very important. This paper presents a laser scanning and Building Information Modeling (BIM) based quality assessment technique that automatically measures the dimensional properties of atypical precast concrete elements. In this study, a new algorithm is developed to match the scanned data obtained from a laser scanner with the as-designed model of precast concrete elements. Validation experiments are conducted on actual atypical precast concrete elements to identify the effectiveness of the proposed technique. The test results show that the dimensional errors between the scanned points and the as-designed model have a 2.6 mm, which is satisfactory accuracy for successful dimensional quality assessment of precast concrete elements.

Keywords: Laser scanning, Building Information Modeling (BIM), dimensional quality assessment, atypical precast concrete elements

1 Introduction
Precast concrete element based construction is a popular construction method that uses the principles of standardization and modularization. Over the last few decades, precast concrete elements have become a popular component for construction projects such as low- and mid-rise apartments, office buildings and bridges. Since success of the precast concrete based construction comes from the dimensional conformability of individual precast concrete elements to their design specifications, checking the dimensional properties of individual precast concrete elements, such as dimensions and positions, is important before assemblage stage. Currently the dimensional quality of precast concrete elements is evaluated manually by certified inspectors and they normally use contact-type devices such as measuring tapes and straightedges. However the manual inspection is time and cost demanding. Moreover, inspection output of the manual inspection is often subjective.

As a non-contact three-dimensional (3D) measurement device, recently terrestrial laser scanners (TLS) have gained popularity due to their merits of accuracy and speed. Contrary to the digital imaging approach, laser scanners directly acquires 3D data with high accuracy (typically 2-6 mm at 50 m

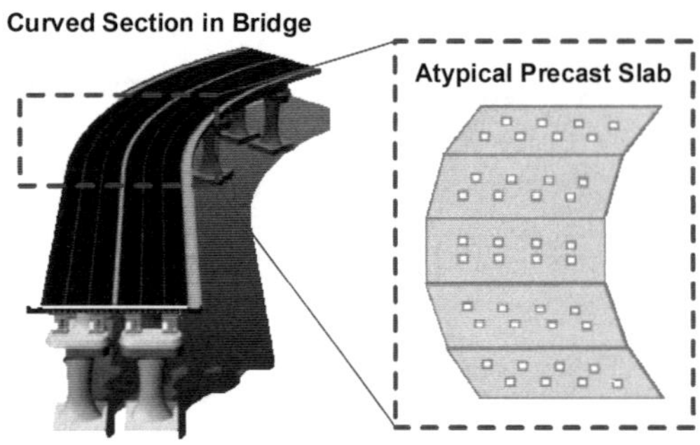

Figure 1. Atypical precast slab based bridge construction

(Olsen et al 2010)) and high point density (up to 960,000 points/sec (FARO 2015)). Due to these merits, several studies have been proposed to validate the feasibility of laser scanning technology for the dimensional quality inspection (Bosche 2010, Han et al 2013). Also our group previously developed a dimensional quality assessment (DQA) technique for precast concrete elements (Kim et al 2014). However, the DQA technique is limited to precast concrete elements with simple rectangular shapes, which is not applicable to non-rectangular precast concrete elements.

This paper presents a technique that automatically measures the dimensional properties of atypical precast concrete element using a TLS. Here, atypical precast concrete elements represent 'diamond' shape elements as shown in Figure 1. In this study, a new algorithm is developed to match the scanned data obtained from a laser scanner with the as-designed model of precast concrete elements. Validation experiments are conducted on actual atypical precast concrete elements to identify the effectiveness of the proposed technique. This paper is organized as follows. First, methodology of the proposed technique is described in Section 2, followed by laboratory test in Section 3. Finally, this paper concludes with a summary and future works in Section 4.

2 Methodology

Figure 2 shows the procedure of the proposed technique which consist of five steps. First, data acquisition is made by a TLS positioned at the above center of a precast concrete element. Due to this position assumption, the entire surface of the

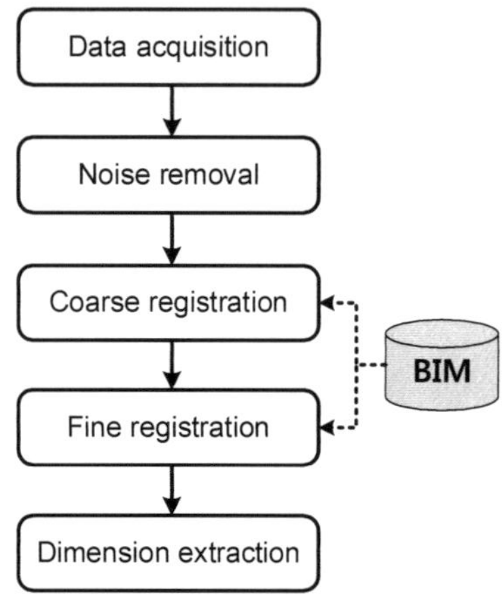

Figure 2. Procedure of the proposed automated dimensional quality inspection technique

precast concrete element can be scanned in a single scan. The next steps are described in detail in next sub-sections.

2.1 Noise removal

Once point cloud data are acquired by the TLS, noise removal is undertaken to remove noise data and retain valid points representing the target object. Figure 3 illustrates three kinds of data contained in a point cloud, in which point $(i-2)$ and point $(i-1)$ are valid points on the target object surface, point $(i+1)$ and point $(i+2)$ are background points, and point i is a mixed pixel. In this study, background points and mixed pixels are assumed as noise data to be eliminated. Background point occurs when a laser beam fully lies on the background rather than the target object. Mixed pixel occurs when a laser beam is separated into two parts and lies on two different surfaces, target object and background (Hebert et al 1991).

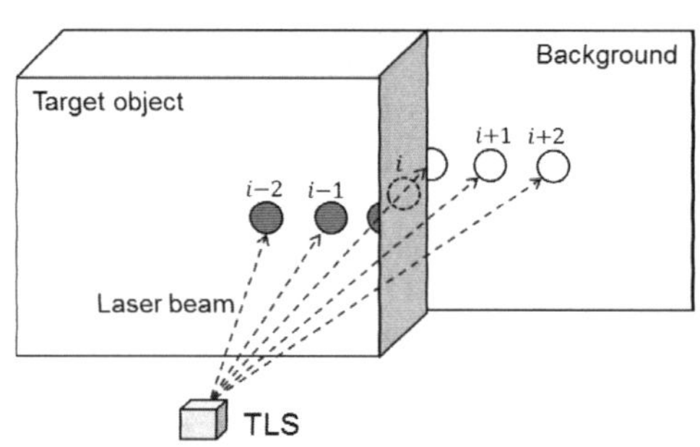

Figure 3. Three kinds of data contained in a point cloud

In this study, a density-based clustering algorithm namely Density-Based Spatial

Clustering of Applications with Noise (DBSCAN) is adopted to remove the background points and mixed pixels from point cloud data (Ester and Martin 1996). DBSCAN is based on two parameters (ε and minPts) and three fundamental concepts (core point, directly density-reachable, and density-reachable). The three fundamental concepts are defined based on the parameters ε and minPts. A point p is a core point if p has at least 'minPts' points within the distance between p and ε. A point q is directly density-reachable from p if p is a core point and the distance from p to q is less than the distance between p and ε. Point q is density-reachable from p if there exists a sequence $p_1, p_2 \dots p_n$ of points with $p_1 = p$ and $p_n = q$ where each p_{i+1} is directly density-reachable from p_i. The DBSCAN algorithm visits each point in a dataset. If one point is a core point, all the points which are density-reachable from the core point as well as the core point itself are included in a cluster. If one point is not a core point and it is not density-reachable from any core point, it is labeled as noise.

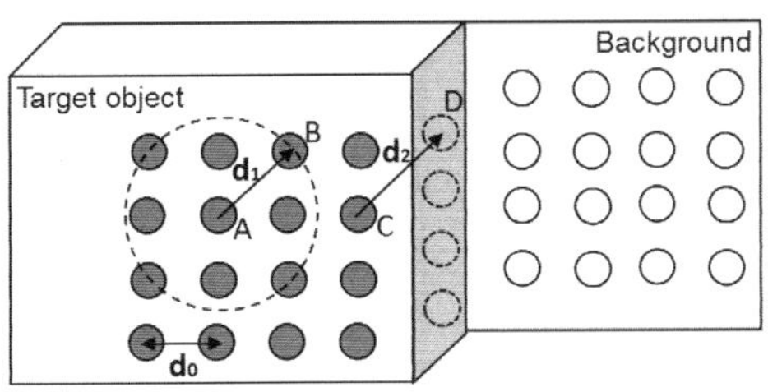

Figure 4. Noise removal based on DBSCAN

Figure 4 shows an example of point cloud data, where filled circles represent valid points, empty solid circles represent background points, and empty dashed circles represent mixed pixels. Assume that all the valid points and background points are evenly distributed respectively and they have the same distance, which is denoted as d_0, between two adjacent points. DBSCAN is applied to this point cloud with minPts set as 8 and ε set as d_1, which is the distance between two adjacent valid points in diagonal direction (e.g. points A and B as shown in Figure 4). As a result, point A becomes a core point because it has 8 surrounding points which have a distance smaller than or equal to ε, so that a cluster is started which will include all the valid points finally. Since point D is a mixed pixel, the distance between points C and D, denoted as d_2, is larger than ε. Therefore, point D is not density-reachable from A and it is not included in this cluster. After applying DBSCAN, all the valid points are included in one cluster; all the background points are included in another cluster; and mixed pixels are labeled as noise.

However, the assumption that valid points are evenly distributed in aforementioned example is not correct. In reality, distance between two adjacent points d_0 depends on the distance from TLS to target object and the incident angle between laser beam and the normal vector of target object surface. Therefore, ε should not be smaller than d_{max}, which denotes the theoretical maximum value of the distance between any two adjacent valid points in diagonal direction. Moreover, considering that the target object surface may not be smooth, d_0 may vary according to local surface condition. Therefore, a safety factor is taken into consideration and ε is set as $1.2d_{max}$.

Once all clusters are found in a point cloud, the cluster of points which have the shorter distances to TLS are taken as valid points and represent the target object, whereas background points which have the longer distances from TLS is considered as noise data to be removed.

2.2 Coarse registration

Once only the scan point of the target object is extracted from the noise removal step, coarse registration is undertaken. This process roughly matches the as-built object with the as-design object. Note that the as-built object is expressed by a point cloud and the as-design object is expressed by BIM model. The as-built object is transformed by a three-dimensional (3D) transformation including three translations and three rotations in order to minimize the distance between as-built and as-design objects.

Considering that the target object in this study is the top surface of an atypical precast concrete slab, which is a quasi-2D object. Thus, the problem of finding a 3D transformation can be simplified to finding a 2D transformation. There are three sub-steps for the coarse registration. (1) Generation of the least squares fitting plane of the as-built object. (2) Projection of the 3D points into the fitting plane and extraction of the boundary corners of the as-built object. Here, the boundary corners are obtained from employing line (Ballard 1981) and corner (Canny 1986) detectors on the range image generated from the projected 2D point cloud. (3) Overlap of the extracted boundary corners with the corresponding boundary corners of the as-design object, which means two objects have same center point. Note that the plane of the as-design object is set as the x-y plane of a new Cartesian coordinate system. Therefore, the problem to be solved is to find best 2D transform of the as-built object so that the moved one is closely positioned to the as-design object. To this end, an iterative search is conducted. Figure 5 illustrates the method of finding the best 2D transformation.

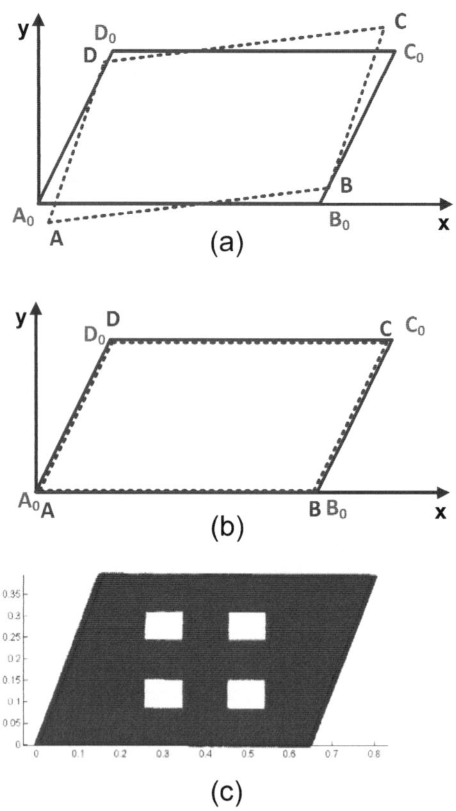

Figure 5. Coarse registration between as-built and as-design objects: (a) The as-built (dotted red line) and as-design (solid blue line) boundaries; (b) Best matching between as-built and as-design boundaries and (c) Transformation of the as-built object by the best matching 2D transformation.

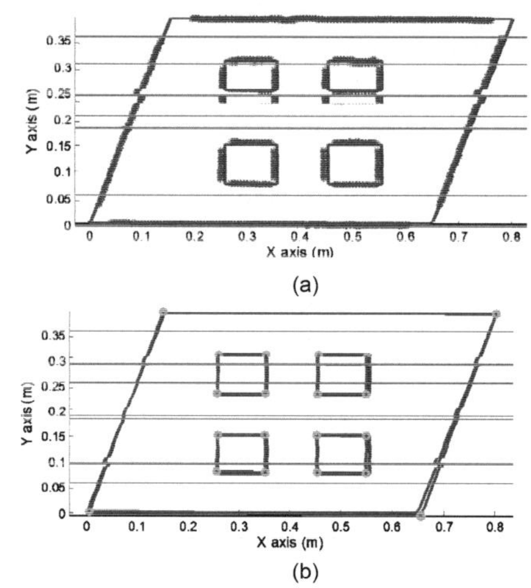

Figure 6. Fine registration between as-built and as-design objects: (a) Extraction of each edge points for the main slab and shear pockets; (b) Best matching between as-built and as-design objects through transformation of the as-built object by the best matching 2D transformation.

In each iteration, generating a different 2D transformation and transforming the as-built boundary corners by this transformation are performed. Then finding the least distance from the as-built boundary corners to the corresponding as-design boundary corners is conducted. After finding the least distance for each boundary corner, the mean square of all the distances is calculated. When the mean square is minimized, the transformation for the best matching is found. Then, the as-built object is transformed by this transformation in order to best match the as-design object as shown in Figure 5(c).

2.3 Fine registration

As next step, fine registration is followed. This process uses shear pocket information with purpose of better registration between the as-built and as-design objects. The key difference between coarse and fine registration is the usage of shear pocket information for object matching. There are two sub-steps for this process. (1) Extraction of all the corners of the as-built object is conducted. Here, all the corners include the corners of the shear pockets positioned inside the as-built object. First, by utilizing the 'vector-sum' algorithm (Kim et al 2014), the edge scan points of the as-built object are extracted. Then, the extracted edge points are divided and assigned to each line of the main slab and shear pockets of the as-design object as shown in

Figure 6(a). Finally the corners of the slab and shear pockets are computed by fitting the edge points of each line into a line and intersecting these lines. (2) Compensation for dimension loss at edges is conducted. To cope with the mixed-pixel phenomenon as mentioned in Section 2.1, an edge loss compensation model (Tang et al 2009) is employed to compensate for dimension loss occurred at edges of the object. (3) Overlap of the dimension-compensated corners of the as-built object with the corresponding corners of the as-design object is carried out. The detail process of finding best 2D transformation is same as that of coarse registration.

3 Laboratory test on concrete slab

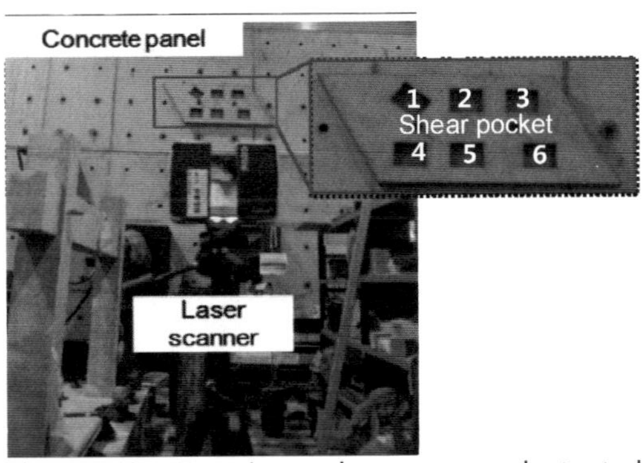

Figure 7. Experimental setup and tested specimen

To examine the effectiveness of the proposed DQA technique for atypical precast concrete elements, experiments on actual precast concrete panel were conducted. The overall test configuration and the investigated precast concrete panel are shown in Figure 7. The bottom surface of the precast concrete panel with dimensions of 1.5 m × 0.7 m × 0.1 m was fixed on a concrete wall with a height of 5 m and then scanned by a TLS. In this experiment, a diamond precast slab was used as test specimen and the TLS was positioned at 10m distance from the specimen and 2.5 m height from the ground, resulting in a vertical incident angle of 14°. On the specimen surface, there are six rectangular shear pockets with identical dimensions of 200 mm * 150 mm. In order to identify that the proposed DQA technique can inspect any abnormal errors exceeding the allowable tolerance, two dimensional abnormalities were introduced on the surface of the specimen, which are (1) clockwise rotation of # 1 shear pocket by 53°, and (2) position shift of # 6 shear pocket to the right by 100 mm.

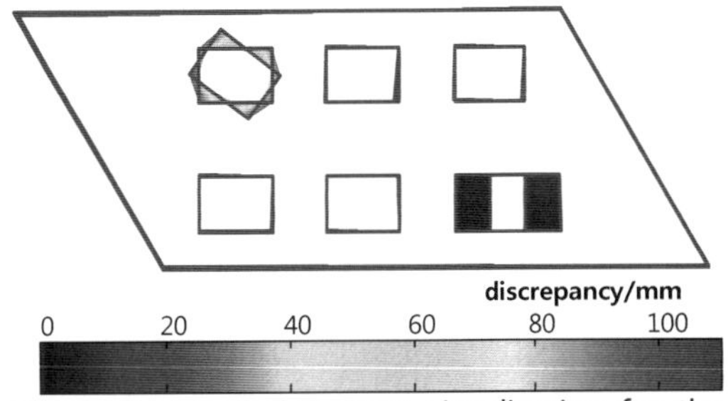

Figure 8. Dimension error visualization for the actual precast slab test

Figure 8 shows the dimension error result. The distance between all the 20 as-design corner points and their corresponding as-built corner points are calculated one by one. The average distance is 2.6 mm and the artificially introduced two abnormal dimensions are successfully identified by the proposed DQA technique.

4 Conclusion

This paper presents a laser scanning and Building Information Modeling (BIM) based quality assessment technique that automatically measures the dimensional properties of atypical precast concrete elements. In this study, a new algorithm is developed to match the scanned data obtained from a laser scanner with the as-designed model of precast concrete elements. Validation experiments are conducted on actual atypical precast concrete elements to identify the effectiveness of the proposed technique. The test results show that the dimensional errors between the scanned points and the as-designed model have a 2.6 mm, which is satisfactory accuracy for successful dimensional quality assessment of precast concrete elements.

However, this study still has some limitations. (1) The proposed DQA technique is limited to atypical elements having straight-line edges, so further study to apply for curved atypical elements is necessary. (2) Comparison of the dimensions from the as-built object with those from actual manual measurements is needed to better identify the accuracy of the proposed DQA technique.

Acknowledgements

This work was supported by a grant (Grant No. 13SCIPA01) from the Smart Civil Infrastructure

Research Program) funded by the (Ministry of Land, Infrastructure and Transport of the Korea Government).

References

Ballard, D (1981) Generalizing the Hough transform to detect arbitrary shapes, Pattern recongnition, 13 (2). pp. 111-122.

Bosche, F. (2010) Automated recognition of 3D CAD model objects in laser scans and calculation of as-built dimensions for dimensional compliance control in construction, Advanced Engineering Informatics, 24. pp. 107-118.

Canny, J. (1986) A computational approach to edge detection, IEEE Transaction on Pattern Analysis and Machine Intelligence, 8. pp. 679-698.

Ester, M., Kregel, H., Sander, J., Xu, Xiaowei (1996) A density-based algorithm for discovering clusters in large spatial databases with noise, Proc. Of KDD-96.

FARO, Focus-3D Technical Specification, *FARO Inc.* (2015)

Han, S., Choe, H., Kim, S., et al (2013) Automated and efficient method for extraction of tunnel cross sections using terrestrial laser scanned data, Journal of Computing in Civil Engineering, 27 (3). pp. 274-281.

Hebert, M., Krotkov, E. (1991) 3-D measurements from imaging laser radars: how good are they?. Proc. of the IEEE/RSJ International Workshop on Intelligent Robots and Systems, Osaka, Japan, Nov. 3-5. pp. 359-364.

Kim, M., Sohn, H., Chang C. (2014) Automated dimensional quality assessment of precast concrete panels using terrestrial laser scanning, Automation in Construction, 45. pp. 163-177.

Olsen, N., Kuester, F., Chang, B., Hutchinson, T. (2010) Terrestrial laser scanning-based structural damage assessment, *Journal of Computing in Civil Engineering*. 24 (3). pp. 264-272.

Tang, P., Akinci, B., Huber, D. (2009) Quantification of edge loss of laser scanned data at spatial discontinuities, Automation in Construction, 18 (8). pp. 1070-1083.

Coping with lists in the ifcOWL ontology

Pieter Pauwels, pipauwel.pauwels@ugent.be
Ghent University, Ghent, Belgium,

Walter Terkaj, walter.terkaj@itia.cnr.it
Institute of Industrial Technologies and Automation (ITIA), Milano, Italy

Thomas Krijnen, t.f.krijnen@tue.nl
Technical University of Eindhoven (TU/e), Eindhoven, Netherlands

Jakob Beetz, j.beetz@tue.nl
Technical University of Eindhoven (TU/e), Eindhoven, Netherlands

Abstract
Over the past few years, several suggestions have been made of how to convert an EXPRESS schema into an OWL ontology. The conversion from EXPRESS to OWL is of particular use to architectural design and construction industry, because one of the key data models in architectural design and construction industry, namely the Industry Foundation Classes (IFC) is represented using the EXPRESS information modelling language. In each of these conversion options, the way in which lists are converted (e.g. lists of coordinates, lists of spaces in a floor) is key to the structure and eventual strength of the resulting ontology. In this article, we outline and discuss the main decisions that can be made in converting `LIST` concepts in EXPRESS to equivalent OWL expressions. This allows one to identify which conversion option is appropriate to support proper and efficient information reuse in the domain of architecture and construction.

Keywords: Semantic Web, Industry Foundation Classes, Resource Descriptions Framework

1 Introduction

The representation of aggregation data types (e.g. lists) is still not explicitly addressed in the Web Ontology Language (OWL - Hitzler et al. (2012)), even if it plays a key role in several applications. Other ontology languages, such as the Knowledge Interchange Format (KIF[1] - Genesereth and Fikes (1992)), or modelling languages like EXPRESS (ISO 10303-11, 2004) propose built-in solutions to deal with lists and sets of data. These data structures are particularly relevant also to support the conversion of data models formalised using other languages into an OWL ontology, so that the data model integration features offered by semantic web technologies (Berners-Lee et al., 2001) can be exploited. An example is represented by the conversion of an EXPRESS schema into an OWL ontology. This is of particular use to architectural design and construction industry, because one of the key data models in architectural design and construction industry, namely the Industry Foundation Classes (IFC), is represented using the EXPRESS information modelling language. An OWL version of IFC, named ifcOWL, would provide a number of advanced semantic technologies to experts in architectural design and construction that are currently seldom available or used in this domain, e.g. reasoning capabilities (inference) and semantic search (Beetz et al., 2009; Schevers and Drogemuller, 2005; Agostinho et al., 2007; Pauwels et al., 2011; Pauwels and Van Deursen, 2012).

The IFC EXPRESS schema (Liebich et al., 2013) includes several aggregation types, which are intensively used to describe geometry, among others. In the case of geometry, the EXPRESS schema relies mainly on the `LIST` data type, which accommodates an ordered aggregation. Also property sets and relational

[1] http://logic.stanford.edu/kif/specification.html

objects often use aggregation data types (in those cases unordered `SET` data types) to link one type instance to a number of other type instances. There are a number of ways in which such aggregation types can be converted into an OWL expression. In the case of `SET` data types, it is typically most appropriate to convert the instances of these `SET` data types into a number of non-functional data property instances, as is proposed by Pauwels and Terkaj (2015a, 2015b). However, the conversion of ordered collections (`LIST` and `ARRAY` data types) often results in representations of an undesirable form, making the resulting RDF graphs following an ifcOWL specification hard to use. In particular, using the simplest conversion routine based on the RDF terms `rdf:list - rdf:first - rdf:rest` (Brickley and Guha, 2014; Dean and Schreiber, 2004) results in an ontology that is in the OWL Full profile (see Hitzler et al. (2012)). An ontology that is in the OWL Full profile cannot be used to exploit the desirable inference and semantic search functionalities in the domain of architectural design and construction. Alternative options, in which a custom `ifc:list` construct is used, typically result in similar complex and verbose graph structures. In this paper, we review the conversion options suggested in literature, and highlight the relevance of the problem for the architectural design and construction industry. Additionally, we introduce two new options to approach the problem, aiming to find an appropriate way to cope with this issue in the usage of IFC and ifcOWL.

2 The ifcOWL ontology

Building information modelling (BIM) is one of the most notable efforts in recent years regarding information management in construction industry (Eastman et al., 2008). BIM environments allow one to semantically describe any kind of information about the building in one information model. The Industry Foundation Classes (IFC) standard (ISO 16739, 2013), developed and maintained by the buildingSMART[2] organisation, aims at supporting these activities by providing a central "conceptual data schema and an exchange file format for BIM data" (Liebich et al., 2013). Using the IFC data model and instance serialisation formats, BIM data can be exchanged between software applications covering a wide range of use cases (e.g. 4D planning, 5D cost calculation, CFD simulation, structural analysis).

The IFC data model is represented as a schema in the expressive EXPRESS data specification language defined in ISO 10303-11:2004 that *"consists of language elements which allow an unambiguous data definition and specification of constraints on the data defined and by which aspects of product data can be specified"* (ISO 10303-11, 2004). The EXPRESS data specification language is very powerful since it allows one to define in detail data types, entities, attributes, cardinality restrictions, type restrictions, complex rule expressions, complex derivation expressions, and complex functions. As a single element can be described in diverse ways by each BIM environment, the export and import possibilities to and from IFC should guarantee that each BIM environment is able to map its own descriptions to a generally understandable IFC format, thus improving interoperability of information.

The semantic web initiative (Berners-Lee et al., 2001) shares some of the formal specification goals that IFC is targeting for in construction industry. Namely, it allows one to describe shared conceptualisations of information in a flexible and generic language that takes the form of directed labelled graphs. Each node in such a graph represents a concept or object in the world and each arc in this graph represents the logical relation between two of these concepts or objects. A graph can be constructed using the Resource Description Framework (RDF) data model (Schreiber and Raimond, 2014). RDF graphs can be given an improved semantic structure using RDF vocabularies or ontologies (RDFS, Brickley and Guha (2014); and OWL, Hitzler et al. (2012)).

There is a considerable parallel between the buildingSMART effort towards the specification and standardisation of IFC for construction industry, and the W3C effort towards the specification and standardisation of RDF for web data. On a schema level, EXPRESS has several similarities to OWL and IFC instance files result in graph-like structures that make RDF a suitable capturing format. However, there are differences between the languages. For instance, Barbau et al. (2012) emphasise the lack of formal semantics in EXPRESS, arguing that a logic-based language, such as OWL, brings a number of modelling advantages in knowledge

[2] http://www.buildingsmart.com/

representation and semantic data sharing. Additionally, Beetz et al. (2009) stress the limits of EXPRESS with respect to the reuse of existing ontologies and interoperability with semantic web tools. On the other hand, EXPRESS provides complex elements which are not commonly available in regular OWL language profiles. For example, EXPRESS explicitly allows one to represent 'enumeration data types', 'select data types', a considerable number of well-specified 'aggregation data types' (namely, bags, sets, lists and arrays), and complex procedural statements (WHERE rules, RULE declarations and FUNCTION declarations). So, both languages have unique features, strengths, weaknesses and distinct levels of expressiveness.

Listing 1: EXPRESS specification of `IfcCartesianPoint`.

```
1 ENTITY IfcCartesianPoint
2  SUBTYPE OF (IfcPoint);
3    Coordinates : LIST [1:3] OF IfcLengthMeasure;
4  DERIVE
5    Dim : IfcDimensionCount := HIINDEX(Coordinates);
6  WHERE
7    CP2Dor3D : HIINDEX(Coordinates) >= 2;
8 END_ENTITY;
```

The many parallels between the data modelling approaches in IFC and RDF make it feasible to publish IFC instance data as RDF graphs and thus harnessing the benefits and features of both languages. The formalisation of IFC data as RDF graphs requires the conversion of the IFC schema, defined as an EXPRESS schema, to an OWL ontology. Various research initiatives proposed conversion approaches from an EXPRESS schema to an OWL ontology. Schevers and Drogemuller (2005) proposed a first unidirectional conversion map from EXPRESS to OWL, taking IFC as a reference example and highlighting some of the key issues to be addressed. Agostinho et al. (2007) proposed a generic mapping between EXPRESS and OWL within a broader Model Morphism initiative. Beetz et al. (2009) proposed a semiautomatic method for converting EXPRESS schemas to OWL files in order to enhance the applicability and re-usability of the IFC standard. Barbau and colleagues specified a set of generic rules for the automated conversion from EXPRESS to OWL within the OntoSTEP initiative (Krima et al., 2009; Barbau et al., 2012). Another conversion tool was presented by Pauwels and Van Deursen (2012).

Currently, two initiatives have been set up to further develop the specification of an ifcOWL ontology, for its use in the context of the architectural design and construction industry. The first initiative is the Linked Building Data community group hosted at the World Wide Web Consortium (W3C)[3]. This group aims at listing and specifying the use cases around building data in RDF, thus helping the development of the required ontologies, including ifcOWL. The second initiative is the Linked Building Data working group, which is part of the 'Technical Room' within BuildingSMART[4]. This group aims primarily at providing and maintaining a recommended ifcOWL ontology as an additional BuildingSMART specification.

3 The aggregation data types in the EXPRESS schema of IFC

The conversion of EXPRESS aggregation data types plays an important role in the generation of the ifcOWL ontology. In particular, the `LIST` and `ARRAY` data types in EXPRESS represent ordered collections of elements (ISO 10303-11, 2004; p. 23). In contrast to an `ARRAY`, which is always fixed in size, a `LIST` can be unbounded. Furthermore, it is possible to nest `LIST` data types, thus creating two- or more-dimensional aggregations (`LIST OF LIST`). The EXPRESS current schema of IFC4 is limited to one- and two-dimensional aggregations.

As a reference, we will consider the example of the `IfcCartesianPoint` entity in the IFC4 schema (see Listing 1). `IfcCartesianPoint` has an attribute named `Coordinates` (line 3 in Listing 1), which refers to a `LIST` of at least one and at most 3 instances of `IfcLengthMeasure`. The `WHERE` rule given in Listing 1 (line 7) additionally specifies that the highest index (`HIINDEX`) of the `Coordinates` property should be 2 or more. This implies that the `Coordinates` property should refer to a

[3] http://www.w3.org/community/lbd/

[4] http://www.buildingsmart.org/lbd

LIST of 2 or 3 instances of IfcLengthMeasure (2D versus 3D).

The importance of IfcCartesianPoint in an IFC model can be appreciated by considering an example, representing the Book Tower in Ghent (Belgium)[5]. This IFC model counts 417033 entity instances, of which 45085 are instances of IfcCartesianPoint (10,6%). There are numerous other lists in the IFC model, therefore the conversion of lists (and other aggregation data types) has a major impact on the eventual graph, in particular in terms of semantic precision and computational performance. Lengthy representations of LIST types result in very precise and correct definitions, but they require notably more time to be loaded in-memory and used. If performance matters significantly, then it might be a better option to use less precise representations of the same information that can be loaded considerably faster.

4 Conversion Procedures

In the following sections, we investigate a number of conversion procedures. We hereby distinguish between:

- Conversion to the regular rdf:List concept natively available in RDF
- Conversion to general purpose list concepts
- Conversion to customised concepts
- Conversion to customised concepts referring to portions of Well-Known Text (WKT)

The existing conversion procedures listed in the previous section typically take the second approach. The Turtle syntax (Beckett and Berners-Lee, 2011) will be used to present the fragments of OWL ontology in the following sections, while referring to the namespaces defined in Listing 2. Note that the 5 namespaces in lines 5 to 9 in Listing 1 are dummy namespaces that are used to distinguish between the ontologies and approaches used in the following sections of this paper. Only one of them should eventually be used and it should reside under namespace www.buildingsmart-tech.org/ifcOWL#. Also the namespace at line 10 is a dummy namespace that represents the instance graph of a BIM model in IFC.

Listing 2: Definition of namespaces used in the remainder of this paper.

```
1    @prefix rdf: <http://www.w3.org/1999/02/22-rdf-syntax-ns#> .
2    @prefix rdfs: <http://www.w3.org/2000/01/rdf-schema#> .
3    @prefix owl: <http://www.w3.org/2002/07/owl#> .
4    @prefix xsd: <http://www.w3.org/2001/XMLSchema#> .
5    @prefix ifcowl1: <http://www.buildingsmart-tech.org/ifcOWL1#> .
6    @prefix ifcowl2: <http://www.buildingsmart-tech.org/ifcOWL2#> .
7    @prefix ifcowl3: <http://www.buildingsmart-tech.org/ifcOWL3#> .
8    @prefix ifcowl4: <http://www.buildingsmart-tech.org/ifcOWL4#> .
9    @prefix ifcowl5: <http://www.buildingsmart-tech.org/ifcOWL5#> .
10   @prefix ifcinst:
         <http://www.linkedbuildingdata.net/20150504_ListInstances#> .
```

4.1 Procedure 1: standard RDF lists

Lists (or any ordered sequence) cannot be easily represented in an RDF graph, because RDF relies on a triple structure that inherently allows one to link only two concepts, not collections of multiple concepts. Lists are thus typically represented in RDF by linking each concept to the next using rdf:List, rdf:first and rdf:rest declarations (Brickley and Guha, 2014; Dean and Schreiber, 2004). When using this construct in an OWL ontology, however, the OWL profile becomes OWL Full, thus impeding the use of reasoning engines that rely on Description Logics (DL – Baader and Nutt, 2003). In addition, the conversion into an OWL Full ontology results in verbose representations for the instantiations of the LIST concepts in the ontology. An instance of IfcCartesianPoint, which is expressed in a regular IFC STEP Physical File Format (SPFF) as in Listing 2, results in the expression given in Listing 3.

Listing 2: Example IfcCartesianPoint instance described according to the IFC EXPRESS schema.

```
1 #37=IFCCARTESIANPOINT((0.,0.,-350.));
```

[5]http://smartlab1.elis.ugent.be:8889/IFC-repo/20110616_bookTowerGhent.ifc

One can clearly see that the OWL expression in Listing 3 is far more verbose and complex (24 lines equivalent to 21 triples) compared to the SPFF representation in Listing 2. Considering the number of lists that are defined in the IFC EXPRESS schema and instantiated in IFC files, the impact on complexity and data volume is high.

Listing 3: Representation of the example `IfcCartesianPoint` instance in Listing 2, following the first conversion procedure documented here.

```
ifcinst:IfcCartesianPoint_37
   rdf:type ifcowl1:IfcCartesianPoint ;
         ifcowl1:Coordinates_of_IfcCartesianPoint
      ifcinst:IfcLengthMeasure_List_371 .
ifcinst:IfcLengthMeasure_List_371
   rdf:type rdf:List ;
   rdf:first ifcinst:IfcLengthMeasure_371inst ;
   rdf:rest ifcinst:IfcLengthMeasure_List_372 .
ifcinst:IfcLengthMeasure_371inst
   rdf:type ifcowl1:IfcLengthMeasure ;
   ifcowl1:has_double “0.0”^^xsd:double .
ifcinst:IfcLengthMeasure_List_372
   rdf:type rdf:List ;
   rdf:first ifcinst:IfcLengthMeasure_372inst ;
   rdf:rest ifcinst:IfcLengthMeasure_List_373 .
ifcinst:IfcLengthMeasure_372inst
   rdf:type ifcowl1:IfcLengthMeasure ;
   ifcowl1:has_double “0.0”^^xsd:double .
ifcinst:IfcLengthMeasure_List_373
   rdf:type rdf:List ;
   rdf:first ifcinst:IfcLengthMeasure_373inst;
   rdf:rest rdf:nil .
ifcinst:IfcLengthMeasure_373inst
   rdf:type ifcowl1:IfcLengthMeasure ;
   ifcowl1:has_double “-350.0”^^xsd:double .
```

4.2 Procedure 2: custom list concepts

An alternative option consists in defining a new general purpose `LIST` concept for OWL, as considered throughout most of the conversion procedures that were outlined in Sect. 2. By doing so, it is possible to remain in the OWL DL profile, instead of OWL Full, which allows one to use reasoning or inference engines. This is a major improvement over the above *Procedure 1*, because logical inference is one of the most important additional features provided by OWL that is not available in regular other data modelling approaches. We distinguish four different proposals in defining such list concepts:

- the OWLList by Drummond et al. (2006)
- the Ordered List Ontology (OLO) by Abdallah and Ferris (2010)
- the approach followed in OntoSTEP by Krima et al. (2009) and Barbau et al. (2012)
- the approach proposed in the ifcOWL ontology by Pauwels and Terkaj (2015a, 2015b)

These approaches are quite similar in handling lists. As an example, Listing 4 shows how the `IfcCartesianPoint` given in Listing 2 can be converted using the approach proposed by Pauwels and Terkaj (2015a).

Although the mentioned approaches are viable alternatives that allow one to build an ifcOWL ontology in OWL DL, their results do not improve *Procedure 1* in terms of compactness and computational efficiency. Indeed, the instance representation given in Listing 4 is about as long as the representation in Listing 3. The differences between Listing 3 and 4 are at line numbers 6 (see `ifcowl:hasListContent`), 7 (see `ifcowl:hasNext`), 13, 14, and 20. These particularly added properties replace the standard `rdf:first`, and `rdf:rest` statements in Listing 3 which would make the ifcOWL ontology OWL Full. The OWLList (Drummond et al., 2006) and OntoSTEP (Krima et al., 2009; Barbau et al., 2012) approaches make the same suggestion, even if using different names for the properties. The OLO approach (Abdallah and Ferris, 2010) additionally allows one to directly define the index of each slot in the list; however, it is also possible to explicitly state the precedence relationship between slots and in this case OLO becomes very similar to the previously mentioned approaches.

4.3 Procedure 3: conversion into more meaningful concepts

A third option that could be considered is to add *entirely new* concepts that are customised for the specific list. For example, in the case of the `IfcCartesianPoint` (Listing 2), it is possible to add a number of new properties to directly refer to the single elements in a list of two or three coordinates (`IfcLengthMeasure` concepts), thereby implicitly allowing to distinguish between 2D and 3D `IfcCartesianPoint` concepts. The results of the application of the *Procedure 3a* is reported in Listing 5, where the object property `ifcowl2:Coordinates_of_IfcCartesianPoint` (line 3 in Listing 4) is replaced by three separate object properties that point directly to the appropriate `IfcLengthMeasure` instances (line 3-5 in Listing 5).

Furthermore, one might also design a procedure in which the *object* property `ifcowl2:Coordinates_of_IfcCartesianPoint` (line 3 in Listing 4) is replaced by three separate *datatype* properties, as shown in Listing 6. The datatype properties point directly to the appropriate literal values of type `ifcowl4:IfcLengthMeasure` (line 3-5 in Listing 6), which is then defined as an equivalent class (`owl:equivalentClass`) of `xsd:double`. Such a formal representation is a major improvement over the representations presented in Listing 3 and 4 (and 5) in terms of length, complexity and readability. The resulting RDF graphs following this conversion approach can thus be loaded

Listing 4: Representation of the example IfcCartesianPoint instance in Listing 2, following the conversion procedure as documented in Pauwels and Terkaj (2015a)

```
1  ifcinst:IfcCartesianPoint_37
2     rdf:type ifcowl2:IfcCartesianPoint ;
3     ifcowl2:Coordinates_of_IfcCartesianPoint ifcinst:IfcLengthMeasure_List_371 .
4  ifcinst:IfcLengthMeasure_List_371
5     rdf:type ifcowl2:List ;
6     ifcowl2:hasListContent inst:IfcLengthMeasure_371inst ;
7     ifcowl2:hasNext inst:IfcLengthMeasure_List_372 .
8  ifcinst:IfcLengthMeasure_371inst
9     rdf:type ifcowl2:IfcLengthMeasure ;
10    ifcowl2:has_double "0.0"^^xsd:double.
11 ifcinst:IfcLengthMeasure_List_372
12    rdf:type ifcowl2:List ;
13    ifcowl2:hasListContent  ifcinst:IfcLengthMeasure_372inst ;
14    ifcowl2:hasNext ifcinst:IfcLengthMeasure_List_373 .
15 ifcinst:IfcLengthMeasure_372inst
16    rdf:type ifcowl2:IfcLengthMeasure ;
17    ifcowl2:has_double "0.0"^^xsd:double .
18  ifcinst:IfcLengthMeasure_List_373
19    rdf:type ifcowl2:List ;
20  ifcowl2:hasListContent ifcinst:IfcLengthMeasure_373inst;
21  ifcinst:IfcLengthMeasure_373inst
22    rdf:type ifcowl2:IfcLengthMeasure ;
23    ifcowl2:has_double "-350.0"^^xsd:double .
.
```

and used far more efficiently. In addition, the resulting RDF graph is also more meaningful, as the relations between the IfcCartesianPoint concept and its coordinates are made explicit.

However, it must be noted that the ifcOWL3 ontology and the ifcOWL4 ontology used in

Listing 5: Representation of the example IfcCartesianPoint instance in Listing 2, following the conversion Procedure 3a that explicitly adds new semantic concepts

```
ifcinst:IfcCartesianPoint_37
   rdf:type ifcowl3:IfcCartesianPoint ;
   ifcowl3:xCoordinate_of_IfcCartesianPoint ifcinst:IfcLengthMeasure_371inst ;
   ifcowl3:yCoordinate_of_IfcCartesianPoint ifcinst:IfcLengthMeasure_372inst ;
   ifcowl3:zCoordinate_of_IfcCartesianPoint ifcinst:IfcLengthMeasure_373inst .
ifcinst:IfcLengthMeasure_371inst
   rdf:type ifcowl3:IfcLengthMeasure ;
   ifcowl3:has_double "0.0"^^xsd:double .
ifcinst:IfcLengthMeasure_372inst
   rdf:type ifcowl3:IfcLengthMeasure ;
   ifcowl3:has_double "0.0"^^xsd:double .
ifcinst:IfcLengthMeasure_373inst
   rdf:type ifcowl3:IfcLengthMeasure ;
   ifcowl3:has_double "-350.0"^^xsd:double .
```

Listings 5 and 6 have concepts that are beyond the original EXPRESS schema. Indeed, the new properties cannot be mapped to definitions in the EXPRESS schema where there is only 'a list with ordered coordinates', thus hindering the use of general purpose SPFF to RDF (and vice versa) converters. Moreover, *Procedure 3b* makes direct use of datatypes, thus discarding the 'objectification' pattern that was proposed in Schevers and Drogemuller (2005) and used in Beetz et al. (2009), Barbau et al. (2012), and Pauwels and Terkaj (2015a). This objectification pattern is required to correctly convert SELECT

Listing 6: Representation of the example IfcCartesianPoint instance in Listing 2, following a conversion Procedure 3b that explicitly adds new semantic concepts

```
ifcinst:IfcCartesianPoint_37
   rdf:type ifcowl:IfcCartesianPoint ;
   ifcowl4:xCoordinate_of_IfcCartesianPoint "0.0"^^ifcowl4:IfcLengthMeasure ;
   ifcowl4:yCoordinate_of_IfcCartesianPoint "0.0"^^ifcowl4:IfcLengthMeasure ;
   ifcowl4:zCoordinate_of_IfcCartesianPoint "-350.0"^^ifcowl4:IfcLengthMeasure.
```

data types in EXPRESS to equivalent expressions in OWL. Hence, there is a risk that the proposal in Listing 6 leads to infeasible representations of SELECT data types in OWL. Namely, it might become possible that a SELECT data type in OWL can be instantiated and refer to a SELECT data type which is at that point both a datatype (Listing 6) and an OWL class wrapping a data type (Listing 5), which is infeasible in OWL DL (see also Pauwels and Terkaj, 2015a).

4.4 Procedure 4: well-known text (WKT)

The suitability and usefulness of describing extensive collections of, for example, Cartesian points using notations compatible with DL mechanisms can be considered limited in many use cases. Namely, using general purpose inference mechanisms to address complex computational geometry problems will limit the performance or will be impossible without dedicated (procedural, non-DL) functions as provided by geometry kernel libraries. When interacting with such structures, most applications will map and transform them into more efficient, intermediary structures. Even if dedicated support for ordered collections in reasoning and query engines might be expected in the future, the verbosity of standard approaches discussed in sections 4.1 and 4.2 will most certainly hamper their efficient use at larger scales on data volume to be processed alone.

Therefore, a fourth procedure considered here relies on the usage of well-known text (WKT - ISO/IEC 13249-3 (2011)). This proposal has been made in the geospatial domain[6], where large amounts of geometrical information must

---

[6] http://www.geoapi.org/3.0/javadoc/org/opengis/referencing/doc-files/WKT.html

be represented both efficiently (short) and in a semantically meaningful manner. In this proposal, numeric values that are part of a particular concept or entity (e.g. a Cartesian point) are represented using (1) a keyword in upper case followed by the parameters of the object in brackets. This procedure applied to the case of the `IfcCartesianPoint` results in the formal representation given in Listing 7.

This formal representation clearly is an even larger improvement over the representations presented in Listing 3 and 4 (and 5 and 6) in terms of length, complexity and readability. The advantage compared to *Procedure 3* is that this approach can likely remain closer to the original EXPRESS schema: there are no additional concepts and the instance representation in Listing 2 is highly similar to the instance representation in Listing 7. A possible loss in terms of semantic precision could be at least partially softened by formally defining a customised *datatype* that is pointed to by `ifcowl5:Coordinates_of_IfcCartesianPoint`, instead of purely relying on informal agreements between the end users. In the case of Listing 7, for example, one could use `ifcowl5:wktIfcLengthMeasure`, instead of `ifcowl5:wktLiteral`. However, it remains to be seen if the correctness of these datatype values can be checked by semantic inference engines. Yet, such a trade-off between semantic precision and computational efficiency needs to be considered for domains with lots of numeric value aggregations, such as the geospatial domain and the geometric parts of the construction industry.

The mapping to WKT offers a plausible alternative to coordinate components, because the equivalents for these concepts exist in the WKT specification. Higher order geometrical representations also have WKT equivalents. For example, the `IfcPolyline` entity, a representation item consisting of a single attribute typed as a `LIST` of `IfcCartesianPoint`, can accurately be expressed as a `LINESTRING` WKT. Such an approach would reduce the number of nodes in the RDF graph even more, as multiple `IfcCartesianPoint` instances would be folded into a single WKT string object. This procedure can be followed up to higher order faceted boundary representations and the `IfcTriangulatedFaceSet` that is newly introduced in IFC4.

However, note that, with the existing set of WKT definitions, the representations that can be expressed are limited to polyhedral surfaces. For a more advanced string serialisation of curved face boundaries, one could look, for example, at the SVG standard, but it is likely that serialising a full-fledged BRep model into a string is beyond the scope of an ifcOWL serialisation. In addition, needless to say, for entities that do not pertain to the geometrical nature of a product, for example the `IfcMaterialLayerSet`, which features an ordered list of `IfcMaterialLayers`, no equivalent WKT concepts can be found, nor would they be meaningful as flattening them into textual strings would hinder graph-based querying of these concepts.

Listing 7: Representation of the example IfcCartesianPoint instance in Listing 2, following a conversion Procedure 4 that relies on the use of WKT

```
ifcinst:IfcCartesianPoint_37
rdf:type ifcowl5:IfcCartesianPoint ;
ifcowl5:Coordinates_of_IfcCartesianPoint "POINTZ(0.0 0.0 -
350.0)"^^ifcowl5:wktLiteral  .
```

5 Conclusion

As indicated at the outset of this paper, information technologies (IT) for the domain of architectural design and construction typically relies on a lot of aggregations (lists, sets, arrays, bags) for the representation of numeric values. A clear example is the intensive use of `LIST` expressions in IFC files. Indeed, the EXPRESS schema of IFC heavily relies on `LIST` data types. These data types do not map well on formal representations in OWL, simply because there is limited support for ordered aggregation types in OWL.

When considering *Procedure 3a* and *3b* as part of the same procedure, we presented four different procedures that can be used to represent aggregation types in OWL for the particular case of the Industry Foundation Classes (IFC). From the outline of these four procedures, it is clear that a trade-off needs to be made between semantic precision and computational efficiency. The procedures that result in the semantically most precise representations (*Procedure 1* and *2*) also result in lengthy and overly complex representations, yet they are the closest equivalents to the original EXPRESS schema. The procedures that result in computationally more efficient representations (*Procedure 3a*, *3b*, and *4*), on the other hand, could result in sloppier data representations, which could in turn result in errors, flaws and mistakes in the applications relying on that data. Yet, as many have concluded in the geospatial domain, this might be the only option to make the use of RDF graphs and OWL ontologies feasible for the architectural design and construction industry.

In further research, we will apply the two last conversion procedures to all the applicable data types in the IFC schema and analyse what this results in for an appropriate number of sample IFC files. This research will allow one to fully appreciate the viability of both approaches as alternatives to the conversion procedure that is currently used (` *2*).

References

Abdallah, S.A., and Ferris, B. (2010). The Ordered List Ontology 0.72 - Namespace Document 23 July 2010, http://purl.org/ontology/olo/core#, accessed April 2015.

Agostinho, C., Dutra, M., Jardim-Goncalves, R., Ghodous, P., Steiger-Garcao, A. (2007). EXPRESS to OWL morphism: making possible to enrich ISO10303 modules. In: Loureiro, G., and Curran, R. (Eds.). Complex Systems Concurrent Engineering, London: Springer, pp. 391–402.

Baader, F., and Nutt, W. (2003). Basic description logics. In: Baader, F., Calvanese, D., McGuinness, D.L., Nardi, D., Patel-Schneider, P.F. (Eds.). Description Logic Handbook: Theory, Implementation, and Applications, Cambridge: Cambridge University Press, pp. 47–100.

Barbau, R., Krima, S., Rachuri, S., Narayanan, A., Fiorentini, X., Foufou, S., Sriram, R.D. (2012). OntoSTEP: Enriching product model data using ontologies, Comput. Aided Design 44, pp. 575–590.

Beckett, D., Berners-Lee, T. (2011). Turtle - Terse RDF Triple Language - W3C Team Submission 28 march 2011, W3C Team Submission, http://www.w3.org/TeamSubmission/turtle/, accessed April 2015.

Beetz, J., Van Leeuwen, J., and de Vries, B. (2009). IfcOWL: a case of transforming EXPRESS schemas into ontologies, Ai. Edam. 23, pp. 89–101.

Berners-Lee, T., Hendler, J., and Lassila, O. (2001). The semantic web, Sci. Am. 284, pp. 35–43.

Brickley, D., and Guha, R.V. (2014). RDF Schema 1.1 - W3C Recommendation 25 February 2014, W3C Recommendation, http://www.w3.org/TR/rdf-schema/, accessed April 2015.

Dean, M., and Schreiber, G. (2004). OWL Web Ontology Language Reference - W3C Recommendation 10 February 2004, W3C Recommendation, http://www.w3.org/TR/owl-ref/, accessed April 2015.

Drummond, N., Rector, A., Stevens, R., Moulton, G., Horridge, M., Wang, H., Sedenberg, J. (2006). Putting OWL in order: Patterns for sequences in OWL. In: OWL Experiences and Directions (OWLEd 2006).

Eastman, C.M., Teicholz, P., Sacks, R., and Liston, K. (2008). BIM handbook: a guide to building information modeling for owners, managers, architects, engineers, contractors, and fabricators. Hoboken: Wiley.

Genesereth, M.R., and Fikes, R.E. (1992). Knowledge Interchange Format Version 3.0 Reference Manual, Technical Report Logic-92-1, Logic Group at the Computer Science Department of Stanford University, http://logic.stanford.edu/kif/specification.html, accessed April 2015.

Hitzler, P., Krötzsch, M., Parsia, B., Patel-Schneider, P.F., and Rudolph S. (2012). OWL 2 Web Ontology Language Primer (Second Edition) - W3C Recommendation 11 december 2012, W3C Recommendation, http://www.w3.org/TR/2012/REC-owl2-primer-20121211/, accessed April 2015.

International Organization for Standardization (2004). ISO 10303-11: Industrial automation systems and integration - Product data representation and exchange - Part 11: Description methods: The EXPRESS language reference manual, http://www.iso.org/iso/iso catalogue/catalogue_tc/catalogue detail.htm?csnumber=38047, accessed April 2015.

International Organization for Standardization (2011). ISO/IEC 13249-3:2011 Information technology - Database languages - SQL multimedia and application packages - Part 3: Spatial, http://www.iso.org/iso/iso_ca-talogue/catalogue_tc/catalogue_detail.htm?csnumber=53698, accessed April 2015.

International Organization for Standardization (2013). ISO 16739: Industry Foundation Classes (IFC) for data sharing in the construction and facility management industries, http://www.iso.org/iso/catalogue_detail.htm?cs-number=51622, accessed April 2015.

Krima, S., Barbau, R., Fiorentini, X., Sudarsan, R., Sriram, R. (2009) OntoSTEP: OWL-DL ontology for STEP, National Institute of Standards and Technology, Technical Report NISTIR 7561.

Liebich, T., Adachi, Y., Forester, J., Hyvarinen, J., Richter, S., Chipman, T., Weise, M., Wix, J. (2013). Industry Foundation Classes IFC4 official release, http://www.buildingsmart-tech.org/ifc/IFC4/final/html/index.htm, accessed April 2015.

Pauwels, P., and Van Deursen, D. (2012). IFC/RDF: adaptation, aggregation and enrichment. In: Report of the First International Workshop on Linked Data in Architecture and Construction, pp. 2–5.

Pauwels, P., and Terkaj, W. (2015a). EXPRESS to OWL for construction industry: towards a recommendable and usable ifcOWL ontology, Automat. Constr. (submitted).

Pauwels, P., and Terkaj, W. (2015b). ifcOWL: The EXPRESS to OWL conversion pattern, https://www.w3.org/communi-ty/lbd/ifcOWL/, accessed April 2015.

Schevers, H., and Drogemuller, R. (2005). Converting the Industry Foundation Classes to the Web Ontology Language. In: Proceedings of the 1st International Conference on Semantics, Knowledge and Grid, pp. 556–560.

Schreiber, G., and Raimond, Y. (2014). RDF 1.1 Primer - W3C Working Group Note 24 june 2014, W3C Working Group Note, http://www.w3.org/TR/2014/NOTE-rdf11-primer-20140624/, accessed April 2015.

Towards an integrated decision tool for evaluation of energy performance during building and plant design

A. Beltrami, alberto.beltrami@unibg.it
University of Bergamo, Dept. of Engineering and Applied Science, Dalmine (BG), Italy
Plymouth University, Building Performance Analysis Group, Drake Circus, PL4 8AA, Plymouth, UK

R.V. Jones, rory.jones@plymouth.ac.uk
Plymouth University, Building Performance Analysis Group, Drake Circus, PL4 8AA, Plymouth, UK

P. de Wilde, pieter.dewilde@plymouth.ac.uk
Plymouth University, Building Performance Analysis Group, Drake Circus, PL4 8AA, Plymouth, UK

M. Picco, marco.picco@unibg.it
University of Bergamo, Dept. of Engineering and Applied Science, Dalmine (BG), Italy

M. Marengo, marco.marengo@unibg.it
University of Bergamo, Dept. of Engineering and Applied Science, Dalmine (BG), Italy
University of Brighton, School of Computing, Engineering and Mathematics, Lewes Road, BN2 4GJ, Brighton, UK

Abstract
This work presents the creation of a dynamic energy model able to simulate, with a reasonable workload, a very large number of integrated building-plant systems with different scales and resolutions, in order to have a design support for architects and designers, reducing their modeling effort and errors. The model includes the dynamic simulation of the building envelope, all the heating plant subsystems, and all the plant components relating to the production of domestic hot water, the latter with possible solar thermal integration.
Starting from a detailed model created with the calculation engine Trnsys, the paper explores simplifications that can considerably reduce the number of necessary inputs for the simulations, thus minimizing the modeling, implementation and simulation runtime of the model, while still maintaining an acceptable degree of accuracy with respect to the computational results and real energy consumptions. The model is benchmarked by means of a case study comprising three different residential apartments with very high thermal performances, subjected to a complete monitoring of all energy consumption. The results show that the accuracy of the integrated model is within 16% of the real monitored consumptions, even for extreme cases such as the one presented.

Keywords: dynamic energy simulation, building and plant energy performance, decision tool.

1 Introduction

The daily operation of commercial and residential buildings is responsible for roughly one-third of the world's primary energy consumption. Because buildings are typically operated for many years, there is great potential for reducing global energy needs through the design of more energy-efficient buildings (Urban et al., 2006).
Computer modeling and simulation is a powerful technology for addressing some of the many interacting architectural, mechanical, and civil engineering issues in buildings. Building Performance Simulation (BPS) can help in reducing greenhouse gas emissions and in making substantial improvements towards lower fuel consumption and higher comfort levels, by treating buildings and their thermal systems as optimized entities, and not as the sum of a number of separately designed and optimized sub-systems or components (Hensen, 2011). Experience with real buildings has shown that low-energy design is not intuitive and that

simulations should therefore be an integral part of the design process (Hayter et al. 2001).
In fact, the efficiency of energy conservation measures cannot be studied in isolation because the interaction between components can have a substantial effect on the efficiency of each individual component. The impact of climate conditions and occupant behavior add to the complexity and make it almost impossible to predict performance without use of computational tools (de Wilde and Augenbroe, 2009).
However, architects and designers are still finding it difficult to use even basic tools (Punjabi et al., 2005). Findings confirm that most BPS tools are not compatible with architects' working methods and needs (Attia et al., 2009; Gratia et al., 2002), and even when simulation experts are part of the design team, modeling efforts and analysis of results typically are out of sync with the dynamics of the rest of the design process, leading to integration issues.
On a generic level, needs related to the design process can be easily identified as time and accuracy. Accuracy is an essential prerequisite for every analysis used for decision-making and becomes significantly more relevant during the design process of buildings, where decisions taken can have serious implications for future energy use and can affect building performance and operation for a large number of years. Accurate energy analysis requires time but this is in contrast with the necessity to minimize the time requirements to make it compatible with design times. A way to reduce time requirements could be the introduction of default values and databases for inputs, with the possible risk of reducing the model detail level and degree of freedom, themselves influencing the accuracy or relevance of the final result (Picco et al., 2013). In the context above, the research presented in this paper defines the creation of a configurable dynamic energy model able to simulate, with a reasonable workload, a very large number of integrated building-plant systems with different design scales and resolutions, including the dynamic simulation of the building envelope, all the heating plant subsystems, and all the plant components relating to the production of domestic hot water. This integrated and dynamic simulation model allows various simulations to be more easily initiated at various stages of design, instead of being used only in the final step of design validation, when most decisions concerning the building have already been made.
The objective of the work presented in this paper is to explore the main features of the model and to show its application to three different residential apartments characterized by very high energy performances and monitored energy consumptions, comparing the latter with the ones coming from the simulations.

2 Integrated and dynamic building – plant system model

The first step of the work has been the creation of an "adaptable and dimensionless" detailed and integrated dynamic building-plant system model.
The calculation engine used for this purpose is Trnsys (Trnsys version 17.00.0019). The model, as previously defined, allows the simultaneous simulation, for a maximum number of 15 different heated thermal zones, with detailed representation of the building envelope, heating plant (with all subsystems), and the hot domestic water systems. If needed, additional thermal zones can still be simulated with an "ideal load" approach.
In the specific Trnsys3D tool, a three-dimensional representation of the entire building can be created, as well as all relevant shadowing objects comprising all the adjacent building structures and the specific solar obstructions.
To characterize the various zones, each one is defined in terms of materials and layers of walls and windows, thermal bridges, internal gains, temperature set-points, heating schedule, external and boundary conditions. To define these items, the TRNBuild tool is used, which is the Trnsys tool specifically dedicated to the characterization of the building envelope.
The dynamic operation of the heating plant and the domestic hot water system are modeled through the Trnsys components called "Types", all connected according to an input – output logic (Fig.1).

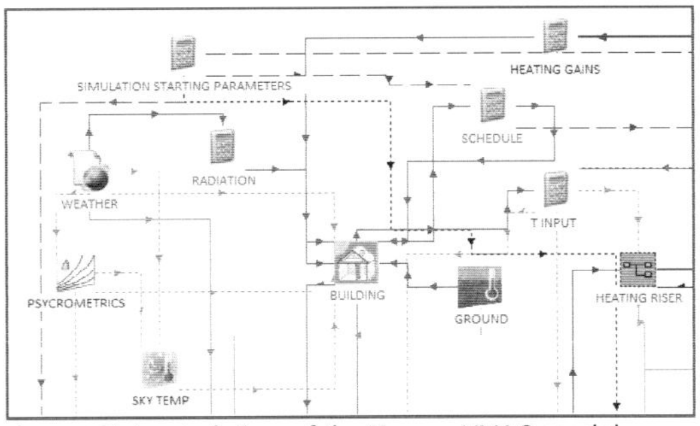

Figure 1 Extracted view of the Trnsys HVAC model

Within Trnsys each Type can be considered as a "black box", which processes input data as a function of defined algorithms, starting from user-defined parameters, and producing output data. The task of each Type is to solve simple problems, and their interconnection allows the user to study higher-level issues.

In the model described here, each Type corresponds to a single component of the building plant.

The hydraulic base system scheme that is simulated by the integrated model can be divided into two main different constituent parts or sub-systems:

- Sub-system A: this represents plant configurations composed of only one single generator with internal Domestic Hot Water (DHW) heat exchanger, for DHW and/or heating (HS).

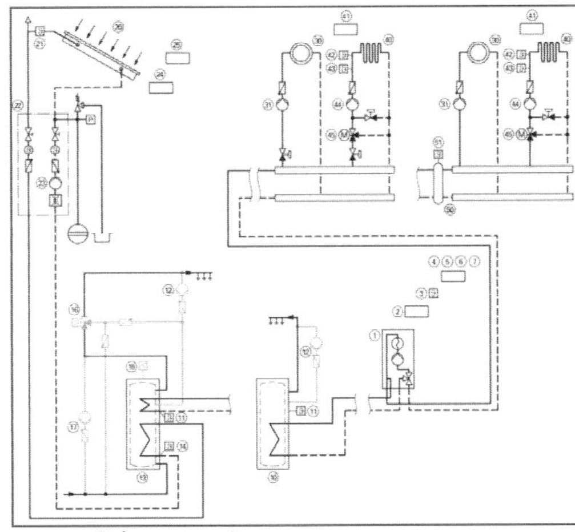

Figure 2 Sub-system A

- Sub-system B: this represents plant configurations composed of one or multiple generators with external DHW heat exchanger, for DHW and/or heating (HS).

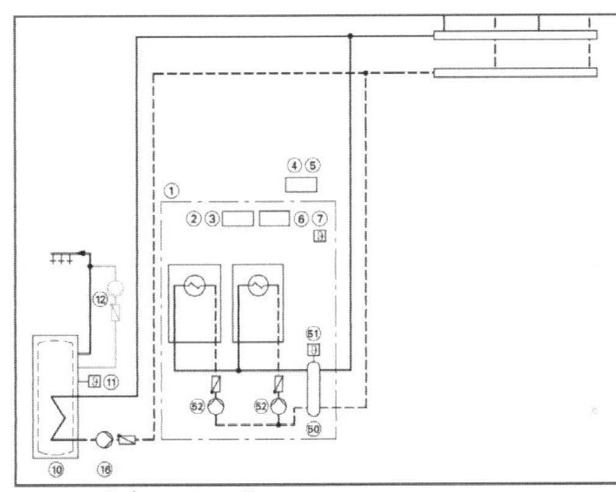

Figure 3 Sub-system B

In the two schemes there can be, for the

Table 1 Hydraulic base system schemes

			DOMESTIC HOT WATER (DHW)					
		No HDW	Instantaneous production		Storage production			
			No solar integr.	Solar integr.	No solar integration		Solar integration	
			Priority	Priority	Priority	No priority	Priority	No priority
	No HS	/	A1	A2	A3	/	A4	/
HEATING SYSTEM (HS)	Direct HS	A5	A8	A11	A14	/	A17	/
	Hydraulic separator HS	A6	A9	A12	A15	/	A18	/
	Storage HS	A7	A10	A13	A16	/	A19	/
	Direct HS & DHW	B1	/	/	B4	B7	B10	B13
	Hydraulic separator HS & DHW	B2	/	/	B5	B8	B11	B14
	Storage HS & DHW	B3	/	/	B6	B9	B12	B15

domestic hot water:
- Instantaneous production, with priority;
- Storage capacity, with or without priority;
- Solar integration;

For the Heating system, there can be a:
- Heating system without hydraulic separator, in other words: a direct loop from the generation;
- Heating system with hydraulic separator or storage (the heating storage can replace the hydraulic separator in Fig.2 and Fig.3);

All these possible simulation combinations are summarized in Table 1, generating an option space that consists of 34 different system schemes starting from only one dynamic and integrated Trnsys model.

As specified above, the model is highly "adaptable" because the 34 different base system schemes can be split into a lot of other different combinations. In fact each scheme is suitable to have the following variations:
- for the emission and internal control subsystems the base model still allows flexible simulation of the behavior of radiators, radiant panels, fan coils, district heating heat exchangers, and variation between On-off, P, PI or PID control;
- for the distribution subsystem there can be different pipe lengths, materials and insulations, with the fluid moved by pumps with fixed or variable speed, the latter with control at constant or proportional pressure;
- for the storage subsystem there is the possibility to change volumes, internal heat exchanger properties, and stratification effects;
- for the generation subsystem the simulation allows for variation of one or multiple cascade/ integrated generators, with different generator types, like boiler supplied with traditional or renewable fuels, heat pumps, cogeneration systems;

The model can also be defined as "dimensionless" due to its adaptability (thanks even to the sizing and simplification protocols described later) to three different design scales, each characterized by a different "resolution", intended as the ability of the model to group multiple components into a unique one, especially for the emission subsystem.

In fact it can be used in the following three design conditions:
- Small scale and high resolution design, for the simulation of an independent apartment, commercial unit or building floor, where each thermal zone is composed of only one room and where each real emission device is individually simulated;
- Medium scale and medium resolution design, for the simulation of an apartment building or a multi-floor building, where each thermal zone is respectively equal to one apartment or one floor and where the real emission devices are summarized and simulated with only one emission device with equivalent features;
- Large scale and small resolution design, for the simulation of district heating, where one thermal zone is equal to one building and its emission device is the district heating heat exchanger;

In conclusion, the single detailed dynamic model provides a starting point for a range of simulations at different levels of scale and resolutions.

3 Sizing and simplification protocols

The model described above represents the highest degree of simulative details with a high number of outputs made available at each time-step (up to about 1700 outputs), from the operating temperatures in all components to the unsteady heat balance regulating each component and the cumulative efficiencies of the various sub-systems installations. It allows to check the actual operation of the entire dynamic building-plant system at any variation of all possible internal and external conditions, taking into account each instant the interaction of all the components.

On the other side a large number of parameters and inputs has to be set for the simulations. In fact, the most detailed model is composed by a total number of 221 types, with about 1400 parameters and 1150 inputs required to describe their features.

In order to reduce the number of necessary variables for the simulations (note that the input-output connections of the types reduce themselves the variables to be set roughly to the number of parameters only), to minimize the modeling, implementation and simulation runtime of the model and to extend it to all the design scales, a "sizing protocol" and a "simplification protocol" have been created.

The "sizing protocol" is composed of a spreadsheet able to do the complete sizing and characterization of all TRNSYS Types used for the plant components, starting from the user's loads (the "ideal" heating load can derive from a dynamic simulation carried out only for the building envelope), going through a stationary plant design and ending with the highlighting

of all inputs and parameters required by the detailed and integrated dynamic model.
The "simplification protocol" is composed of the following two possible simplifications:
- S1: Building envelope simplification;
- S2: Heating plant simplification;

Starting from the first (S1), the whole simplification process is composed by eight consecutive steps to generate a simplified model from a detailed model (Fig.4), where each step tackles one major aspect of the building model description.

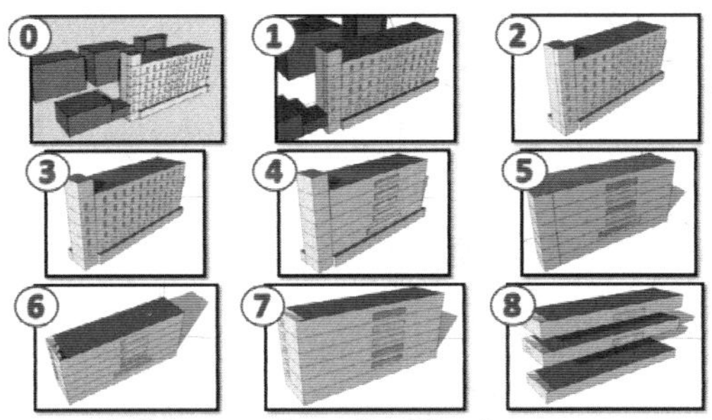

Figure 4 Building envelope simplification

It is divided into the following steps:
- Step 1- Simplified construction: reduction of the number of constructions to only 6 archetypes reflecting the average transmittance of each type of dispersant surface considered for the whole building
- Step 2- Removal of external obstructions: elimination of all the external shading elements modeled;
- Step 3- Zone lumping: characterization of each floor of the building with one single thermal zone.
- Step 4- Simplified transparent surfaces: modeling, for each floor, only one window for each cardinal direction that considers all of the windows present in that direction;
- Step 5- Single floor standardization: elimination of all accessory areas and defining of all zones (floors) with a single geometry. Zone parameters and internal gains are also made constant with the exception of underground and under-roof floors, if present.
- Step 6- Squaring zone: definition of each zone as an element composed of only six surfaces, making up a box (the main information to maintain as close as possible to the full model are the dispersant surfaces).
- Step 7- Standardization of fenestrations: characterization of all the windows facing one direction by the same parameters regardless of the floor, always considering all of the windows present in that direction.
- Step 8- Number of modeled floors: Reduction of the model to a minimum number of floors by allowing the creation of 3 zones only for any type of building (with the exception of the unheated underground and under-roof floors, if present), simulating the remaining as a multiplier of the above.

This first simplification process has been already tested and validated by Picco et al (2013) for different kinds of buildings, featuring differences always within the margin of 20% between the most detailed model and the most simplified model and a large decrease of the work load related to the building modelling (from days to hours).

About the heating plant simplification, three different simplifications has been identified:
- S2.1- Internal control with external energy input: this simplification involves the replacement, in the detailed model, of the component related to the simulation of the building behavior with a type constituted by an external data file that gives, at each time-step, the ideal thermal useful energy demand of each zone considered.

The latter, coming from a dynamic simulation carried out only for the building envelope, represents the new external input of the environmental control subsystem, no longer based on the internal temperature of the zone, assumed equal to the set point temperature as boundary condition for the emission subsystem.
- S2.2- External efficiency for emission and control subsystems: this simplification allow to characterize all the different kinds of emission and control subsystems only with their constant or variable efficiency, derived from standard values universally adopted.
- S2.3- Heating plant resizing: the reduction of a certain number of real zones to a single thermal zone coming out from the first simplification process S1 is necessarily accompanied by a new sizing of the plant, in particular of the emission and distribution subsystems, now sized starting from the sum of the loads related to the real zones.

The whole simplification process has been already tested for a small scale design consisting of a residential unit located in a semi-detached existing house, subjected to a renovation design (Beltrami et al. 2015).

The model, composed of seven different thermal zones or rooms and the base system scheme A7, has been used for the development of the most detailed model and for the application of the simplification protocols to a

small scale case study with common concrete structure and medium energy performances.
The results indicate the accuracy of the most simplified model in terms of energy needs, power curves and subsystem efficiencies is very high, with a difference from the most complete analysis always below the 12% for all the output parameters and with a workload for the preparation of the model and the simulation reduced to one half (from six days to three days) and equal or even less than the time necessary to perform a complete traditional stationary simulation.

4 Case study

This paper applies the generic model to a specific, challenging case study: a recently built apartment building in the UK which has been designed to high energy efficiency standards, and which is subject to monitoring. This allows the validation of the model with a high performance building, making sure this is able to represent advanced dwellings. The availability of metered data provides a baseline for validation which is not available for any hypothetical cases.
In fact the case study consists of a recently built apartment building comprising 15 flats, three of which subjected to a complete monitoring of all energy consumptions and activities.
In particular the dynamic simulations have been carried out for the whole building-plant system of each of this latter three single units, with a small scale design (each room equal to one thermal zone) and a base system scheme A5.
Following the description of the case study and the achieved results.

4.1 Building description

The building studied is an apartment building comprising 15 flats, built in 2012 and situated in Torquay, UK.
The building consists of four floors, the basement for the car park, ground, first and second floors intended for residential purposes and each composed of five apartments along a central hallway (Fig.5).

Figure 5 Building second floor plant

The whole building is characterized by a net total floor area of 1921 m^2 and a net total volume of 5255 m^3, while each apartment has 8 heated rooms, a useful floor area of 77 m^2 and a net total volume of 208 m^3.
The building has an innovative steel-wood structure able to reduce thermal bridges and especially construction times. The building layers are also uncommon, designed to have the best thermal, hygrometric and acoustic performances.
In particular, the dispersant surfaces have been designed in order to have high thermal and hygrometric performances.
In fact all the surfaces are composed by several different layers and materials, with a transmittance equal to 0.10 W/m^{2}K for the external walls, 0.11 W/m^{2}K for the external ceilings, 0.13 W/m^{2}K for the external floors, 0.55 W/m^{2}K for the external doors and 1.2 W/m^{2}K for the external windows or transparent surfaces.
In addition, the internal partitions have been designed to have the best acoustic performances, based on the so called "Robust details", an online handbook that brings together the best layers in terms of acoustic performances, already tested and recognized by the English building legislation.
The separating walls and floors are composed by multiple layers and they have low transmittance, equal to 0.21W/m^{2}K and 0.18 W/m^{2}K respectively. The HVAC plant provided for each apartment is composed by an independent mechanical ventilation system (whose main aim is to ensure proper air change in the winter season and to avoid overheating during the summer) and an independent aluminium radiators heating system, powered by a 28kW combined condensing natural gas boiler, used even for the instantaneous production of the domestic hot water.
A climate control for the supply temperature of the heating plant is provided, together with an

internal regulation composed by thermostatic valves able to reduce or increase the flow rate of the heat transfer fluid to the radiators. All the isolated distribution network piping is placed inside the heated environments in order to reduce losses to a minimum value.

As previously specified, three apartments of the building, situated on the second floor, have been subjected to monitoring of energy consumptions and activities.

In particular, in addition to the outside temperature and relative humidity, for each apartment the following data, with a five minutes timestep, have been monitored:

- Occupancy (with Passive InfraRed sensor) of central hallway and living room;
- Window opening in main and second bedroom;
- Balcony door opening in living room;
- Temperature and Relative Humidity in living room and main bedroom;
- Total gas and electricity consumptions;

Even if the apartments have the same dimensions, structural, thermal and HVAC features, and even if the consumptions are very low respect when compared with a standard residential unit, the occupant's influence during the real management of the apartment is very high, as shown by the monitored gas consumptions for the heating system, completely different for the three users (Fig.6).

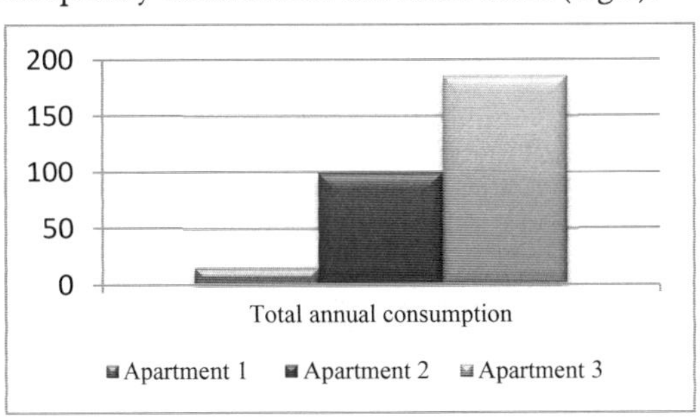

Figure 6 Total monitored gas consumptions (m^3)

4.2 Simulations

In order to apply the integrated and dynamic building - plant system model to the three apartments with monitored data, the three-dimensional modeling of the entire building has been created, as shown in the following Fig.7. In particular every room has been modeled for the three apartments while only one thermal zone has been created for the other apartments and boundary zones.

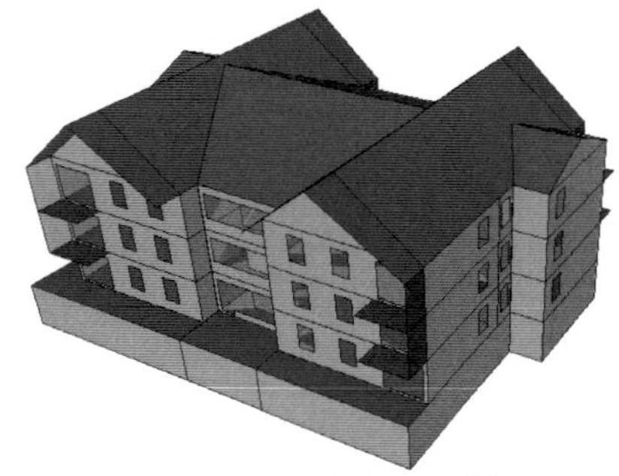

Figure 7 Complete model for building envelope (Trnsys3D)

After, the characterization of the entire building envelope in Trnbuild tool has been performed and finally three different dynamic simulations have been carried out, each one applying the integrated model only for one apartment, simulating the others boundary thermal zones only with an "ideal load" approach (i.e. no HVAC systems really simulated).

In particular the main assumptions done in the whole process has been the following:

- Plymouth 2002 weather file has been used (the closest available weather file), correcting it with the real temperature and relative humidity coming from the monitored data.
- Set point temperature for the heating system of each apartment equal to the average internal temperature monitored in the same unit (for the three apartments) or equal to the global average internal temperature monitored (for the other apartments);
- Solar factor or g-value of all the transparent surfaces equal to 0.265 and internal shading devices able to considerably reduce the external solar radiation fraction directly transmitted to the internal environment;
- Continuous air change due to infiltrations equal to 0.06/h and increase of the latter to 0.15/h when the inside temperature is higher and the outside temperature is lower than the one monitored, in order to reflect the real opening and closing of the external doors and windows.
- Continuous air change volume due to the mechanical ventilation, for all the apartments except the apartment 3, equal to 85.1 kg/h, and increase of the latter to 170.2 kg/h in the summer. For these apartments the temperature of the incoming air in the winter season is equal to the one coming from an heat recovery with an efficiency of 87%, while in the summer season is equal to the one coming either from the heat recovery or directly from the outside, when the conditions for the

activation of the heat recovery bypass are satisfied (note that air change volume, heat recovery efficiency and bypass logic have been derived from the constructor details);

- Continuous air change volume due to the mechanical ventilation, for only the apartment 3, equal to 170.2 kg/h, both in the winter and in the summer season. For this apartment the temperature of the incoming air is always equal to the one coming either from the heat recovery or directly from the outside, the latter when the conditions for the activation of the heat recovery bypass are satisfied (in this case the temperature set point for the activation of the bypass is supposed lower than the same for the others apartments in order to permit the bypass to be activated even in the winter season);
- Internal electric gains of each apartment equal, for the three apartments, to the total electric consumptions monitored in the same unit, minus the energy related to the electric showers, whose activation is supposed for the monitoring timesteps with higher consumptions. For the other apartments the internal electric gains are supposed equal to the average of the three above.
- Internal occupancy provided, for each apartment, only for the two thermal zones with PIR sensor, the central hallway and the living room. When the PIR sensor has registered a positive occupation of the area during the monitoring timestep, it has been supposed to have one person in the hallway and two people in the living room.

As for the other variables the occupancy on-off value for the three main apartments derives directly from the monitored data, while for the other apartments an average value of the latter is provided.

- The monthly gas consumption of the three main apartments, used to compare real and simulations results, is directly derived from the monitored data, removing from the global monthly consumption the one related to the domestic hot water, this equal to the average gas consumption of the summer months (from May to September);
- Applying of the integrated and dynamic building – plant system model to the three apartments with monitored data with the adoption of the heating plant simplifications S2.1 and S2.2 and recovery of all the losses and internal energy changes related to the distribution subsystem because the isolated distribution network piping is placed inside the heated environments.

4.3 Results

Due to the high number of available outputs, the comparison between the simulation results and the monitored data has been restricted to the output parameters able to describe the main thermal behavior of the building. So, the comparison has been proceeded, for each of the three apartments, for:

- Trend of the average internal temperature during the winter season (controlled temperature) and during the summer season (temperature controlled only through the mechanical ventilation);
- Monthly gas consumption for heating;

The results are the following:

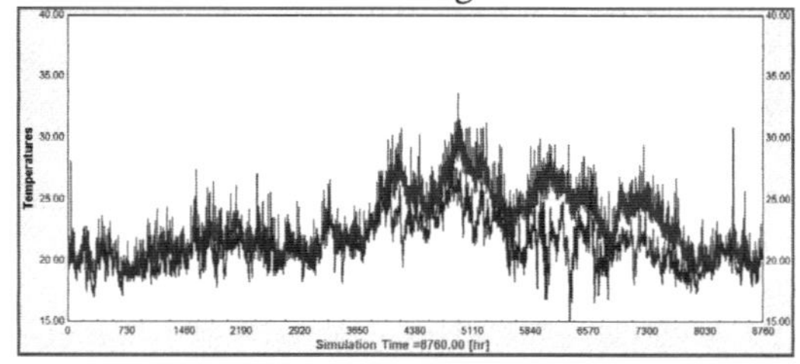

Figure 8 Apartment 1 internal monitored (violet line) and simulated (blue line) average temperature (°C).

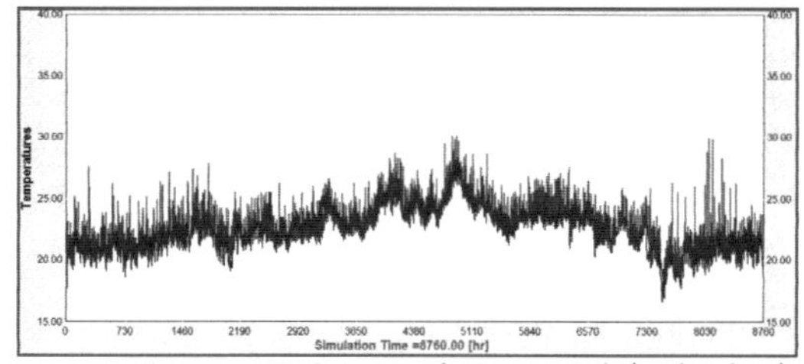

Figure 9 Apartment 2 internal monitored (violet line) and simulated (blue line) average temperature (°C).

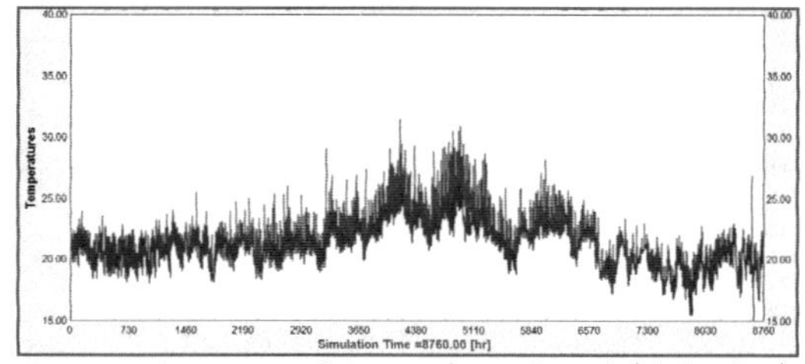

Figure 10 Apartment 3 internal monitored (violet line) and simulated (blue line) average temperature (°C).

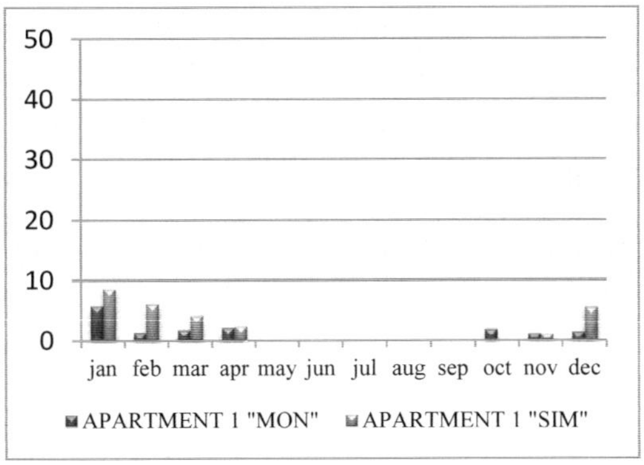

Figure 11 Apartment 1 monitored ("MON") and simulated ("SIM") monthly gas consumptions (m^3).

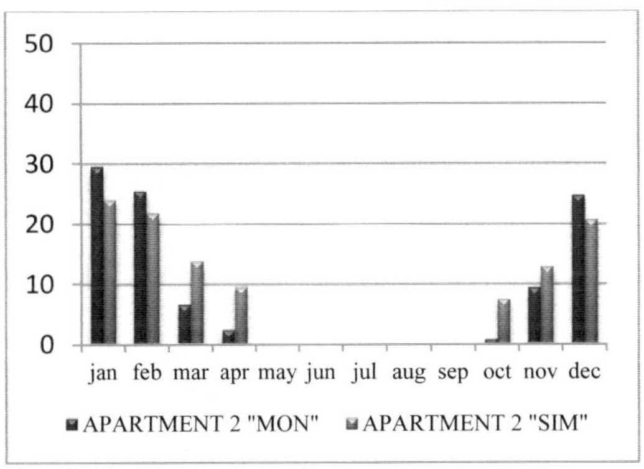

Figure 12 Apartment 2 monitored ("MON") and simulated ("SIM") monthly gas consumptions (m^3).

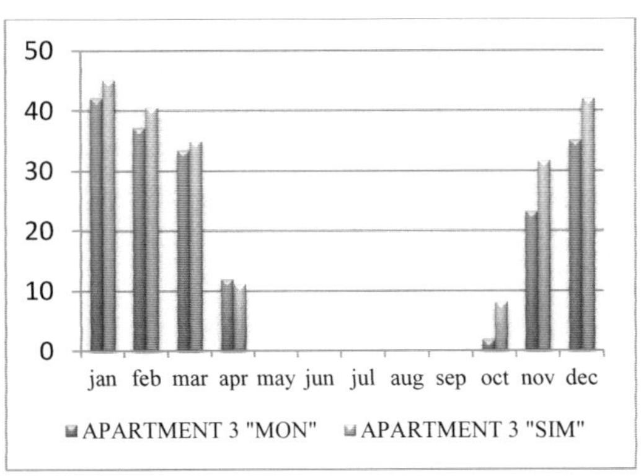

Figure 13 Apartment 3 monitored ("MON") and simulated ("SIM") monthly gas consumptions (m^3).

It can be stated that:

- The simulation trend of the average internal temperature during both the winter and the summer season reflect in a very reliable way the same as in the monitored data, especially for apartments 2 and 3.

Only for the first apartment the simulation sometimes overestimates the internal temperature.

- Even the trend of the monthly gas consumption between the simulated and monitored data is similar for all of the apartments. In particular the average annual consumption coming from the simulation is 11% overestimated compared to the real one for the apartment 2, while 16% overestimated for the apartment 3. The percentage overestimation of the gas consumption for the apartment 1 is higher but it doesn't matter because the consumption of that unit is practically zero both in the monitoring an in the simulations.

Then taking into account that:

- The simulated building is characterized by very high thermal performances and low energy consumptions (the gas consumption for heating of the apartment 3 is approximately equal to one-tenth of that for a common residential unit);
- The heat balance that describes each unit is very sensitive even to small variations of each component, from the different solar gains due to different exposures to the presence or absence of people, the management of the electrical equipment and to the different possible adjustments of all HVAC components;
- The apartments are indeed characterized by very different consumption from each other, showing how the occupant's influence during the real management of the apartment is very high;
- Nonetheless the assumptions made for the applying of the dynamic simulations have been extended without distinctions to all apartments;

the results obtained through the application of the dynamic and integrated model can be considered excellent as the latter is able to predict the behavior of the whole building-plant system for extreme cases such as the one presented above.

5 Conclusions

This paper presents a detailed simulation model of actual dwellings in the UK, which can easily be configurated to study a range of design alternatives (both in terms of systems and system attributes) throughout the design process of building plants for similar buildings.

In particular the "adaptable and dimensionless" integrated model described in the paper is able to provide a complete energy simulation with a very high accuracy and a workload equal or

even less that the time necessary to perform a complete stationary simulation for an high number of different building-plant systems in different design scales and conditions.
In fact the model has been developed to help architects and designers to adress time/accuracy issues , both in terms of quality and low engineering costs.

Acknowledgements
The authors thank the graduating student M. Cagliani for his work and inputs on this project. The authors would also like to express gratitude to the anonymous housing association that provided access to the buildings as well as additional funding for the Post-Occupancy Evaluation of the dwellings.

References
Attia, S., et al., 2009. Architect friendly: a comparison of ten different building performance simulation tools. Building simulation 2009, Eleventh International IBPSA Conference Glasgow, Scotland July 27-30, 2009.
Beltrami, A., Picco, M., Marengo, M., 2015. Comparison of energy simulations for a residential unit: a rapid method for an integrated decision tool. Paper accepted for Building Simulation Applications 2015, 2a IBPSA Italy conference, Bolzano, Italy, February 4-6, 2015.
de Wilde, P. and G. Augenbroe, 2009. Energy modelling. In: D. Mumovic and M. Santamouris (eds), A Handbook of Sustainable Building Design and Engineering. London: Earthscan, 51-61.
Gratia, E., De Herde, A., 2002. A simple design tool for the thermal study of an office building. Energy and Buildings, 34: p. 279-289.
Hayter, S.J., Torcellini, P.A., Hayter, R.B., Judkoff, R. 2001. The Energy Design Process for Designing and Constructing High-Performance Buildings. Clima 2000/Napoli 2001 World Congress - Napoli (I), 15-18 September 2001.
Hensen, J.L.M. and R. Lamberts, eds. 2011. Building performance simulation for design and operation. Abingdon: Spon Press.
Jordaan, I., 2005. Decisions under uncertainty: probabilistic analysis for engineering decisions. Cambridge: Cambridge University Press.
Picco, M., Lollini, R., Marengo, M., 2014. Towards energy performance evaluation in early stage building design: A simplification methodology for commercial building models. Energy and Buildings, Volume 76, June 2014, Pages 497-505.
Punjabi, S., Miranda, V., 2005. Development of an integrated building design information interface. IBPSA Building Simulation 2005, Ninth International IBPSA Conference, Montréal, Canada, August 15-18, 2005.
Urban, B., Glicksman, L., 2006. The MIT Design Advisor – A fast, simple tool for energy efficient building design. Simbuild 2006 Second National IBPSA-USA Conference Cambridge, MA August 2-4, 2006.

Dynamic Blind Control: A Simulation Approach for Energy Efficiency

Rodrigo Leal, rodrigomfl@hotmail.com
Intituto Superior Técnico, Universidade de Lisboa, Portugal

Francisco Regateiro, francisco.regateiro@tecnico.ulisboa.pt
Intituto Superior Técnico, Universidade de Lisboa, Portugal

Maria Gomes, maria.gloria.gomes@tecnico.ulisboa.pt
Intituto Superior Técnico, Universidade de Lisboa, Portugal

Abstract
With the increasing energy demand energy efficiency is becoming increasingly more important. Automated blind control is one of the ways to waste less energy in a building. With multiple studies finding that manual control is inefficient, further study on automated blind controls is needed. This paper proposes some control strategies for automated blinds and comparing the different energy consumptions.

Keywords: Blind Automation, Energy Efficiency, Building Performance Simulation

1 Introduction

Energy efficiency has been receiving considerable attention. One particular focus of attention concerns the big growth in electric energy demand, besides 1.3 billion people worldwide with no access to electric energy. The IEA (International Energy Agency) predicts a 50% growth in this demand until 2030 due to the industrial development and population growth. According to IEA, electric energy consumption in buildings represents 32% of the total energy consumption worldwide. The ECF (European Climate Foundation) states that 75% of buildings are residential buildings and of the other 25%, 23% are office buildings. Moreover, in spite of existing less office buildings, in Europe these consume around 306 kWh/m^2 whereas residential buildings consume around 200 kWh/m^2, i.e., office buildings consume about more 50% than residential buildings. Considering that energy efficiency may be improved in residential buildings, ADENE (the Portuguese Agency for Energy) recommends three most cost-effective fields of intervention: insulation (roof, walls, and floor), solar systems, DHW system (domestic hot water).

Human beings evolved over thousands of years being subjected to various time cycles. As a consequence we developed biological clocks that allow us to follow the progress of each cycle. One of these clocks is known as the circadian clock, which follows the daily period, which is related to daylight. Desynchronization between the circadian clock and the external environment can be caused by little exposure to sunlight, which can negatively affect health. (Boyce et al., 2003; Gery and Koeffler, 2010; Golombek et al., 2013; Pauley, 2004)

One study found a positive correlation between increased sunlight and higher academic performance in various schools (HESCHONG MAHONE GROUP, 1999a) and another study found a positive correlation between increased solar lighting and more sales at various stores (HESCHONG MAHONE GROUP, 1999b). This latest study suggests a possible positive correlation between solar lighting and productivity in other areas of work.

Manually operated blinds tend to be operated once a day and stay in that position for the remainder of the day.(Galasiu and Veitch, 2006; Zhang and Barrett, 2012)

A study to 468 blinds for 4 days (Kim et al., 2009) found that over 50% of the blinds were not operated during the day, adding to this value the blinds used only once during the day the percentage rises to 95%.

In Vine et al., 1998 was concluded that automated blind control methods were less accepted by the users when compared with manual control. In spite of that the manual control users reported more glare related discomfort situations with both electric and natural lighting.

Following the previous paragraphs, there is a need for further study and development of methods for automated control blind systems.

One of the limitations of automated blind control is the high variability user preferred comfort values.(Galasiu and Veitch, 2006; Newsham, 1994)

In EN ISO 13790, 2006 for design purposes the radiation value of 300 W/m^2 is used as reference value to blind operation.

In Newsham, 1994 the value 233 W/m^2 was used as maximum solar beam intensity allowed on the user, upon which the blinds would be activated. The value was enough to avoid user discomfort.

In Oh et al., 2012 Energy Plus automated blind simulations were ran in which one of the goals was to keep the DGI value near the window below 22. Using radiation measurements it was concluded that incident window solar radiation values below 50 W/m^2 didn't cause visual discomfort.

Energy Plus documentation suggests 22 as office maximum DGI value.(Ernest Orlando Lawrence Berkeley National Laboratory, 2013a)

da Silva et al., 2012 ran automated blind simulations in which the blinds were closed or opened depending on DGI values. Two different cases were simulated one using the value 20 and the other using the value 24 as the reference values for blind operation.

The most cited recommended minimum work surface illuminance level were 300 lux and 500 lux, the last one being the more cited between the two.(Olbina and Hu, 2012; Reinhart, 2004; Tzempelikos and Athienitis, 2007)

In DiBartolomeo et al., 1996 a blind control algorithm was used to block direct radiation as its first priority. Its second priority was to guaranty that the work surface illuminance was between 485 lux and 675 lux with maximum daylight. If the daylight wasn't enough to fulfil the lighting need an electric light would activate.

In Kim et al., 2009 automated blind control was done taking into account the exterior illuminance. One of the strategies was more energy conservative and closed the blinds when the exterior illuminance was 16 klux and opened otherwise. The other strategy was more aimed at user comfort and closed the blinds at 25 klux except between 12:00 and 13:00 when the operation value dropped to 16 klux.

In Reinhart and Voss, 2003 several offices were tested with automated blinds which closed when exterior illuminance was higher than 28 klux and lower otherwise. Many users didn't accept the automatic blind closing. As such it was suggested that a better control method would be to raise the blinds is the external illuminance was lower than 28 klux but only close it if the external illuminance surpassed 50 klux.

2 Setting

A simulation based approach allows testing and comparing of numerous types of control, different geometric conditions like façade orientation amongst others and different seasons.

A one person office modeled in Energy Plus was used to run the simulations.

2.1 Office

This office was modeled in Cláudio Ribeiro Faustino, 2012, but modified and updated for this paper.

The office is located on the second floor of a three floor building, the Civil Engineering complex in IST in Lisbon, Portugal. The façade is oriented due east, has a 66% glazed area and it's the only outside facing surface. With ceiling height of 3,15 m and a floor area of 14,06 m^2 it has a volume of 44,30 m^3.

In this model the venetian blinds were horizontal. A "WindowMaterial:Blind" object was created where the necessary data to build a blind in EP was inputted. Based in blinds used in other studies (Gomes et al., 2012) it was considered a slat with 8 cm of width, 6,8 cm spacing between slats and a medium level of reflectance of 0,4. The thickness value used was 1 mm and was based on the value in the EP example file "WindowBlindMaterials.idf".

For temperature control it was specified a dual point thermostat to maintain the temperature between 20ºC e 25ºC. It was created a "ThermostatSetpoint:Dualsetpoint" object with the field "Heating Set point Temperature Schedule Name" with a schedule which the value was 20 during work hours and with the field "Cooling Set point Temperature Schedule Name" with a schedule which the value was 25 during work hours.

To meet the minimum lighting needs of the user it was created an object "Daylighting:Controls". This object needed the input of the reference point in which the lighting measures would be made, in this case was considered to be the center of the work surface. The work surface was at 0,8 m of height and its center was 0,9 m from the window. As a minimum illuminance value to be guaranteed by the electric lighting it was inputted 500 lux. When daylight illuminance was lower than 500 lux the electric lighting would be activated. The lighting control was simple on/off. Furthermore these automatic lights only worked on a specific schedule, in this case during work hours.

2.2 Environmental conditions

As said before because it is a simulation it is possible to consider multiple environmental conditions. In this paper only a few were explored.

Although the original office had its façade facing east, simulations were run for both east and south facade orientation. Both orientations have different limitations. East is where the sun rises and as such in the morning the sun is very low in the sky, which exposes most of the office to direct radiation if not protected. South is where the sun moves in the afternoon and where it stays longer. In spite of being higher in the sky it's when its effect is felt with more intensity resulting in higher levels of radiation.

Although many values used in the model were in compliance with the Portuguese regulation the running period was not. The running period used was summer, between June 21st and September 21st, this was done so it would be easier to compare results with simulations ran in other countries.

In this model venetian blinds were the solar protection of choice for both being very popular in offices and for being very versatile and adapting easily two the users' needs(Zhang and Barrett, 2012). The venetian blind were exterior blinds because these are more suited to summer time.

2.3 Control Strategies

Table 2 shows the nine blind control strategies that were considered.

Strategies 1, 2 and 3 don't represent preferences or comfort needs of the users. In spite of that these strategies were considered for representing extreme cases.

Strategy 4 was considered for comparisons purposes. Lisbon's latitude is about 38□ and a fixed 45° slat angle should provide similar result to strategy 8.

Strategy 5 considers what is specified if the Portuguese regulation ("Despacho n.º 15793-K/2013," 2013). In the regulation for calculating the cooling needs the approach is to consider the solar protection device active for a fraction of the time which depends on the orientation of the window in which it is installed. On table 1 there are all the values of the decimal fraction of daytime in which the device is considered to be active. In EP the fraction of time in which the blinds were active coincided with the period of the day in which the radiation more inconvenient depending on the orientation. For the east orientation that period began at sunrise and for the south orientation that period's midpoint coincided with the midpoint of day time.

Table 1 Portuguese regulation values

Window orientation	Daytime fraction in which is active
N	0
NE/NW	0,4
S	0,6
SE/SW	0,7
E/W	0,6
H	0,9

Strategies 6 and 8 activate or deactivate the blinds based on a specific set point. Strategy 6 works by activating the blinds if solar radiation incident on the window is higher than 300 W/m^2. The radiation measured was the global solar radiation, meaning the diffuse radiation plus the direct radiation. With strategy 8 the blinds are activated when DGI value are higher than 22. The point at which DGI values are measured is a reference point with the same coordinates as the work surface center but at 1,2 m of height and is orientated 90□ clockwise from the window.

Strategy 7 only operates the slat angles. The slat angle has the cut-off value, which allows the maximum slat opening whilst blocking direct solar radiation. The calculation of the cut-off angle is purely a geometrical problem and can be done with a simples equation.(Gomes et al., 2014) In EP this is done with a built-in slat control system called "block beam solar".

Table 1 Blind control Strategies

Strategy	Description
1	Blinds are not active
2	Blinds are active and slats are closed
3	Blinds are active and slats are at 90 □
4	Blinds are active and slats are at 45 □
5	Blinds are active and slats closed for 60% of daytime
6	Blinds are active if global radiation (direct + diffuse) is higher than 300 W/m^2
7	Blinds are active and slat angle is the cut-off value
8	Blinds are active when DGI is higher than 22

Strategies 1 through 5 are baseline strategies, meaning that they were used to compare results to other strategies. Strategies 6 through 9 are proposed control strategies which can be used in real case scenarios.

2.4 Software

Energy Plus calculates cooling and/or heating loads to maintain a certain temperature taking in account the electrical consumption, the operation of heating and/or cooling systems, lighting levels, among others. This is done by simulating the building model and the respective systems as described in language FORTRAN90 when exposed to various weather conditions.

Energy Plus has various types of automated blind control, these can be controlled via an operating time period (schedule) and/or methods that focus on specific objectives: to minimize the cooling load limiting solar gain, minimizing the heat load closing overnight to isolate (good for very insulating blind materials) and open during the day to take advantage of solar gain, minimize heating or cooling loads exclusively through the insulating properties of the material of blinds and blind control through an index comfort lowering the blinds when it is exceeded and many other types of control.

The program also allows you to control the slat angle of the Venetian blinds in three ways: fixed angle at a given value, angle controlled by a time (can change only once every hour) and block direct radiation.

Although there are many control strategies within the program, there are several limitations, such as: limited data available for blind and slat angle control; interval between control actions; blind only opens completely or closes completely.(Ernest Orlando Lawrence Berkeley National Laboratory, 2013a, 2013b, 2013c)

To do custom simulations and/or overcome some of the limitations there are tools within the program like the EMS (Energy Management System) and software's which can co-simulate with Energy Plus lime BCVTB (Building Controls Virtual Bed) and MLE+ (a toolbox from Matlab). The simulations will be done in Energy Plus, some co-simulated with MLE+ and some with the use of the EMS.

2.4.1 Energy Management System

The EMS is a high level control method which allows the development of custom control routines with the users own code. It allows access to several sensors and actuators in EP. The output file "eplusout.rdd" has a list of all the sensors accessible and the output file "eplusout.edd" has a list of all the available actuators. Both of this files can be requested as outputs by creating an "Output:VariableDictionary" object.

Of the control strategies 1 of them were accomplished using EMS.

Strategy number 5 used a custom control method since EP doesn't allow for shading devices to be controlled with external illuminance. For this it was used an external illuminance sensor and an actuator to close the blinds.

3 Results and discussion

The results in tables 3 and 4 show some general tendencies for east and south orientations.

The same strategy has larger energy consumption when the façade is facing east.

As expected strategy 1 and strategy 2 consume the most and least amount of energy respectively in both orientations.

Also as expected strategy 3 has larger energy consumption than strategy 4, although that difference is more relevant in the east orientation.

In both orientations and in strategies 6 through 9 electric lighting never represents more than 9 % of total energy consumption.

Table 3 Energy consumption when façade is due east

Strategy	HVAC (kW.h)	Electric Lighting (kW.h)	Total (kW.h)
S1	1324,5	1,9	1326,3
S2	177,5	59,0	236,4
S3	604,5	18,5	623,0
S4	279,8	31,8	311,6
S5	561,1	25,6	586,7
S6	338,5	21,3	359,8
S7	374,8	21,0	395,8
S8	979,4	14,9	994,3

Table 4 Energy consumption when façade is due south

Strategy	HVAC (kW.h)	Electric Lighting (kW.h)	Total (kW.h)
S1	864,1	1,6	865,7
S2	153,9	59,0	212,9
S3	324,3	10,9	335,2
S4	220,6	21,3	241,9
S5	179,2	49,3	228,5
S6	309,8	30,0	339,9
S7	321,0	16,6	337,6
S8	864,1	1,6	865,7

3.1 East

Strategy 8 is the second most energy demanding strategy in this orientation.

From strategies 6 through 8, 6 and 7 by that order are the less energy demanding strategies and both of them have lower energy consumptions than strategy 5.

3.2 South

In this orientation both strategy 1 and strategy 8 have the same energy consumption. As DGI levels never exceed 22 the blinds are never active.

Strategies 7 and 3 also have similar consumptions. The angle necessary to block direct radiation in this orientation is close to 90 □ during large portion of the simulation time.

As in the east orientation between strategies 6 through 8, strategy 8 is the most energy demanding. Strategies 7 and 6 are the least energy demanding but need almost double the energy consumption of strategy 5.

4 Conclusion

Of the proposed blind control strategies, 6 and 7 are the most energy efficient. Strategy 6 based in a set point valor of 300 W/m2 and strategy 7 providing a slat angle that blocks direct sunlight while letting in diffuse sunlight. Both of these strategies are simples and relatively easy to implement.

Although this paper does not take into account the comfort of the user which is a very important factor in any type of automated blind control. Because this is a simulation based approach there are also others factors not considered in this paper like user preference variability, user acceptance, user manual overwrite.

This is a simple approach to energy efficiency for some proposed blind control strategies.

4.1 Future Work

As stated earlier user comfort plays a big part in any blind control strategy as such the same analysis done with metrics to quantify the users comfort would be a more useful tool. As it would take into account user acceptance and consequently evaluate its applicability.

Some of the EP limitations can be partially overcome with the use of software's like MLE+ or BCVTB. Custom programs could allow for the blinds to be partially active and not just completely open or completely closed. Custom programs could also allow the adjustment of slat angles to meet specific indoor conditions, which is not possible with EP.

One of the advantages of the simulations environment is all the possibilities in which the simulation can occur. In this paper only a few possibilities were explored. Winter, other latitudes, different slat reflectance's, interior blinds and split blinds would require different approaches and meet other needs.

References

Boyce, P., Hunter, C., Howlett, O., 2003. The Benefits of Daylight through Windows. Rensselaer Polytechnic Institute.

Cláudio Ribeiro Faustino, 2012. Influência dos Vãos Envidraçados no Desempenho Energético de Edifícios. Universidade técnica de Lisboa, Lisboa.

Da Silva, P.C., Leal, V., Andersen, M., 2012. Influence of shading control patterns on the energy assessment of office spaces. Energy Build. 50, 35–48. doi:10.1016/j.enbuild.2012.03.019

Despacho n.º 15793-K/2013, 2013.

DiBartolomeo, D.L., Lee, E.S., Rubinstein, F.M., Selkowitz, S.E., 1996. Developing a Dynamic Envelope/Lighting Control System with Field Measurements. J. Illum. Eng. Soc. 26, 146–164.

EN ISO 13790, 2006. Energy performance of buildings — Calculation of energy use for space heating and cooling.

Ernest Orlando Lawrence Berkeley National Laboratory, 2013a. Input Output Reference.

Ernest Orlando Lawrence Berkeley National Laboratory, 2013b. Getting Started with EnergyPlus.

Ernest Orlando Lawrence Berkeley National Laboratory, 2013c. EnergyPlus Engineering Reference.

Galasiu, A.D., Veitch, J.A., 2006. Occupant preferences and satisfaction with the luminous environment and control systems in daylit offices: a literature review. Spec. Issue Daylighting Build. 38, 728–742. doi:10.1016/j.enbuild.2006.03.001

Gery, S., Koeffler, H.P., 2010. Circadian rhythms and cancer. Cell Cycle 9, 1097–1103.

Golombek, D.A., Casiraghi, L.P., Agostino, P.V., Paladino, N., Duhart, J.M., Plano, S.A., Chiesa, J.J., 2013. The times they're a-changing: Effects of circadian desynchronization on physiology and disease. Spec. Issue Time Percept. 107, 310–322. doi:10.1016/j.jphysparis.2013.03.007

Gomes, M.G., Rodrigues, A.M., Bogas, J.A., 2012. Numerical and experimental study of the optical properties of venetian blinds. J. Build. Phys.

Gomes, M.G., Santos, A.J., Rodrigues, A.M., 2014. Solar and visible optical properties of glazing systems with venetian blinds: Numerical, experimental and blind control study. Build. Environ. 71, 47–59. doi:10.1016/j.buildenv.2013.09.003

HESCHONG MAHONE GROUP, 1999a. Daylighting in Schools.

HESCHONG MAHONE GROUP, 1999b. Skylighting and Retail Sales.

Kim, J.-H., Park, Y.-J., Yeo, M.-S., Kim, K.-W., 2009. An experimental study on the environmental performance of the automated blind in summer. 6th Int. Conf. Indoor Air Qual. Vent. Energy Conserv. Build. IAQVEC 2007 Sendai Jpn. 28-31 Oct. 2007 44, 1517–1527. doi:10.1016/j.buildenv.2008.08.006

Newsham, G.R., 1994. Manual control of window blinds and electric lighting: implications for comfort and energy consumption. Indoor Environ. 3, 135–144.

Oh, M.H., Lee, K.H., Yoon, J.H., 2012. Automated control strategies of inside slat-type blind considering visual comfort and building energy performance. Cool Roofs Cool Pavements Cool Cities Cool World 55, 728–737. doi:10.1016/j.enbuild.2012.09.019

Olbina, S., Hu, J., 2012. Daylighting and thermal performance of automated split-controlled blinds. Build. Environ. 56, 127 - 138. doi:http://dx.doi.org/10.1016/j.buildenv.2012.03.002

Pauley, S.M., 2004. Lighting for the human circadian clock: recent research indicates that lighting has become a public health issue. Med. Hypotheses 63, 588–596. doi:10.1016/j.mehy.2004.03.020

Reinhart, C.F., 2004. Lightswitch-2002: a model for manual and automated control of electric lighting and blinds. Sol. Energy 77, 15 - 28. doi:http://dx.doi.org/10.1016/j.solener.2004.04.003

Reinhart, C.F., Voss, K., 2003. Monitoring manual control of electric lighting and blinds. Int. J. Light. Res. Technol. 243–260.

Tzempelikos, A., Athienitis, A.K., 2007. The impact of shading design and control on building cooling and lighting demand. Sol. Energy 81, 369 - 382. doi:http://dx.doi.org/10.1016/j.solener.2006.06.015

Vine, E., Lee, E., Clear, R., DiBartolomeo, D., Selkowitz, S., 1998. Office worker response to an automated Venetian blind and electric lighting system: a pilot study. Energy Build. 28, 205 - 218. doi:http://dx.doi.org/10.1016/S0378-7788(98)00023-1

Zhang, Y., Barrett, P., 2012. Factors influencing occupants' blind-control behaviour in a naturally ventilated office building. Build. Environ. 54, 137–147. doi:10.1016/j.buildenv.2012.02.016

Towards an optimal topology for hybrid energy networks

Wiet Mazairac, l.a.j.mazairac@tue.nl
Eindhoven University of Technology, The Netherlands

Robbe Salenbien, robbe.salenbien@vito.be
Flemish Institute for Technological Research, Belgium

Bauke de Vries, b.d.vries@tue.nl
Eindhoven University of Technology, The Netherlands

Abstract
Existing networks do not have the quantitative and qualitative capacity to facilitate the transition towards distributed renewable energy sources. Irregular production of energy over time at different locations will alter the current patters of energy flow, necessitating the implementation of short- and long-term changes in the energy distribution network. To determine the optimal topology of a future multi-carrier hybrid energy distribution network an optimization model is currently under development.

Keywords: multi-carrier energy networks, network topology optimization, energy conversion, linear programming

1 Introduction

The world is changing, and with it the energy markets are changing. Fossil fuel reserves are gradually depleting and therefore the extraction of oil, coal and natural gas will become more complicated, more expensive and more unreliable. Furthermore the consumption of fossil fuels has a major impact on our environment and climate. The transition towards renewable energy technologies reduces the need for fossil fuels and therefore also the impact on our environment and climate at the cost of fluctuations in energy production, which are inextricably linked to renewable sources. The current energy distribution system, which was designed to distribute energy produced by few producers among many consumers, is not able to cope with many production units, is not able to cope with units simultaneously or alternately both producing and consuming energy and is also not able to cope with fluctuations in energy availability and energy prices. The development of a network that can cope with these problems and provides the flexibility to switch from carrier anywhere in the network is of great importance to secure the future supply of energy.

Hybrid energy networks provide such flexibility. Unlike a conventional energy distribution network, i.e. an electric power network, a natural gas network or a district heating network, which operates independently form others, a hybrid energy network consists of multiple energy carriers between which conversion is possible. When one of the energy carriers suddenly becomes unavailable, hybrid energy networks introduce the ability to adapt by local or central conversion of an available form of energy into the required form of energy. When local conversion is possible, hybrid energy networks also introduce the ability to select a specific form of energy for transportation independent from the form of energy produced or the form of energy required.

This paper presents the ongoing PhD research project in which an approach is being developed to determine the optimal layout of a hybrid energy distribution network. This approach determines the location of energy distribution lines, conversion and storage units, given the location of energy producers and consumers in order to find the optimal balance between capital, operational and maintenance costs on the one hand and revenue on the other hand.

This paper is divided into three parts. The first part describes the topology optimization of single-carrier energy distribution networks. Both algorithms found in literature and algorithms developed within the PhD project are covered. The second part describes the topology optimization of multi-carrier networks. Algorithms described in the first part are extended in order to support more than one carrier and in order to support conversion between different carriers. The third part describes how energy fluctuations over short and long periods can be taken into account during the optimization of hybrid energy networks. Although this part is still under development, it will most likely result in the distribution of energy storage units over the area of interest and a reduced maximum capacity of distribution lines.

2 Single-carrier energy distribution network topology optimization

Although the goal of this PhD project is to optimize the topology of multi-carrier energy networks, first the topology optimization of single-carrier networks was addressed. Two different optimization methods were applied, the cross-entropy method, which is a heuristic optimization method and the linear programming method, which requires all equations to be linear. The optimization algorithm under development is versatile and therefore the linear program for the optimization of multi-carrier networks in section 3 is described in more detail than the linear program for single-carrier networks in this section.

2.1 Cross-entropy method

The cross-entropy method (Rubenstein & Kroese 2004) relies on the consecutive generation of collections of random data samples or in this case, collections of random district heating networks. The quality of each randomly generated network is evaluated and the parameters of the random mechanism are updated based on the outcome of that evaluation. Therefore the quality of the last collection is most likely higher than the quality of any of the preceding collections.

The cross-entropy method allows for separation between the optimization algorithm itself and the algorithms that determine the quality of a solution generated by this heuristic method. This separation provides the opportunity to apply more detailed, non-linear physical and economical equations to determine the quality of a randomly generated network. These are equations to determine (1) investment costs, (2) operational costs, (3) thermal losses, (4) heat generation costs and (5) heat revenue.

The equation to determine the investment costs (1) is derived from (Frederiksen & Werner 2013) and compared with investment costs related to recent district heating projects implemented by VITO, the Flemish Institute for Technological Research.

$$C_{inv.} = 4840 + 350r \; [\tfrac{€}{m}] \qquad (1)$$

The (2) operational costs depend on the pumping power and therefore the operational costs depend on the pressure losses in the network. The Darcy-Weisbach equation (2) is applied to determine the pressure losses in a district heating network. An iterative approach is required to determine the Darcy friction factor, equation (3). When flows and pressure losses are known, the pumping power can be determined by equation (4).

$$\Delta p = f_D \frac{l}{d}\frac{\rho V^2}{2} \; [Pa] \qquad (2)$$

$$f_D = \frac{1,325}{\left\{\ln\left[\left(\frac{\epsilon}{3,7d}\right)+\left(\frac{5,74}{Re^{0,9}}\right)\right]\right\}^2} \; [1] \qquad (3)$$

$$P = \frac{\Delta PQ}{\eta} \; [W] \qquad (4)$$

To determine (3) thermal losses in a heating network generated by the cross-entropy method each distribution line is divided into many short segments **(Figure 1)** and (4) is applied to calculate the heat flow from each segment.

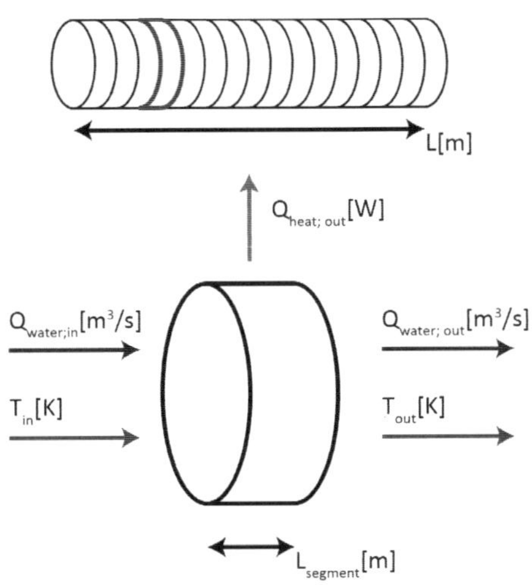

Figure 1 Application of the finite element method to determine the thermal losses in an district heating energy distribution line

$$\varphi_{l\ tot} = \frac{\theta_i - \theta_e}{R_{l\ tot}} \cdot L\ [W] \qquad (5)$$

Heat generation costs (4) depend on i.a. the availability of industrial waste heat, the availability of geothermal heat and fossil fuel prices. In the Netherlands, heat revenue (5) is related to the price of the natural gas, since a consumer connected to a district heating network is protected from additional costs compared to a consumer connected to the natural gas network.

For each randomly generated network investment costs, operational costs, costs related to thermal losses, heat generation costs and heat revenue are added to determine the quality of the network in order to generate a higher quality collection in the next iteration. Here quality is related to costs, however quality can also be related to any other objective, e.g. environmental impact or comfort. The cross-entropy method is stopped when the quality of the generated networks no longer increases.

2.2 Linear programming method

The linear programming method relies on the optimization of linear objective function, subject to linear equality and linear inequality constraints, which means that the non-linear equations described in the cross-entropy section need to be linearized. Compared to the cross-entropy method in which a clear separation between the optimization algorithm and the model is observed, which provides flexibility during development of the model, this separation is less clear in the case of linear programming.

(Dorfner & Hamacher 2014) describes how the linear programming method is applied to find the optimal layout of a district heating network. This publication however does not explain how to linearize the equations to determine investment costs, operational costs and thermal losses. In order to determine the optimal layout of a district heating network under different conditions a straightforward method was developed to linearize these non-linear equations.

In (Dorfner & Hamacher 2014) investment costs, operational costs and thermal losses vary when the thermal capacity of a distribution line varies. For each specific scenario (1) supply temperature, (2) return temperature, (3) maximum pressure drop (4) thermal properties of the distribution pipe and (5) relation between the diameter and the costs of the distribution pipe are determined in advance.

Figure 2, figure 3 and figure 4 show the result of the linearization method. **Figure 2** shows the relation between capacity and costs of a distribution pipe, **figure 3** shows the relation between capacity and friction loss, which relates to pumping power and **figure 4** shows the relation between capacity and heat loss. The least squares method is applied to find a linear approximation. When a pipe capacity is not expected to be part of the final solution, this pipe capacity is disregarded when applying the least squares method to reduce the error of the linear approximation.

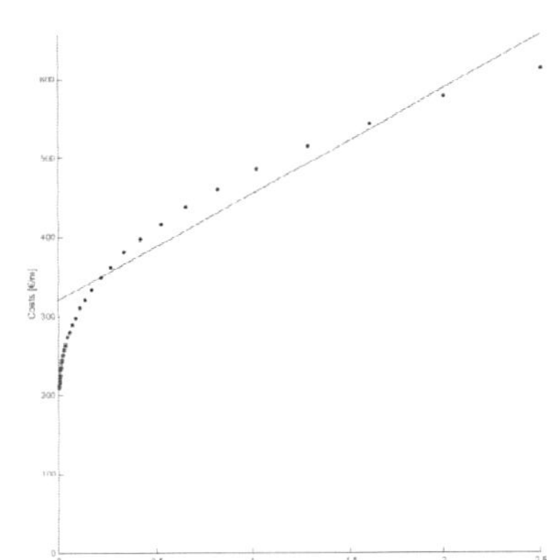

Figure 2 Linearization of costs as a function of the capacity

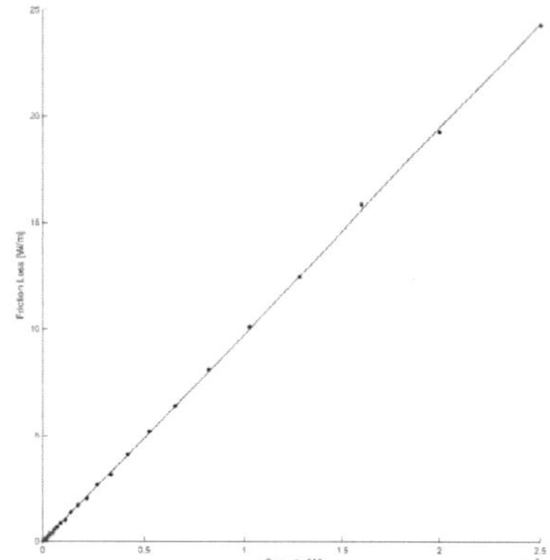

Figure 3 Linearization of friction losses as a function of capacity

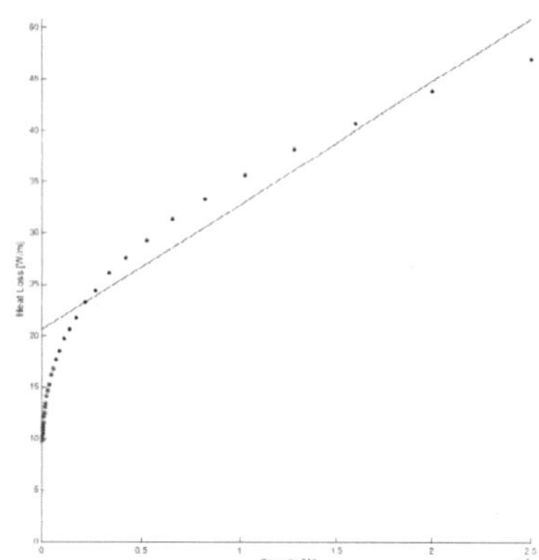

Figure 4 Linearization of heat losses as a function of capacity

2.3 Conclusions

Both the cross-entropy method as the linear programming method return plausible results, however validation is required to confirm this and also to determine the error as a result of the linear approximation. Although the cross-entropy method allows for the optimization of a more detailed model, process time increases exponentially with the size of problem. Also, a heuristic optimization approach, in contrast to the linear programming method, is not guaranteed to find the optimal solution. For these reasons the linear optimization approach will be applied to find the optimal topology of multi-carrier hybrid energy distribution networks, although some small experiments have been conducted in which the cross-entropy method was applied.

3 Multi-carrier energy distribution network topology optimization

The algorithms applied to find the optimal topology of single-carrier networks can be applied to find the optimal topology of multi-carrier networks. In order to do so, these algorithms are expanded to cope with multiple energy carriers and conversion of energy, which results in an increased solution space.

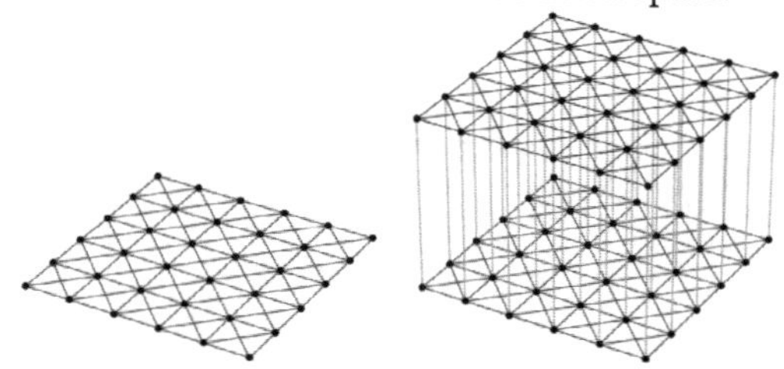

Figure 5 Solution space of a single-carrier (left) and a multi-carrier network (right)

The solution space of a single-carrier network consists of a single set of edges **(figure 5, left)**. Each edge represents a possible location for an energy distribution line. The solution space of a multi-carrier network, with in this example two carriers, consists of three sets of edges **(figure 5, right)**. Each red edge represents a possible location for an energy line, which distributes the first energy carrier. Each blue edge represents a possible location for an energy line, which distributes the second energy carrier. Each green line represents a possible location for an energy converter, which transfers energy between carriers.

In **figure 5** each edge represents two opposite directed edges. A directed edge allows energy to flow in only one direction. Accordingly each green edge in **figure 5** represents two potential converters. The first converter transfers energy from the first carrier to the second carrier. The second converter transfers energy from the second carrier to the first carrier.

In reality the red and blue edges share the same location, however, for clarity, they are drawn separately. Also, in contrast to the lengths of the red and the blue edges, the lengths of the green edges, representing the converters, have no meaning.

3.1 Cross-entropy method

First the cross-entropy method is applied to find the optimal topology of a multi-carrier energy system. Although process time increases exponentially with the size of the problem, this method is applicable to smaller problems.

In **section 2.1** equations relating to (1) investment costs, (2) operational costs, (3)

thermal losses, (4) heat generation costs and (5) heat revenue were introduced. These equations apply to district heating networks. Similar equations are required for the second network, in his case the electric power network. These equations relate to (6) investment costs, (7) operational costs, (8) energy loss to resistance, (9) electric power generation costs and (10) electricity power revenue. Finally, similar equations are required for the conversion units. These equations relate to (11) investment costs, (12) operational costs and (13) energy conversion losses.

Figure 6 represents a problem that can be solved by applying the cross entropy method. The edges part of the upper half represent possible locations for heat distribution lines. The edges part of the lower half represent possible location for electric power lines. The vertical lines represent possible locations for conversion units.

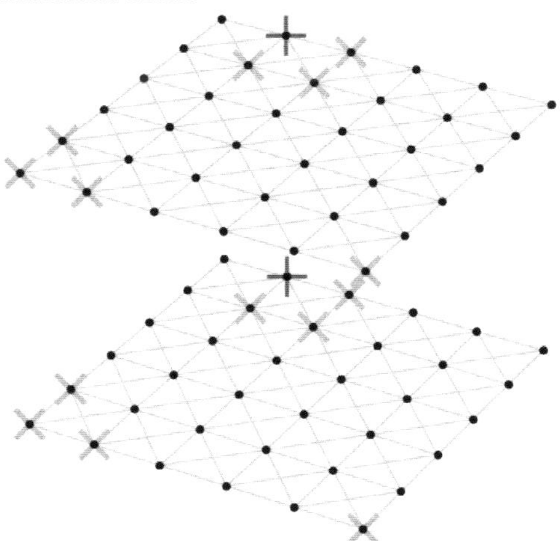

Figure 6 Multi-carrier network problem. Magenta colored nodes (+) represent production units. Cyan colored nodes (x) represent customers

The magenta colored node (+) part of the upper mesh represents an electric energy production unit. The cyan color nodes (x) part of the upper mesh represent electric energy customers. The magenta colored node (+) part of the lower mesh represent a heat production unit. The cyan colored nodes (x) part of the lower mesh represent heat customers.

Four hypothetical scenarios were examined by the cross-entropy method. In scenario (a) conversion units are relatively expensive and energy revenues are high. In scenario (b) conversion units are relatively inexpensive and energy revenues are high. In scenario (c) energy revenues are low. In scenario (d) conversion units are reasonably priced compared to energy revenues.

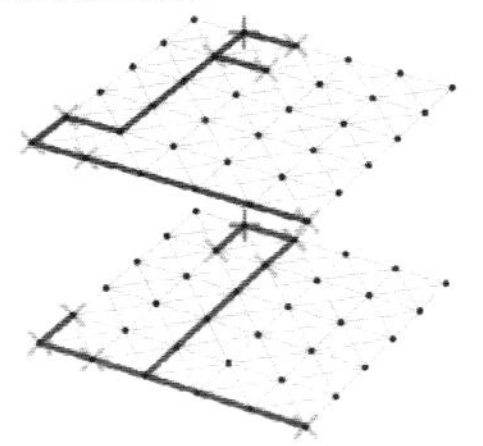

Figure 7 Optimal network in scenario (a)

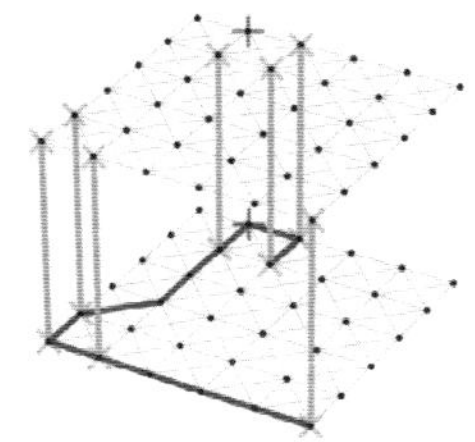

Figure 8 Optimal network in scenario (b)

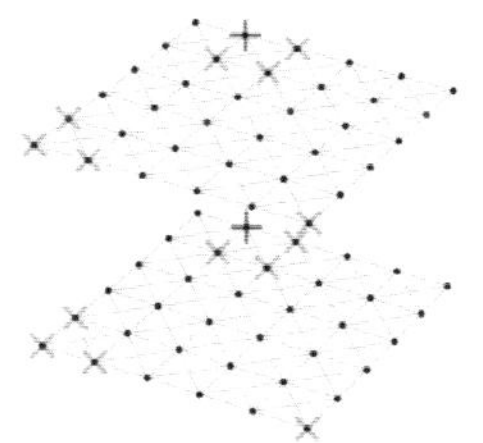

Figure 9 Optimal network in scenario (c)

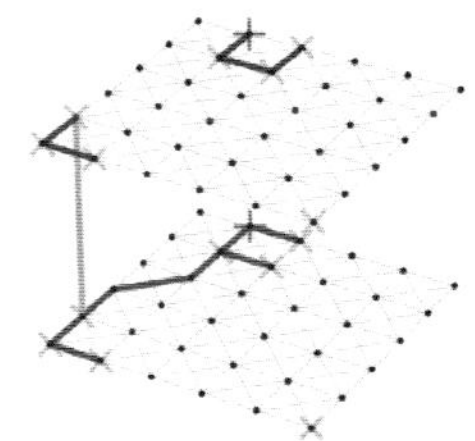

Figure 10 Optimal network in scenario (d)

Figure 7, 8, 9 and 10 shows the multi-carrier networks generated by the cross-entropy method for the four scenarios. In scenario (a) expensive energy units and high energy revenues result in two separate, fully connected networks **(figure 7)**. In scenario (b) inexpensive energy units and high revenues result in one fully connected network. Instead of constructing a second network, energy conversion units provide the second form of energy **(figure 8)**. In scenario (c) energy revenues are too low to make an energy distribution network profitable **(figure 9)**. In scenario (d) customers close to the production unit are directly connected to both production units. A distant group of consumers is directly connected to one production unit. The other form of energy is obtained through conversion. The single, distant consumer is not connected, because that connection would not be profitable **(figure 10)**.

3.2 Linear programming

A district heating network with a high-temperature, high-pressure primary network and a low-temperature, low-pressure secondary network can be regarded as a multi-carrier network. Area substations transfer energy between the primary and the secondary network. The multi-carrier topology optimization algorithms described in this paper can be applied to any combination of carriers, including a multistage district heating network.

3.2.1 Sets

Let $G(V,E)$ be the graph that represents the solution space. Let V be the set of vertices v_i, representing starting points, end points and crossings of possible future energy distribution lines and energy converters. Let E be the set of directed edges e_{ij} representing possible future energy distribution lines and energy converters. Every possible future energy distribution line and energy converter is represented by two direct edges, e_{ij} and e_{ji} **(figure 5, right)**.

3.2.2 Parameters

Table 1 summarizes all model parameters. Different types of parameters can be distinguished, e.g. economical (c, r), technical (θ) and parameters that describe the existing situation (l, ϵ).

Table 1 Model parameters

Name	Description
$c_{so^c}^{fix}$	Source, fixed investment costs
$c_{so^c}^{var}$	Source, variable investment costs
$c_{so^c}^{om}$	Source, operation and maintenance costs
c_d^{fix}	Drain, fixed investment costs
c_d^{var}	Drain, variable investment costs
c_d^{om}	Drain, operation and maintenance costs
c_c^{fix}	Converter, fixed investment costs
c_c^{var}	Converter, variable investment costs
c_c^{om}	Converter, operation and maintenance costs
c_e^{fix}	Edge, fixed investment costs
c_e^{var}	Edge, variable investment costs
c_e^{om}	Edge, operation and maintenance costs
$c_{so_i^c}^{en}(t_n)$	Energy generation costs
$r_{d_i}^{en}(t_n)$	Energy revenue
k	Derived cost parameter
u	Derived revenue parameter
$\theta_{c_i}^{fix}$	Converter, fixed energy losses
$\theta_{c_i}^{var}$	Converter, variable energy losses
$\theta_{e_{ij}}^{fix}$	Edge, fixed energy losses
$\theta_{e_{ij}}^{var}$	Edge, variable energy losses
α	Annuity factor for investment costs
τ	Time factor
$l_{e_{ij}}$	Edge length
$\epsilon_{so_i^c}$	Source is already connected
ϵ_{d_i}	Drain is already connected
ϵ_{c_i}	Converter already exists
$\epsilon_{e_{ij}}$	Edge already exists
$p_{so_i^c}^{out,lim}$	Source, available capacity
$p_{c_i}^{lim}$	Converter, available capacity
$p_{e_{ij}}^{lim}$	Edge, available capacity
$p_{d_i}^{demand}(t_n)$	Drain, demand

3.2.3 Variables

Table 2 summarizes all model variables. Different types of variables can be distinguished, e.g. variables that represents the decision to connect a source or drain and the decision to install a converter or distribution line (x), the power in and out of system components as a function of time $(p(t_n))$ and the peak powers (p^{max}).

Table 2 Model variables

Name	Range	Description
z	$\mathbb{R}$	System costs
$x_{so_i^c}$	{0,1}	Source, decision variable
$x_{d_i^{nc}}$	{0,1}	Drain, decision variable
x_{c_i}	{0,1}	Converter, decision variable
$x_{e_{ij}}$	{0,1}	Edge, decision variable
$p_{so_i^c}^{out}(t_n)$	$\mathbb{R}_0^+$	Source, power out
$p_{d_i^{nc}}^{in}(t_n)$	$\mathbb{R}_0^+$	Drain, power in
$p_{c_i}^{in}(t_n)$	$\mathbb{R}_0^+$	Converter, power in
$p_{c_i}^{out}(t_n)$	$\mathbb{R}_0^+$	Converter, power out
$p_{e_{ij}}^{in}(t_n)$	$\mathbb{R}_0^+$	Edge, power in
$p_{e_{ij}}^{out}(t_n)$	$\mathbb{R}_0^+$	Edge, power out
$p_{so_i^c}^{max}$	$\mathbb{R}_0^+$	Source, maximum power
$p_{d_i^{nc}}^{max}$	$\mathbb{R}_0^+$	Drain, maximum power
$p_{c_i}^{max}$	$\mathbb{R}_0^+$	Converter, maximum power
$p_{e_{ij}}^{max}$	$\mathbb{R}_0^+$	Edge, maximum power

3.2.4 System costs function

The system costs **function (6)** sums the costs of the system components, the energy production costs and the energy reveneus.

$$z = k_{SO^c} + k_{D^{nc}} + k_C + k_E + k_{SO^c}^{en} - u_{D^{nc}}^{en} \quad (6)$$

3.2.5 Component costs functions

Function (7) returns the sum of the fixed and variable investment costs of the sources. The fixed and variable investment costs depend on the existence and capacity of the sources. **Function (8) and (9)** return the annualized fixed investment costs and the annualized variable investment costs of the sources.

$$k_{SO^c} = \sum_{so_i^c \in SO^c} \left[k_{so_i^c}^{fix} * x_{so_i^c} + k_{so_i^c}^{var} * p_{so_i^c}^{max}\right] \quad (7)$$

$$\forall so_i^c \in SO^c : k_{so_i^c}^{fix} = c_{so^c}^{fix} * \alpha * \left(1 - \epsilon_{so_i^c}\right) + c_{so^c}^{om} \quad (8)$$

$$\forall so_i^c \in SO^c : k_{so_i^c}^{var} = c_{so^c}^{var} * \alpha * \left(1 - \epsilon_{so_i^c}\right) \quad (9)$$

Function (10) returns the sum of the fixed and variable investment costs of the drain. The fixed and variable investment costs depend on the existence and capacity of the drains. **Function (11) and (12)** return the annualized fixed investment costs and the annualized variable investment costs of the drains.

$$k_{D^{nc}} = \sum_{d_i^{nc} \in D^{nc}} \left[k_{d_i^{nc}}^{fix} * x_{d_i^{nc}} + k_{d_i^{nc}}^{var} * p_{d_i^{nc}}^{max}\right] \quad (10)$$

$$\forall d_i^{nc} \in D^{nc} : k_{d_i^{nc}}^{fix} = c_{d^{nc}}^{fix} * \alpha * \left(1 - \epsilon_{d_i^{nc}}\right) + c_{d^{nc}}^{om} \quad (11)$$

$$\forall d_i^{nc} \in D^{nc} : k_{d_i^{nc}}^{var} = c_{d^{nc}}^{var} * \alpha * \left(1 - \epsilon_{d_i^{nc}}\right) \quad (12)$$

Function (13) returns the sum of the fixed and variable investment costs of the converters. The fixed and variable investment costs depend on the existence and capacity of the converters. **Function (14) and (15)** return the annualized fixed investment costs and the annualized variable investment costs of the converters.

$$k_C = \sum_{c_{ij} \in C} \left[k_{c_{ij}}^{fix} * x_{c_{ij}} + k_{c_{ij}}^{var} * p_{c_{ij}}^{max}\right] \quad (13)$$

$$\forall c_{ij} \in C : k_{c_{ij}}^{fix} = c_c^{fix} * \alpha * \left(1 - \epsilon_{c_{ij}}\right) + c_c^{om} \quad (14)$$

$$\forall c_{ij} \in C : k_{c_{ij}}^{var} = c_c^{var} * \alpha * \left(1 - \epsilon_{c_{ij}}\right) \quad (15)$$

Function (16) returns the sum of the fixed and variable investment costs of the edges. The fixed and variable investment costs depend on the existence and capacity of the edges. **Function (17) and (18)** return the annualized fixed investment costs and the annualized variable investment costs of the edges.

$$k_E = \sum_{e_{ij} \in E} \left[k_{e_{ij}}^{fix} * x_{e_{ij}} + k_{e_{ij}}^{var} * p_{e_{ij}}^{max}\right] \quad (16)$$

$$\forall e_{ij} \in E : k_{e_{ij}}^{fix} = c_e^{fix} * l_{e_{ij}} * \alpha * \left(1 - \epsilon_{e_{ij}}\right) + c_e^{om} * l_{ij} \quad (17)$$

$$\forall e_{ij} \in E : k_{e_{ij}}^{var} = c_e^{var} * l_{e_{ij}} * \alpha * \left(1 - \epsilon_{e_{ij}}\right) \quad (18)$$

3.2.6 Energy costs function

For each source **function (19)** returns annualized energy production costs.

$$\forall so_i^c \in SO^c : \forall t_n \in T : k_{so_i^c}^{en}(t_n) = c_{so_i^c}^{en}(t_n) * \tau * \Delta t \quad (19)$$

3.2.7 Energy revenues function

For each drain **function (20)** returns the annualized energy revenues.

$$\forall d_i \in D : \forall t_n \in T : u_{d_i}^{en}(t_n) = r_{d_i}^{en}(t_n) * \tau * \Delta t \quad (20)$$

3.2.8 Vertex constraints

Constraint (21) ensures that for every vertex and for every moment in time the amount of power that leaves that vertex at a certain moment in time is at least as large as the amount of power that enters that vertex at the same moment in time. N_i is the set of vertices adjacent to vertex i.

$$\forall v_i \in V : \forall t_n \in T : \sum_{m \in N_i^e} \left[p_{e_{im}}^{in}(t_n)\right] + \sum_{m \in N_i^c} \left[p_{c_{im}}^{in}(t_n)\right] + p_{d_i}^{in}(t_n) \leq \sum_{m \in N_i^e} \left[p_{e_{mi}}^{out}(t_n)\right] + \sum_{m \in N_i^c} \left[p_{c_{mi}}^{out}(t_n)\right] + p_{so_i^c}^{out}(t_n) \quad (21)$$

3.2.9 Edge constraints

Constraint (22) represents the difference in power into and out of an energy distribution line. **Function (23)** returns a derived parameter which relates to the variable energy losses and **function (24)** returns a derived parameter which relates to the fixed energy losses in the energy distribution line.

$$\forall e_{ij} \in E : \forall t_n \in T : \eta_{e_{ij}} * P_{e_{ij}}^{in}(t_n) - P_{e_{ij}}^{out}(t_n) = \delta_{e_{ij}} * x_{e_{ij}} \quad (22)$$

$$\forall e_{ij} \in E : \eta_{e_{ij}} = 1 - l_{e_{ij}} * \theta_{e_{ij}}^{var} \quad (23)$$

$$\forall e_{ij} \in E : \delta_{e_{ij}} = l_{e_{ij}} * \theta_{e_{ij}}^{fix} \quad (24)$$

3.2.10 Power constraints

Constraint (25) registers the peak power of every source. The peak power of a source has great influence on the variable investment costs. **Constraint (26)** ensures a source's peak power never exceeds its predefined limit.

$$\forall so_i^c \in SO^c : \forall t_n \in T : p_{so_i^c}^{out}(t_n) \leq p_{so_i^c}^{out,max} \quad (25)$$

$$\forall so_i^c \in SO^c : p_{so_i^c}^{out,max} \leq p_{so_i^c}^{out,lim} * x_{so_i^c} \quad (26)$$

Constraint (27) registers the peak power of every converter. The peak power of a converter has great influence on the variable investment costs. **Constraint (28)** ensures a converter's peak power never exceeds its predefined limit.

$$\forall c_{ij} \in C : \forall t_n \in T : p_{c_{ij}}(t_n) \leq p_{c_{ij}}^{max} \quad (27)$$

$$\forall c_{ij} \in C : p_{c_{ij}}^{max} \leq p_{c_{ij}}^{lim} * x_{c_{ij}} \quad (28)$$

Constraint (29) registers the peak power of every energy distribution line. **Constraint (30)** ensures a line's peak power never exceeds its predefined limit.

$$\forall e_{ij} \in E : \forall t_n \in T : p_{e_{ij}}^{in}(t_n) \leq p_{e_{ij}}^{max} \quad (29)$$

$$\forall e_{ij} \in E : p_{e_{ij}}^{max} \leq p_{e_{ij}}^{lim} * x_{e_{ij}} \quad (30)$$

Constraint (31) ensures that when a consumers is connected demand will always be met.

$$\forall d_i^{nc} \in D^{nc} : \forall t_n \in T : p_{d_i^{nc}}^{in}(t_n) = p_{d_i^{nc}}^{demand}(t_n) * x_{d_i} \quad (31)$$

Equations and constraints (6) up to (31) define a mixed integer linear program which was implemented in MathWorks MATLAB and solved by IBM ILOG CPLEX Optimization Studio.

In **figure 11**, which shows the result of the optimization process, analogous to previous examples, the magenta node (+) represents the heat production units, the cyan nodes (x) represent the heat customers, the red lines represent the primary network, the blue lines represent the secondary network and the green lines represent the area substations.

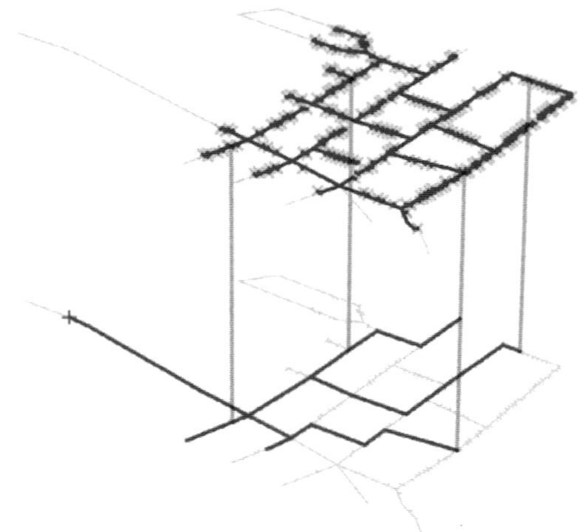

Figure 11 Optimal multi-stage district heating network. The red graph represents the primary network, the blue graph represents the secondary network. The green graph represents the area substations.

4 Conclusions

Both the cross-entropy method as the linear programming method return plausible results, however validation is required to confirm this and also to determine the error as a result of the linear approximation. The solution space of a multi-carrier problem increases with the number of carriers and is therefore at least twice as large as the solutions space of a single carrier problem. Accordingly, as a result of better performance, the linear programming method is more applicable than the cross-entropy method when dealing with multi-carrier problems.

5 Outlook

The optimization methods described in this paper return plausible results. Introduction of other carriers, e.g. natural or hydrogen gas, requires collecting data on those carriers and related conversion techniques. Introduction of many distributed renewable energy production units, e.g. rooftop pv-panels, requires collecting data on the location and power of those techniques.

Implementation of renewable energy techniques is inseparable from energy storage. Dynamic modelling and optimization over time is required to determine the location, capacity and power of potential storage units. To make this possible, first, the existing optimization method needs to be extended in order to remember a storage unit's state. Second, charge and discharge profiles need to be added to the optimization model.

A discrete optimization model, opposite to a continuous one, will reduce the complexity of the problem and will increase the likelihood obtaining an optimal topology within reasonable time. For each discrete step, all storage units' states are stored. A storage unit's state will determine if that storage unit is able to store or discharge energy over the time of the next discrete step.

In order to take into account simultaneity, which influence the required maximum capacity of storage units and distribution lines, unique consumption profiles need to be assigned to all consumers. Privacy policies and technical barriers prevent network operators and energy providers to provide detailed information on the amount of energy consumed over time. To solve this problem a hidden Markov model (HMM) is under development that generates unique consumption profiles. In this HMM the hidden, unobserved states reflect a low, medium or high consumption of energy at a specific time. The sequence of hidden states is predicted by observing time. This results in a collection of unique consumption profiles, **figure 12**.

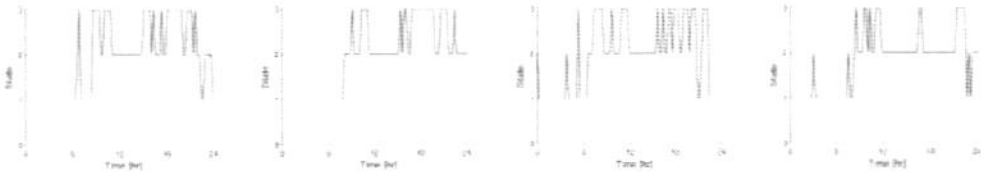

Figure 12 Multiple consumption profiles generated by a Hidden Markov Model

These extensions provide the possibility to determine the optimal topology of a future multi-carrier hybrid energy network, taking into account distributed generation with the possibility to decide between local and central storage.

References

Rubenstein, R.Y. and Kroese, D.P. [2004]. The Cross-Entropy Method: A United Approach to Combinatorial Optimization, Monte-Carlo Simulation and Machine Learning, Springer-Verlag.

Frederiksen, S. and Werner, S. [2013]. District Heating and Cooling, Studentlitteratur AB.

Dorfner, J.; Hamacher, T. [2014]. Large-Scale District Heating Network Optimization, Smart Grid, IEEE Transactions on, vol.5, no.4, pp.1884,1891

Towards extending IFC with point cloud data

Thomas Krijnen, t.f.krijnen@tue.nl
Jakob Beetz, j.beetz@tue.nl
Eindhoven University of Technology, The Netherlands

Sebastian Ochmann, ochmann@cs.uni-bonn.de
Richard Vock, vock@cs.uni-bonn.de
Raoul Wessel, wesselr@cs.uni-bonn.de
Institute of Computer Science II, University of Bonn, Germany

Abstract

In this paper we suggest an extension to the Industry Foundation Classes model to integrate point cloud datasets. The proposal includes a schema extension to the core model allowing the storage of points either as Cartesian coordinates, points in parametric space of a surface associated with a building element or as discrete height fields projected as grids onto (building element) surfaces. To handle considerable amounts of data, we further suggest to employ the Hierarchical Data Format (HDF) as an efficient serialization format as an additional alternative to clear text encoded ISO 10303 part 21 files. Based on prototypical implementations we show early results of population files and discuss potential benefits of dedicated compression algorithms.

Keywords: Point clouds, Industry Foundation Classes, Building Information Modelling, HDF

1 Introduction

A point cloud model is a large set of unstructured 3d points that carries detailed geometric and appearance information of scanned objects in an *implicit* manner acquired in bulk in automated processes. Information in the Industry Foundation Classes (IFC) file format on the other hand, represents detailed *explicit* knowledge and design intent most often modelled manually.

In IFC, a building is described as a semantically rich assembly of building elements, which can be represented by various forms of geometry, including 2D and 3D line drawings, Constructive Solid Geometry (CSG), Boundary Representations (BRep) and tessellated meshes. However, these three-dimensional representations are just one of the aspects conveyed in an IFC model. In addition, attributes related to thermal or acoustic performance, costing or intended use of spaces etc. can be added.

In many common data formats for the storage of point cloud data, such as E57 (ASTM, 2011), PCD (Rusu & Cousins, 2011), metadata is attached to individual data sets. This metadata for example includes scanner positions or weather conditions that allude to aspects of the perceived physical world. In general however, the point data itself contains no grouping, decomposition or other information that relates the points to the semantic meaning of the real-world object that was scanned.

The magnitude of the data, which is typically found in point cloud data sets and IFC model populations, can be dramatically different for the two file types. A meaningful IFC file can have file sizes in the order of a few megabytes, if geometrical representations and property values are properly reused and especially when the file contains implicit rather than tessellated geometry. Depending on the amount of detail and precision, point cloud scans can easily amount to gigabytes of data.

1.1 IFC and point clouds combined

Despite the fundamental differences in the two data carriers, there is a growing interest in the use of point cloud data in the architecture engineering and construction industry. Point clouds are a viable tool to precisely document a structure as it is physically built, rather than as it has been designed, and to detect differences between these 'as-planned' and 'as-built' states is interesting for many use cases.

Superimposing, reconstructing, comparing and integrating 'as-planned' and 'as-built' models of buildings and other structures has been the subject of many research and development efforts (Bhatla, Choe, Fierro, & Leite, 2012; Pu & Vosselman, 2009). Practical use cases include the monitoring of construction processes (Bügler et al. 2014; Yang et al. 2015; Teizer 2015; Braun A 2015) or indoor navigation (Khoshelham & Elberink, 2012). The increasing availability of affordable acquisition technology such as aerial and terrestrial laser scans (Pu & Vosselman, 2009; Tang, Huber, Akinci, Lipman, & Lytle, 2010), image based approaches (Bhatla et al., 2012) or combinations (Brilakis et al., 2010) as well as the necessary processing and storage resources have contributed to this spike in interest amongst practitioners and researcher alike. (Braun A, 2015; Bügler, Ogunmakin, Teizer, Vela, & Borrmann, 2014; Teizer, 2015; Yang, Park, Vela, & Golparvar-Fard, 2015)Especially in the domain of digital preservation there is a confluence in the desire to document the design intent and intended use along with the physical edifice as it is delivered and changes over time (Dietze et al., 2013). The often intricate details of historical buildings including detailed plaster works, for which a definition using parametric surfaces is beyond what is typically the scope of the modelling effort in IFC.

From these converging interests the need for a unified and harmonized storage model of the two data carriers using open and semantically rich standards arises. A number of advantages can be identified for the use and creation of such integrated datasets in a single file format: Being able to store a single file as a harmonized storage model of semantically rich IFC data and detailed geometrical point cloud data, brings administrative benefits by not having to implement, maintain and synchronise two distinct data carriers. More importantly, the ability to document and annotate the point cloud using the semantically rich constructs in the IFC file allows the focused search, selection and use of point clouds. As an example, a subset of the points can be specified to describe the surface of a particular wall element. This relation could e.g. be semi-automatically detected by the geometrical proximity of the points to the individual `IfcRepresentationItems` associated to the respective element. This relation assigns meaning to the set of points, i.e. that they describe a wall, and by descending into the relationships of the IFC population model, users can relate additional information like material properties associated with these points. On the other hand, point cloud data enriches the information on the wall found in the original, explicitly modelled IFC data by providing insight into the exact placement, shape and details of the wall, material irregularities and geometrical deformations.

1.2 Benefits for point cloud visualisation

Except for very small point clouds, their visualization requires the usage of certain acceleration structures like Octrees (Meager 1980) or k-d-trees (Bentley 1975), as the entire amount of data is not manageable even by modern graphics hardware. Especially when points are browsed online, for example in a digital preservation system, the streaming nature of data transmission imposes additional constraints on effective clustering in order to conserve bandwidth and reduce load times.

With the ever increasing amount of data that state-of-the-art acquisition devices like laser scanners are able to provide, point clouds hardly fit even into workstations' main memories. The idea behind acceleration structures is to (hierarchically) structure the point clouds into cells, each one only containing a certain part of the points. During visualization it is determined which cells can be seen by the virtual observer regarding her/his point of view. Only those points are rendered that lie within the frustum.

As point clouds are inherently unstructured, the traditional acceleration trees are not tailored semantically to the data in a way that e.g. one cell would correspond to exactly one room. Instead, the cell borders' positions rather arbitrarily cut through semantic structures. This can lead to an overhead of points being rendered despite being invisible because of e.g. being positioned behind a wall that blocks the current view.

Associating points to IFC entity instances as illustrated in Figure 1 would enable to overcome such limitations and offer the possibility to construct semantically-driven and therefore intelligent acceleration structures.

The spatial subdivision structure common in IFC files, by which a building is decomposed into individual building storeys and spaces, can be harnessed as a spatial indexing structure into the otherwise unstructured point cloud data. As such, point clouds can potentially be more efficiently visualised as the spatial segmentation derived from the IFC files can help to cull away points that the viewpoint of someone exploring the dataset.

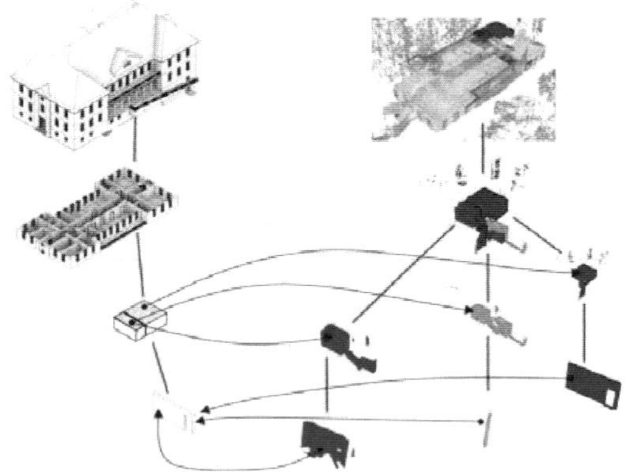

Figure 1 Decomposition relationships in hybrid data sets

Employing a hierarchical structure to point cloud data, which at some level, associates points with an `IfcSpace`, the visibility of points can be reduced to those belonging to the room the virtual observer is located in. In case of open doors and windows this can be extended with neighbouring rooms, related via `IfcSpaceBoundaries`. With an additional layer of classic acceleration structures or building element level associations within these room-cells, different viewing directions can be handled efficiently as well.

1.3 Benefits for point cloud compression

With the increasing resolutions of 3D acquisition devices, researchers have investigated possibilities to efficiently compress point clouds. Ideal point cloud compression techniques would enable high compression ratios without sacrificing decompression speed, the ability to decompress localized segments without decompressing the entire file and streaming levels of detail.

Universal entropy-based methods like e.g. (Ziv & Lempel, 1978) that perform well on data like text turn out to be less suited for point cloud compression as they cannot detect and exploit hidden underlying geometric structures in the, unstructured point cloud.

Several methods like (Botsch, Wiratanaya, & Kobbelt, 2002; Huang, Peng, Kuo, & Gopi, 2008; Schnabel & Klein, 2006) use an Octree to approximate the actual surface that is underlying the sampled point cloud.

Conversely, in this paper we assume a point cloud is paired with an IFC file with geometrical representation for its building elements. As such, the proposal in this paper follows a shape-proxy-based compression method, for example as outlined in (Digne, Chaine, & Valette, 2014; Golla, Schwartz, & Klein, 2014; Schnabel, Möser, & Klein, 2008). The key to an efficient compression is to find shape proxies that explain a large amount of measured points in order to store the points not as triplets of {x, y, z} coordinates, but instead as a projected height field on the shape proxies, as such reducing the dimensionality of a point to only a single component that specifies deviation from the surface at a specific grid point.

The assumption is that representations of IFC entities will yield better localized surfaces than structures that are estimated from the point cloud data itself, hence yielding higher compression ratios.

In this paper, we discuss existing practices of serializing IFC data models, the presentation of our proposed schema extension and a brief overview of the HDF5 file format, a novel binary serialization form of IFC, introduced in this paper. In the following sections the implications of various serialization options are discussed based on concrete measurements from a prototypical implementation.

2 Existing solutions and general approaches

To bridge the disparate approaches, in IFC and point cloud processing, different technical solutions are introduced and discussed in the following sections. On a schema level, the solution approach suggested here consists of three components, which can be layered to obtain a near optimal storage of point clouds: a) points can be recorded either in Cartesian coordinate space or in surface-parametric space b) the points within a bounded surface-parametric space can be discretized and interpolated into a (albeit lossy) grid-based height field superimposed on bounding surfaces of building elements such as walls, floors or ceilings c) floating point numbers within a bounded range such as surface {u,v} values or offsets from the association surface can be recorded in a discretized integer numerator notation, with a single denominator for an entire set of points.

Alongside the data structures introduced into the IFC schema itself a second mechanism is suggested to allow the efficient processing of realistic data set sizes of several Gigabytes as they are expected in typical workflows involving point cloud measurements and processing. In this paper we suggest the use of the Hierarchical Data Format 5 (HDF 5) (Folk, Heber, Koziol, Pourmal, & Robinson, 2011) to allow the efficient handling of large quantities of data.

2.1 Existing data structures

In version 4 of the IFC specification (buildingSMART 2014) the `IfcCartesianPointList3D` entity has been added as a subtype of the `IfcGeometricRepresenationItem` to the schema. In principle this allows the representation of point clouds such as acquired from laser scans directly into a model population as an unbounded, two-dimensional array of `IfcLengthMeasures` values (`LIST [1:?] OF LIST [3:3]`). However, no additional attributes are defined that allow to capture information regarding e.g. the level of detail or further data dimensions to individual points such as colors or normals as is common in many dedicated point cloud formats.

Another approach is the use of bitmap structures already present in the schema. However, embedding large blobs of binary data into IFC files can deteriorate the ease of exchanging files. Therefore, the ability to use compression algorithms to reduce the size implications of the texture can be essential. On the other hand, linking to external data may be problematic as it dictates to preserve an unaltered copy along with the data. Lastly, the prevalent serialization formats of IFC are human readable file formats, deviating from this, by embedding compressed blobs in the file breaks with this promise. Similarly, using a foreign format to compress data dictates the availability of additional routines to interpret data.

2.2 Existing Serialization formats.

To date, the most common serialization format of IFC instance models is the ISO 10303 part 21 (Step Physical File Format, SPF). It has been designed to maximize interoperability, not storage efficiency. Its clear text encoding uses 8-bit (1 byte) values corresponding to the graphic characters of ISO 8859-1 referred to as "Latin 1" and produces large files using e.g. 8 bytes for the number "123.4567" encoded as a character string. The same number can be encoded in 4 bytes (32 bits) using IEEE 754 single precision floating points. Note that sequences of text encoded numbers need to be separated by a comma, whereas boundaries of binary number representations are known by definition of their datatypes. In addition, the time required to parse binary data is significantly lower than clear text counterparts as the binary equivalents map directly to registers implemented in hardware.

An XML encoding in UTF-8 as standardized in ISO 10303 part 28 would require 16 bit per character and at the opposite end, storage space for binary representations could be further brought down using 'half' precision 16 bits shorts or 8 bit 'minifloats'. Variable bit length floating point numbers optimized for the needed accuracy could further decrease file sizes but the implementation effort would render such approaches impractical.

Structurally, SPF also lacks capabilities such as built-in indexing for random access to e.g. read only a certain LOD of a point cloud from a particular room on a certain building story without having to parse the complete file first.

3 Proposed data structure

The proposed schema extension, fully published in an open repository[1], follows the conventions in the existing IFC schema. For example the separation of product level instances from their representations. The proposal also incorporates lessons learned from existing blob instances for image textures in the IFC schema and avoids the inefficient EXPRESS binary attribute type. Our proposed approach incorporates state of the art point cloud compression techniques while allowing variable precision ratios and levels of detail for different purposes or elements. The suggested approach is modelled with the prevalent serialization formats in mind, but allows a transition to a more efficient serialization in the HDF5 format.

3.1 Decomposition

The general approach suggested is the addition of a new Entity type `IfcPointCloud` as a subtype of the abstract `IfcRepresentationItem` base definition. This allows the coherent extension of well-established modeling approaches by allowing the assignment to arbitrary populations of `IfcProducts` and its subclasses. By providing an additional label to

[1] https://github.com/DesignSystemsEindhoven/IFCPointCloud

indicate the level of detail, different resolutions of point clouds can be stored in parallel to allow the incremental access of rough approximations to fine-grained detail when needed by end-users. Using existing data types derived from `IfcNormalisedRatioMeasure`, colors from panoramic pictures taken by some laser scanner models as well as direction vectors indicating reflection normals during the scan can optionally be stored alongside the positions of points and can be captured in attributes of the `IfcPointCloud` structure.

In addition to storage structure itself, an `IfcPointCloudElement` entity allows the assignment of several `IfcPointCloud` instances to achieve the structural advantages described in section 2. Similarly to the `IfcProxy` entity, its main use is that of a placeholder and grouping element. It can also be used as a virtual element that carries all point cloud structures for which no other explicit association could be identified. This includes superfluous data from furniture, or drapes that has not been cleaned from the data sets as well as noise by scanner reflections in glass panes or targets outside the building such as foliage as illustrated in Figure 2. Coordinates in the `IfcPointCloud` elements themselves make up the bulk of the average expected data sets. We suggest one of three possible types of representations described in the following sections.

3.2 3D Cartesian coordinates

Re-using the existing two dimensional array, `IfcCartesianPointList3D` elements can be used to capture the coordinates of `IfcPointClouds` using the established mechanism of nested local coordinate systems relative to the site or storey of a building. This allows capturing the positions at arbitrary precision rates beyond the accuracy of commonly employed terrestrial laser scanners.

3.3 Parametric surfaces

To further increase the efficiency of storage and deepen the semantic connection of a point cloud segment and the building element it describes, the schema extension incorporates the storage of points in the form of *parametric* coordinates `{u,v}` on an association surface `S`, with an offset `w` along the surface normal of `S` evaluated at `{u,v}`. The entity is named `IfcParameterValueList`. When paired with other serialization techniques, described in section 3.5, parametric storage will require less storage space, as opposed to coordinates in Cartesian space, an `IfcRectangularTrimmedSurfaces` can be used to map the range of floating point values to defined boundaries. Here, 'rectangular trimmed' surface means a rectangular in the parametric `{u,v}` space also applicable to cylindrical, spherical or b-spline surfaces.

Figure 2 Visualization of associated and unassociated points. Associated points are colored according to their parametrization, unassociated points, describing abutting constructions, reflections and furniture, colored in gray

3.4 Height fields

As an extension to the approach of parametrization described in section 3.3, a third option are height fields which store points as discretized grid cells, illustrated in Figure 3. As such, the `{u,v}` components in parametric space are defined at the intersection of the grid axes and per point only the `w` component needs to be stored in an entity named `IfcGridOffsetList`. Hence, the dimensionality required to represent a single point is reduced from three, for either `{x,y,z}` or `{u,v,w}`, to one, `{w}`, which is the offset from the surface.

Two ways of constructing such grids are proposed. Firstly, the existing `IfcGrid` entity is leveraged and allows arbitrary grids, including radial and irregular grids, to be constructed from a list of arbitrary curves. These axes should be defined as `IfcPCurves` to maintain the invariant that these curves are guaranteed to lie on the association surface. Secondly, to reduce the overhead of `IfcGrid` definitions for a simple rectangular grid a new entity `IfcSurfaceGrid` is introduced that models a rectangular grid on an association surface by means of a regular spacing interval and number of axes in both the `u` and `v` direction.

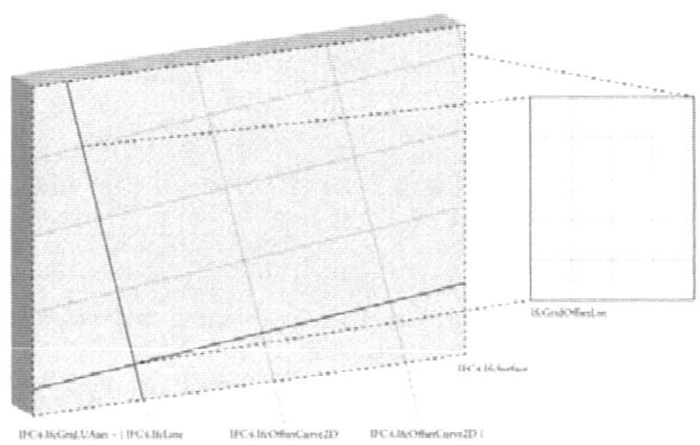

Figure 3 Schematic representation of an instantiated IfcGridOffsetList

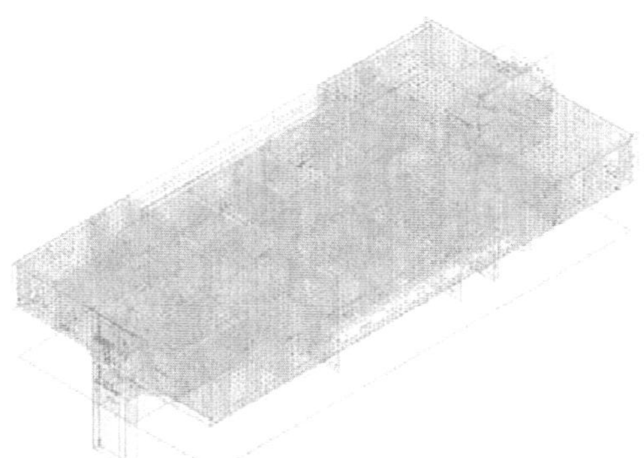

Figure 4 Coarse visualization of a collection of IfcGridOffsetLists in 3d and their underlying parametrization surfaces.

3.5 Floating point discretization

Two approaches have been presented in sections 3.3 and 3.4 that model point cloud coordinates in bounded parametric spaces. The space is bounded in the `{u,v}` direction by means of an `IfcRectangularTrimmedSurface`. The `w` direction is bounded by two additional attributes that specify the minimum and maximum deviation from the surface for a set of point cloud coordinates.

With the range of values bounded by a lower and upper bound, the range can be discretized using a fixed number of steps and expressed as an integer numerator with known denominator. A floating point number is represented as $(-s) \times d \times \beta^e$, with, in case of typical IEEE 754 single precision, 23 bits for the significand d, 8 bits for the exponent e, 1 sign bit s and base β 2. If the range of values is limited to `[0.0, 1.0]` a number with similar, but uniform, precision can be formalized as $d/(2^n - 1)$, with n being the amount of bits for the significand and hence can be represented using an integer number. If the parametric range `[u1, u2]` corresponds to 1m and n is either 8 bits or 16 bits, the equivalent of an `unsigned byte` or `unsigned short` in standard computer architectures, the obtained precision is respectively $1\text{m}/255 \approx 4\text{mm}$ and $1\text{m}/65535 \approx 0.02\text{mm}$. For on-site measurement with terrestrial laser scanners this usually exceeds the accuracy of common hardware and satisfies tolerances for potential use cases such as e.g. precast concrete elements (Kim, Cheng, Sohn, & Chang, 2015) or steel. Also note that parametric ranges can be arbitrarily subdivided by instantiating multiple `IfcRectangularTrimmedSurfaces`, over the building surface geometries, facilitating arbitrary precision even for integer numeral representations.

With this in mind a discrete and a continuous variant for each of the abstract base classes `IfcParameterValueList` and `IfcGridOffsetList` is created, either supplying `{u,v,w}` and `{w}` values as floating point numbers or as integer numerals. An indication of the advantage of such an approach, even in SPF serialization can be found in Listing 1.

```
((0.04918746,0.1925387,0.8992467))
((12,49,229),255)
```

Listing 1. Comparison of clear text encoding for floating point numerals

4 Proposed serialization format HDF

Using the schema extension described above, point clouds can be serialized as SPF, the prevalent clear text IFC serialization format. However, we recommend the use of the Hierarchical Data Format (HDF) (Folk et al., 2011) for an efficient handling of large datasets. HDF is used for more than 20 years in different engineering and scientific communities to cope with large amounts of data including e.g. physics, astronomy and medical datasets. It is an open standard with mature portable implementations in many languages that allows efficient I/O (see figure 5). It provides flexible mechanisms for data modeling in a transparent, self-documenting way that makes it an accepted candidate for long-term preservation (Bertin-Mahieux, Ellis, Whitman, & Lamere, 2011; Gray et al., 2005) and interoperability (Choi & Folk, 2007; Dougherty et al., 2009) use cases. With the ISO 10303 part 26, a standard exists that specifies mappings of STEP schemas from EXPRESS into HDF 5 as well as the serialization of instance model populations.

Apart from the storage space advantages that comes with a binary format, HDF also adds a number of additional advantages over part 21 SPF workflows. Firstly, the underlying data schema and meta data is transported along with the instance files.

Secondly, the hierarchical nature of HDF and its indexing mechanisms, illustrated in figure 5 allow fast random access and slices through large datasets and facilitate lazy loading approaches. This is of particular interest for point cloud data workflows where often only partial datasets ('progressive' LODs, spatial compartments, element clusters) need to be processed.

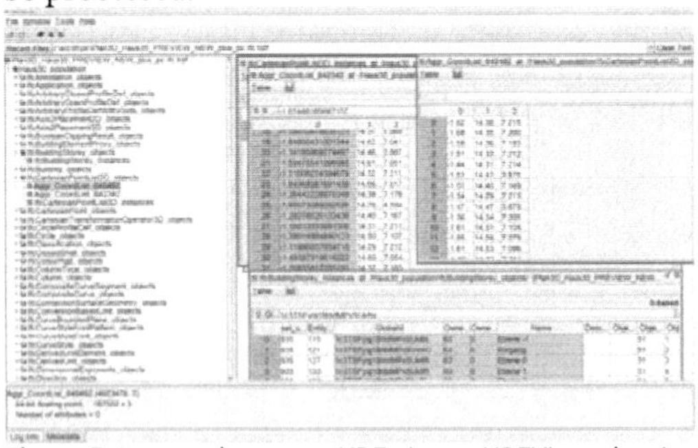

Figure 5 A general purpose HDF viewer, HDFView, showing an IFC instance model population with point clouds. The outline on the left shows the hierarchical nature of HDF, in which the mapping approach results in a separate dataset for every entity type. In addition, large aggregate-valued attributes can be stored in an individual dataset as well, using HDF's dataset referencing mechanism.

4.1 Prototype implementation and test results

In this section we provide an overview of the prototypical implementation that we have developed to validate the feasibility for the suggested approach.

4.2 Test data set

The test data sets used for the tests described in this paper are based on the "Haus 30" data set. The dataset contains a professionally modelled IFC representation of an historic building near Berlin, Germany with five stories. The complete building has been using a laser scanner. The data tested here comprises 40 internal scanner positions sampled down to approx. 15 million individual points. These have been registered with the IFC representation and when stored as an E57 require about 201 MB of storage space.

4.3 Software Prototype

A number of conversion tools have been implemented, that extract the raw point clouds from the source files, register point cloud clusters to building elements, structure them using different options of the proposed schema and serialize them either as SPF or HDF5. For visual control, a viewer prototype has been built that allows additional analytical visualizations of e.g. deviations etc. Only open source libraries such as IfcOpenShell, h5py, Point Cloud Library (PCL), e57lib, NumPy, Scipy and OpenCascade have been used during the implementation and the prototypes themselves are available the open source software repository. Permutations of different combinations have been generated to compare the resulting files, measure access times etc.

4.4 Performance indicators

The performance indicators used during the test are mainly focused on the impact of different data modelling approaches on file sized and runtime behavior such as access times.

From the comparison of file size, presented in figure 6, several observations can be made. Firstly, note that the e57 file (column 0), which has been the source document for the point clouds, is comparable in size to the 32bit uncompressed HDF serialization (5) when the non-Cartesian point information is deducted. This is to be expected as both carry the same number of points in the same 32bit floating point format.

In addition, the compressed SPF serialization (2) in byte count, does not deviate sfrom the binary HDF file (4). In fact, SPF is not very inefficient with regard to byte count. For example, an SPF entity instance reference like `#123` can take more space in HDF as it is described as a compound structure of two unsigned integers, according to ISO 10303-26 6.10.4. In addition SELECT and OPTIONAL EXPRESS attributes in HDF need to be initialized for all possible concrete implementations, no matter the actual attribute value, as HDF does not allow missing data, as described in ISO 10303-26 6.9.3.4. On the other hand, the zip compression quite effectively minimizes the otherwise massive overhead of repeated IFC entity names throughout the SPF file, such as the thousands of occurrences of `IFCCARTESIANPOINT`. However, the compressed SPF file provides an undesirable solution as the file needs to be decompressed in its entirety and offers no mechanisms to retrieve subsets. This however is feature built-into HDF by means of its hierarchical nature and block-level compression and decompression.

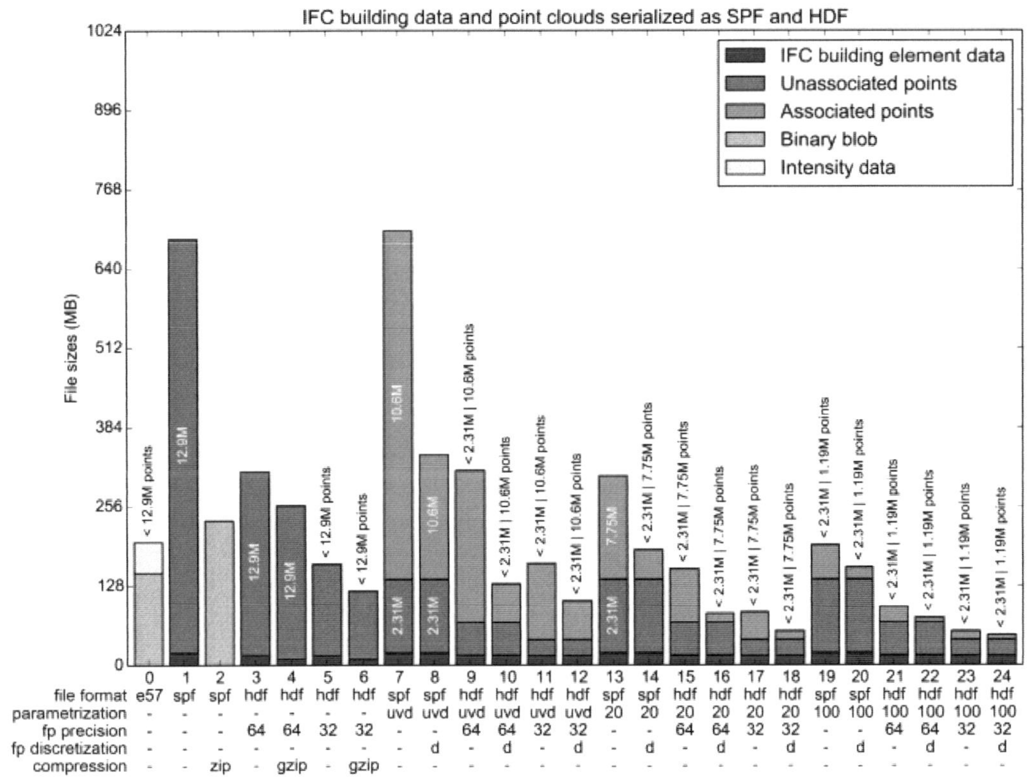

Figure 6. Overview of various forms of serialization for point clouds and building data.

The introduction of associatiosn between point clouds segments and building elements comes with a minimal cost, as association entities need to be populated as is visible in cases (3) and (9) in figure 6. However, as discussed in section 3.5 the parametrization onto bounded surfaces allows the use of an integer discretized notation for the parametrized components. Combined with a precision loss under typical scanner's resolution, this yields a tremendous file size reduction in both SPF (7-8) and HDF (9-10). At this point the HDF file (10) is smaller than the original e57 file, carrying the same number of points, enriched with the complete IFC building model instantiation.

An additional layer of compression can be gained from the grid discretization as described in section 3.4. A grid size of 20mm and 100mm is shown in (13-18) and (19-24) respectively. When using the discretized notation for the floating point numbers, even in SPF a low resolution associated point cloud can be embedded in the IFC file of smaller file size than the building data itself, as can be seen in the red and green parts of (20). Such a low resolution (100mm) point cloud totaling to roughly 1.2 million points is probably not useful to assess exact surface properties of the building elements, but might be sufficient for facility management purposes to assess the exact location, rotation and existence of building elements.

5 Conclusion

In this paper a novel extension is introduced that provides a harmonized storage of point cloud models and IFC files, using an extension to the IFC schema. The method presented follows state of the art point cloud compression techniques. In addition, their application in this context deepens the semantic relation between building elements and point clouds, as points are parametrized onto the building surface they describe. Lossy compression is introduced by means of discretized notation of floating point numerals and surface discretization into rectangular and irregular free-form grids.

A prototypical implementation has shown that using this schema, coarsely subsampled point clouds can be embedded in the prevalent clear text serialization form of IFC. In order to facilitate the storage of industry standard large point cloud datasets, a novel serialization form using the HDF file format is proposed, which follows existing ISO standards to serialize EXPRESS instance models.

6 Future work

At the time of writing, the prototypical implementation only compresses associated points, as the existing building element surfaces are used as shape proxies to parametrize the point cloud. State of the art point cloud compression techniques can be applied to the unassociated points as well, in order to find surfaces not lying on building elements, that can be used for parametrization.

HDF5 allows several compression schemes, including user-defined compression methods. These would allow much higher compression ratios by exploiting structural knowledge of the point cloud or by introducing additional lossiness in the compression methods. In the prototypical implementation only gzip compression is used. Especially the point clouds segments stored as height maps projected on parametric surfaces might be suitable for specific-purpose compression methods, such as jpeg or png, which can exploit and filter unperceivable differences.

A more rigorous study of the precision implications of the various constructs introduced in this paper will result in best practices for future implementers of the proposed standard extension. In addition, it

Figure 7 A height map derived from a point cloud projected onto a building element. Advanced grids, rectangular decomposition and specific-purpose

might yield a more successful compression level when this knowledge is used to apply rectangular decomposition methods on the parametrized surface in order further constrain the parametric range based on localized point cloud densities and in order to decompose faces with internal boundaries, for example from walls with opening elements.

Following current modelling standards in IFC, several cardinal properties should be defined and should be standardized in an `IfcPropertySet`, similar to how predefined properties are provided for building elements. This should include properties such as weather conditions that influence the scan quality. Preferably, existing metadata structures, for example as standardized by ASTM, should be tstarting point. This requires no further work in the EXPRESS schema extension definition itself, as the `IfcPointCloudElement` by subtyping `IfcProduct` already allows `IfcPropertySets` to be related.

When more metadata about scanner positions and models is known, it could be worthwhile to assess whether the projection of points onto parametric surfaces conforms to a re-usable pattern. In this case a precise `IfcGrid` can be derived, reused for multiple point cloud associations, minimizing the precision loss by point cloud interpolation onto grids and maximizing the compression ratio.

Lastly, future research will indicate how the associated point cloud structure presented in this paper can be paired with other spatial indexing structures to further advance the localized extraction of point cloud segments and spatial querying techniques.

Further experiments will be conducted to harness and reuse the general purpose decomposition and aggregation relationships of the IFC to implement octrees and kd-trees to further enhance structure and accessibility of the data.

Acknowledgements

This work has been partially funded by the EU FP7 project "DURAARK", grant agreement 600908.

References

ASTM. (2011). E2807 – 11 Standard Specification for 3D Imaging Data Exchange, Version 1.0 1 . ASTM.

Bertin-Mahieux, T., Ellis, D. P. W., Whitman, B., & Lamere, P. (2011). The Million Song Dataset. *ISMIR 2011: Proceedings of the 12th International Society for Music Information Retrieval Conference, October 24-28, 2011, Miami, Florida*, 591–596.

Bhatla, A., Choe, S. Y., Fierro, O., & Leite, F. (2012). Evaluation of accuracy of as-built 3D modeling from photos taken by handheld digital cameras. *Automation in Construction*, *28*, 116–127. doi:10.1016/j.autcon.2012.06.003

Botsch, M., Wiratanaya, A., & Kobbelt, L. (2002). Efficient High Quality Rendering of Point Sampled Geometry. In *Proceedings of the 13th Eurographics Workshop on Rendering* (pp. 53–64). Aire-la-Ville, Switzerland, Switzerland: Eurographics Association.

Braun A, T. S. (2015). A concept for automated construction progress monitoring using BIM-based geometric constraints and photogrammetric point clouds.

Brilakis, I., Lourakis, M., Sacks, R., Savarese, S., Christodoulou, S., Teizer, J., & Makhmalbaf, A. (2010). Toward automated generation of parametric BIMs based on hybrid video and laser scanning data. *Advanced Engineering Informatics*, *24*(4), 456–465. doi:10.1016/j.aei.2010.06.006

Bügler, M., Ogunmakin, G., Teizer, J., Vela, P. A., & Borrmann, A. (2014). A comprehensive methodology for vision-based progress and activity estimation of excavation processes for productivity assessment. In *Proceedings of the 21st International Workshop: Intelligent Computing in Engineering (EG-ICE), Cardiff, Wales.* Retrieved from http://www.cms.bgu.tum.de/publications/2014_Buegler_EG-ICE.pdf

Choi, V., & Folk, M. (2007). Investigations into using HDF5 as an alternative to STEP for finite element modeling data. In *Proceedings of the 9th NASA-ESA Workshop on Product Data Exchange, National Aeronautics and Space Administration, Santa Barbara, CA.*

Dietze, S., Beetz, J., Gadiraju, U., Katsimpras, G., Wessel, R., & Berndt, R. (2013). Towards Preservation of semantically enriched Architectural Knowledge. In *Proceedings of the 3rd International Workshop on Semantic Digital Archives (SDA 2013)* (Vol. 1091, pp. 4–15). Valetta, Malta: CEUR. Retrieved from http://ceur-ws.org/Vol-1091/

Digne, J., Chaine, R., & Valette, S. (2014). Self-similarity for accurate compression of point sampled surfaces. *Computer Graphics Forum*, *33*(2), 155–164. doi:10.1111/cgf.12305

Dougherty, M. T., Folk, M. J., Zadok, E., Bernstein, H. J., Bernstein, F. C., Eliceiri, K. W., ... Best, C. (2009). Unifying Biological Image Formats with HDF5. *Commun. ACM*, *52*(10), 42–47. doi:10.1145/1562764.1562781

Folk, M., Heber, G., Koziol, Q., Pourmal, E., & Robinson, D. (2011). An overview of the HDF5 technology suite and its applications. In *Proceedings of the EDBT/ICDT 2011 Workshop on Array Databases* (pp. 36–47). New York, NY, USA: ACM. doi:10.1145/1966895.1966900

Golla, T., Schwartz, C., & Klein, R. (2014). Towards Efficient Online Compression of Incrementally Acquired Point Clouds. In J. Bender, A. Kuijper, T. von Landesberger, H. Theisel, & P. Urban (Eds.), *Vision, Modeling & Visualization.* The Eurographics Association. doi:10.2312/vmv.20141271

Gray, J., Liu, D. T., Nieto-Santisteban, M., Szalay, A., DeWitt, D. J., & Heber, G. (2005). Scientific Data Management in the Coming Decade. *SIGMOD Rec.*, *34*(4), 34–41. doi:10.1145/1107499.1107503

Huang, Y., Peng, J., Kuo, C.-C. J., & Gopi, M. (2008). A Generic Scheme for Progressive Point Cloud Coding. *IEEE Transactions on Visualization and Computer Graphics*, *14*(2), 440–453. doi:10.1109/TVCG.2007.70441

Khoshelham, K., & Elberink, S. O. (2012). Accuracy and Resolution of Kinect Depth Data for Indoor Mapping Applications. *Sensors*, *12*(2), 1437–1454. doi:10.3390/s120201437

Kim, M.-K., Cheng, J. C. P., Sohn, H., & Chang, C.-C. (2015). A framework for dimensional and surface quality assessment of precast concrete elements using BIM and 3D laser scanning. *Automation in Construction*, *49, Part B*, 225–238. doi:10.1016/j.autcon.2014.07.010

Pu, S., & Vosselman, G. (2009). Knowledge based reconstruction of building models from terrestrial laser scanning data. *ISPRS Journal of Photogrammetry and Remote Sensing*, *64*(6), 575–584. doi:10.1016/j.isprsjprs.2009.04.001

Rusu, R. B., & Cousins, S. (2011). 3D is here: Point Cloud Library (PCL). In *2011 IEEE International Conference on Robotics and Automation (ICRA)* (pp. 1–4). doi:10.1109/ICRA.2011.5980567

Schnabel, R., & Klein, R. (2006). Octree-based Point-cloud Compression. In *Proceedings of the 3rd Eurographics / IEEE VGTC Conference on Point-Based Graphics* (pp. 111–121). Aire-la-Ville, Switzerland, Switzerland: Eurographics Association. doi:10.2312/SPBG/SPBG06/111-120

Schnabel, R., Möser, S., & Klein, R. (2008). Fast vector quantization for efficient rendering of compressed point-clouds. *Computers & Graphics*, *32*(2), 246–259. doi:10.1016/j.cag.2008.01.014

Tang, P., Huber, D., Akinci, B., Lipman, R., & Lytle, A. (2010). Automatic reconstruction of as-built building information models from laser-scanned point clouds: A review of related techniques. *Automation in Construction*, *19*(7), 829–843. doi:10.1016/j.autcon.2010.06.007

Teizer, J. (2015). Status quo and open challenges in vision-based sensing and tracking of temporary resources on infrastructure construction sites. *Advanced Engineering Informatics*, *29*(2), 225–238. doi:10.1016/j.aei.2015.03.006

Yang, J., Park, M.-W., Vela, P. A., & Golparvar-Fard, M. (2015). Construction performance monitoring via still images, time-lapse photos, and video streams: Now, tomorrow, and the future. *Advanced Engineering Informatics*, *29*(2), 211–224. doi:10.1016/j.aei.2015.01.011

Ziv, J., & Lempel, A. (1978). Compression of individual sequences via variable-rate coding. *IEEE Transactions on Information Theory*, *24*(5), 530–536. doi:10.1109/TIT.1978.1055934

Identifying Thermal Microgrids on the Basis of Spatialized Fuzzy Logic and Metamodelling

Philipp Geyer, mailto:,p.geyer@kuleuven.be
Architectrual Engineering, KU Leuven, Belgium

Fabian Ritter, fabian.ritter@tum.de
Computational Modelling and Simulation, TU München, Germany

Abstract
Microgrids have high potential in future energy supply and its efficiency. However, establishing microgrids within a building stock is a complex task as characteristic of buildings in terms of energy demand and supply systems need to match. For this purpose, the paper proposes an identification method for assistance in pre-planning that bases on a spatialized fuzzy logic in combination with metamodelling to represent key building characteristics. The method, which is intuitively applicable, identifies potential building groups for microgrids based on key factors window size, insulation and compactness as well as age of the heating system, emissions and spatial location. It is demonstrated by means of the data of a small Swiss building stock.

Keywords: Automated network identification, spatial fuzzy logic, metamodelling or surrogate modelling.

1 Introduction

Microgrids are a promising solution for a sustainable energy supply of building stocks. They allow for the intelligent management of energy demand and excess between buildings, for the sharing of plants and other infrastructure, which reduces peak loads and cost for installation and maintenance as well as for exploiting heat sources of the building. However, microgrids strongly rely on the condition and use of the buildings, on the distances of the buildings to each other and on locally available renewable energy sources. Therefore, the identification of well-working configurations of microgrids in building stocks is a complex task.

For this complex task, computer assistance has a high potential to help planners in identifying well-performing configurations. Building stock databases with information on heat demand and location of the buildings are the basis for this identification. Additional information, e.g., on the age of the heating system, the condition of the envelope improves the results. The identification of thermal microgrids requires to find closely located buildings with certain properties that are at the moment selected by experience. Of most interest is the replacement of old heating systems that will be probably replaced in near future or of heating systems with high CO_2 emissions. These are basic criteria that are considered in the presented study. Further identification criteria in future research could include available waste heat or solar thermal potential of roofs as well as a more detailed analysis, which parameters lead to the best microgrid configurations.

However, often no data on energy consumption and emissions are available and only simplified building geometry and construction information are known in the building stock database. For building stocks with hundred up to 10.000 of buildings, detailed energy analysis of each building including energy simulation are not adequate. Nonetheless, for identifying microgrids, information on annual energy demand, CO_2 emissions and required peak power are essential. Therefore, simplified energy performance assessment methods are required.

The paper provides a method for the identification of potential microgrids and describes a spatialized fuzzy logic approach for this purpose in Section 3. The approach defines closeness and other criteria as fuzzy functions. These functions form a fuzzy logic that is able to identify candidate buildings for thermal microgrids in a database with geospatial information and heating energy demand and further properties of the buildings. This approach allows the identification well-performing microgrid configurations. For the derivation of energy demand and CO_2 emissions, which acts as vital basis for the spatialized fuzzy logic, Section 4 introduces the response surface method (RSM), which is one important technique of metamodelling, to build a quick-responding substitute model for the heating energy demand and peak power. This allows to determine these chief performance indicators for thermal microgrids from simple building data on geometry and construction for a large number of buildings. Parametric simulation of a generic indoor space dependent on the three key factors, which are window size, insulation and compactness, provides the supporting data for the performance metamodel. Section 5 applies the whole methodology to the building stock of the Swiss village Zernez and identifies 15 potential microgrid configurations including CO_2 savings and necessary investments for individual and for grid heating solutions.

2 State of the Art

2.1 Building Stock Analysis

For designing microgrids, the prediction of the energy consumption in building stocks is required. For such predictions with related emissions and for evaluating scenarios and strategies, building stock models are important. Swan and Ugursal (2009) and Kavgic et al. (2010) review the state of the art techniques of building stock modelling in research including the existing models and approaches and their use for policy making. The typical parameters that these models build on are categories of building age, type of building, heat distribution type, energy source, construction or refurbishment year and type of building. Furthermore, different classification methods are applied to buildings stock data. Usually, the parameters in the building stock data are used to derive groups and to assign measures for energy efficiency. A typical example is the type-age classification that has been developed for Germany by the Institut für Wohnen und Umwelt (IWU) and recently extended to Europe (IWU, 2012).

In terms of more sophisticated data analysis techniques, different approaches related to energy use in building stocks exist. Clustering is an essential technique to identify similar buildings. Santamouris et al. (2007) apply clustering to a database of 320 schools in Greece and determine groups based on normalized energy consumption. Gaitani et al. (2010) identify typical building properties and parameters of the schools using k-means clustering. Jones et al. (2001) cluster a building stock by properties, such as heated ground floor area, facade, window to wall ratio. Yamaguchi et al. (2007) identify district types and provide typical energy performance by simulating buildings in a representative district. Moreover, as part of the research project 'Zernez Energia 2020', which also serves as the data source for the case study in the paper, Geyer et al. (2014) have recently developed a method to cluster buildings based on the performance of retrofit measures.

However, all these classification approaches mostly focus on energy demand and retrofit actions and use mainly non-spatial parameters for classification. None of them considers the suitability of buildings for microgrids including both non-spatial properties and spatial data. Thermal microgrids however strongly rely on spatial considerations; their performance depends on the number and distance of buildings included. Due to the many different possible combinations of connections between buildings the extension of the clustering method based on retrofit performance for the identification of thermal microgrids would cause high computational loads. For this reason, we utilize fuzzy logics as presented below.

2.2 Metamodelling

A prominent method of metamodelling for quick-responding models and interpolating between samples is the response surface methodology (RSM). Box and Draper (2007) comprehensively describe the method and its application, which includes not only polynomial modelling methods but also suitable Design of Experiments (DoE) tables, usually serving to gain supporting experimental layouts for the model. Forrester et al. (2008) give a general introduction to the use of metamodelling in engineering, including radial basis functions, kriging, and support vector regression in addition to the traditional polynomial RSM. Simpson et al. (2001) provide a comparison of such techniques. The preference of RSM in this study relies on the simple engineering-related form of the method resembling basic curve fitting.

In engineering, especially with a focus on simulation results, there exists a tradition of using metamodels, which frequently follow the RSM. Chlela et al. (2009) and Jaffal et al. (2009) applied traditional RSM to the setup a metamodel for the thermal performance of a building. They compared different types of DoE tables and their benefit for establishing a metamodel. However, their setup is not related to a specific design decision and involves many factors leading to a complex design space, which is difficult to fit by means of a traditional polynomial metamodel. Ekren and Ekren (2008) used RSM for the layout of a hybrid renewable energy system and its optimisation. Gholap and Khan (2007) performed a similar task for heat exchangers for refrigerators and used it for optimisation. Goel et al. (2007) present a systematic approach to approximate the Pareto front in optimisation by RSM and applied the method to a rocket injector design problem. Cheng et al. (2013) built a metamodel based on neural networks for a nonlinear complex model of fuel cells. Zhang et al. (2012) built an RSM metamodel for the cost of energy production for the planning of wind farms and reduced the cost by optimisation. Georgopoulou and Giannakoglou (2010) used metamodels to assist evolutionary algorithms in power generating unit commitment problems with probabilistic unit outages to reduce computation time. Geyer and Schlüter (2014) introduce a method for automatically adapting the metamodel structure for the more precise representation of building performance for a single building. However, there does not exist a building stock approach for assessing heat loads and heating power peaks by RSM.

3 Clustering Based on Fuzzy Logic

3.1 Fuzzy Logic Method

The identification of microgrids is based on a spatialized fuzzy logic approach comprising criteria to select buildings suitable for a thermal microgrid. The basis is usual fuzzy logic as described by Harris (2006). The criteria are defined as fuzzy functions using the form of one-sided triangular fuzzy functions. This is the general form of these functions:

$$\mu(x, x_1, x_2) = \begin{cases} x <= x_l & 0 \\ x > x_l \wedge x < x_u & \dfrac{x - x_l}{x_u - x_l}, \\ x >= x_u & 1 \end{cases} \quad (1)$$

where x is the value to be assessed and x_l and x_u are the lower and upper limit of the ramp.

Whereas such fuzzy functions only deal with parameters of one building, microgrids involve more than one building and their spatial relation. The use of spatial information in fuzzy functions extends the evaluation for this purpose to a spatialized fuzzy logic. As a first example, a membership function of closeness of two buildings is set up. This spatial extension of the membership function uses a Euclidian distance d:

$$d(B_1, B_2) = \sqrt{(x_2 - x_1)^2 + (y_2 - y_1)^2}, \quad (2)$$

where x and y are the corners coordinates with the least distance of two buildings B_1 and B_2; an additional algorithm determines the closest corners to be used for this purpose. The pairwise comparison for all buildings forms the distance matrix $\boldsymbol{D}$ that has the size n^2 for n buildings. The application of the membership function $\mu_{is\ close}$ on $\boldsymbol{D}$ identifies all pairs of buildings that are close enough for forming a microgrid. With two further membership function for the heating system age and the emissions, the assessment of the buildings stock data is carried out. Figure 1 shows the three membership functions, the first for the emissions $\mu_{high\ emissions}$, the second for the age of the heating system $\mu_{old\ heating\ system}$ and the third for the distance $\mu_{is\ close}$. Weighting is implicitly possibly by the shape of these fuzzy functions and by later selecting the defuzzification threshold.

After the evaluation of the data by the three membership functions, a fuzzy logic function serves to identify candidates for microgrids. This function selects building pairs that have high emissions or an old heating system and that are at the same time close enough to each other for a microgrid. The fuzzy logic function for this purpose is

$$\mu_{micro\ grid\ affine} = (\mu_{much\ emissions} \vee \mu_{old\ heating\ system}) \wedge \mu_{is\ close} \quad (3)$$

The application of the resulting membership function $\mu_{micro\ grid\ affine}$ to the database delivers the microgrid-affine matrix ***M*** with the building pairs suitable for microgrids; the matrix has the same dimensions as the distance matrix, which is $n2$.

3.2 Cluster Identification Algorithm

Among these pairs that are found by the fuzzy logic, the identification of connected groups of buildings is required that spatially form a cluster and thus potentially one microgrid. A further algorithm identifies these clusters among the pairwise matrix ***M*** and adds up the distance and the heat demand per cluster; these data allow to assess the performance of the microgrid. A simple algorithm determines the connectivity of candidate buildings and forms groups from them. It starts from the first building in the database assigns it to a group together with all buildings that it is connected to. Once a building is assigned to a group it is not considered anymore. The next group starts with the next unassigned building. When all buildings are assigned, the groups with only one building are eliminated. This process assigns all microgrid-affine buildings to exactly one cluster

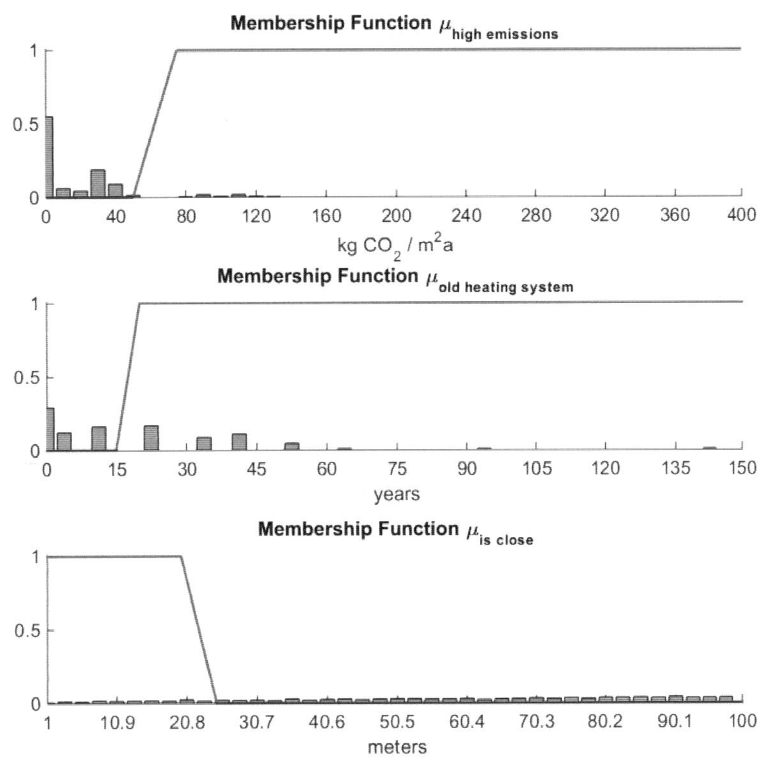

Figure 1: Membership functions for the criteria combined with percentage histograms of the respective values in the database of the Swiss Village Zernez.

Table 1 Configuration of design variables

Design variable	-1	0	+1
Insulation standard (i)	U_{wall} = 2.0 W/m²K U_{window} = 1.85 W/m²K	U_{wall} = 0.32 W/m²K U_{window} = 1.25 W/m²K	U_{wall} = 0.14 W/m²K U_{window} = 0.65 W/m²K
Compactness (A/V) (ii)	1.67 m^{-1}	1.0 m^{-1}	0.84 m^{-1}
Glazing factor	0.3	0.6	0.9

(iii)

4 Using Metamodels for Building Stock Assessment

In the case study of Zernez, described in Section 5, energy consumption is known by the extensive data base. However, such a situation is normally not given. Therefore, metamodeling serves to construct the performance from simple parameters of building geometry and construction. Such parameters are usually known by plans, maps and owner interviews. The metamodel allows to determine an approximate energy demand based on typical characteristics: insulation standard, compactness and glazing factor.

4.1 Metamodelling Method

In the traditional RSM approach, the structure of the equations is static considering that second-order polynomials and either no or only first-order interaction represent the response in the design space. A usual form is

$$y = f(x_1, x_2), \quad (4)$$

where x_i are the design vectors, which contain the parameter values for each variable, and y is the target value, in this particular case the simulation results for the parameter combinations. The metamodel is then represented as

$$\hat{y} = \beta_0 + \beta_1 x_1 + \beta_2 x_2 + \beta_3 x_1^2 + \beta_4 x_2^2 + \beta_5 x_1 x_2 + \varepsilon = g(x), \quad (5)$$

where β_i are the fitting coefficients, ε is the modelling error and ŷ is the response.

To enable metamodeling, a selected number of supporting points have to be calculated. There are three ways of achieving the responses for the supporting points: (1) calculation, for example based on known physical behaviour; (2) measured through experiments; (3) simulation. In this research, we focus on metamodeling using simulation, because of the lack or poor availability of measured data and the high influence of the behaviour of the people living in the examined area.

Therefore, a parametric simulation model has been developed using MatLab and EnergyPlus. In this particular case, we developed a three factor design using (i) the insulation standard (U-values of windows, outer walls and roof), (ii) the compactness (outer surface to volume ratio) and (iii) the glazing factor.

Normally, DoE serves for determining a subset of supporting points that provide as much as possible information with as least as possible experiments. However, in this case, for calculating the polynomial metamodel of second degree corresponding to equation (5), at least three variation steps (design points) of each factor are necessary. This leads to a minimum of $3^3 = 27$ simulations for the metamodel, which allows for a full factorial exploration of the design space. The each factor is normalized to a range of -1 to 1. Therefore, the evaluation of the parametric simulation model is performed at the steps -1, 0 and 1 to ensure the most accurate model due to the highest distribution of design points in the examined design space. The ranges for the design variables, thus representing the steps of the design space, are chosen as shown in Table 1.

The simulation results calculated for supporting the detection of microgrids are the overall heating energy demand (including warm water) and the maximum heating peak power. The results show a heating energy demand in the range from 51 to 443 kWh/m²a and a maximal heating peak power from 20 to 180 W/m². The metamodel is then gained from regression (minimizing the quadratic mean error) whereby the absolute error is calculated with following equation:

$$\varepsilon = \frac{1}{n}\sum(\hat{y} - y)^2, \quad (6)$$

where $\hat{y}$ are the results of the metamodel and y are the simulation results. Additionally, the simulation results using the in between steps -0.5 and 0.5 are generated to perform a simple cross validation and to evaluate the metamodel at these points as shown in Figure 2.

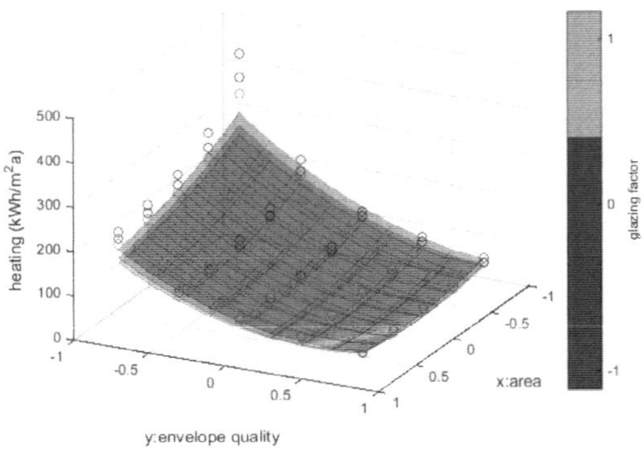

Figure 2: The me2tamodel of the three factor design of the energy use displaying the surfaces for low (blue), medium (red) and high (green) glazing factors and the simulation results (points).

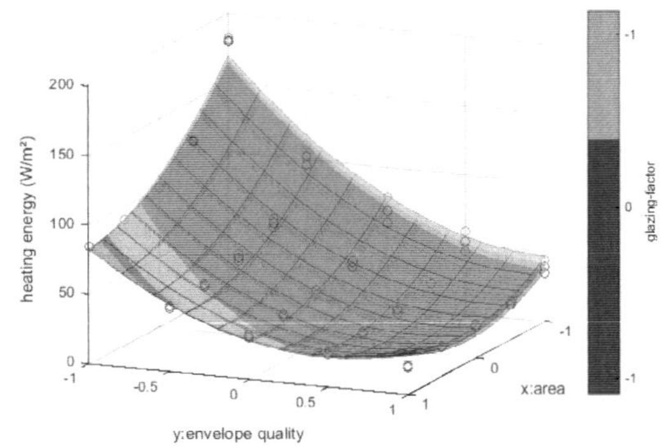

Figure 3: The metamodel of the three factor design of the heating load displaying the surfaces for low (blue), medium (red) and high (green) glazing factors and the simulation results (points).

Table 2 Conversion and efficiencies factors for heating system technologies

Heating system technology	Conversion factor in kg CO_2/kWh	Efficiency
CHP	0,023	0,85
Electric or electric and wood	0,371	0,95
Ground-souce heat pump	0,066	0,95
District heating (wood)	0,022	0,90
Wood	0,017	0,80
Air-source heat pump	0,061	0,95
Solar thermal / Wood	0,007	0,85
Oil	0,290	0,85
Oil and wood	0,126	0,85
Oil and electric	0,391	0,85

The metamodel is calculated for both, the energy consumption and the maximal heating load. The results show a maximal error of 65% for the metamodel of the energy consumption. The metamodel is still used, because most of the values are below an error of 10% and the maximal error only occurs at one border of the design space (see also Figure 2).

In case of the peak heating power, the metamodel is of higher accuracy with a maximal error of 20% with almost all values below 10% (see also Figure 3).

Using conversion factors, the metamodels delivers also an estimate of the CO_2 emissions based on the heating energy demand in kWh/m²a. In the test case, the energy demand is used to determine the CO_2 emission for the different heating systems according to Table 1.

5 Test Case

An application to the building stock data of the village Zernez serves to test the method. The data for this application origin from the research project Zernez Energia 2020. Zernez Energia 2020 is an ambitious low emission project of the village Zernez in the Southeast of Switzerland in collaboration with ETH Zurich. In this project, extensive data on the 309 buildings located in the village have been collected. From this database, the method uses the building geometry to determine the compactness, the share of windows in the façade as well as the insulation standard of the envelope.

An ongoing study will deliver more detailed results on thermal microgrids for this building stock (Schlüter et al. 2015). This study only uses the energy consumption from the year 2013 included in database without metamodelling. It will include more detailed analyses of the performance of microgrids then that provided in the following.

5.1 Applying the Method on the Zernez Data

As first step, the energy demand and the CO_2 emissions to be expected result from using the metamodel described in Section 4. As basis for the metamodel, geometric data from the database are utilized. The response of the metamodel is gained without further user interaction. The outcome of this step is the basis for applying the microgrid identification method described in Section 3. This second step uses two additional information categories from the database: the age of the heating system and the location of the buildings.

As a result, the method identified 15 possible clusters that are candidates for planning microgrids. Table 3 shows the size of clusters $n_{Buildings}$, an estimation of the pipe length in the network $l_{network}$, the reduction of CO_2 emissions by exchanging existing heating systems by microgrid heat pump technology, the investments for the individual heat pumps and for microgrids and the investment savings achievable by the microgrid solution of a thermal microgrid solution with one central heat pump compared to individual heat pumps. The estimation of the network length $l_{network}$ uses a linear regression based on some planning examples in the size range for Zernez made by the ETH research team that lead to the following dependency on the sum of distances within a cluster $d_{cluster}$:

$$l_{network} = 0.4 \sum d_{cluster} + 120\,\text{m}. \quad (7)$$

The investment costs c_{inv} derive from the required peak power P_{peak} and the pipe length $l_{network}$:

$$c_{inv} = 9{,}000\ \text{CHF/kW}\ P_{peak} + 29000\ \text{CHF} + 1000\ \text{CHF/m}\ l_{network}. \quad (8)$$

This is a simplified assumption relying on practical experience that describes the economy of scale of heat pumps and on average piping costs as described by Frederiksen and Werner (2013). However, it does not consider further advantages such as higher efficiency of bigger heat pumps by using more elaborate technology, the possibility of reducing the peak power by intelligent scheduling and the possible heat exchange between consumers.

The savings by the microgrid compared to individual heat pumps range from 3% to 37%. These savings rely on the economy of scale of the heat pumps exceeding costs for the network. Only for the largest network (Cluster 11) with 31 buildings and 1.3 km network length, the network infrastructure is more expensive then these savings. Table 3 including the diagram shows that the solution is most profitable for small clusters. This proves the benefit of the thermal microgrid idea.

6 Conclusion

In sum, the method presents a means to identify microgrids in building stocks with spatially distributed nodes of different characteristics. Currently, the method has been applied for thermal microgrid identification considering the heat demand of buildings derived from simple geometric characteristics as well as some selected construction data. Deliberately, the approach only uses simple data, such as insulation standard, compactness and size of windows, because they are normally quickly available by owner statements, plans etc. In this situation, metamodelling serves as a well-scaling method to derive yearly energy demand, peak heating power and CO_2 emissions from these data. The method has been identified as suitable with enough accuracy to substitute energy simulation models, which are connected with high effort. It can serve to determine the energetic behaviour of large building stocks considering detailed dynamic effects that rarely other methods than simulation are able to analyse.

Table 3: Left: Results of clustering for the Zernez building stock using the metamodel for CO2 assessment; Right: Diagram showing the savings over the peak power of the microgrids.

Cluster	$n_{Buildings}$	$l_{Network}$	Heating Power in kW	Head Demand in kWh/a	Reduction by HP(s) in CO2 t/a	Investment individual heat pumps in thou. CHF	Investment microgrid with one HP in thou. CHF	Investment savings by microgrid
1	8	84	149	363.385	84	1.158	1.039	10%
2	3	5	32	75.359	24	142	89	37%
3	4	19	284	670.889	30	1.414	1.346	5%
4	19	427	516	1.297.987	214	3.309	3.214	3%
5	3	8	26	59.671	14	351	301	14%
6	5	42	253	639.448	94	1.538	1.463	5%
7	5	19	86	236.776	92	920	822	11%
8	15	328	175	415.826	121	2.024	1.946	4%
9	2	5	38	90.883	11	199	175	12%
10	2	4	19	43.607	14	231	206	11%
11	31	1.327	948	2.271.626	271	6.819	7.277	-7%
12	2	5	19	54.533	4	962	938	3%
13	2	1	27	72.039	47	362	334	8%
14	6	44	162	428.876	101	1.609	1.508	6%
15	3	5	55	141.713	49	684	630	8%

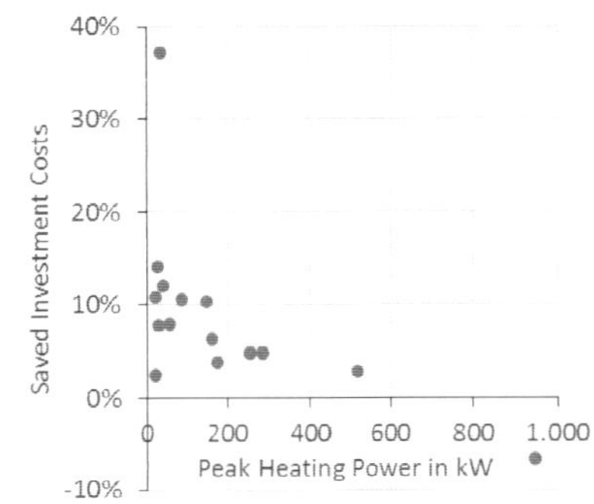

The subsequent application of the spatialized fuzzy logic identifies buildings with suitable properties for the network as candidates for possible networks. It is important to emphasise that the results from this identification are a proposal for a microgrid that needs to be checked and further developed by an engineering expert. The method is aimed as pre-planning assistance rather than replacing a planning process and its expert. Compared to other clustering methods, this approach is an intuitively applicable method with good and quick available results. The only use of pairwise comparison for determining spatial reasoning reduces the computational load and provides high potential for scaling the method up. The fuzzy functions allow the intuitive direct encoding of characteristics needed for networks. Finally, it is important to note that in case all necessary data are available it is also possible to apply the spatialized fuzzy logic directly without metamodelling.

Future research will deal with more extensive applications of the method. First, this includes the consideration of thermal energy sources, such as waste heat, geothermal or solar thermal sources. This requires a second microgrid-affine matrix as extension of the cluster identification algorithm. Second, in analogy, the application for network identifications of other energy carriers has high potential. One possibility would be the development of electric smart grid structures based on expected demand patterns, renewable potentials of PV and wind power and storage facilities to balance supply and demand, to reduce transport loads in cables and to avoid losses and overloads. In this way, the spatialized fuzzy logic can contribute to the identification and establishment of smart grids and microgrids by grouping suitable suppliers and demanders to well-performing configurations.

Acknowledgements

The test case data origin from the Zernez 2020 research project, which partly is funded by the Swiss Commission for Technology and Innovation (CTI). We acknowledge thankfully the contributions of the research groups of ETH Chairs of Architecture and Building Systems, Prof. Dr. Arno Schlüter, of Architecture and Urban Design, Prof. Kees Christiaanse, Michael Wagner (project lead) and Building Physics, Dr. Jan Carmeliet, Dr. Kristina Orehounig. Furthermore, required characteristics of microgrid candidates were developed in discussion with Prof. Schlüter and Sasha Cisar.

References

Box GEP, Draper NR (2007): Response surfaces, mixtures, and ridge analyses - Wiley series in probability and statistics, Wiley, Hoboken, NJ.

Cheng SJ, Miao JM, Wu SJ (2013): Use of metamodeling optimal approach promotes the performance of proton exchange membrane fuel cell (PEMFC), Applied Energy 105(0), pp. 161-169, http://dx.doi.org/10.1016/j.apenergy.2013.01.001.

Chlela F, Husaunndee A, Inard C, Riederer P (2009): A new methodology for the design of low energy buildings, Energy and Buildings 41(9), pp. 982-990, http://dx.doi.org/DOI: 10.1016/j.enbuild.2009.05.001.

Ekren O, Ekren BY (2008): Size optimization of a PV/wind hybrid energy conversion system with battery storage using response surface methodology, Applied Energy 85(11), pp. 1086-1101, http://dx.doi.org/10.1016/j.apenergy.2008.02.016.

Forrester AIJ, Sóbester A, Keane AJ (2008): Engineering design via surrogate modelling : a practical guide - Progress in astronautics and aeronautics ; 226, Wiley, Chichester.

Frederiksen S, Werner S (2013): District heating and cooling, Studentliteratur, Lund.

Gaitani N, Lehmann C, Santamouris M, Mihalakakou G (2010): Using principal component and cluster analysis in the heating evaluation of the school building sector, Applied Energy 87(6), pp. 2079-2086, http://dx.doi.org/10.1016/j.apenergy.2009.12.007.

Georgopoulou CA, Giannakoglou KC (2010): Metamodel-assisted evolutionary algorithms for the unit commitment problem with probabilistic outages, Applied Energy 87(5), pp. 1782-1792, http://dx.doi.org/10.1016/j.apenergy.2009.10.013.

Geyer P, Schlüter A (2014): Automated metamodel generation for Design Space Exploration and decision-making – A novel method supporting performance-oriented building design and retrofitting, Applied Energy 119(0), pp. 537-556, http://dx.doi.org/10.1016/j.apenergy.2013.12.064.

Geyer P, Schlüter A, Cisar S (2014): A Performance-Based Clustering Method for Retrofit Management of Building Stocks, eg-ice Workshop 2014, Cardiff.

Gholap AK, Khan JA (2007): Design and multi-objective optimization of heat exchangers for refrigerators, Applied Energy 84(12), pp. 1226-1239, http://dx.doi.org/10.1016/j.apenergy.2007.02.014.

Harris J (2006): Fuzzy Logic Applications in Engineering Science - Microprocessor-Based and Intelligent Systems Engineering, Springer Netherlands.

IWU (Institut Wohnen und Umwelt) (2012): Typology Approach for Building Stock Energy Assessment. Main Results of the TABULA project, www.building-typology.eu, accessed Dec 2014.

Jaffal I, Inard C, Ghiaus C (2009): Fast method to predict building heating demand based on the design of experiments, Energy and Buildings 41(6), pp. 669-677, http://dx.doi.org/10.1016/j.enbuild.2009.01.006.

Jones PJ, Lannon S, Williams J, Modelling building energy use at urban
scale, in: Proceedings of the 7th International IBPSA conference, Rio de Janeiro, Brazil, 2001, pp. 175–180.

Kavgic M, Mavrogianni A, Mumovic D, Summerfield A (2010): A review of bottom-up building stock models for energy consumption in the residential sector, Building and Environment 45(7), pp. 1683-1697, http://dx.doi.org/10.1016/j.buildenv.2010.01.021.

Santamouris M, Mihalakakou G, Patargias P, Gaitani N (2007): Using intelligent clustering techniques to classify the energy performance of school buildings, Energy and Buildings 39(1), pp. 45-51, http://dx.doi.org/10.1016/j.enbuild.2006.04.018.

Schlüter A, Geyer P, Cisar S (2015): Analysis of Geo-referenced Building Data for the Identification and Evaluation of Thermal Microgrids, Proceedings of the IEEE, Special Issue Microgrids and Energy Efficient Buildings, submitted.

Simpson TW, Poplinski JD, Koch PN, Allen JK (2001): Metamodels for Computer-based Engineering Design: Survey and recommendations, Engineering with Computers 17(2), pp. 129-150, http://dx.doi.org/10.1007/PL00007198.

Swan LG, Ugursal VI (2009): Modeling of end-use energy consumption in the residential sector: A review of modeling techniques, Renewable and Sustainable Energy Reviews 13(8), pp. 1819-1835, http://dx.doi.org/10.1016/j.rser.2008.09.033.

Yamaguchi Y, Shimoda Y, Mizuno M (2007): Proposal of a modeling approach considering urban form for evaluation of city level energy management, Energy and Buildings 39(5), pp. 580-592, http://dx.doi.org/10.1016/j.enbuild.2006.09.011.

Zhang J, Chowdhury S, Messac A, Castillo L (2012): A Response Surface-Based Cost Model for Wind Farm Design, Energy Policy 42(0), pp. 538-550, http://dx.doi.org/10.1016/j.enpol.2011.12.021.

Generation of a hierarchic structure via 3D-topology optimisation using black and white filtering

Sjonnie Boonstra, s.boonstra@student.tue.nl
Eindhoven University of Technology, The Netherlands

Hèrm Hofmeyer, h.hofmeyer@tue.nl
Eindhoven University of Technology, The Netherlands

Abstract

Commonly used building structures often show a hierarchic layout of structural elements. It can be questioned whether such a layout originates from practical considerations, e.g. related to its construction, or that it is (relatively) optimal from a structural point of view. This paper investigates this question by using topology optimisation in an attempt to generate a commonly used timber floor. The optimisation is conducted using 3D-volume elements so the topology can differentiate over the height, making a hierarchic layout at least possible. First results show indeed a hierarchic layout, however the floor surface is non-continuous, due to low density areas, reducing its practical applicability. Black and white filtering is proposed via a Heaviside function to avoid the low density areas. Although some implementation issues exist, this function results in a more continuous floor surface, suggesting that a hierarchic layout is optimal from a structural point of view.

Keywords: 3D-topology optimisation, hierarchic structures, Heaviside function

1 Introduction

Hierarchic layouts of structural elements are commonly found in building structures such as floors, walls and roofs.

A hierarchic structure consists of sets of structural elements and arranges a flow of forces hierarchically from the last set on which an external load acts via intermediate sets to the primary set which is connected to a supportive structure. The flow of forces is stepwise being concentrated by each set with the aim to transfer a distributed load to a few specific locations. For example, a roof can be spanned by primary beams, secondary beams, tertiary beams and finally the roof cladding, see Error! Reference source not found..

Using hierarchic layouts of structural elements could very well be practical, e.g. in terms of construction speed and preventing errors. Namely, its aspects of repetition allow for standardized building methods, and errors are spotted more easily in a repeating system. However, a hierarchic layout of structural elements could also be explained if it would be (relatively) optimal from a structural point of view. Therefore, in this paper topology optimisation will be used in an attempt to generate a commonly used timber floor. The optimisation is conducted using 3D-volume elements so the topology can differentiate over the height, making a hierarchic layout at least possible.

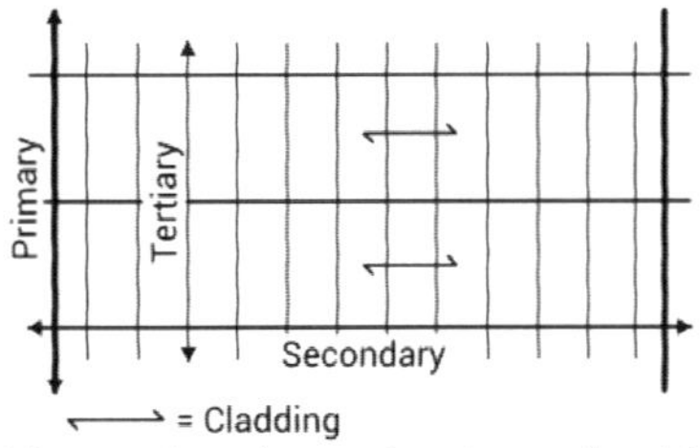

Figure 1, schematic view of a hierarchic roof layout

In the next two sections, first research on stiffened plate optimisation will be discussed, for stiffened plates suggest that hierarchical layouts are indeed related to optimised structural behaviour, then a brief introduction will be given on the subject of topology optimisation.

1.1 Stiffened plate optimisation

Plates are often stiffened by ribs in a parallel or (orthogonally or diagonally) grid layout, and these stiffened plates have become increasingly popular because of their low weight and the high load capacity for both in-plane and out-of-plane loading. As such, research has been carried out on the optimisation of stiffened plate layouts e.g. for the layout and shape of stiffeners in 2D-structures (Bojczuk & Szteleblak 2008); via parametric optimisation of grid-stiffened composite panels under transverse loading (Jadhav & Mantena 2007); and by studying compressively loaded composite stiffened plates (Iuspa & Ruocco 2008, Kang & Kim 2005).

Above, optimisation of stiffened plates is gradient-based, using design variables for e.g. the number of ribs, their shape or height. However, Lam & Santhikumar (2003) use topology optimisation to introduce new ribs and to determine the rib sizes.

As a conclusion, rib stiffened plates are extensively researched and optimised for both in-plane and out-of-plane loading, but this is not the case for the "from the ground up" generation of a (rib-stiffened) plate to distribute a specified load.

1.2 Topology optimisation

Topology optimisation predicts for each element in a finite element model an optimal relative mass density, such that an objective (e.g. total strain energy) reaches a (local) minimum, given a certain load case.

1.2.1 Algorithms

An often referenced gradient-based optimisation algorithm has been published by Sigmund (2001), its code efficiency been updated in Andreassen et al. (2011). Evolutionary optimisation algorithms are used as well, e.g. the level-set method (Yulin & Xiaoming 2004) and a multi-objective genetic algorithm (Bandaru & Deb 2015).

1.2.2 Filtering

Part of a topology optimisation algorithm involves the determination of the objective's sensitivity to the variation of element densities. Hereafter, filtering techniques average the element sensitivities (or densities) with their neighbouring elements, i.e. often to prevent so-called checkerboard patterns. Sigmund (2007) introduces new morphology based filters, e.g. eroding, dilating, opening and closing morphology filters, and compares these with existing filters like density filtering, sensitivity based filtering, and filters based on a Heaviside filter.

1.2.3 Applications

Topology optimisation has been used to optimise all sorts of artefacts, e.g. bridges, aircraft wings, chairs and tables, statues, etc., proving optimality of their shapes (Christiansen et al. 2015). Other research uses topology optimisation for design process simulation e.g. for automated building spatial and structural design (Hofmeyer & Davila Delgado 2015).

More specifically, plate optimisation via topology optimisation exists (Bojczuk & Mróz 2009, Lam & Santhikumar 2003), however element formulations are based on plate theory. These plate theory elements are 2D, which consequently do not allow for differentiation of the density over the height. The influence of different types of the plate formulation has been researched as well (Long et al 2009).

Technically, to reduce computational time, symmetry can be used (Rozvany 2011), and useful analytical benchmarks can be found in (Rozvany 1998). Related to this a derivation of an analytical solution is found in (Lewiński et al. 1994).

It can be concluded that a number of techniques exist for topology optimisation, which have been used on a variety of design problems. However, the potential optimality of a 3D floor structure has never been investigated.

2 Topology optimisation

Topology optimisation is usually carried out by discretising a volume into finite elements with a density. The topology optimisation algorithm then gradually varies the density of each element until the objective has been achieved. In this paper, a topology optimisation algorithm from literature (Sigmund 2001) has been implemented in C++. Although improvements for this algorithm, as found in Andreassen et al. (2011), are useful and efficient, they are not (yet) implemented into the program used here. Thus the optimisation problem for the algorithm can be formulated as in function **(1)**.

$$\left.\begin{aligned}&\min_{x}:\\&c(\mathbf{x}) = \mathbf{U}^{\mathbf{T}}\mathbf{K}\mathbf{U} = \sum_{e=1}^{n}(x_e)^p \mathbf{u}_e{}^{\mathbf{T}}\mathbf{k}_e\mathbf{u}_e\\&\text{subject to:}\\&\frac{V(\mathbf{x})}{V_0} = f\\&\mathbf{KU} = \mathbf{F}\\&0 < x_{\min} \le x_e \le 1\end{aligned}\right\}\quad (1)$$

The objective is the minimisation of compliance c, which is the total strain energy over all elements. In the objective function, e is a finite element identifier, x_e is the relative density of the element, p is the penalisation factor (using the power-law approach), $\mathbf{u}_e$ is the displacement vector of an element and $\mathbf{k}_e$ is the element's stiffness matrix. Respectively from top to bottom the constraints are as follows: the volume fraction remains constant; equilibrium of forces; the density of an element must be higher than 0 and lower than or equal to 1. In these functions, $V(\mathbf{x})$ and V_0 are the material volume and the design volume respectively, f is the design volume fraction that is allowed to be occupied by material, $\mathbf{K}$ is the global stiffness matrix, $\mathbf{U}$ is the global displacement vector and $\mathbf{F}$ is the force vector.

The algorithm starts by computing the modified stiffness matrices of elements, see function **(2)**.

$$\forall_e\left\{\mathbf{k}_e \rightarrow x_e^p\mathbf{k}_e\right\} \quad (2)$$

The global stiffness matrix is then assembled and $\mathbf{KU} = \mathbf{F}$ is solved. Accordingly, the compliance can be calculated with the displacement field of the structure known, see $c(\mathbf{x})$ in function **(1)**. The sensitivity of the compliance to the variation of an element's relative density can now be calculated with equation **(3)**.

$$\partial c(\mathbf{x})/\partial x_e = -p x_e^{p-1}\mathbf{u}_e^{\mathbf{T}}\mathbf{k}_e\mathbf{u}_e \quad (3)$$

A so-called mesh-independency filter modifies the sensitivity of an element on the basis of the sensitivity, density, and distance of surrounding elements, effectively averaging the sensitivities over a specified domain, function **(4)**.

$$\begin{aligned}&\frac{\widehat{\partial c}(\mathbf{x})}{\partial x_e} = \frac{\sum_{f=1}^{N}\hat{H}_f x_f\left(\partial c(\mathbf{x})/\partial x_f\right)}{x_e\sum_{f=1}^{N}\hat{H}_f}\\&\hat{H}_f = r_{\min} - dist(e,f)\\&\{f \in N \mid dist(e,f) \le r_{\min}\}\\&e = 1,2,\ldots,N\end{aligned}\quad (4)$$

In the function above, element e is considered and the sensitivities of all other elements f within a radius r_{min} are weighted on the basis of their density x_f and their distance to the considered element with factor $\hat{H}_f$.

Lastly, elements obtain a new density x_e^{new} as shown below in formula **(5)**.

$$\begin{aligned}&x_e^{new} = x_e\sqrt{\frac{\widehat{\partial c}(\mathbf{x})/\partial x_e}{\lambda}}\\&but:\\&x_e^{new} \ge \max(x_{\min}, x_e - m)\\&x_e^{new} \le \min(1, x_e + m)\end{aligned}\quad (5)$$

The value of x_e^{new} is limited to 1 (full density) and should be larger than x_{min}, itself slightly larger than 0, to prevent a singular element stiffness matrix. The change in relative density is limited to m to obtain smooth changes in the topology, and is usually set to 0.2. The total sum of all densities is scaled to equal the design volume fraction f (see function **(1)**) by a bi-sectioning algorithm that finds the value of the Lagrangian multiplier λ, equal for each element.

The algorithm described above is repeated until the maximum norm of the difference between the old and new density vector is lower than a predefined threshold (usually 0.01).

3 Generation of a hierarchic structure (timber floor)

To investigate whether some building structures are hierarchic because as such they are (relatively) optimal with regards to structural behaviour, here topology optimisation (which finds a locally optimal distribution of structural mass) will be used in an attempt to generate a commonly used timber floor, specified below.

3.1 Design variables

3.1.1 Floor design

A commonly used timber floor is presented here that consists of beams with a cross-section equal to 38 mm × 235 mm and with centre-to-centre distances equal to 300 mm. The span length equals 5.0 m, and the underlayment has a thickness of 18 mm. The modulus of elasticity is 6000 N/mm² and the Poisson's ratio is assumed to equal 0.3. The floor is loaded with a uniformly distributed load p_d equal to 3.0 kN/m² and is simply supported, see **Figure 2**.

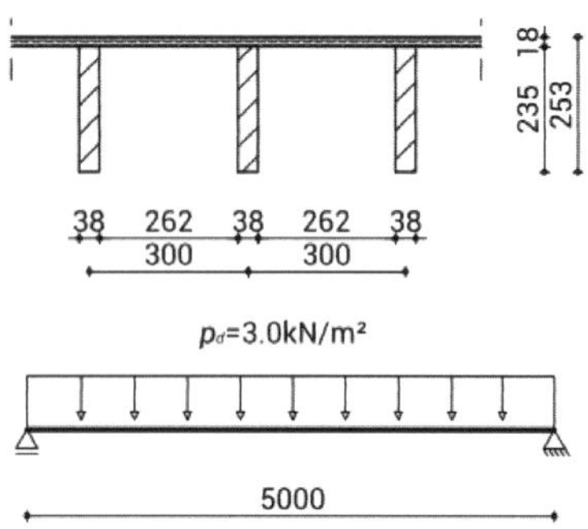

Figure 2, Top: cross-section floor structure. **Bottom:** mechanical scheme floor beam.

3.1.2 Design volume

For topology optimisation, a design volume can be defined using the floor design above. Symmetry is used (Rozvany 2011) to reduce computing costs by first modelling half the floor beams' span length and secondly simulating 2 parts of this: one being a (left) side part and one being an intermediate part. As such a whole floor can be visualised by using a left side part, intermediate parts, and a mirrored left side part, mirroring all these over the floor's span middle line. When modelling a left side part the grey font boundary condition of the intermediate part is omitted, see **Figure 3**.

Cubic finite elements are used for the correct functioning of the mesh-independency filter, which works spherically with radius r_{min}.

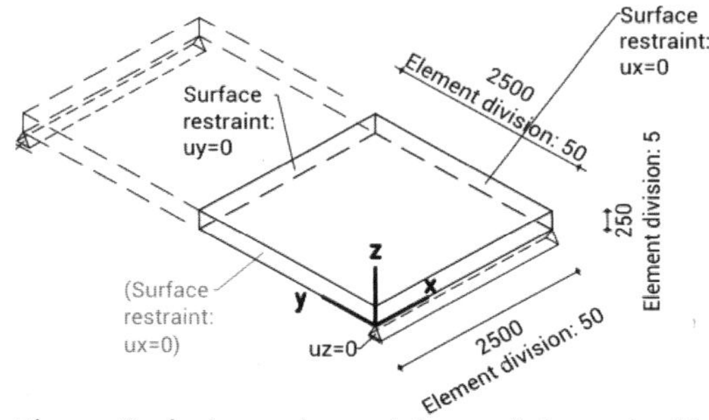

Figure 3, design volume: intermediate part with all indicated side surface restraints, left side part results when grey font restraint is omitted.

3.1.3 Settings for topology optimisation

A penalisation factor of p=3, a Young's modulus of E=6000 N/mm², and a Poisson's ratio of ν=0.3 are used. However, the volume fraction and filter size are varied accordingly **Table 1**.

Table 1, different topology optimisation settings for the floor design volume

	Volume fraction f	Filter size r_{min}
Simulation 1	0.5	1.5
Simulation 2	0.5	1.1
Simulation 3	0.2	1.5
Simulation 4	0.2	1.1

The values used in simulation 1 are more or less standard in topology optimisation and are often used when no specific results are desired. The volume fraction $f=0.2$ resembles the practical volume fraction of the timber floor in section 3.1.1. The filter size $r_{min}=1.1$ is used to be able to generate smaller structural elements, e.g. slender beams.

3.2 Results

Simulation results are shown in **Figure 4** to **Figure 7**, by showing the simulated left and intermediate parts mirrored over the floor's span middle line. Relative densities are visualised via red (high density) to blue (low density) colour map. Transparency is used for the low density elements to make the occurring 3D-structures visible, and a bottom view is applied because a closed plate could be expected on the top, which may obstruct the view of the generated structure. Finally, cross-sections over the length of the floor are shown to the right of the results.

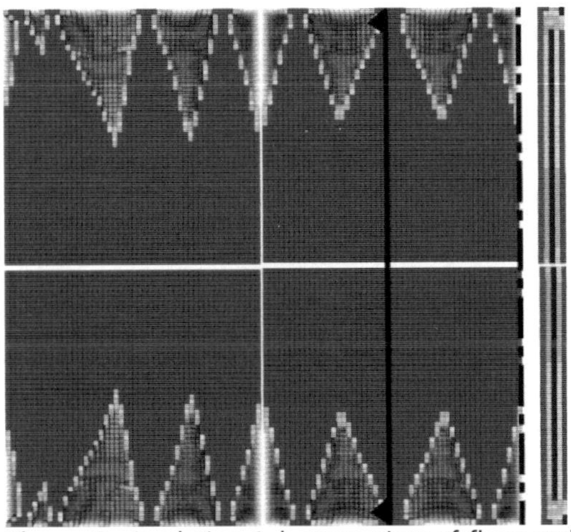

Figure 4, simulation 1, bottom view of floor and cross-section of a beam, volume fraction 0.5, filter size 1.5.

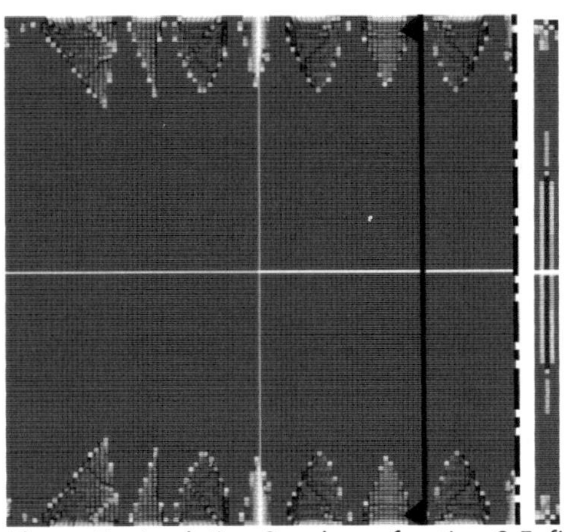

Figure 5, simulation 2, volume fraction 0.5, filter size 1.1.

3.3 Discussion of results

Simulations 1 and 2 (with a high volume fraction) generated a sandwich structure. Although some beam ends seem to branch out of the sandwich top and bottom layer (looking at the top or bottom), there are no beam webs present at these beam ends for simulation 1. However, the smaller filter size in simulation 2 introduces webs at the beam ends.

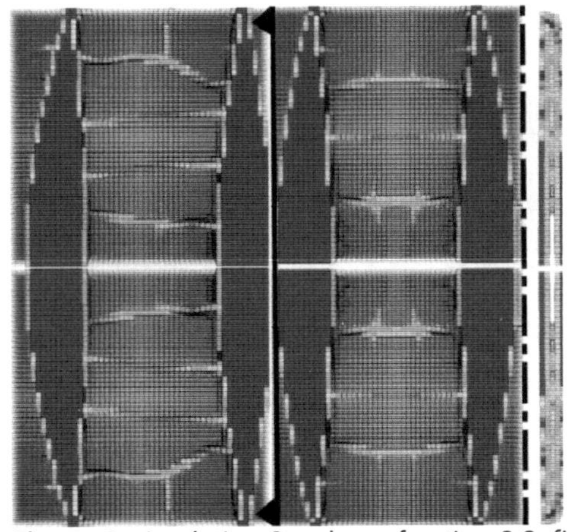

Figure 6, simulation 3, volume fraction 0.2, filter size 1.5.

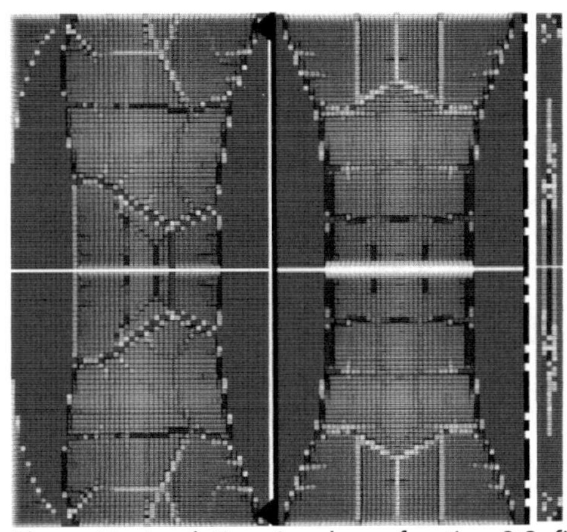

Figure 7, simulation 4, volume fraction 0.2, filter size 1.1.

Taking away material from the optimisation, by using a lower volume fraction, yields different results, see simulation 3 and 4. Beams with cigar shaped flanges appear, however no webs are present at the middle of the beam's span. Besides the primary beams also secondary and tertiary beams/arches appear, which clearly makes for a hierarchical structure, see **Figure 8**. Reducing the filter size in simulation 4 generates a solution with a finer distribution of beams. A large filter size thus seems to suppress the development of a hierarchy and beam webs.

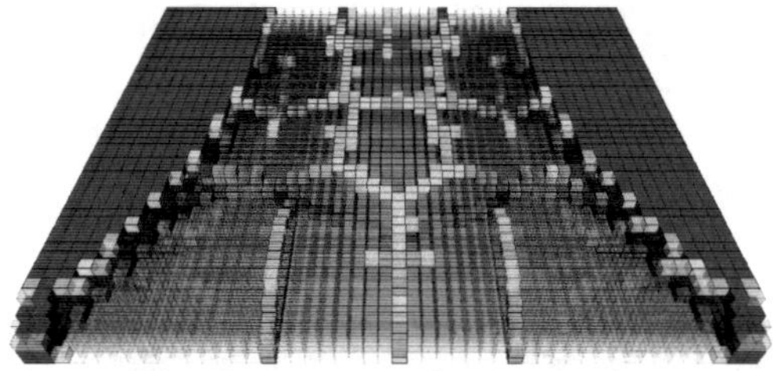

Figure 8, bird's-eye view of a intermediate part of simulation 4 shows primary beams, secondary arches, and tertiary beams.

These results are promising with respect to the generation of a hierarchic structure, however not regarding the practicality of the floor design. This because very low density elements appear at the top surface, which suggest voids or holes where loads are acting. Structurally this may be correct, as stacked low density elements can still bear relatively large loads, however this cannot be practically constructed.

To prevent these low density elements from appearing, two solutions can be imagined. The first solution is the introduction of a boundary condition that enforces the densities of elements on which an external load acts to e.g. 1.0. However, this is similar to steering the algorithm directly to generate a desired solution.

The second solution is to only allow a discrete density distribution. In literature a solution with a discrete density distribution is referred to as a black and white solution, which can be obtained via a black and white filter (Sigmund 2007). Here black and white filtering is selected to attempt to generate a floor structure without voids or holes.

4 Black and white filtering

Several black and white filter types exist (Sigmund 2007). First, morphology based filters can be used, which are based on techniques used in image processing and analyses. Secondly, a Heaviside filter can be applied, which is based on the Heaviside step function. Lastly, the mean sensitivity and bi-lateral sensitivity methods exist, which are modifications of the standard sensitivity filter.

A comparison has been made between several filters for topology optimisation, including black and white filters (Sigmund 2007). Each filter is valued for its effect on the topology optimisation performance, i.e. the minimal compliance, the discreteness of the relative density values, and the number of iterations. For discreteness, a measure has been used as shown in equation **(6)**. Here, 0% means a fully discrete density distribution (only values 0 and 1 exist) and 100% means a fully homogeneous density distribution. As equation **(6)** has been developed for a volume fraction equal to 0.5, here a modification for other fractions is proposed in equation **(7)**.

$$M_{nd} = \sum_{e=1}^{n} \frac{4x_e(1-x_e)}{n} \cdot 100\% \qquad (6)$$

$$M_{nd} = \sum_{e=1}^{n} \frac{x_e(1-x_e)}{n \cdot f(1-f)} \cdot 100\% \qquad (7)$$

In the equations above M_{nd} is the measure of discreteness and x_e is the physical density of an element, and f equals the design volume fraction.

4.1 Filter selection

Of the three filters mentioned above, the Heaviside filter is the only filter that explicitly aims at generating a solution with a discrete density distribution. And although so far there seem to be no large differences in the discreteness results of the Heaviside filter and other morphology and sensitivity based filters, this might not be the case with future problems or the problem studied here.

Besides, the Heaviside filter, along with the sensitivity based filters, is easy to implement in the optimisation algorithm presented, whereas the morphology filters require some extensive reprogramming of the algorithm. Finally, a ready-to-use implementation of the Heaviside filter is available (Andreassen et al. 2011).

Thus the Heaviside filter is selected here, and its implementation and benchmarking are discussed below.

4.2 Implementation of the Heaviside filter

A Heaviside step function is a discrete function, shown in function **(8)**. New density types are introduced here: the <u>intermediate</u> density $\tilde{x}_e$ is a density used to couple the <u>design</u> density x_e to the <u>physical</u> density $\bar{x}_e$, the latter used in finite element analyses and visualisation.

$$\bar{x}_e = \begin{Bmatrix} 0 \text{ for } \tilde{x}_e < 0 \\ 1 \text{ for } \tilde{x}_e \geq 0 \end{Bmatrix} \qquad (8)$$

Implementation of this Heaviside step function would lead to abrupt changes in the topology design, which is not desirable using a gradient-based method. Therefore a modified Heaviside function is introduced in (Guest et al. 2004), equation **(9)**, this section follows the implementation by Andreassen et al. (2011).

$$\bar{x}_e = 1 - \exp(-\beta \cdot \tilde{x}_e) + \tilde{x}_e \cdot \exp(-\beta) \quad (9)$$

This modified Heaviside function is a continuous function that converges to equation **(8)** when factor β increases. The value of β starts with 1 and will be doubled after some criterion has been reached.

This new approach to compute the physical density affects the sensitivity of the compliance to the change of an element's density. The new sensitivity can, however, now be calculated with the modified Heaviside function and using the chain rule, see equations **(10)** & **(11)**.

$$\frac{\partial c(\bar{\mathbf{x}})}{\partial \tilde{x}_e} = \frac{\partial \bar{x}_e}{\partial \tilde{x}_e} \cdot \frac{\partial c(\bar{\mathbf{x}})}{\partial \bar{x}_e} \quad (10)$$

$$\frac{\partial \bar{x}_e}{\partial \tilde{x}_e} = \beta \cdot \exp(-\beta \cdot \tilde{x}_e) + \exp(-\beta) \quad (11)$$

The sensitivities resulting from equation **(10)** are filtered, using function **(4)**, the filtered sensitivities are then used to calculate the values of x_e^{new} according function **(5)**.

Finally, the intermediate densities are found by using a density filter on $\mathbf{x}^{new}$ as shown in function **(12)**, for H_f see function **(4)**.

$$\tilde{x}_e = \frac{\sum_{f=1}^{N} \hat{H}_f x_f^{new}}{x_e^{new} \sum_{f=1}^{N} \hat{H}_f} \quad (12)$$

For clarity the general modification made to the algorithm is illustrated in a simple flow chart, see **Figure 9**, filtering of sensitivities is omitted in these flow charts.

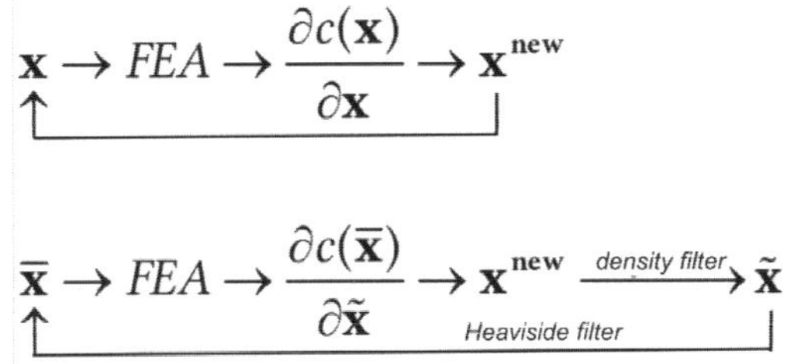

Figure 9, top: standard algorithm in section 2, **bottom:** algorithm with Heaviside filter section 4.2.

No general accepted updating scheme for factor β exists, and the development of this scheme is presented in the next section.

4.3 Benchmarking the Heaviside filter

A documented benchmark for topology optimisation is the MBB-beam as shown in **Figure 10**. Usually symmetry is used to reduce calculation costs. Topology optimisation for the beam yields a truss-like structure as shown in **Figure 11**.

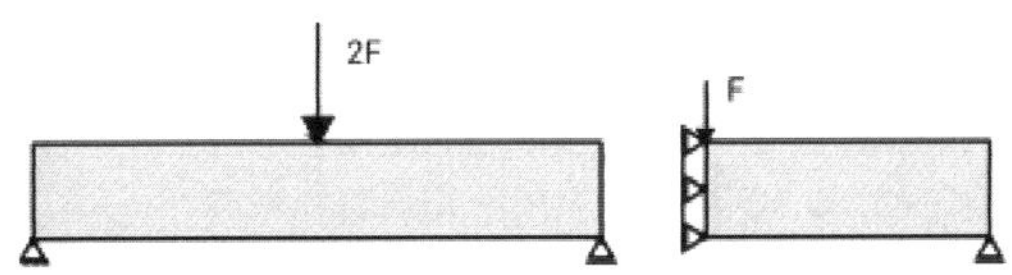

Figure 10, MBB-beam on the left and modelled part on the right.

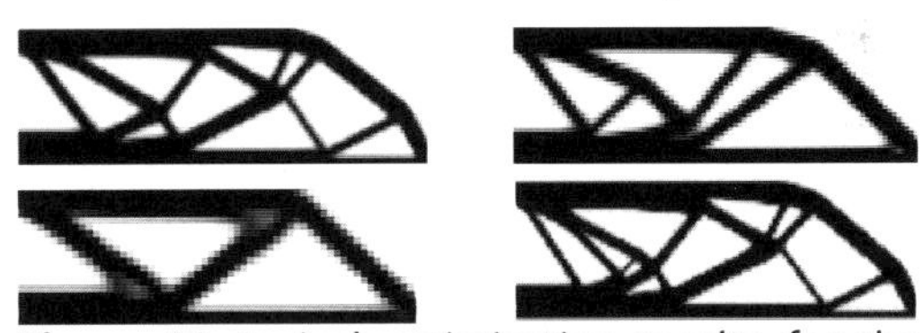

Figure 11, typical optimisation results for the MBB-beam for different topology optimisation settings generated using the code in Sigmund (2001).

The benchmarks of the implemented Heaviside filter have been performed here with an MBB-beam divided in 120 by 40 cubic elements, having a rib size equal to 25 mm, with a volume fraction of f=0.5, Young's modulus of $E=30000$ N/mm^2, Poisson's ratio $\nu=0.3$, a filter size of 1.5 times the element size and penalisation factors p=3 or $p=4$. The β-factor for the Heaviside filter will be updated after every 20 iterations or earlier if the change in element design densities has become sufficiently small (0.01). Factor β will be subject to updating until it reaches a value of 512, the optimisation will afterwards continue until the change in design densities has become sufficiently small (0.01). The solution is shown in **Figure 12** and yields a measure of discreteness of M_{nd} = 0.68%.

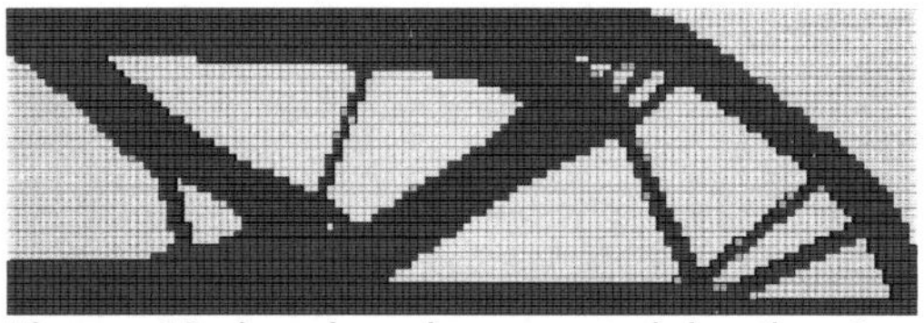

Figure 12, benchmark generated by the C++ program including a Heaviside filter, *p*=4.

The program yields an optimal solution with the Heaviside function implemented, however its results only resemble the benchmark with a penalisation factor of *p*=4 instead of the more commonly used *p*=3. Thus, before investigating the effect of a Heaviside function (with *p*=4) on the timber floor simulations, it should first be investigated what the isolated effect is of changing *p*=3 to *p*=4 to the floor simulations. Therefore a simulation 5 has been carried out – without Heaviside filter- on the floor using *p*=4, Young's modulus *E=6000 N/mm²*, Poisson's ratio *v=0.3*, volume fraction *f*=0.2, filter size r_{min}=1.5, see **Figure 13**. As no large differences are found for the floor for *p*=3 versus *p*=4, it will be tried to avoid low density elements in the floor simulations by using the Heaviside filter using *p*=4 as well.

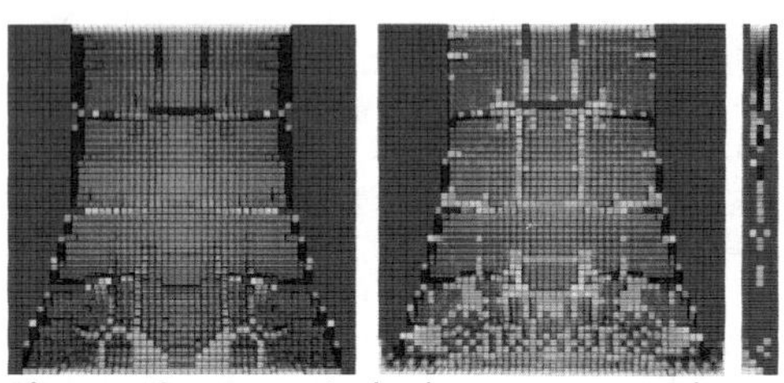

Figure 13, respectively: bottom, top and cross-section of an intermediate part of simulation 5, *p*=4, without Heaviside filter.

5 Generation of a hierarchic structure (timber floor) with a Heaviside filter

Simulations on the floor volume in this section are performed with a penalisation factor of *p=4*, young's modulus *E=6000 N/mm²* and a Poisson's ratio *v=0.3*, the volume fraction and filter sizes are given in **Table 2**. The factor β is updated according the same conditions described under section 4.3. Simulation 7 is performed with a higher volume fraction since the elements at the top surface of the floor would already occupy a fraction of 0.2 of the design volume.

Table 2, simulations and settings for the optimisation of the floor design volume with Heaviside filter

	Volume fraction *F*	Filter size r_{min}
Simulation 6	0.2	1.1
Simulation 7	0.35	1.1

5.1 Results

The results of the simulations at a high β-factor are inefficient and yield higher compliance than earlier iterations, see **Figure 14** for some typical results. During the optimisation process there is a turning point where the floor design loses its beams resulting in a sudden change in topology, and after the turning point the optimisation algorithm cannot find an optimal layout anymore.

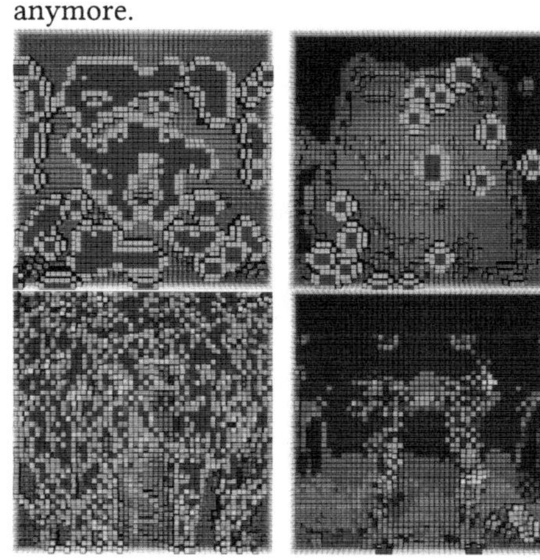

Figure 14, some typical results at a high β-factor.

There are still usable results when looking just before the turning point: **Figure 15** and **Figure 16** show the results of simulations 6 and 7 just before the topologies become distorted.

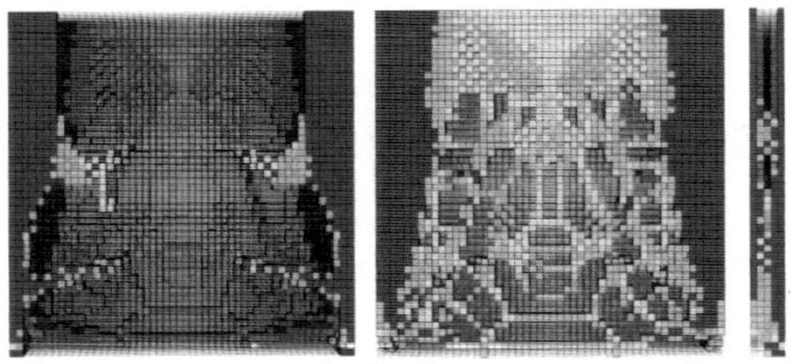

Figure 15, respectively: bottom, top and section of an intermediate part for simulation 6, result at iteration 100, β=16, M_{nd}=35,20%

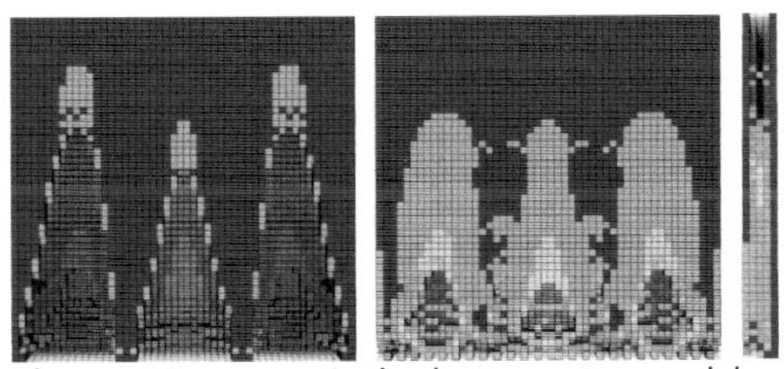

Figure 16, respectively: bottom, top and beam section of an intermediate part of simulation 7, result at iteration 89, β=16, M_{nd}=35,57%

5.2 Discussion of results

The unfinished results in **Figure 15** and **Figure 16** show similar characteristics as observed in simulations 1 to 4, however now more material has grouped at the top side of the plate. So far, the Heaviside filter seems indeed to slightly close the gaps in the floor topology. It should be noted that some verification simulations have been carried out with another implementation (Liu & Tovar, 2014), yielding similar results.

6 Conclusions

In this paper hierarchic structures are defined and it is questioned whether a hierarchic layout of structural elements could be explained to be (relatively) optimal from a structural point of view. Then 3D-topology optimisation is proposed to research this question.

A standard topology optimisation algorithm has been implemented in C++ and used on a 3D floor volume first. The results show hybrid structures, consisting of beams and sandwich structures, and a hierarchical layout is visible in the form of primary, secondary and tertiary beams or arches.

However, the standard optimisation algorithm resulted in floors with non-constructible and unusable surfaces due to low element densities. To solve this issue, black and white filtering in the form of a Heaviside filter was proposed and implemented. The C++ program shows then that a gradual Heaviside filter seems to close the openings in the floor's surface. However after a certain number of iterations results become unusable.

So far it has been shown that optimisation may lead to hierarchic structures for plates. A thorough understanding of the optimality of hierarchic structures is not yet obtained and requires further research.

6.1 recommendations

Future research could focus on the further implementation of the black and white filter in the C++ software. A Heaviside filter has been implemented, however it results in unexpected outcomes after several iterations, and the loaded (floor) surface is not yet covered with structural elements (i.e. with elements with high density). Also other types of black and white filters may have to be considered. A better understanding of the penalization factor regarding black and white filtering should be obtained as well. And the influence on the optimisation result of the β-updating scheme should be investigated with regards to the Heaviside filter.

An further understanding of the optimality behind hierarchy should be obtained by performing more simulations of different floor shapes, with finer mesh distributions and an appropriate black and white filter.

References

Andreassen, E., Clausen, A., Schevenels, M., Lazarov, B. S., & Sigmund, O. (2011). Efficient topology optimization in MATLAB using 88 lines of code. *Structural and Multidisciplinary Optimization, 43*, 1–16. doi:10.1007/s00158-010-0594-7

Bandaru, S., & Deb, K. (2015). Evolutionary Multi-Criterion Optimization, *9018*, 79–93. doi:10.1007/978-3-319-15934-8

Bojczuk, D., & Mróz, Z. (2009). Topological sensitivity derivative and finite topology modifications: Application to optimization of plates in bending. *Structural and Multidisciplinary Optimization, 39*, 1–15. doi:10.1007/s00158-008-0333-5

Bojczuk, D., & Szteleblak, W. (2008). Optimization of layout and shape of stiffeners in 2D structures. *Computers and Structures, 86*, 1436–1446. doi:10.1016/j.compstruc.2007.05.005

Christiansen, A. N., Bærentzen, J. A., Nobel-Jørgensen, M., Aage, N., & Sigmund, O. (2015). Combined shape and topology optimization of 3D structures. *Computers & Graphics*, *46*, 25–35. doi:10.1016/j.cag.2014.09.021

Guest, J. K., Prévost, J. H., & Belytschko, T. (2004). Achieving minimum length scale in topology optimization using nodal design variables and projection functions. *International Journal for Numerical Methods in Engineering*, *61*(2), 238–254. doi:10.1002/nme.1064

Hofmeyer, H., & Davila Delgado, J. M. (2015). Co-evolutionary and Genetic Algorithm Based Building Spatial and Structural Design. *AIEDAM - Artificial Intelligence for Engineering Design, Analysis and Manufacturing*, accepted for publication, April 2, 2015.

Iuspa, L., & Ruocco, E. (2008). Optimum topological design of simply supported composite stiffened panels via genetic algorithms. *Computers and Structures*, *86*, 1718–1737. doi:10.1016/j.compstruc.2008.02.001

Jadhav, P., & Mantena, P. R. (2007). Parametric optimization of grid-stiffened composite panels for maximizing their performance under transverse loading. *Composite Structures*, *77*, 353–363. doi:10.1016/j.compstruct.2005.07.015

Kang, J. H., & Kim, C. G. (2005). Minimum-weight design of compressively loaded composite plates and stiffened panels for postbuckling strength by Genetic Algorithm. *Composite Structures*, *69*, 239–246. doi:10.1016/j.compstruct.2004.07.001

Lam, Y. C., & Santhikumar, S. (2003). Automated rib location and optimization for plate structures. *Structural and Multidisciplinary Optimization*, *25*, 35–45. doi:10.1007/s00158-002-0270-7

Lewiński, T., Zhou, M., & Rozvany, G. I. N. (1994). Extended exact solutions for least-weight truss layouts—Part I: Cantilever with a horizontal axis of symmetry. *International Journal of Mechanical Sciences*, *36*(5), 375–398. doi:10.1016/0020-7403(94)90043-4

Liu, K., & Tovar, A. (2014). An efficient 3D topology optimization code written in Matlab. Structural and Multidisciplinary Optimisation, 50, 1175-1196. doi:10.1007/s00158-014-1107-x.

Long, C. S., Loveday, P. W., & Groenwold, A. a. (2009). Effects of finite element formulation on optimal plate and shell structural topologies. *Finite Elements in Analysis and Design*, *45*(11), 817–825. doi:10.1016/j.finel.2009.06.027

Rozvany, G. (1998). Exact analytical solutions for some popular benchmark problems in topology optimization. *Structural Optimization*, 42–48. doi:10.1007/BF01197436

Rozvany, G. I. N. (2011). On symmetry and non-uniqueness in exact topology optimization. *Structural and Multidisciplinary Optimization*, *43*, 297–317. doi:10.1007/s00158-010-0564-0

Sigmund, O. (2001). A 99 line topology optimization code written in matlab. *Structural and Multidisciplinary Optimization*, *21*(1999), 120–127. doi:10.1007/s001580050176

Sigmund, O. (2007). Morphology-based black and white filters for topology optimization. *Structural and Multidisciplinary Optimization*, *33*, 401–424. doi:10.1007/s00158-006-0087-x

Yulin, M., & Xiaoming, W. (2004). A level set method for structural topology optimization and its applications. *Advances in Engineering Software*, *35*, 415–441. doi:10.1016/j.advengsoft.2004.06.004

An Optimization Strategy for 3D Concrete Printing

Rob Wolfs, r.j.m.wolfs@tue.nl
Eindhoven University of Technology, The Netherlands

Theo Salet, t.a.m.salet@tue.nl
Eindhoven University of Technology, The Netherlands

Abstract
The development of automation techniques shifts the building industry towards CAD/CAM oriented design. This requires the relations between design and construction to be considered in each step of the design process. However, the nature of these relations is still largely unknown for new techniques and the amount of involved parameters is great. One of these new, upcoming techniques is 3D printing. A research model has been developed, which allows 3D concrete printing to be studied in an efficient way. The model is set up in a parametric environment, combining a structural analysis with an optimization module based on the simulated annealing algorithm.

Keywords: CAD/CAM, 3D Concrete Printing, Optimization, Simulated Annealing

1 Introduction

The on-going developments of automation techniques in the building industry require each discipline in the construction cycle to change their approach. Design (CAD) and construction (CAM) are no longer separate, but must be considered as connected from early sketching to realization. One of these new automation techniques is 3D printing. In case of 3D concrete printing, the connection consists of the relationship between the different components involved: printing strategy, the printed material (concrete) and the printed objects. However, the nature of these relations is generally unknown, which may result in a time consuming trial-and error approach to find the desired printing strategy if one or multiple parameters change. A graduation project on 3D printing of concrete structures has been carried out at the Department of the Built Environment of the Eindhoven University of Technology. The project aimed at contributing to the development of the technique, by designing a method to study and optimize the relationships between the components involved in 3D concrete printing in an efficient way. The topics discussed here are based on the findings of this project (Wolfs 2015).

2 Research Model

A research model has been constructed to study the concrete printing technique without the need for a trial-and-error approach. The structure of this model is depicted in **Figure 1**.

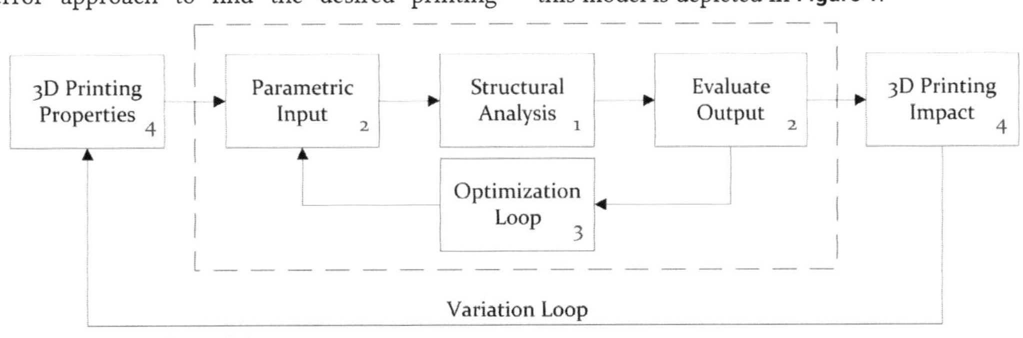

Figure 1 Research Model

The core of the research model is a structural analysis module [1], realized in FEM software Abaqus. This allows the structural behaviour of printed objects to be studied for varying shapes, as it includes orthotropic behaviour which is a typical result of the layered production method. Considering the developments of new printable materials like fibre-reinforced concrete, non-linear elastic material properties are also incorporated in the FEM model.

The input and output modules [2] are set up in a parametric environment, which provides the user with the possibility to easily vary parameters and their relations. The input can be categorized in geometry, boundary conditions, and material parameter sets. All of these are modelled in Grasshopper, a graphical algorithm editor which comes as a plugin for Rhinoceros.

The great number of connected parameters results in a large amount of combinations and variations. To avoid the need for an exhaustive search on desirable combinations of settings, an optimization module is incorporated in the research model [3]. This module uses the output of the structural analyses to find the desired input settings.

In addition to the parameters in the input component, a set of printer properties is added to the model. They consists of a user defined printing strategy, i.e. printing speed, layer size and printing environment. These properties are placed in a variation loop. By changing the print strategy in a stepwise manner, entering the optimization loop for each step, the impact of 3D printing can be studied [4].

As Grasshopper is a propagation-based system, it restricts the use of cyclic algorithms (i.e. 'loops') without the use of additional plugins. To keep full control of both the optimization and variation loop, these modules are written in programming language Python. Additionally, Python can be used to control the structural analysis in Abaqus.

3 Optimization Algorithm

Because of the early stage of research 3D concrete printing is in, little is known about the behaviour of the components involved and their relations. When evaluating one or multiple printing parameters and searching for a certain goal, it is initially unknown how the range of the parameters' values is related to the optimum value. Moreover, the evaluation function, i.e. the way the chosen values relate to the optimum (the fitness of each solution), is usually strongly non-linear and may contain local optima. Fortunately, optimization algorithms have been improved over the past years. Methods have been developed that take these issues into account, like the simulated annealing (SA) algorithm.

3.1 Simulated Annealing

The simulated annealing algorithm was inspired from thermodynamics and metal work. Annealing involves heating and cooling a material, altering its properties by changing its structure on molecular level. Once the material is cooled down, this new structure is locked in, along with its newly obtained properties. If the temperature is dropped too quickly, irregularities may occur which are trapped in the newly created structure as well (Jacobson 2013).

The SA algorithm has a fictitious temperature variable, similar to this heating and cooling process. This variable starts high, and the slowly 'cools down' as the algorithm runs. At high temperature the algorithm is often allowed to accept worse solutions than the currently best one, more or less similar to a random search. It is therefore able to jump out of local optimums in the early stage of execution, like depicted in **Figure 2**. The chance of accepting worse solutions is reduced as the temperature drops, i.e. as the algorithm has completed more iterations. This allows the algorithm to narrow the search space. (Michalewizc & Fogel 2000).

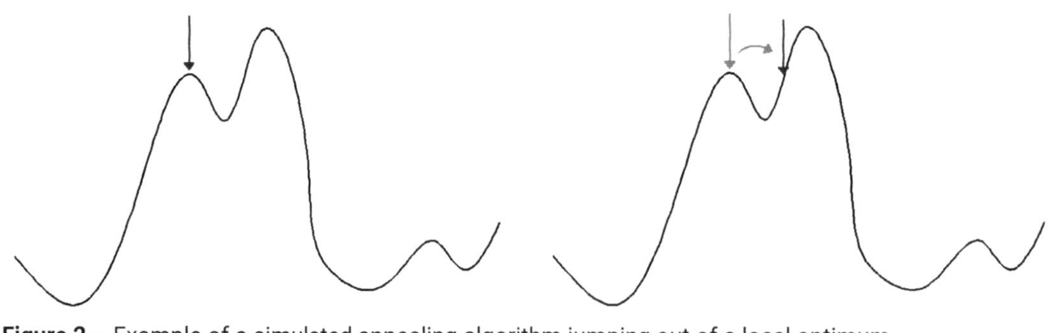

Figure 2 – Example of a simulated annealing algorithm jumping out of a local optimum

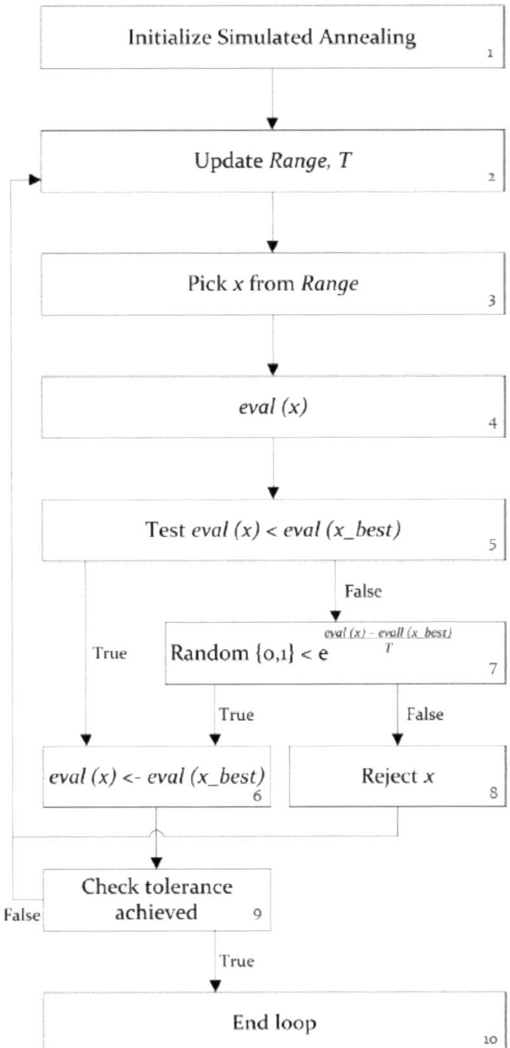

Figure 3 – Flowchart of simulated annealing as used in the research model

3.2 Implementation in Research Model

The optimization module of the research model is based on the SA algorithm. The procedure is given in **Figure 3**. Each function of the algorithm will be explained stepwise based on this flowchart.

As the simulated annealing algorithm gets initiated [1], the variable and goal of the optimization loop have to be fixed, along with a certain number of parameters. The target module is parametrized in Grasshopper and allows the users to choose these parameters of interest: the variable to be optimized can be the applied loading, the printed geometry, or material properties. The chosen optimization goal is based on the structural behaviour of the printed object, and can be either the occurring stresses or displacements.

Next, the algorithm parameters are chosen. The maximum amount of iterations is fixed, and so is the initial domain and temperature [2]. Finally, the tolerance is set. Once the algorithm has found a solution that is within this range of accuracy, it terminates the loop.

The algorithm is now initialized and choses a random point *x* within initial domain {*R1, R2*} [*3*]. The value *x* is then evaluated by the function *eval(x),* which corresponds to a structural analysis in Abaqus [*4*]. This analysis will show the maximum occurring stresses or deformations and compares them with the predefined goal. The result of this evaluation function is compared to the currently best solution [*5*]. If the occurring result is indeed better, *eval(x)* becomes the currently best solution *eval(x_best)* [*6*]. When *eval(x)* < *eval(x_best)* returns a *False* statement, a new function is called upon. This part of the algorithm determines if a worse solution is accepted or not, based on the difference between the current and best solution, and the fictitious temperature parameter *T*. The probability of acceptance is chosen as a random value in the domain {0, 1} [7]. This number is compared with the evaluated point in Python as follows:

```
p = math.exp((eval(x) –
eval(x_best))/ T)
if random.random() < p:
        eval(x_best) = eval(x)
```

Once this statement returns *True*, the value is accepted as *eval(x_best)* [*6*]. When it returns *False,* the solution is discarded [8]. After these steps, the solution being either better or worse, the algorithm will return to its starting point and repeat the same steps. Before doing so however, it checks a termination condition; in this case the required tolerance of the solution [*9*]. If the tolerance is achieved, the algorithm ends, showing the result, the corresponding best value of *x* and the tolerance percentage of the solution [*10*].

If the tolerance is not achieved, the temperature *T* is updated before restarting the algorithm. The nature of this update function can be varied: both the order of the function and the size of steps may vary between analyses. Subsequently, the choice of function strongly influences the probability of accepting worse solutions. In case the analysed problem is largely unknown or contains a high amount of local optima, it may be desired to slowly decrease the temperature during the run. On the other hand, when the problem is well-known, the temperature function may drop rapidly such that the algorithm converges quickly to the optimum solution. For the implementation in this research model, the temperature update function is taken as linear decreasing. Each step *k* in temperature drop is therefore equal, but the step size can be varied by selecting the total number of iterations *I*. The resulting temperature function in Python language is shown below.

```
def update_temperature(T, k):
        return T_int - (k * (T_int
  / I) )
```

To study the concrete printing technique an additional functionally has been added to the algorithm. The behaviour of the parameters of interest and the relationship between them is generally unknown. For this reason, the initial domain {*R1, R2*} is taken very large at first, to prevent a too small choice of range that doesn't incorporate the optimum solution. However, as the algorithm runs, the problem gradually becomes clearer. Keeping the domain large would result in a time consuming optimization run, which negates the benefit of this smart algorithm. Thus, at a user defined point in the loop, the algorithm will narrow the initial domain to {R3, R4} step by step based on the current best solutions. This allows the algorithm to converge to an optimum solution much faster, even when the problem is initially unknown.

The values of R3 and R4 are based on the best and second best known solution, which continuously update during the run, as the figures below illustrate. The horizontal axis concerns the domain, in which a parameter x may be chosen. The vertical axis lists the fitness of each solution *eval(x)*. The optimum solution corresponds with an unknown optimum variable *x_optimum:* the target of the algorithm.

Figure 4 shows that if this expected optimum is somewhere in between the currently best two solutions *x1* and *x2*, i.e. the best evaluation value is below the target and the second best is above or vice versa, the range will be straightforwardly reduced.

However, if the initial range was chosen too small and both values are on one side of the target, the new range is less obvious. **Figure 5** shows how the algorithm uses the distances between the two best values *x1* and *x2*, to compute the trend of the solutions. This can then be used to estimate the distance Δx between the currently best value and the optimum one. However, as this assumes the problem to be linear, the range is taken as twice this distance $2\Delta x$ to incorporate for non-linear optimization problems.

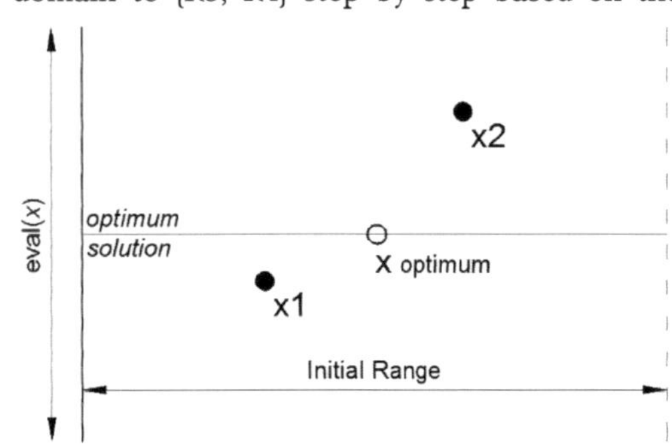

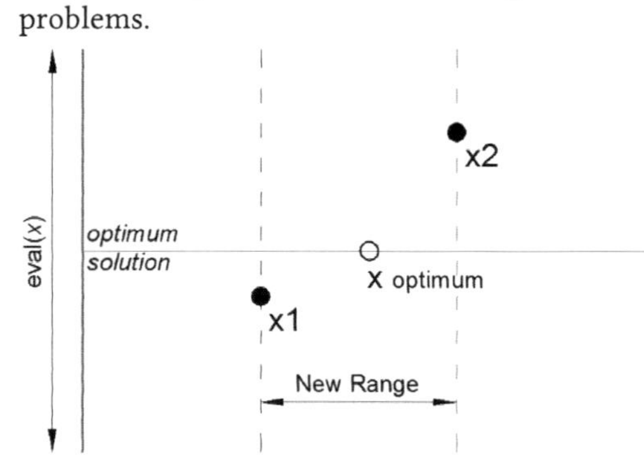

Figure 4 – Reduction of range, using the two best known evaluation values on two sides of the optimum

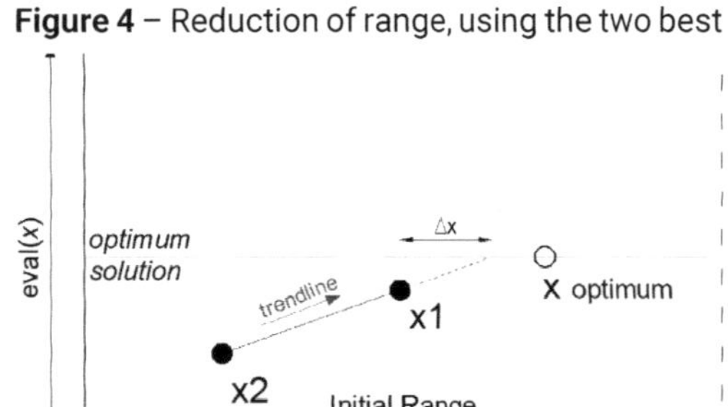

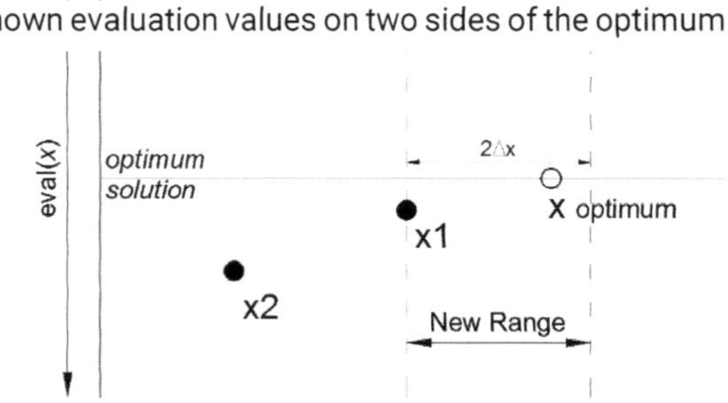

Figure 5 – Reduction of range, using the two best known evaluation values on one side of the optimum

It is noted that when using optimization algorithms, the balance between computational time and accuracy comes into play. Besides, accepting solutions is partially based on chance. Especially in case of largely unknown problems, as is this case for this study, either much iterations and exact solutions, or a quick evaluation and somewhat inaccurate solutions may be the result. For this early stage of research the latter is preferred.

4 Example

The research model is demonstrated by varying the printing strategy of a 3D printed orthogonal concrete wall. The printing speed, layer size and printing environment (in-situ or pefab) are varied in a stepwise manner. For each step, the optimization loop is entered, which seeks toward the maximum loading capacity of the wall. As the optimization loop runs, the results of each step are sent back to Grasshopper in real time, allowing the user to keep track of the progress. Finally, the optimized result in presented, which is done for each step in the variation loop. These results can be combined and presented in a graphical way, to show the impact of 3D printing on the design process. An example is given in **Figure 6**. This graph shows the normalized printing speed on the horizontal axis, versus the normalized loading capacity on the vertical axis. Each dot represents the result of an optimization loop.

5 Conclusions

The example analyses of the model show that the impact of 3D printing should not be underestimated, as the chosen printing strategy clearly influences the required mechanical properties or geometry, and vice-versa. The presented research model provides an efficient way to study 3D concrete printing, without the need for a time-consuming trial and error approach. The modular and parametric environment of the research model are set up such, that they can easily be replaced or edited by fresh data on existing or newly developed print techniques, as the following years will provide much more (experimental) research on 3D concrete printing.

It is recommended that future research will be carried out to extend and renew models like presented here, to support upcoming automation techniques like 3D concrete printing and apply them on a large scale in the building industry.

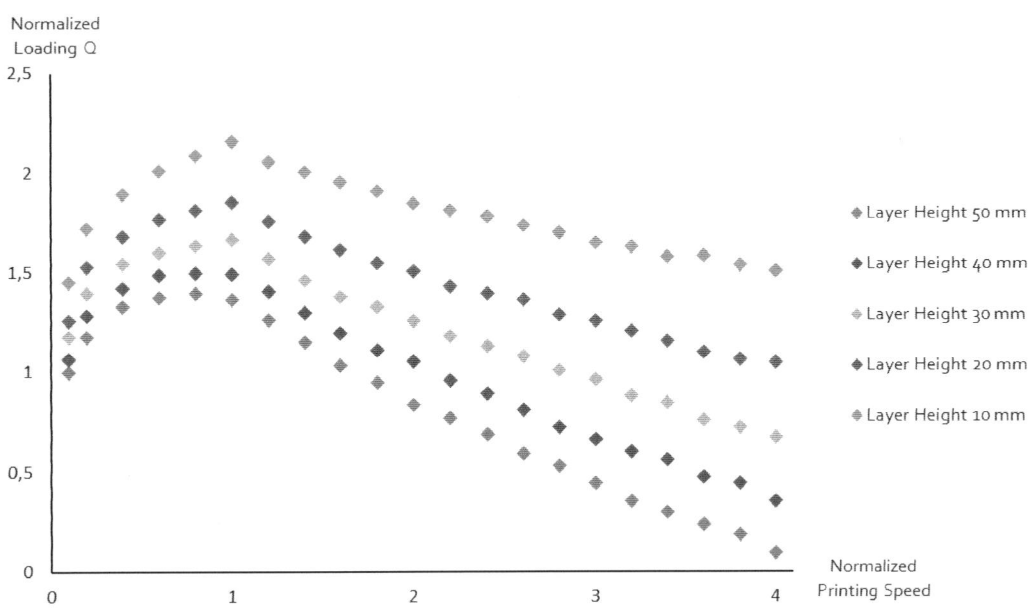

Figure 6 – Optimization results of printing speed versus loading capacity for varying layer height

References

Jacobson, L. (2013). *Simulated Annealing for beginners*. Retrieved January 2015, from theprojectspot.com.
Michalewicz, Z. & Fogel, D. (2000) *How to Solve It: Modern Heuristics*. Berlin: Springer.
Wolfs, R (2015). *3D Printing of Concrete Structures*. Master's thesis. Eindhoven University of Technology.

Author Index

Name	mail	paper id	Affiliation
Philipp Geyer	p.geyer@kuleuven.be	41	Architectrual Engineering, KU Leuven, Belgium
Kay Smarsly	kay.smarsly@uni-weimar.de	28	Computing in Civil Engineering, Bauhaus-Universität Weimar, Germany
P. de Wilde	pieter.dewilde@plymouth.ac.uk	37	Plymouth University, Building Performance Analysis Group, Drake Circus, PL4 8AA, Plymouth, UK
A. Beltrami	alberto.beltrami@unibg.it	37	University of Bergamo, Dept. of Engineering and Applied Science, Dalmine (BG), Italy Plymouth University, Building Performance Analysis Group, Drake Circus, PL4 8AA, Plymouth, UK
Barbara Strug	barbara.strug@uj.edu.pl	9	Jagiellonian University, Poland
Fabian Ritter	fabian.ritter@tum.de	41	Computational Modelling and Simulation, TU München, Germany
Andreas Schumann	andreas.schumann@rub.de	23	Ruhr—University Bochum, Germany
Richard Vock	vock@cs.uni-bonn.de	40	Institute of Computer Science II, University of Bonn, Germany
Thomas Krijnen	t.f.krijnen@tue.nl	35, 40	Technical University of Eindhoven (TU/e), Eindhoven, Netherlands
Szymon Gajek	szymon.gajek@gmail.com	16	Jagiellonian University, Kraków, Poland
Theo Salet	t.a.m.salet@tue.nl	55	Eindhoven University of Technology, The Netherlands
Jakob Beetz	j.beetz@tue.nl	35, 40	Technical University of Eindhoven (TU/e), Eindhoven, Netherlands
Seif Dalil Safei	seif.dalilsafei@epfl.ch	11	Swiss Federal Institute of Technology (EPFL), Lausanne, Switzerland
M. Picco	marco.picco@unibg.it	37	University of Bergamo, Dept. of Engineering and Applied Science, Dalmine (BG), Italy
Rob Wolfs	r.j.m.wolfs@tue.nl	55	Eindhoven University of Technology, The Netherlands
Wojciech Palacz	wojciech.palacz@uj.edu.pl	16	Jagiellonian University, Kraków, Poland
Gordon Horn	gordon.horn@rub.de	23	Ruhr-University Bochum, Germany
Christopher Kropp,	christopher.kropp@rub.de	27	Ruhr-Universität Bochum, Germany
Hoon Sohn	hoonsohn@kaist.ac.kr	33	Korea Advanced Institute of Science and

			Technology, Republic of Korea
Ewa Grabska	ewa.grabska@uj.edu.pl	16	Jagiellonian University, Kraków, Poland
Stefania C. Radopoulou	scr58@cam.ac.uk	22	University of Cambridge, Cambridge, UK
André Borrmann	andre.borrmann@tum.de	15	Chair of Computational Modeling and Simulation, Technische Universität München, Germany
Kateryna Sigalov	kateryna.sigalov@rub.de	26	Ruhr-Universität Bochum, Bochum, Germany
Veronika Hartmann	veronika.hartmann@uni-weimar.de	28	Computing in Civil Engineering, Bauhaus-Universität Weimar, Germany
Simon Daum	simon.daum@tum.de	15	Chair of Computational Modeling and Simulation, Technische Universität München, Germany
M. Marengo	marco.marengo@unibg.it	37	University of Bergamo, Dept. of Engineering and Applied Science, Dalmine (BG), Italy University of Brighton, School of Computing, Engineering and Mathematics, Lewes Road, BN2 4GJ, Brighton, UK
R.V. Jones	rory.jones@plymouth.ac.uk	37	Plymouth University, Building Performance Analysis Group, Drake Circus, PL4 8AA, Plymouth, UK
Min-Koo Kim	kmk0125@kaist.ac.kr	33	Korea Advanced Institute of Science and Technology, Republic of Korea
Georg Suter	georg.suter@tuwien.ac.at	31	Design Computing Group, Center for Geometry and Computational Design, TU Wien, Vienna, Austria
Robbe Salenbien	robbe.salenbien@vito.be	39	Flemish Institute for Technological Research, Belgium
Markus Konig	koenig@inf.bi.rub.de	23	Ruhr—University Bochum, Germany
Qian Wang	wangqian@kaist.ac.kr	33	Korea Advanced Institute of Science and Technology, Republic of Korea
JoonWoo Park	joonwoonpark@kaist.ac.kr	33	Korea Advanced Institute of Science and Technology, Republic of Korea
Diogo Simoes	simoes_diogo@hotmail.com	1	Dep. Civil Engineering and Architecture, University of Lisbon, Lisbon, Portugal
Walter Terkaj	walter.terkaj@itia.cnr.it	35	Institute of Industrial Technologies and Automation (ITIA), Milano, Italy
Wiet Mazairac	l.a.j.mazairac@tue.nl	39	Eindhoven University of Technology, The Netherlands
Raoul Wessel	wesselr@cs.uni-bonn.de	40	Institute of Computer Science II, University of Bonn, Germany
Grażyna Ślusarczyk	gslusarc@uj.edu.pl	9	Jagiellonian University, Poland
Pieter Pauwels	pipauwel.pauwels@ugent.be	35	Ghent University, Ghent, Belgium,
Hèrm Hofmeyer	h.hofmeyer@tue.nl	44	Eindhoven University of Technology, The Netherlands
Bauke de Vries	b.d.vries@tue.nl	39	Eindhoven University of Technology, The Netherlands
Sebastian	ochmann@cs.uni-bonn.de	40	Institute of Computer Science II, University of

Ochmann			Bonn, Germany
Markus König	koenig@inf.bi.rub.de	26, 27	Ruhr-Universität Bochum, Bochum, Germany
Kristina Georgieva	kristina.georgieva@rub.de	23	Ruhr-University Bochum, Germany
Ian F.C. Smith	ian.smith@epfl.ch	11	Swiss Federal Institute of Technology (EPFL), Lausanne, Switzerland
Alcinia Z. Sampaio	zita.sampaio@tecnico.ulisboa.pt	1, 32	Dep. Civil Engineering and Architecture, University of Lisbon, Lisbon, Portugal
Christian Koch	christian.koch@nottingham.ac.uk	23, 27	University ofNottingham, United Kingdom
Tom Lahmer	tom.lahmer@uni-weimar.de	28	Optimization and Stochastics, Bauhaus-Universität Weimar, Germany
Rodrigo Leal	rodrigomfl@hotmail.com	38	Intituto Superior Técnico, Universidade de Lisboa, Portugal
Maria Gomes	maria.gloria.gomes@tecnico.ulisboa.pt	38	Intituto Superior Técnico, Universidade de Lisboa, Portugal
Francisco Regateiro	francisco.regateiro@tecnico.ulisboa.pt	38	Intituto Superior Técnico, Universidade de Lisboa, Portugal
Sjonnie Boonstra	s.boonstra@student.tue.nl	44	Eindhoven University of Technology, The Netherlands
Nicolas Veuve	nicolas.veuve@epfl.ch	11	Swiss Federal Institute of Technology (EPFL), Lausanne, Switzerland
Ioannis Brilakis	ib340@cam.ac.uk	22	University of Cambridge, Cambridge, UK
Edgar Berdeja	edberdeja@sapo.pt	32	Dep. Civil Engineering and Architecture, University of Lisbon, Lisbon, Portugal

Contact

TU Eindhoven
Design Systems Group

++31 40 247 2280
eg-ice-2015@tue.nl

European Group For Intelligent Computing in Engineering (eg-ice)
c/o Andre Borrmann
Arcisstrasee 21
80333 Munich
Germany

ISBN 978-1-5108-0956-7
9 781510 809567

CURRAN ASSOCIATES INC.
proceedings
.com